CLARE
AND THE GREAT WAR
JOE POWER

The
History
Press
Ireland

First published 2015

The History Press Ireland
50 City Quay
Dublin 2
Ireland
www.thehistorypress.ie

British Library Cataloguing in Publication Data.
A catalogue record for this book is available from the British Library.

ISBN 978 1 84588 872 5

Typesetting and origination by The History Press
Printed and bound in Great Britain by TJ International Ltd.

CONTENTS

Private Patrick Halloran, saying goodbye to his mother and sister at Ennistmon railway station. (Courtesy of Ger, 'Guss', O'Halloran)

I dedicate this work to the memory of all those who suffered during the Great War, especially my two uncles, Private John Power, Clare Castle, Royal Dublin Fusiliers, who was killed during the Battle of the Somme on 13 November 1916; and Private Timothy Power, Clare Castle, Royal Army Medical Corps, who never recovered from 'shell-shock' suffered on the battlefields of the Western Front.

ACKNOWLEDGEMENTS

I wish to acknowledge the contribution of many people who have assisted me in this project. First of all, I am grateful to Mrs Edel Glynn and family of Kilrush for allowing me access to their valuable records, which give a huge insight into the role of recruitment organisers such as C.E. Glynn during 1915 and 1916. My thanks are also due to the following people who helped and assisted my researches: the family of the late Peadar MacNamara of Inch, who generously shared his research into the First World War in Clare, along with photographs and other records; Dr Michael Linnane, Shannon, who gave me some of the Linnane papers and a copy of a portrait of his grandfather, Councillor P.J. Linnane, JP; Eric Shaw, Clare Castle, has kindly shared many photographs and newspaper clippings and a prison letter from George Perry; Jane Tottenham, Mount Callan, gave me information about Capt. Tottenham; Paul O'Brien, Kilrush, drew my attention to some photos in the Glynn Collection; Ada and Frank Power, Clare Castle, reminded me of family letters and photographs; Brian Honan, Cappa, Kilrush, showed me his extensive collection of First World War memorabilia and gave me some relevant postcards from prisoners of war. Besides these, thanks are due to the following: the staff of Clare County Research Library, Ennis; Mr John Rhattagan, curator of the Clare Museum, Ennis, for information on Jack Barrett; the staff of the National Library, Kildare Street, Dublin; the staff of the National Archives, Bishop Street, Dublin; Bishop O'Reilly for allowing me access to the Killaloe Diocesan Archive, Westbourne, Ennis; the librarian and staff NUI, Galway; the staff of Limerick Diocesan Archives, especially David Bracken; and the staff of Mary Immaculate College, Limerick, have all been very helpful. The staff of Kilrush Community School have been very helpful, especially Colleen Galvin, who has helped enormously in storing my researches safely; Oliver Hawes, Cobh, generously gave me information and photographs of his grandfather Joe Hawes, leader of the Connaught Rangers Mutiny, 1920; Con Woods, Newmarket-on-Fergus, gave me information on Jack Fox; Sean Spellissy, Ennis, has generously allowed me to use his photographs of old Ennis; David Browne gave the photos of the Clare Hunt at Buncraggy per Eric Shaw; Gerard 'Guss' O'Halloran, Ennistymon, kindly allowed me to use the photo of Patrick Halloran of Ennistymon; Cormac O'Comhrai sent me a photo of Capt. Tom Corry DCM; I am greatly indebted to John Power, Clare Castle, for his invaluable help with photographs; Gerald Dunne of Quin also helped with me greatly with photographic services; I am very grateful to the Hon. Grania Weir (*née* O'Brien), for allowing me to see and use her family papers, especially, the war diary of her father, the Hon. Donogh O'Brien, later 16th Baron Inchiquin; Dr Hugh Weir gave me information on the current status of the Church of Ireland in County Clare; and Dr Ger Browne, Ennis, has been very generous in sharing his knowledge and research into the Great War; I am very grateful to the Galvin family, Ennis, for the photo of Nurse Nellie Galvin, MM, and some information on her career; I wish to express my sincere thanks to Ronan Colgan and Beth Amphlett of The History Press Ireland for accepting and publishing my work. Finally, I must thank my wife Fionnuala and my daughters, Maria, Rachel and Bronwyn for their support during my researches and writing of this labour of love.

INTRODUCTION

This study of the Great War in County Clare examines the impact of the war upon the people of Clare during these crucial years in Ireland's history. The political, social, economic and cultural effects of the war are studied to show how the war affected the people of Clare and how they reacted to the conflict. The study is organised on a chronological basis, highlighting the major political and military developments, both at home and abroad, during each year of the conflict.

In 'Prelude to War' the political state of the county in 1914 is examined, with the hopes of the nationalists, expecting Home Rule in 1914, contrasting with the fears of the unionist minority that Home Rule would bring sectarian conflict. Many people genuinely feared that the introduction of Home Rule would spark off a civil war in Ireland.

The significant question of recruitment for the war is studied in detail and the role of the local press, of government propaganda, of the Catholic and Protestant Churches, of John Redmond's Home Rule Party, of local recruitment officers, and of Sinn Féin are all examined.

Local newspapers were hugely significant in forming public opinion at that time, as David Fitzpatrick, citing a British intelligence report, states: 'Owing to the fact that the standard of education is very low, the press has great influence in the country districts; the views of the people being drawn from the local paper, the priest and the national schoolmaster.' The *Clare Champion* and its opposition papers, the *Saturday Record* and the *Clare Journal*, were the main local papers circulating in the county. Of course, other papers, such as the unionist *Irish Times* and the nationalist *Irish Independent* and the *Freeman's Journal*, were also sold in the county, but were probably only bought by a much smaller clientele, representing the middle and upper classes. These local papers, both

nationalist and unionist circulating in the county are examined thoroughly to
see how they moulded public opinion.[1]

The involvement of Clare soldiers in the major military engagements in
several theatres of war is recorded mainly through letters they sent home to
family and friends in Clare, some of which were published in the local papers,
though they may have been heavily censored, while others were used for
propaganda purposes. Although Dungan noted, 'few ordinary soldiers wrote
diaries or memoirs or even letters deemed worthy of being kept,'[2] the letters
from a couple of Clare priests, especially those from Fr Moran of Tulassa, to his
friend, Councillor P.J. Linnane, JP of Ennis, are most informative of the terrible conditions of war faced by the men of Clare. His letters also give a very
good insight into the faith and morale of the men at the front, who faced
death on a daily basis.

A few significant people had enormous impact upon public opinion in
the county, men such as the previously mentioned Councillor P.J. Linnane, JP,
chairman of Ennis Council; the MPs for West and East Clare, Col Arthur Lynch,
MP, and Mr Willie Redmond, MP; the Catholic Bishop of Killaloe, Dr Michael
Fogarty, and his friend, Dr E. O'Dwyer, Bishop of Limerick; and the Church
of Ireland Bishop of Killaloe and Kilfenora, Dr T. Sterling Berry. Besides these
politicians and churchmen, the role of prominent members of the unionist
community in Clare, such as Lord Inchiquin of Dromoland, President of the
Clare Unionist Club, is highlighted and contrasted with that of significant
republican activists, such as Michael Brennan of Meelick. Wealthy business
people such as the Glynns of Kilrush, especially H.R. Glynn and his brother
C.E. Glynn, who was recruitment officer for West Clare, had a significant
impact on recruitment during 1915 and 1916.

The crucial impact of the 1916 Rising is scrutinised, examining the reaction
of the local media and the opinions of the local bishops, politicians, and other
significant people in the county to the Rising. The major sea-change in Irish
political life afterwards, 'the spirit of 1916', is reflected in the famous East Clare
by-election of 1917, caused by the death of Willie Redmond, MP, resulting in
the election of Eamon de Valera. The 1916 Rising also caused a sharp decline
in recruitment.

There was a real fear of famine, and this, combined with the growing power
and influence of Sinn Féin, with widespread 'cattle drives' and other agrarian
agitation, made County Clare virtually ungovernable and subject to martial
law in 1918. The conscription crisis galvanised all shades of public opinion
to resist its introduction. The sinking of the SS *Leinster* in October caused the
deaths of at least eight Clare civilians, including six women. Towards the end
of the war the devastating impact of the 'Spanish Flu' brought more heartbreak
and deaths to the county.

The penultimate chapter looks at the way in which the men who fought were largely ignored and forgotten by Irish society after independence, until fairly recent times; though some of the survivors in Clare honoured their dead comrades in Remembrance Day ceremonies for many years afterwards. This chapter also scrutinises the great amnesia in the historiography of the war in County Clare by local historians and journalists.

The concluding chapter summarises the main developments over the four-and-a-quarter years of the conflict and the impacts of the war on the people of Clare, with analysis of mortality etc. It shows how the county was radically transformed and politically convulsed during these years of the Great War.

The Towns and Villages of County Clare

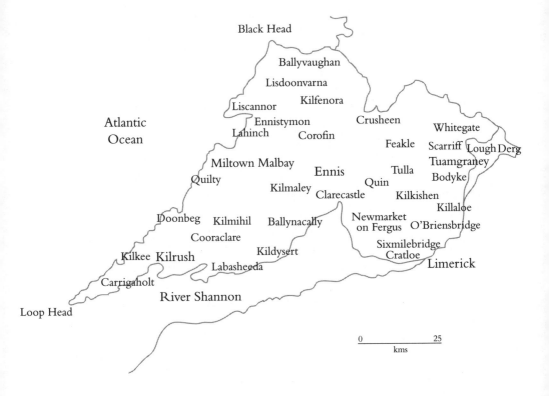

1

PRELUDE TO WAR: 'A NATION ONCE AGAIN'

The Holy season of Christmas was celebrated with all due solemnity befitting such an occasion. Walking through the streets on Christmas Eve one was impressed by the absence of drunkenness and the orderly behaviour and manner of the people. Looking around the thronged streets you here and there espied a batch of men chatting and the merry ring of their voices, coupled with the beautifully decorated and well-lighted windows, impressed one with the hope that there are brighter days for Ireland. It was truly a happy Christmas in every sense of the word happy, because the demon of intemperance was banished from our minds, and the men and boys of Ennis, especially the labour element, deserve to be congratulated for their sobriety and the good example they have shown.

This editorial in the *Clare Champion* of 3 January 1914 described a peaceful time in Ennis during the Christmas season of 1913 and the editor expressed the hope that there would be 'brighter days for Ireland' in the coming year. Little did the editor realise that the 'happy' Christmas of 1913 was to be the last 'happy' Christmas for many years to come because of the Great War and the War of Independence in Ireland. The hopes for 'brighter days in Ireland' were to be dimmed by a looming crisis over the Home Rule Bill for Ireland. Furthermore, while the 'demon of intemperance' may have been absent from the streets of Ennis on Christmas Eve and during the Christmas season, the demons of war were unleashed upon the people of Ireland in August 1914, with horrific consequences for many Clare people over the next ten years.

While the joys and happiness of Christmas with goodwill to all may have been genuinely felt and expressed, there was, beneath the veneer of Christmas cheer, a simmering and volatile political tension in Clare liable to explode at any time due to the forthcoming Home Rule Bill.

Religious Tolerance

County Clare was one of the most Catholic counties in Ireland. The vast majority of County Clare people were Catholic and nationalist. The Census of 1911 records a population of 104,232, of whom 98.14 per cent were Catholic. There were 1,709 Episcopalians, 166 Presbyterians, 38 Methodists and 14 of other religions in the county, totalling 1,932 non-Catholics, comprising only 1.84 per cent of the population. Though they were small in number, the Protestants were an elite group in society, composed of the old landed gentry, and much of the professional elite of the county, being prominent in law, county administration, the local magistracy, banking, trade and medicine. The majority of County Clare people, about 65 per cent, worked in primary industries, especially farming.

While the vast majority of the population of Clare may have desired Home Rule and may have been eagerly anticipating its introduction in 1914, concerns were expressed by some of the unionists, who had reservations about their future under a Home Rule administration. Some business interests were also concerned about their economic prospects after independence.

When the Third Home Rule Bill was proposed in 1912, the Protestants and unionists of Clare were alarmed and they held several meetings in January to voice their concerns and to oppose the Bill. The meetings were held at Dromoland Castle and were chaired by Lord Inchiquin, while Henry V. MacNamara, JP, DL, of Ennistymon acted as secretary to the Clare Unionist Club. Lord Inchiquin and Lord Dunboyne of Knappogue Castle were elected respectively as president and vice-president of the Clare Unionist Club.

At the meetings Henry V. MacNamara, DL, defended the speeches that were made by himself and other members of the Clare Unionist Club, including Col George O'Callaghan Westropp and Revd Mr McLaurin, at a Unionist Party meeting in Hollywood, County Down during late 1911, which he said were misrepresented in the press. Nevertheless, the Clare unionists, by their presence and their speeches against Home Rule, fomented northern Protestant prejudices in Ulster. Mr MacNamara claimed that the Protestants of Clare were being persecuted by the Land League and not, as was stated in 'malicious press reports', by the Catholics of some isolated districts in Clare and elsewhere. MacNamara stated that the people of outlying districts, both Catholics and Protestants, were being persecuted by the United Irish League and if the Protestants did not bow to the dictates of the United Irish League, then their lives were made unbearable. MacNamara was referring to 'cattle drives' (when cattle and other animals were driven off the lands by people seeking to force the break-up of the estates and the division of the estates among the tenant farmers) and other agrarian outrages committed against the landlords of Clare, which were common at that time in Clare as part of the Land War. It was also asserted at the meeting by Mr W.W. Fitzgerald that the Ancient Order of Hibernians (AOH) was a disloyal, secret, sectarian organisation led by Mr Joseph Devlin, MP, a prominent member of the Home Rule Party.

These assertions of sectarianism in Clare against the Protestant minority were repudiated by several prominent Protestants over the next few years, but, despite these assertions, the allegations did not go away and were still deeply felt and believed by some Protestants. Mr Charles MacDonnell, JP, DL, a landlord from New Hall, near Clare Castle stated:

> I have read a report of the Unionist Party meeting at Hollywood and what was said there by my fellow Clare unionists. In justice to the people of Clare, I consider that I, a Protestant, am in duty bound to make public the fact that during that part of my lifetime I spent in this county, no Roman Catholic has ever in any way interfered with, or upbraided me, on the subject of my religion – and I know of others who will say the same ... I consider this county remarkably free from religious intolerance. I have never experienced it myself, nor have I known a co-religionist to suffer from it.

The secretary to Clare County Council, F.N. Studdert, a Protestant, testified in the *Clare Record* of 14 October 1911:

> Adverting to previous letters written on above subject, I would like to state publicly as a county official of fourteen years standing, that the word 'religion' has never been mentioned to me, officially, or otherwise by any Roman Catholic in this county ... I am proud to state that I have as many sincere and true Roman Catholic friends as Protestant friends.

Mr H.B. Harris, JP, a prominent member of the Protestant community in Clare, who was elected as vice-chairman of Ennis Town Council in 1899-1900, wrote to the press on 15 November 1911:

> I fear Ireland is becoming almost intolerable just now, especially in the south and west, owing to these discussions on religious intolerance. If there were any justification for such a cry one would not feel so much, but residing as Protestants in the County Clare, in the midst of a Catholic population, we are living evidence of their good sense, good nature, and kindly disposition. My best friends,

outside my own family circle, are Catholics, and it is indeed painful for me to meet my neighbours with this charge of intolerance appearing in the public press from day to day, and made by those who should know better.

There are hundreds of business people scattered all over Ireland who could not succeed without the patronage of their Catholic neighbours ... and having such a vast area as Clare in the occupation of Catholics, we still enjoy life, free from annoyances, meeting with our Catholic neighbours in fair or market, dealing in this, that or other shop without any friction, sitting together on the bench to administer the law, and all meetings at marriage functions, christenings, and funerals, just as if we belonged to the same church, giving honour to whom honour is due, no matter what his or her creed or politics might be.[1]

Another Protestant, Mr A. Capon of Church Street Ennis, stated that he had lived in Ennis for twenty-nine years and had been in business for fifteen years, with most of his customers being Catholic. The fact that he had been elected to the Ennis Urban Council for nine years was proof, he said, that there was no sectarianism in Clare. Mr Doherty, who was elected to Kilkee Town Council, and Mr James Greer, who was elected in Kilrush, both Protestant, asserted vigorously in letters to the *Saturday Record* in January and February 1914 that there was no sectarianism in Kilkee or Kilrush or in Clare.

Mr Doherty from Kilkee wrote:

I feel it a duty to protest against the false charges of intolerance made by unionist speakers in Ulster and elsewhere against Irish Catholics. I am a Protestant living in West Clare, which has a population of 98% Catholic, yet, this community, intensely Catholic as it is, has elected me for six years as a member of Kilkee Town Commissioners. In one of the contests for this body, I was elected at the head of the poll. A greater honour still has been conferred by unanimously electing me for the fourth time, chairman of Kilkee Town Commissioners, the only Protestant member of that body.

Never have I known a Protestant to be injured in person, property, position or repute because of his religion. It is a vile slander of Irish Catholics to accuse them of intolerance and I challenge the accusers to prove their charge, even by one solitary case of intolerance.

I ask my co-religionists in the west and south of Ireland to come out manfully and condemn these wicked slanders of our Catholic fellow countrymen. We have lived without religious differences amongst Catholics and they have always treated us with respect. I certainly think it is a duty of every self-respecting Protestant to speak out now and put an end to a campaign of malice against a generous and kindly Catholic people.

About a week later, Mr Green emphatically stated that he had never experienced sectarianism in Clare either:

> I cannot allow this opportunity to pass without again vindicating the high reputation for toleration and friendliness enjoyed by my Catholic neighbours in this county. This has been markedly evidenced last month in my election to Kilrush Urban Council at the head of the poll by a substantial majority ... as a matter of fact religion is rarely mentioned here except by Protestants ... Religious intolerance is a thing with which, during my ten years sojourn here, I have never met. In conclusion, there never was a greater scandal against the Catholics of the south (so far as Clare is concerned at any rate), than the charge of religious persecution.[2]

Despite these assertions of religious toleration in Clare and that the Protestant minority should not fear the prospect of Home Rule, the matter was again raised in controversial circumstances in April and May 1914 when Canon S.C. Armstrong, rector of Kilrush, wrote an article that was published in the April edition of the *Howth Parish Magazine*, dealing with the life and work of a Church of Ireland clergyman in the west of Ireland. In this article Canon Armstrong stated that the local branch of the AOH in Kilrush had shown 'open hostility' towards the Protestants of the town. It is worth quoting the article in full as it gives a Protestant perspective on life in West Clare in 1914 as a Church of Ireland minister. He outlines the challenges facing the declining Protestant community and their fears of 'Rome rule':

> Kilrush Parish County Clare
> I have been asked to write a short article for your magazine dealing with the life and work of a clergyman in the west of Ireland. I trust that these few particulars may prove interesting, though they are necessarily contracted so that they do not take too much available space. I should have liked to have said something of this neighbourhood, and especially of the river.
>
> 'Rose cloud and purple cloud
> Purple cloud and rose,
> Kerry shore and Clare shore,
> Where the river flows –
> Trembling in purple twilight
> Paling as the daylight goes;
> Golden burst of rain cloud,
> Low rocks and golden sky,

> Flats of shining seaweed,
> And a wild bird's cry;
> Slowly as the river widens
> One black sail goes drifting by.'

(By AVC in *Irish Gardening*)

But I must forbear, County Clare has attained a most unenviable reputation for murders and outrages, but I am glad to say this western portion is remarkably peaceable. There are wicked and lawless people in every community, but the inhabitants of Kilrush and neighbourhood are, as a rule, orderly and well behaved. There is no open display of religious animosity, except on the part of a few extremists – such as the members of the AOH.

The Roman Catholics, who number over 98% of the population, treat us courteously. A Protestant clergyman is never insulted in the back streets of Kilrush. Many of our people live in isolated situations, surrounded by Roman Catholic neighbours, but they are not molested in any way on account of their religion. The better class in the town are very friendly and many of them are extremely liberal-minded. For instance, they like to help the annual feast and Christmas tree for our school children. They give donations and come to the entertainment. Some even attend our missionary sales and spend their money freely.

I have seen large numbers of well-behaved and attentive Roman Catholics in our church at a funeral service. Notwithstanding this friendly and liberal spirit, to which I gladly testify, it is natural and inevitable that our small Protestant community should feel isolated, and especially in the case with those of us who have lived in other places where numbers were more equal. It is hard for those who live surrounded by their co-religionists to realise the depressing effects of this.

The 'atmosphere' is intensely Roman Catholic and there is a deeply-rooted conviction in the minds of our people that, had Rome the power, it would fare badly with us. To the Church of Rome we are heretics, and she has always taken a rough and ready way with them.

Our parish church is a handsome modern building one hundred years old. In the churchyard are the ruins of a very ancient one. Thanks to the zeal and energy of my predecessor, Canon Hyde, the internal appointments are all that could be desired and there are three very beautiful stained glass windows erected to the memory of members of the Vandeleur family. But, alas, while there is seating for 300, we count 49 a fair congregation. About 30 years ago the parishioners numbered about twice as many as now and the dwindling process goes on year by year.

Our school is always a matter of great anxiety to us. We find it very difficult to keep up the necessary average attendance of ten. If a coastguard or a policeman, who had children attending our school, is removed, we have to use all possible influence in high quarters to try and get another with a family sent in his place. Then, when there are elder boys, the parson has sometimes to turn schoolmaster in order to teach them subjects outside the National School Board curriculum, or else they are sent to the Christian Brothers School.

I look upon the school as vital to our small western parishes. Without a school in which our children can be trained in church doctrine and principles, a parish is humanly speaking doomed. Even if no direct attempt is made to influence their faith, the mere fact of our children associating day by day with overwhelming numbers of Roman Catholic companions is necessarily most injurious.

Not only has the parson sometimes to turn schoolmaster, but he has often to start a marriage bureau. Our church in the west has lost heavily in years gone by from mixed marriages. The children of such unions are almost invariably brought up Roman Catholics. The pressure brought to bear upon the Protestant parent is tremendous, so strong to be resisted in nearly every case. If our church families are not to die out, the young people must marry in their own faith. Rarely, where numbers are so small, can suitable mates be found in the parish. Some of us think it our duty to communicate our wants in this line to our brother clergy and to try and bring about suitable introductions with a view to matrimony. Such 'marriages of convenience' may be sadly wanting in that romantic process called 'falling in love at first sight', but are they not contracted in the very highest circles, and have we not a happy precedent in the happy union of Rebekah and Isaac? I have known such marriages turn out (seemingly), quite as satisfactory as others which have given Cupid a lot of archery practice.

There is an old saying: 'it is better to wear out than to rust out'. The clergyman in the small country parish has light work in comparison with his city brother. He is in no danger of 'wearing out'; if he wants to keep fit, he must guard against the insidious attacks of the 'rusting' process. Work in a large parish must be done systematically and regularly. In the small one there is the temptation to put off to tomorrow what can be done today, and so what can be done any day is in danger of being left undone. In the large parish there is always the stimulus of co-workers and intellectual discourse. In the small one the clergyman enjoys few or none of these great advantages, and must fight against deadly lethargy. The two positions differ widely in many respects, but it is a deep truth that every job has its compensations.

The thought is all sustaining. The 'few sheep in the wilderness' are precious in the eyes of the Chief Shepherd, and if the pastor in whose charge they have been placed but strive to tend them faithfully, he will, in due time, receive his Master's 'well done' and enter into the joy of his Lord.'

S.C. Armstrong (Canon)

(NB the editor of the *Howth Parish Magazine*, the Revd Mr Powell, added that the Parish of Kilrush had, for the past two years, received half of the Collection for Poor Parishes at the Harvest Collection in Howth.)

This published article was brought to the attention of the AOH in Kilrush and Canon Armstrong was forced to publish a retraction of what he had written and to apologise for making the false allegation, which, he said, 'was not founded on fact'.[3]

Another insight into religious tolerance in Clare was published in late July 1914, describing a visit to Ennis by a body of English trade unionists on Tuesday 19 May:

We visited Ennis, Co. Clare and we found here Protestant children attending Catholic schools in preference to the National Schools. It was also pointed out to us that the most successful businessmen in Ennis were Protestants, which goes to show that religious bigotry or intolerance does not exist in Clare. In fact two Protestant farmers had written to the Ennis papers a few months ago and stated that they knew of no ill-feeling between Catholics and Protestants.

I also visited Mr Scott, Presbyterian minister, and he said that he received nothing but kindness from his fellow townsmen and the priests were amongst his best friends. He also spoke of the prosperity of the Protestants in the district.

I visited Fr Hogan, Catholic priest and he stated that if he wished to influence the people in politics, they would take no notice of him, and this I know to be true. He also told me that they had been the friends of the peasant class, who were being oppressed by the landlords.

Mr Capon, secretary to the Oddfellows Club, told our delegation that the priests told the people not to join the Oddfellows Club, as it was a secret society. When I mentioned this to Fr Hogan, he stoutly denied such statements, 'as they all knew that the Oddfellows were no such thing'.

Mr-----, a unionist, told us at a meeting in the evening that he would not mind being represented by a nationalist, if they would only put forward capable men and not drunkards incapable of governing themselves. It had been repeatedly stated to us that the priests would deal out punishment to their flock if they did not vote as they told them, and I asked at this meeting what the punishment consisted of, but the answer I got was that there was no such thing. It was rather significant that this was the only meeting during our tour that the Catholics were not misrepresented and abused, because there happened to be a prominent Catholic landowner and lawyer amongst the unionists present.

Our representative waited on Mr Capon in reference to the statement attributed to him to the effect 'that the priests told their people not to join the Oddfellows Club, as it was a secret society'; and having discussed the question was given the following written answer by Mr Capon:

'I could not say, but my opinion was that there were a certain number of priests in the county who had an idea in their heads that the Oddfellows were a secret society, and therefore, if these gentlemen had that idea, what might you expect from other people?

I was further asked how long I had been in this county, and I told them on and on since 1885, and I gave them a description of the way in which I was treated, but they have not had the decency to report that, as it would appear too good for them.' [4]

(Note, as mentioned above, Mr Capon, a Protestant had been in business in Ennis for fifteen years and most of his customers were Catholic. Furthermore, he had been elected to Ennis Urban District Council for nine years.)

Sport and Social Life

Despite these fears, deep-rooted convictions and reservations of the unionist community in County Clare, the social life of the gentry was carried on as before; with hunt balls and other social gatherings. The County Clare Hunt Ball was 'a glittering social occasion' held at the Courthouse, Ennis, attracting over seventy couples, who danced almost until dawn. On the day after the ball, members of the Clare Hounds held a meet at Buncraggy, where they had 'a capital day chasing hares from Buncraggy to Island McGrath and back after a brilliant hunt of one hour and twenty minutes'. Another high society social occasion at that time was the New Years' Eve dance held at Moyriesk, the home of Mrs R.H. Crowe. The guests included the elite of the county and many army officers from Cork, Limerick and Galway as well as from Clare.[5]

Another ball was organised by the AOH at the Courthouse, Ennis, in February 1914, which was also a great social occasion for the Catholic community of the county. Other Christmas and New Year dances were held in places such as St Michael's Hall, Kilmihil and at Kilkee and Kilrush.

The Clare Hunt at Buncraggy, 16 November 1911.
(Photos by A. Holmes, courtesy of the late James McMahon and David Browne)

The sporting traditions of the county carried on as usual, with a wide variety of sports being played. Chief among these sports were the country pursuits of hunting, fishing and fowling. Race meetings were held at Ennis, Quilty, Miltown Malbay and Lahinch, which were usually held during the summer holidays, while the Clare Hunt annual point-to-point was held at Clonmoney, Newmarket-on-Fergus, at Easter. Besides these, there were agricultural shows at the County Agricultural Show in Ennis held on 15 August and at Kildysart in mid-September, along with a horticultural show held at Ennis in June.

There were coursing clubs at Ennis – Clare Castle, Cooraclare, Miltown Malbay and at Newmarket-on-Fergus. Lahinch was the premier golf club, where the South of Ireland Championship was held. Besides this there were clubs at Ennis, Spanish Point, Kilkee and Killaloe. There were several soccer clubs in the county, mainly based in Ennis, associated with British garrisons, police and transport companies. Athletics meetings were held at Clare Castle, the Ennis Showgrounds and at places such as Corifin and Scarriff.

Sports clubs such as tennis, cricket and hockey clubs were scattered through-out the county. These sports clubs, like golf, catered for the middle and upper class groups in society and so had a relatively high Protestant membership.

The salmon fishing season opened on 1 March 1914. Fishing conditions on that day were not good as 'the weather was wet and cold and the water was high'. The honour of catching the first salmon on the River Fergus went to John Kerin, who caught a 9lb 8oz specimen. The following anglers, mostly local gentlemen, had the following catches: M. Kennedy, 9lb10oz; M. Stacpoole, 9lb; F.N. Studdert, 11lbs 9oz; and W.F. Crowe, 11lbs.

GAA clubs were established in every parish in the county and besides the county competitions, occasional hurling tournaments were held, such as at Clare Castle on 1 March, which was held to raise funds for the local Land and Labour Band, which was founded in 1902. Another sports meeting was promoted at Clare Castle in April under GAA rules for the purpose of paying off the debt on the curate's house. Among the events was the tug-of-war championship of Clare. However, the sport-ing highlight of the year undoubtedly was that the Clare Senior Hurling team won the All-Ireland title for the first time in September 1914.[6]

Fowling was regularly carried on at a couple of estates in the county, such as at Lord Inchiquin's at Dromoland and at Mr Stacpoole's of Eden Vale. This sport was also carried on in the Tottenham estate on Mount Callan and on the Broadford Hills. The sport was usually engaged in by the estate owners and their friends among the gentry. The season extended from November until February each year, with several shoots before and after Christmas. The records of shooting at Eden Vale for the 1913-14 season show that there were four shoots, with an average gun-line of six guns; and there were total bags of 231 pheasants and 116 woodcock.[7]

THOMAS McGRATH, O'Callaghan's Mills;   Subs.—JOHN RODGERS, Tulla;   JOHN FOX, Newmarket;   PATRICK McDERMOTT, Whitegate;   PATRICK MOLONY, Feakle. GUERIN, Newmarket;   PATK. McINERNEY, O'Callaghan's Mills;   W. CONSIDINE, Ennis;   AMBY POWER (Capt.), Quin;   MICHAEL FLANAGAN, Quin;   ROBERT DOHERTY, Newmarket;   JAMES CLANCY, Newmarket;   BRENDAN CONSIDINE, Ennis;   M. MOLONY, Ennis;   ED. GRACE, O'Callaghan's Mills;   JOE POWER Quin.   SHAM SPELLISSY, Ennis.   J. SHALLOO, O'Callaghan's Mills.

Clare All-Ireland hurling
champions, 1914. (Courtesy of John Power)

There was, however, significant interruption of all major sporting events in the county that year when an outbreak of foot-and-mouth disease in the country forced the cancellation of all sporting events between 16 March and 28 April. This highly contagious bovine disease also had a significant impact upon the farming economy during this time, with all fairs and markets being cancelled.[8]

The Gaelic League was revived in the county when a meeting, chaired by Revd A. Clancy, PP, was held at the town hall in Ennis on 14 February. Later in the year a huge *Feis an Chlair* was held at Ennis in July to promote Irish music, song, and dance in the county. This cultural event attracted huge crowds.[9]

One exciting new source of entertainment was started in Ennis in January 1914, when a company took a five-year lease of the town hall for the purpose of showing films. The weekly or bi-weekly black and white silent movies at the town hall became a major addition to the cultural attractions of the town of Ennis. Besides films, the local people were able to watch newsreels, with scenes of news items broadcast by Pathé News. Most of the new movies were of American or British origin and some were later deemed to be controversial and immoral. The silent movies were dubbed with subtitles to explain the subject matter, and later, live piano music was provided to add to the dramatic effect. Besides the new cinema there were occasional travelling cinemas in Ennis at this time. For instance in April there was a 'Picturechrome' at Keane's Yard, Ennis, with nightly shows during the week at 8 p.m. Admission costs ranged between 1s 6d and 3d.[10]

Law and Order

In 1912 H.V. MacNamara, JP, DL, of Ennistymon had described the landlords of Clare as being 'persecuted' by the activities of the Land League during the continuing Land War. It seems that by 1914 not much had changed and the agitation continued. There were several 'cattle drives' in Clare during the early part of the year, in places such as Kilkishen on Maj. Studdert's property; Shalee, the property of Mr J. Cullinan; Cahercalla, the home of Mr Wyndham F. Crowe, and Gortmore and Cragleigh, the property of Mr Pilkington. There were some successes in this regard; it was announced in February that the Morony estate in West Clare, including the town of Miltown Malbay, had been purchased by the Land Commission, largely through the efforts of Very Revd Canon J. Hannan, PP. Also, in May the Land Commission took over Maj. Studdert's estate in Kilkishen for division.[11]

The issue of law and order was a topical one in the county at this time and the local newspapers carried regular reports on one murder trial, the Derrymore murder, which was frequently aborted and transferred to different courts because of the difficulty of getting a jury to convict, allegedly due to intimidation. The *Clare Champion* reported claims from the prosecution that 'there was a feeling of terror in the district and that witnesses were afraid to come forward'.[12] The problem of securing convictions in Clare was so serious that the matter was raised in the House of Commons. Mr Mitchell Thompson, MP, asked the Chief Secretary in Dublin, Mr Birrell, to state how many cases had the Attorney General had applied to have transferred from County Clare to County Dublin in the King's Bench Division. He also asked whether any steps were being taken to remove the feeling of terror that prevailed in County Clare and prevented fair trials.

In reply, Mr Birrell stated that the Attorney General had applied for changes of venue in four cases from County Clare. The applications were made on the grounds that in the belief of the responsible officials, a fair trial was not likely to be had in County Clare. He added that there was a large extra force of police in the county and special measures had been taken for the protection of life and property. Mr Birrrel was happy to state that the condition of the county was improving.[13]

In the previous year, Willie Redmond, MP for East Clare, stated in the House of Commons in reply to the question of crime in Clare:

From every point of view, Clare was more free of crime than any civilised county in the world. There was very little agrarian crime; but until land purchase was completed there would undoubtedly be excitement and irritability shown. The National Party, however, have done everything in its power to condemn and discountenance crime and outrage of every description.[14]

Perhaps it was a coincidence that Sir Peter O'Brien, 1st Baron Kilfenora, PC, QC, who was born at Carnelly House, Clare Castle, in June 1842, had retired as Lord Chief Justice of Ireland in 1913. He earned the soubriquet, 'Peter the Packer' during the Land War of the 1880s when he, as a Crown Prosecutor, secured the conviction of many people accused of agrarian crimes because of his skill in 'packing' juries. O'Brien died on 7 September 1914, when the Land War was entering its final stages in Ireland due to land purchase.[15]

The Weather

The weather during the year was unusual. The period from April to June was drier than normal. During June the weather was almost continuously dry and warm, and by the end of the month the effect of the prolonged drought was apparent on the crops. In some districts little or no rain had fallen since early May and much inconvenience was caused through shortage of water. By contrast, the second half of the year was unusually wet. The annual rainfall was about 7 inches (8cm) above normal. There were about 4 inches (10cm) of rain in July, but the harvesting months of August and September were wetter than normal. The rain in December was over seven inches (8cm), a record at that time since records were first taken at Carrigoran.

Because of the dry weather, the state of the crops in the county by the end of June was serious. Cereals such as wheat, oats and barley were lighter than normal, with shorter stalks. The potato crop, which was also affected by some frost in early May was also late and both early and mainstream crops were between two and three weeks behind. In many cases first crops of hay were cut and in some areas two crops, but, though the yield was well below average, the quality was good. Yields of other crops such as mangels, turnips and beans were also backward. In addition, pastures were burned and bare and stock such as cattle suffered from shortage of grass. The drought also caused a reduction in milk yields. Because of the fodder crisis, prices of cattle and sheep fell back and farmers had to reduce their herds, selling stock at lower prices. This was a further blow after the foot-and-mouth crisis in April and May.[16]

The Prospects of Home Rule

Besides the weather, the imminent prospect of Home Rule was a major topic of conversation throughout Ireland in early 1914. An editorial in the *Clare Champion* stated, 'there is not a cabin or castle in the country in which the prospects of the Home Rule Bill are not being discussed with the greatest interest'. The editor, on 7 March 1914, was optimistic that Prime Minister Aquith would keep his word: 'Taken on the whole, we think that Mr Asquith will not break faith with the Irish people or destroy his reputation as a statesman, by yielding to the threats of violence and civil war in the north'.

The AOH had branches in towns and villages throughout the county in places such as Ennis, Kilrush, Kilkee, Lahinch, Kilkishen, Ennistymon, Sixmilebridge, Newmarket-on-Fergus, Corofin, Quin, Kilfenora, Scarriff, Feakle, O'Callaghan's Mills, and Mullagh. The membership seems to have been drawn from the Catholic middle classes of the town and country. It was an influential social, business, and political network in the county, which had strong links with the United Irish League and the Home Rule Party. The AOH also had a prominent role in local and national politics, especially during the local elections, which were held during May 1914.

Members in the Ennis branch of the AOH included the president, Mr Sarsfield Maguire, editor of the *Clare Champion*; vice-president, P. Connolly, Ennis Urban Council; treasurer, D. McParland; and secretary, J.F. McHugh, Ennis Urban Council; other members included; J.B. Lynch, solicitor; Dr MacClancy; P. Cullinan; F.C. McMahon; Martin Collopy; J. Clohessy; J. Moroney; J.J. Meade; C. Mungovan; M.J. Carmody; and M.J. Reddan. The Ennis branch built a new hall called Hibernian Hall, which was opened by Mr Joseph Devlin, MP from Armagh, leader of the AOH, who was a prominent member of the Home Rule Party. At the election for a new president of the Ennis branch in July 1915, a total of eighty-four members were present.[17]

There was a great expectation among nationalists that Home Rule was imminent. Home Rule collections were organised throughout Ireland mainly through the parishes. Contributions from each of the parishes were usually headed by the title, 'From the priests and people of …'. This indicated the prominent role of the Catholic clergy in the Home Rule campaign. In Killaloe, V. Revd Canon Flannery, PP,VG, sent a cheque for a sum of £25 7s 6d. In the letter accompanying the cheque, which was published in the *Freeman* as well in the *Saturday Record* of 10 January 1914, he praised John Redmond, 'the closer the contest is coming the more we admire the skill and courage of our splendid representatives. With such a party, led by such a wonderful man, we believe in a few months we will have you at home, building the nation up again in College Green.'

The *Clare Champion* reported on the progress of the Home Rule Bill throughout the early months of the year. Though there were some concerns about
the unionist threats to oppose Home Rule, the editor of the *Clare Champion*,
Mr Sarsfield Maguire, president of the Ennis branch of the AOH, seems to have
been greatly influenced by Joseph Devlin, MP for Armagh, founder and leader
of the AOH, who regularly asserted that Carson's campaign of opposition to
Home Rule was just 'bluff'. This seems to have been the opinion of most of
the nationalists of Clare in the early part of the year. The editorial ended with
mixed feelings of hope and despair, with an 'appalling vista':

> It is quite possible, but by no means certain that the Home Rule question
> will be settled by consent, but there does not now appear to be any doubt
> about the Bill becoming law. One thing is quite certain, that is if the govern-
> ment happened to be defeated and the measure thrown out, the government
> of this country as it stands, would become an impossibility, and disasters
> would follow far worse than even civil war in its most dangerous form in
> the north.[18]

The nationalist hopes of a successful Home Rule Bill being passed in the
British Parliament were further dimmed, when on 9 March John Redmond,
leader of the Home Rule Party, agreed to the government proposal at the
Second Reading of the Bill that six Ulster counties should have the right to
opt out of a Home Rule settlement for all Ireland on a temporary basis for
six years. This, the *Clare Champion* argued, would be Ulster's loss. The *Clare
Champion* editor stated with determination that 'no nationalist would agree to
the permanent exclusion of the six counties!' However, its editorial insisted
that the government should push the measure through no matter what the
consequences for Ulster would be, even the threat of civil war. It still held the
view that Carson and the unionists were bluffing – 'Every nationalist in Belfast
and Ulster knows that there was never a greater game of bluff than the Ulster
Volunteer Movement'.[19]

One of the Clare MPs, Col Arthur Lynch, was very unhappy with Redmond's
concession to the Unionist Party and wrote to him expressing his concern.
He told Redmond that he lacked confidence in Asquith's Liberal government,
which allowed Carson to practice treason with impunity, to win exclusion for
Ulster. He said that Home Rule would be a mockery, 'I know the plea that this
is only a temporary arrangement that the Ulstermen will come in … I do not
believe that they will be won over … even by force! The proposition is absurd …
I see little here but hypocrisy on the part of the government'.[20]

However, political matters took a sinister and more alarming course when
the unionist campaign of opposition, which included much propaganda

suggesting that 'Home Rule would be Rome Rule', became more threatening. There was a sense of shock when the Curragh 'mutiny' took place on 20 March, when the majority of the British officers stationed at the Curragh declared that they would rather resign than lead a military action to suppress the Ulster Volunteer Force. In response to this revelation, the editor of the *Clare Champion* became more militant:

> Are we to accept the veto of the officers' mess? Democracy must either win or perish. We suggest that the nationalists of Ireland should join the National Volunteers and be ready to demonstrate that if the Orange north is ready to use force, they will be prepared to meet it, and if necessary, as Mr Devlin has suggested, settle the Irish question without the intervention of police or military.[21]

The National Volunteers

The increasing unionist threat was a spur to a surge of enlistment into the National Volunteers in the county. When a corps of the National Volunteers was formed during March in Ennis, the *Clare Champion* boasted: 'There was not much bluff and bluster about the formation of a corps of the Irish Volunteers in Ennis!' Within a week the Ennis corps had expanded greatly. The Ennis 'Brian Boru' corps of Volunteers numbered more than 400 men of all classes, including shop assistants, tradesmen and labourers, who drilled with enthusiasm and marched through the town in a strong body.[22]

One of the major local politicians behind the call for the formation of the Clare Volunteers was Councillor P.J. Linnane, JP, chairman of Ennis Urban Council, who stated at a public meeting on 8 March, 'People from all parts of Ireland should help bring about a body which will be second to none in Ireland, for it will be composed of men ready and prepared to stand faithfully and firm to meet any emergency that might arise.'

Councillor P.J. Linnane had been a member of Ennis Urban Council since 1898. He was chairman of the council in 1902 and in 1914. He was one of the founders of the Ennis branch of the United Irish League (the Home Rule Party) in 1902. Indeed, for his political activities he was incarcerated in Limerick Jail for three months in 1902. Linnane Terrace on the Kilrush Road was named in his honour in 1902. He was a significant political figure in nationalist politics in Ennis and indeed throughout County Clare during the war years. Willie Redmond, MP for East Clare, was quite friendly with him and relied upon him for local advice.[23]

The political crisis over Ulster was dramatically transformed on 24 April when a huge quantity of arms and ammunition was illegally imported by the Ulster unionists during what was known as the Larne gun-running. The *Clare*

Journal highlighted, but did not condemn, the 'audacious coup of the Ulster Volunteers'. It highlighted Mr Asquith's statement on the 'unprecedented outrage in Ulster'. The *Clare Journal* also noted that recent government actions, allowing a temporary exclusion of six counties, had caused 'resentment among nationalists'. This was surely a major understatement of the anger among nationalists at the undemocratic behaviour of the unionists and their Tory friends. The *Saturday Record* made no reference to the Larne gun-running. The *Clare Journal* editor held out some hope of a settlement of the crisis by suggesting partition on the lines proposed by Winston Churchill.

On the other hand, the *Clare Champion* strongly condemned the actions of the Ulster Volunteers, referring to the 'Orange outlaws'. The editorial in the *Clare Champion*, putting a brave face on the matter, defiantly stated: 'the fact of 50 or 70 thousand rifles being in the hands of the Orangemen will not turn a hair on the head of a single Northern nationalist!' The editorial also stated trenchantly that 'Carson's demand for the permanent exclusion of six Ulster counties would spell the permanent and total destruction of Home Rule! The nationalists of Ulster would be betrayed and coerced under the heel of Orange ascendancy.' The *Clare Champion* editor expressed the opinion that if Carson had been more reasonable then the Ulster 'problem' would be settled amicably among Irishmen.[24]

These dramatic developments in Ulster showed that the unionists were not bluffing and that the threat of force by them in forming the Ulster Volunteer

The Irish National Volunteers of Ennistymon before the 'split', 1914.
(Courtesy of Peadar McNamara Collection)

'War or Peace', Lucania bicycle advertisement from *Clare Champion*, 25 April 1914.

Force and illegally arming themselves did bring about significant political amendments to the Home Rule Bill. The lessons were not lost on nationalists throughout Ireland and in County Clare. Nationally, between the end of 1913 and July 1914 the number of men enrolled in the Irish National Volunteers increased from about 2,000 to more than 160,000. Belatedly, but enthusiastically, the men of Clare began to answer McNeill's call to join the Irish National Volunteers and over the next few months, corps of volunteers were formed throughout the county and thousands enlisted, while many women from Clare joined the auxiliary organisation of Cumann na mBan.

Between the end of March and June many branches of the Irish National Volunteers were formed throughout the county. Apart from Ennis, branches were formed in Ballycar, Ballyea, Barefield, Bodyke, Carrigaholt, Clare Castle, Clonlara, Corofin, Crusheen, Doonbeg, Doora, Ennistymon, Hurler's Cross, Kilrush, Kilkee, Kilalloe, Kildysart, Kilfenora, Kilmihil, Kilmurry Ibrickane, Labasheeda, Lisheen, Meelick, Miltown Malbay, Newmarket-on-Fergus, O'Callaghan's Mills, Tulla, Quin, Stonehall and Tuamgraney. The Catholic clergy were prominent in forming many of the branches and were specifically mentioned in some cases, such as Fr Hayes, CC in Labasheeda, Fr John O'Dea, CC in Kilnoe and Tuamgraney, and Fr Moloney, CC in Kilkee. Most of these branches were represented at the Convention of Irish National Volunteers in Clare.

As a show of strength, a huge gathering of the National Volunteers of Clare was held in Ennis on 1 June, to demand that the British Government should not attempt to delay or stop the Home Rule Bill from becoming law. The meeting was addressed by the local MPs, Willie Redmond and Arthur Lynch, as well as others. Willie Redmond stated, 'The Volunteer movement has been taken up in every part of Ireland by the most respectable people in the country.' Fitzpatrick states that the number of National Volunteers in the county was over 3,200, divided into sixty companies. A national collection for the Irish National Volunteers Defence of Ireland was held on 16 August. The subscriptions were collected on a parish basis and the subscribers were named and acknowledged in the local press. In Clare Castle a total of £19 12s was collected by the local branch.[25]

The increasing martial spirit in Ireland, with much talk about civil war, even inspired one local businessman to capitalise on this atmosphere to put advertisements in the local paper with the caption 'War or Peace!' Mr James O'Dea of Kildysart, selling bicycles, wrote 'no matter what game is on you will need a Lucana Bicycle'. Little did he or anyone else realise what horrors lay ahead.[26]

Earlier in the year one anonymous local wit, XYZ from Kilmihil, wrote a poem urging the young men of his parish to join the Irish National Volunteers.

The Kilmihil Volunteers

Sons of St Michael awake from your slumbers,
And respond to the call of a nation to be;
Remember that Ireland will soon be a nation,
First flower of the earth and first gem of the sea.

Your ancestors fought to obtain Ireland's freedom,
And shouldered the pike in dark '98;
So, young men of Kilmihil, their loyal descendants,
Muster your clans before it's too late.

Think of the days of the great agitation,
When your fathers were tortured in Limerick jail;
And now on the dawn of Home Rule for dear Ireland,
Be ready to help and take care you don't fail.

The Black North, a mote in the eye of dear Ireland,
Is now causing trouble as it did heretofore;
And Sir Neddy has filled it with big dummy rifles,
The refuse of Turk, Italian, and Boer.

His army is drilling with these deadly rifles,
The echoes resounding all over the land
So, be comrades in arms and rise in your thousands;
Throw the gauntlet at the feet of that mean cowardly band.

Look back and read over our history's sad pages,
Dwell on the heroes of Emmet and Tone;
And with hearts stout and bold, like your fathers of old,
Strike for old Ireland and Ireland alone.

Show Carson in Ulster that we will be a nation,
With a parliament once more in dear College Green;
Then we'll join hands with Ulster and sing Ireland a nation,
And forget the sad memories of days that have been.[27]

The Home Rule Bill was passed in the House of Commons in May 1914, with amendments allowing for the temporary exclusion of six Ulster counties, and it was hoped that it would shortly become law. To mark the occasion there were celebrations and huge demonstrations in all of the main towns and villages of Clare. The National Volunteers paraded to mark the occasion. They were accompanied by brass and reed, fife and drum, or by pipe bands. Many houses were illuminated with candles in the windows, while tar barrels and bonfires were lit in the villages. There was great joy as the enthusiastic crowds sang the famous ballad, which was at that time almost a national anthem, 'A nation once again', written by Thomas Davis in 1840. After the local clergy and politicians had spoken at Clare Castle, there were many cheers for John Redmond and the Home Rule Party.[28]

A Nation Once Again

When boyhood's fire was in my blood
I read of ancient freemen,
For Greece and Rome, who bravely stood
Three hundred men and three men;
And then I pray I yet might see
Our fetters rent in twain
And Ireland long a province, be
A Nation once again!

(Chorus)
A Nation once again,
A Nation once again,
And Ireland, long a province, be
A Nation once again!'

However, these 'celebrations', apparently orchestrated by the local branches of the Home Rule Party, were premature. The prospects for 'brighter days in Ireland' looked unlikely as Ireland seemed to drift towards civil war over the Ulster crisis after the failure of the Buckingham Palace Conference of 21 and 22 July.

To make matters worse, the British Army fired upon the Irish Volunteers who had taken part in the Howth gun-running of 26 July and four civilians were killed at Bachelor's Walk, Dublin. This outraged the Irish nationalists, as they contrasted the attempt to disarm the Irish nationalists with the impunity with which the Ulster Volunteers were treated over the Larne gun-running. The shootings in Dublin were condemned by the local press and by local authorities in Clare. A meeting of the Kilrush Board of Guardians expressed their 'horror and condemnation of the outrage committed by the military on the streets of Dublin.' The atrocity was also condemned at a meeting of Clare County Council. The motion 'viewed with horror and indignation the brutal murder of defenceless people on the streets of Dublin by British soldiers'.[29]

Despite a government ban on the importation of arms there was, it seems, an attempt to import guns into West Clare in early August. As the *Clare Champion* stated:

> … gun-running on an elaborate scale is reported to have taken place at Kilkee. The affair appears to be wrapped in mystery, but from the information which could be gleaned from authoritative quarters, it appears that a well-thought out plan matured in a most successful manner. Since, a number of gun boats have been seen about the coast, and by night their powerful searchlights are illuminating many parts. Liscannor has been visited and searched, but nothing eventuated. The greatest activity prevails amongst Volunteers in the west, and on Tuesday, we have authority to state, that arrangements were made for a landing at Liscannor, which were cancelled and a Kerry port chosen for tactical purposes. We believe that the efficient sea officers were being hoaxed on Tuesday afternoon, when they decided to search for arms at Liscannor, and the Scotland Yard representatives, who are exercising their expert knowledge about Clare and Kerry ports, ought to be better engaged, and with more success at any other occupation, than trying to prevent arms coming into the Volunteers of the south and west.[30]

Fear of Civil War

At the beginning of August there was much talk in Britain and Ireland about the possibility of civil war over Ulster. The local unionists in Clare were becoming apprehensive about their safety and the protection of their homes and properties in the event of Home Rule being implemented. Early in April 1914, H.V. MacNamara, DL, secretary to the Clare Unionist Club, sent a letter to the authorities in Dublin Castle requesting that more military be sent to County Clare to protect the Protestants and unionists against possible attacks from nationalists should the Home Rule Bill be implemented.[31]

The Church of Ireland bishop of Killaloe and Kilfenora seemed to be very worried about the prospect of civil strife. In a remarkable, and in his own words, 'hopelessly optimistic' speech, given at the annual synod of the diocese of Killaloe and Kilfenora at Limerick on Thursday 6 August, the Rt Revd Dr T.S. Berry appealed for peace in Ireland and prayed for the avoidance of civil war in Ireland:

It would be impossible to omit any reference to the very grave crisis through which we are now passing. Surely, with our whole hearts we should pray for the peace of our country, for the avoidance of the horrible calamity of civil strife ... when brother lifts up his hand against brother, we stand face to face with an unparalleled calamity ... obedience to the law of the land is a moral, a Christian duty ...

I would appeal to my lay brothers, should the proposed changes in this country take effect, not to hastily sever their connection with this land by going to reside elsewhere, nor, if they stay, to remain aloof from the new order. I believe as the present crisis passes, a time will come when your cooperation will be welcomed.

I say this because I am convinced that the dominant majority of the part of this country who differ from us in faith do not desire, either to drive us away, or to interfere with our liberties. This may seem to you to be hopeless optimism ...

I have lived on terms of friendship with my neighbours, the clergy and laity of the Catholic Church ... Let us go back to work, steadfast in faith, joyful through hope and rooted in charity ... assured in the knowledge that Providence will guide and protect us ...[32]

Bishop Berry's address was much more optimistic about the prospects for the Protestants under Home Rule than the depressing and pessimistic opinions expressed by Canon Armstrong, rector of Kilrush, in May.

2

'FOR THE FREEDOM OF SMALL NATIONS'

The First World War erupted suddenly at the beginning of August 1914 and, within a short time, began to have a significant impact upon Clare's people, society and economy. Britain declared war on Germany on 4 August 1914 after Germany had invaded Belgium as part of the Schlieffen Plan for the war on France. So, Britain publicly went to war for a high moral purpose – 'for the freedom of small nations' – in defence of neutral Belgium. About forty British Army and Royal Navy reserve officers in Clare as well as all the Clare coast-guard were immediately called up, while others volunteered to join the British forces from a sense of duty and loyalty to their king.

There were emotional scenes at the railway stations of Clare during the middle of August with the departure of the reservists and the regular army men. A batch of about forty men left Ennis Station on 12 August, a number of them from West Clare. The reporter noted 'some pitiful scenes were witnessed among the female relatives of the departing men. The men seemed to be in excellent spirits. Crowds witnessed their departure and there was much excitement'.

The Catholic population of County Clare were initially not as enthusiastic about the war as the small Protestant community, where military service was, in many cases, a family tradition and a duty. But, after John Redmond, leader of the Home Rule Party and of the Volunteers, at a speech at Woodenbridge, County Wicklow on 20 September, encouraged the National Volunteers to enlist and fight in the British Army, saying: 'account yourselves as men, not only for Ireland itself, but wherever the firing line extends, in defence of freedom and religion in this war', many National Volunteers joined up.

However, a small but significant body of nationalists, led by Eoin McNeill, who founded the Irish National Volunteers in November 1913, decided not to follow Redmond's lead; they said they would fight for Ireland's freedom only in Ireland. Initially they were called the Irish Volunteers, but later they became known as the Sinn Féin Volunteers. Those who followed John Redmond's leadership now called themselves the National Volunteers. This was a significant split in the Volunteer movement. The Irish or Sinn Féin Volunteers were to become more significant in 1916 and afterwards. It seems that about 300 members of the National Volunteers in Clare, about 10 per cent, seceded from Mr John Redmond's group and joined the Irish Volunteers.

The local newspapers were initially supportive of the war, but they varied in their enthusiasm. The *Clare Journal*, published on Tuesdays and Thursdays, and the *Saturday Record*, both owned by the Protestant Knox family, were unionist in their attitudes. The *Clare Journal* of 10 August 1914 opined that 'the mother country has never embarked upon a more righteous cause'. On the other hand, the *Clare Champion* (owned by the Galvin family, of Catholic nation-

John Redmond, MP.
(Courtesy of National Library of Ireland)

alist background) of 8 August was initially more reserved about the war: 'the wisdom of her [Britain's] actions can only be tested by time and results'. The editorial called for Irishmen, Protestant and Catholic, to stand together in common cause to win national unity in the face of the common enemy. Three weeks later, an editorial in the *Clare Champion* called upon Britain to withdraw her army from Ireland and to leave the defence of Ireland to the Volunteers, as Redmond had suggested:

A few years ago England's difficulty would be Ireland's opportunity. Today a Liberal government is restoring to Ireland her national independence and the Irish leader is in a position to say that England may withdraw her army and that the National Volunteers and the Ulster Volunteers will protect Ireland. The effect of that will be to unite Ireland – will bring us closer – help us to bury the petty differences and have peace with honour – the time for Ireland has come!

However, John Redmond, perhaps bowing to British military and political pressure, unilaterally announced a new policy at Woodenbridge, County Wicklow on 20 September, urging the National Volunteers to join the British forces. Significantly, there was no supporting editorial in the *Clare Champion* after Redmond's 'Woodenbridge speech'; neither did the *Clare Champion* condemn the new policy. The *Clare Champion* followed Redmond's leadership up until 1916 but, thereafter, took a more republican approach to recruitment and the war.

Both of the Clare MPs, William Redmond, and Col Arthur Lynch, were in favour of recruitment. John Redmond, MP, leader of the Home Rule Party, and Lynch toured the county early in September, urging nationalists to fight for Ireland and the 'freedom of small nations' like Catholic Belgium. The *Clare Champion* of 15 September reported Lynch declaring: 'I want to get to the front to help France, if I can get troops to come with me'. But there was little response to their 'call to arms', even though great emphasis was put on the sufferings of Catholic Belgium in order to win the sympathy of the Irish Catholics.

Within days of the declaration of war the vigilance of local officials such as policemen and members of the coastguard resulted in the arrest of several 'spies' in Clare. One Englishman, who happened to be sketching near Loop Head, was arrested by three members of the local Volunteers, armed with revolvers, who had cycled 14 miles from Kilkee to arrest him as a 'German spy' before he revealed his true identity. A week later the *Clare Journal* of 15 August reported the arrest of three alleged spies in Clare. But, as in the previous week, it turned out that the three men were not spies. Instead they were found to be deserters from a Norwegian ship that had discharged timber in Kilrush. The men, an Englishman, a Welshman and a German,

---

Why
Mr. Wm. Redmond, M.P.
joined the Army.

Mr. William Redmond, M.P. for East Clare, writing to Mr. Linnane, J.P., of Ennis, states :—

That he offered himself to the Irish Brigade because he is absolutely convinced that the future freedom, welfare, and happiness of the Irish people depend upon the part Ireland plays in this War. He adds :

"There may be a few who think that the Germans would not injure Ireland, and that they would even benefit her. I hope the Clare people will rely on no such statements. If the Germans come here—and they will if they reach Great Britain—they will be our masters, and we shall be at their mercy. What that mercy is likely to be, judge by the treatment given to Belgium. If, in the time to come, we in Ireland could not show we had struck a blow for Belgium, then, indeed, I believe that our name would be disgraced. . . . . It would be ungrateful and inhuman if we stood idly by while English, Scotch, and Welsh people were in danger, and their women and children killed in cold blood—as happened in Scarborough. I am far too old to be a soldier, but I intend to try to do my best, for whatever life remains in me, to show that Ireland, at least, is true to her principles, and not in any way ungrateful to her friends throughout the World."

Irishmen ! Follow
Mr. Redmond's example and
ENLIST TO-DAY

'Why Mr. Wm. Redmond, M.P. joined the Army', article from the *Clare Journal*, 19 April 1915.

were arrested in Kildysart, and, after being conveyed to Ennis police barracks, were transferred to Limerick. They were jeered at as 'German spies' in Ennis en route to Limerick Jail.

William Redmond, brother of the Home Rule Party leader, John Redmond, was active in promoting recruitment after his brother made the speech in Woodenbridge, County Wicklow on 20 September urging the National Volunteers to join the British Army. Speaking at a recruitment meeting in Cork in December, he declared that he would not ask men to volunteer unless he was prepared to join them in the British Army: 'And when it comes to the question – as it may come – of asking young Irishmen to go abroad and fight this battle, when I am personally convinced that the battle of Ireland is to be fought where many Irishmen now are – in Flanders, in France – old as I am and grey as are my hairs, I will say: 'Don't go, but come with me'.[1]

Willie Redmond also justified his decision to enlist and the overall recruitment campaign in a letter to a friend, Patrick J. Linnane, an Ennis urban councillor:

> If the Germans come here they will be our masters … look at what hap-
> pened in Belgium, they were invaded and massacred … we must show our
> gratitude to Britain for restoring our parliament by standing by her in her
> hour of need … If we stand idly by and not strike a blow for Belgium then
> indeed, I believe that our name would be disgraced …

Later, from his training camp at Fermoy, Capt. Willie Redmond wrote to Capt. Jorgenson in Kilkenny, elaborating upon and justifying his decision to enlist:

> My views are well-known, I believe every
> interest of Ireland is bound up with the Allies,
> which cause, in my opinion, is the cause
> of liberty, as against German militarism …
> I believe the Home Rule Act is a treaty of
> peace and Ireland is bound to keep her word
> of defending the empire. That is why I and
> thousands of others have joined up … In this
> war the interests of England, Ireland and the

Willie Redmond, MP. (Courtesy of the National Library of Ireland)

empire are identical … Apart from those national and honourable aspects of the war, surely Ireland could not stand by while France and Belgium were being ruined … We are a fighting race and can't be neutral as though we were cowards. I have left my home and joined the Irish Brigade. That action should be at least as eloquent as any speech I could make in Kilkenny'.[2]

Economic and Social Impacts

Many sporting events in the county were cancelled due to the war. One of the most important was the Clare County Agricultural Show, usually held on 15 August. The reason given was that there was a difficulty in getting judges. A sporting event of national significance, the South of Ireland Golf Championship was also cancelled. Horse racing meetings at Ennis and Miltown Malbay were called off as well as a bazaar at Kilkee. On the other hand, GAA sports were not affected. This was fortunate as Clare hurlers won the first All-Ireland in September 1914.[3]

The war brought mixed fortunes to various sectors of the economy of Clare. The agricultural sector entered a long boom period, with rising prices and demand for produce, which continued until about 1919. The earliest manifestation of this was a rising demand for horses for the British Army. Within weeks there were reports of 'extensive purchases of horses for the army', with Capt. O'Grady and Mr T. Lloyd, assisted by Mr P.J. Howard, veterinary surgeon, travelling around the county buying horses for transport and for the cavalry. The price of good horses for military use rose from about £25 to £40 each. Also, there was a substantial rise in the price of cattle at the November Fair of Clare. 'There was a brisk demand for well-conditioned cattle which realised substantial prices. Sheep averaged fifty-five shillings per head. There was also a big supply of horses on sale. There was a brisk demand with remunerative prices'.[4]

Horses for the British Army gathered outside the old RIC Barracks, Ennis.
(Courtesy of Sean Spellissy Collection)

On the other hand, tourism in the holiday resorts of Clare, especially the premier resorts of Kilkee, Lahinch and Spanish Point, as well as Killaloe, was badly
affected. At a meeting of the County Clare Committee for the Prevention of
Distress held in March 1915, a report of the Kilkee sub-committee highlighted
the distress in Kilkee caused by the war:

> On the outbreak of war in early August the banks shut down for a few days. There
> was a great exodus of visitors and the majority did not return. The military men
> and their families left on the declaration of war. The principal hotel shut down,
> while other hotels did poorly and suffered losses. This had fallen on the poor, who
> lived by visitors. There was acute distress due to want of employment'.[5]

One businessman, who seems to have had a vested interest in opposition to
recruitment, put an advertisement in the *Clare Champion* of 19 September
urging Volunteers to remain at home and not join the British Army. He wrote
that Home Rule 'was only a matter of time'. Mr Griffin, the proprietor of a
wholesale and retail draper's outfit in Ennis, had a large stock of Volunteer outfits and kit, approved by the Volunteer HQ. He stated that he had supplied the
Ennis and Doora units of the Volunteers. He did not wish to be left with a large
stock of unwanted Volunteer outfits!

Dr Fogarty, Catholic Bishop of Killaloe. (Courtesy of Peadar McNamara Collection)

The Catholic Church and the Great War

Meanwhile, the Catholic bishop of Killaloe, Dr Fogarty, initially justified the war 'as a sign of God's anger at sinful humanity'. In perhaps one of his first public utterances about the war, at first Mass at the cathedral in Ennis, Bishop Fogarty spoke 'with much feeling' about the war, which he did not condemn. 'It would', he said, 'involve many sacrifices and the poor would necessarily suffer. He deprecated all idea of panic. The banks would be perfectly safe; there was no fear of any financial alarm and no necessity for raising the price of food'.[6] Judging by what the bishop said and from the report of the County Clare committee for the prevention of distress, there must have been a run on the banks in the early days of the war as people panicked and tried to withdraw their money.

Towards the end of the month Dr Fogarty delivered his opinion on the cause of the war. 'It was', he said, 'the anger of God. People throughout Europe had disregarded His power and defied His laws. People worshipped Mammon instead of God.' In a pastoral letter to his flock, Bishop Fogarty stated that the Litany of the Saints should be recited after Mass on the first Sunday of each month for the cessation of the war. He also urged his flock to be charitable in their language about the enemy.[7]

The Irish Catholic hierarchy met at Maynooth in October and they did not condemn the war either. However, they issued a number of resolutions, which were subtly supportive of Britain's war aims and justification for war – that is the freedom of small nations and the German invasion of Catholic Belgium.

They passed four resolutions: 1, that there was a need for Catholic chaplains at the front to cater for the moral and spiritual needs of the many Catholic soldiers in the British Army; 2, that each bishop was to direct his priests to remind their flocks at sermons at Sunday Masses of the sufferings and needs of the 'brave Belgian people'; 3, that the hierarchy protested at the destruction of Louvain; and 4, that a collection be held for the relief of the Catholic people of Belgium. These resolutions appealed to the sympathies of the Catholic people of Ireland for their suffering co-religionists in Belgium and perhaps encouraged them to enlist.

According to Jerome Aan De Wiel, 'in the early months of the war the Church stood by the recruiting sergeant ... only a handful of bishops and priests were opposed to the war'. De Wiel states that twenty-one out of twenty-seven Catholic bishops supported the war, three or four were neutral, and only two bishops publicly opposed the war, the Archbishop of Dublin and the Bishop of Limerick.

One of the bishops who publicly opposed the war was Bishop O'Dywer of Limerick, who urged that Catholics should heed the Pope's call for peace. Bishop O'Dwyer's appeal may not have been heeded initially, but his voice became more influential later in the war. The Diocese of Limerick included part of South East Clare, in the parishes of Meelick, Parteen and Cratloe and Bishop O'Dwyer's call for peace may not have had more influence there initially, but had a much greater impact later.

The Bishop of Galway, Dr Thomas O'Dea, also had ecclesiastical jurisdiction in part of the county in the deanery of Kilfenora, which covers most of North Clare, including places such as Kilfenora, Ennistymon, Lahinch, Liscannor, Lisdoonvarna, Carron and Ballyvaughan. Dr O'Dea, although he initially condemned the war, it was he said 'caused by a lack of brotherly love', preferred ecclesiastical consensus on the issue and did not publicly oppose enlistment. However, in his Lenten pastoral of March 1916 Dr O'Dea seems to have changed his views on the war, suggesting that Ireland should support the allied cause. 'He hoped that

A war poster of 1914/1915.
(Courtesy of Wikimedia Commons)

every Irish Catholic would join.' It was his 'earnest hope that the contribution of blood made by Irishmen to strike down arrogant militarism would not be a wasted measure'. Such a call from their bishop in a pastoral letter must have carried some weight and had some influence on his parishioners in the North Clare area, encouraging some of them to enlist. [8]

The collection for the Catholics of Belgium was held during November and the total sum collected in the diocese of Killaloe amounted to £1,020 14s 0d, what Bishop Fogarty called 'a magnificent contribution'. He went on to say that it would show the Belgian people, who by all accounts are starving, that the Irish people are not unmindful of their sufferings, which we would alleviate if we could; and that neither do we forget the friendly hand so generously extended by that gallant little country to our forefathers in the tearful centuries, now happily passed and gone, of Ireland's crucifixion'. [9]

It is significant that the Catholic hierarchy did not collectively condemn the war, or indeed condemn the real causes of the war, a potent mix of factors such as: Great Power rivalry; imperialism and imperial rivalry, for example in the Balkans and in Africa; the arms race (especially the naval rivalry between

Britain and Germany during the years 1908-1914); the system of great power alliances at the time, Britain, France and Russia in the 'Triple Entente' versus the central powers of Germany, Austria-Hungary and Italy in the Triple Axis; the aggressive and boastful militarism of Kaiser Wilhelm of Germany; and ultra-nationalism, especially in 'powder-keg' regions such as the Balkans. Instead, Bishop Fogarty and the hierarchy focused on the general bland and politically neutral theme of 'sinful humanity' as the cause of the conflict.

Uniting in a Common Cause

The war had the effect of temporarily uniting the Catholic nationalists and the Protestant unionists of Clare in a common cause, the defence of the country. Following John Redmond's appeal for unity of the Ulster Volunteers and the Irish National Volunteers in the common defence of Ireland, several unionists in County Clare responded to the call and offered their military services voluntarily to the Irish National Volunteers. Col George O'Callaghan Westropp sent a letter to the *Clare Journal* urging unionists in Clare to come forward, 'fall into line', and help to train the Volunteers. Following O'Callaghan's call about a dozen British ex-army officers expressed a willingness to train the Volunteers.

Several meetings were held between 13 and 27 August at Carmody's Hotel Ennis, to discuss how they could co-operate in the emergency. The unionist delegation included Sir Michael O'Loghlen of Drumconora, His Majesty's Lieutenant (HML) for Clare, Col O'Callaghan Westropp of Lismehane, O'Callaghan's Mills and Dr W. MacDonnell of Eden Vale; while the nationalist delegates were Mr M O'Shea, Solicitor, Kilrush, who was chairman of the county board of the Irish National Volunteers, Mr Kenneally, chairman of Ennis UDC, Mr M. McNamara, commander of the Ennis Volunteers, J. Ryan and T. Lynch, O'Callaghan's Mills; M. Collins and M. McNamara, Kildysart; J. Kerin, Ennis UDC; M. Murray Newmarket; M. Walsh, Killaloe, D. O'Brien and M. Clair, Ennistymon; P. McNamara, Mr. Dan O'Brien, UC, and Mr J. Kett, Kilkee, chairman of Clare County Council.

Col George O'Callaghan Westropp stated that he had letters of support from many leading unionists in the county, men such as Mr Stacpoole, Eden Vale, Mr Scott, Mr Ball of Fortfergus, Mr O'Brien of Ballyalla, Mr Crowe jnr, of Dromore, Col Henn of Paradise, Col Massy Westropp, 'an officer of great experience, who had already taken over the Clonlara Volunteers', Capt. Molony of Kiltannon, Tulla, Mr Crowe of Moyriesk, and Mr Lefroy of Killaloe. All of these gentlemen were willing to offer their military experience to train the Volunteers.

However, Mr M. McNamara, chairman of the Ennis National Volunteers, stated that a memorandum from HQ stipulated that all those willing to help would have to enrol and join the ranks, like all other Volunteers. There would be no patronage or favouritism, he said. After their enrolment, allowances would be made for their military expertise. This policy did cause some difficulty for the unionist gentlemen, who would not take orders from their social inferiors. O'Callaghan stated that this policy 'was an unspeakably silly proposal'. Maj. Hickman of Fenloe wrote to Col Moore of the National Volunteers in 1914:

> I could not take orders from some who appear to be in authority on the County Board. I feel awfully ashamed of us all in the south not enlisting in the Irish Division. How could a soldier work under the class of the County Board and perhaps take orders from 'Col' Lynch? You know his record no doubt.

Col Lynch, to whom Maj. Hickman referred, was Arthur Lynch, MP for West Clare since 1909. Arthur Lynch was born in Australia in 1861 to an Irish father and Scottish mother. His father was a native of Tirmaclane, County Clare. After attending the University of Melbourne he graduated as an engineer. Then he travelled to Europe and studied for a couple of years at the University of Berlin, where he became fluent in German. After that he pursued a career in journalism and became Paris correspondent of the *British Daily Mail* in 1898. When the Boer War broke out in 1899 he travelled to South Africa as war correspondent for the Parisian newspaper, *Le Journal*. He met Gen. Botha and decided to join the Boers in the fight against the British. He was appointed 'colonel' of the Second Irish Brigade in South Africa. He went to America on a propaganda mission on behalf of the Boers and later returned to Paris.

While he was away, he was elected as a nationalist MP for Galway in 1901. He went to London to take his seat in parliament and was arrested in 1902 and charged with treason for his pro-Boer actions. He was found guilty and sentenced to death in January 1903. However, following international protests, the sentence was commuted to life imprisonment. He was released a year later on 'licence' by the Tory government. He was finally pardoned by King Edward VII in 1907. He then took up medical studies and qualified as a doctor in 1908. In 1909 he was elected unopposed on 4 September as Nationalist MP for West Clare in a by-election caused by the death of Mr James Halpin, Home Rule MP from Newmarket-on-Fergus. To the unionists Col Arthur Lynch was *persona non grata* and was greeted with silence when he first entered the House of Commons. He was to remain as MP for West Clare till the next general election of 1918.

Col Arthur Lynch, MP,
in 1915. (Courtesy of the
Library of Congress)

Given Arthur Lynch's 'disloyal and traitorous' actions during the Boer War, it is understandable why members of the unionist community in Clare would not take orders from him or associate with him. However, these two meetings between the unionists and nationalists of Clare, while helping to promote some form of unity in the face of a major crisis, were not fruitful. Col George O'Callaghan Westropp felt that the meetings 'were overloaded with politicians and other varieties of unpractical windbags'. Unionist interest in the Volunteers cooled, the Volunteers were afraid of being sucked into the regular British Army, the government was unwilling to assign the Volunteers to home defence duties only, and the Protestants and Catholics distrusted each other.[10]

John Redmond's offer to use the Volunteers as a home defence militia was rejected by Gen. Kitchener and the British War Office. Kitchener wanted to raise an army of 100,000 under regular British Army control. The reserve unionist officers in Clare were called up to join British regiments. Furthermore, Lord Kitchener, despite allowing the Ulster Protestants to form their own exclusive 36th Ulster Division, an exclusively Protestant division, based on the organisation of the Ulster Volunteer Force refused to allow the Irish National Volunteers to form a separate Irish Division. Instead, Irish National Volunteers were split up and had to join existing Irish regiments such as the Leinster, Munster, or Connaught regiments, which were formed into the 16th Irish Division.

Furthermore, Gen. Sir Lawrence Parsons, who commanded the new 16th Irish Division, would not accept the vast majority of the leaders of National Volunteers as officers. Parsons insisted that commissions should only go to gentlemen, with officer training corps experience in public schools, universities or at the cadet college in Sandhurst. The result of Parson's policy was that the vast majority of the officers of the 16th Irish Division were Protestants, while the vast majority of the ranks were Roman Catholics. There were a couple of notable exceptions in the early years of the war when people such as Willie Redmond, MP, and Tom Kettle, MP, joined the 16th Irish Division.[11] Later, due to the loss of so many officers, more Catholics, such as Councillor Dan O'Brien from Clare Abbey, who was leader of the Clare Castle National Volunteers in 1914, were granted commissions.

Another significant factor was that the vast majority of the Protestant Ascendancy class, the landed gentry of Clare, mainly joined established British-based regiments, especially in the early stages of the war, when they were called up as reserve officers, while the majority of Irish Catholics joined the Irish regiments, such as the Connaught Rangers, The Royal Munster Fusiliers and the Royal Dublin Fusiliers. Fitzpatrick wrote 'that virtually every county family sent all its able-bodied sons to fight, leaving a lop-sided community at home stacked with women, the very young and the very old. By late 1917, O'Callaghan had lost five cousins killed and nine cousins were wounded'. Capt. Vandeleur of Kilrush and Cahercon had joined the Life Guards; Maj. George MacNamara of Ennistymon joined the Wiltshire Regiment. The Hon. Desmond O'Brien, son of the 14th Baron Inchiquin of Dromoland, joined the Royal Air Force. His nephew, the Hon. Donough O'Brien, eldest son of the 15th Baron Inchiquin of Dromoland, was too young in 1914, but was old enough to enlist in 1916 and, after a few months training in Scotland, was sent to France in October 1916 as an officer with The Rifle Brigade. Richard Hassard Stacpoole of Eden Vale joined the Royal Artillery as a subaltern in May 1915. Two notable County Clare exceptions were Capt. Robert H. Cullinan of Bindon Street Ennis, of the 7th Battalion Royal Munster Fusiliers and Capt. Poole H. Hickman of Kilmore, Knock, who served in the Royal Dublin Fusiliers.[12]

The Battle of Etroux

Following the 'call up' the British regular army was hastily mobilised and a British Expeditionary Force of about 100,000 men was sent to France to assist the French, who were under pressure from the Germans who, by then, had advanced through much of Belgium. By 20 August the bulk of the

British Army was in Belgium, near the mining town of Mons. Two days later, on 23 August, the British had their first military engagement with the German Army in the First Battle of Mons. Some Irish regiments were in action soon after this date and soldiers from the 2nd Battalion of the Royal Munster Fusiliers were fighting the Germans. The British Army made a tactical retreat but the order to retreat did not reach the Munsters in time and they fought a desperate rearguard action on 27 and 28 August.

Hopelessly outnumbered by the Germans, the Munsters suffered huge losses, with at least nine officers and 118 men killed, in addition to many wounded. Outgunned, surrounded and out of ammunition, the surviving Munsters held up the German advance for nearly fourteen hours, but their position was hopeless. Eventually, the surviving four officers and 240 men, many of them wounded, surrendered in the orchard at Etreux on 28 August. They had engaged in a fierce battle against vastly superior German forces, at least six times more numerous. Tom Johnstone, in his history of the Irish regiments in the war, records that the resistance of the Munsters was so heroic that they even won the respect of the Germans. One German officer said that 'men had never fought so bravely'. The Germans allowed the Munsters to bury their dead in a mass grave in the orchard. At least five Claremen died in this action, including Pte John Cunneen from Newmarket-on-Fergus; Christopher Spillane, Ennis; James Williams, Ennis; John O'Connor, Ennistymon; and James Halloran, from Ennis. They were killed at Etroux on their first day of battle. They were probably the first casualties of the Great War from Clare.[13] Because of their heroic stand, Gen. Haig's first army corps was able to retreat safely with few losses.

Among those who surrendered were seven soldiers from Kilrush. They would have spent the rest of their war years in German prisons, unless they were injured when they might have been exchanged for German wounded through the agency of the Red Cross.

Following the return of the prisoners of war in 1919, the War Office carried out an investigation into the conduct of the 2nd Munsters, which concluded that 'The battalion not only held up the attack of a strong hostile force in its original position, thereby securing the unmolested withdrawal of the division, but in retiring drew upon itself the attacks of very superior numbers of the enemy.' As a result, many of them were given military awards, including the DSO for Maj. Bayley, along with several Military Crosses (MC), Military Medals (MM) and Distinguished Conduct Medals (DCM) as a testimony of the bravery of the regiment. According to Johnstone, the survivors 'were warmly congratulated by the Germans on the fine fight they had made at Etreux'.[14]

Propaganda

Soon, the local papers were carrying reports of the war issued by the British and French war offices, copied from the national Irish or British press. These reports were heavily propagandist in tone, passed by the army censors, and one must be aware of the old cliche that 'truth is the first casualty of war'. There were sensational headlines such as 'GERMANS RETREATING';'GREAT RUSSIAN VICTORY';'ENORMOUS GERMAN LOSSES'; 'FIERCE FIGHTING IN BELGIUM';'BRAVE IRISH GUARDS' etc.The newspapers differed in that the *Clare Journal* and the *Saturday Record* gave far more comprehensive reports on the war than the *Clare Champion*.The *Clare Champion* did, however, highlight the call to arms by Redmond and urged the Clare nationalists to rally to the defence of Catholic Belgium.

Within a short while, reports of casualties in the British Expeditionary Force from County Clare began to appear in the local papers. *The Clare Journal* and the *Saturday Record* highlighted the deaths or injuries suffered by prominent members of the landed gentry of Clare, who had been called up for service, such as Maj. Parker, Ballyvalley; the Hon. Lt Butler, brother of Lord Dunboyne, Knappogue; Lt Gore of Derrymore and Capt. Alexander Vandeleur of Kilrush and Cahercon. The local papers also mentioned prominent Clare individuals such as Poole Hickman BL, of Kilmore, Knock, secretary of the Munster Bar, and Dr C.J. Kelly of Trinaderry House, Barefield, who had voluntarily enlisted.

The papers were also delighted to report unusually high rates of enlistment among some poor families. For instance, a Mrs Keane of Kilrush was reported as having five 'gallant' sons serving in the army. Another Kilrush family, the Devers also had five sons in the colours. Mrs Margaret Molony of Newmarket-on-Fergus also had five sons who volunteered, one joined the Royal Dublin Fusiliers and four of them joined the Royal Munster Fusiliers. However, the Clare family that contributed most of their members to the war effort was probably the Halloran family of Ennistymon. Michael Halloran along with five of his sons, John, William, Michael, Jeremiah and Martin, all joined the Royal Munster Fusiliers, while another son named Patrick joined the Connaught Rangers. Unfortunately, Patrick Halloran was fatally wounded at the Second Battle of Ypres on 29 April 1915, but all of the rest of the family survived.[15]

Selected letters from the front were published, which highlighted the conditions of war, the bravery of the soldiers and the need for recruits. One letter, from Pte Edward Toomey to his mother in Kilkee, which was printed in the *Clare Champion* of 26 August, was clearly propagandist and was headed 'We stood our ground to the last':

We have had some very hard fighting; we were in the thick of it all the time. Our regiment was posted to cover the retreat for five days and the Germans were as thick as bees around us all the time. When you are put on duty of that kind there's no question of giving way until your task has been completed and we stood our ground till the last. That meant in some cases we had to be cut up, but we were selected because we could be relied upon to make the best possible show and delay the enemy as long as possible. Some of our detachment had a very rough time in every way, but they carried themselves with a steadiness that won the praise of everybody, and they made the Germans realise that they weren't going to have it all their own way.

The most distinguished soldier, Lt Gen. Sir Thomas Kelly Kenny, a former commander in chief of the British Army, a Catholic native of West Clare, prophesising a long war, urged the necessity of universal conscription in a letter to *The Times*, of London, which was copied in the *Saturday Record* of 14 November 1914:

There is still a word which has not been spoken – compulsion. If the government can assure itself that our present recruiting system will enable us to bring this two, five or even ten year's war to a successful issue it takes on itself the responsibility – not a great consolation to the king's subjects of the empire if we see the Potsdam trained goose step up the Mall. I believe if compulsion is once settled it will clear the way for other great reforms. While I advocate and believe that our only safety is in compulsion for this war, my admiration for the army put into the field under our present recruiting conditions is unbounded. The nation will never forget this noble volunteer army, which has not waited for this measure ...

One unusual letter from a prisoner of war was published in the *Saturday Record* in October under the subtitle of CLAREMAN'S LETTER FROM THE FRONT: Cpl T. Kelly sent a letter to his father, Mr T. Kelly, Clare Castle. Cpl Kelly mentioned that he was 'one of the 500 or 600 Munster Fusiliers taken prisoner on August 27th'. The letter was dated 31 August 1914 and the editor of the *Saturday Record* suspected that it had been heavily censored by the Germans as it painted a rosy picture of the treatment of the prisoners by the Germans:

Of course, I told you I was going to the war in France. Well I left on the 13th August along with my regiment I was 14 days in France and on 27th August the Munster Fusiliers had a great battle with the Germans, where we lost a few men, but there was a lot of us captured by the Germans, about 500 men and I was lucky to be amongst them. Of course I cannot give you any information ... Tell the Hynes' in Ennis that their son is alright. A brother of Paddy Moroney's that works at Howard's in Ennis is alright also ... We are kept as prisoners of war by the Germans till the war is over. The German soldiers are very nice people. They are giving us all the privileges they can and plenty to eat … I will be sorry to leave them …, I think, when we are leaving … but won't I be delighted when I am on the boat for England again. Pray for my safe return soon and sound. You can imagine what it is to be a prisoner of war. I shall laugh when I am telling you by word of mouth … I have a terrible story to tell ye when I get home … I can't give ye any address, being a prisoner. Cheer up, as I am as happy and cheerful as can be.

The letter from Cpl T. Kelly provoked a reply from Lt Col W.B. Butler, who stated, 'Re Clare Castle man's letter from the front in issue of 14 October, I can scarcely believe that any Clare man would feel "lucky" at being taken prisoner. I believe that not only was the German censor close by when the letter was written, but also gave it a final touch up!' [16]

Several other letters were published in the local press and the letters seemed to have been chosen for propaganda purposes. Indeed, they may have been fictitious! They all cited anonymous sources. One allegedly from 'an Ennis man' had sub-headings such as 'a hell upon earth' and 'German cowards before the bayonet'.

The first was from a private in the Connaught Rangers, writing from the General Hospital, near Versailles, Paris:

'GERMAN COWARDS BEFORE THE BAYONET'
My dear James,
I suppose you will be surprised to get this letter … but I take the opportunity as I am only a few hours from England. I suppose you read of this terrible war and an awful war it is. There were terribly hard times for us at the front, fighting days and nights without any rest whatever. We didn't know what a blanket was for the last few weeks, and it is getting frightfully cold now. I am here badly wounded through the left side and right arm. I was lying on the open ground under shrapnel and gunfire for four hours and I thought my time had come. It was a regular hell upon earth, enough to turn you sick, men falling all round you for six long hours. The Gurkhas were on our right and we had to support them and we had Hell to cross the open under a terrible fire from the enemy's trenches. But we drove the Germans back with frightful losses. They are cowards when it comes to the bayonet, and we have to fight them at five to one, so you know what work we have to do to keep them back. The Munsters were cut off in the retreat from Mons – 600 of them went west by a mistake in the signalling. As I write this I am waiting for an operation to remove a piece of shell from my side. I am only here a week, but I expect to be back at the front again soon. There is a lot of Germans wounded here so there is not room for many more. I am the only one from Ennis here, as far as I know, and there are only two more in the Connaughts from Ennis.

A second anonymous letter was entitled: 'FIGHTING FOR A GOOD CAUSE'. According to the paper it was from 'a Clare man serving in the Guards':

> Dear sister, just a line in answer to your kind and welcome letter of the 10th inst. I am sorry to hear that you are not as strong, but cheer up, things will get better when all the Germans are killed ... You will feel very lonely, I am sure when you have three brothers out of your sight, but don't fret, they are fighting for a good cause. I am longing to have a crack at the Germans anyway, my turn is drawing near, and don't fret for me. I know I gave up a good job to come here, but I am quite satisfied. I had a letter from brother C this morning. I heard that brother W was captured, but don't let it upset you as he will be alright. Remember me to all at home. Tell them I am doing fine and I hope the boys are answering Lord Kitchener's call. Tell them I advise them to join and let us wipe the Germans off the map altogether as they are nothing but a lot of curs ... We have a fine body of Irishmen here and we are ready for anything.
>
>   Wishing you all sorts of good luck, your ever loving brother, G

A third anonymous letter was written by 'a young gentleman to his brother in Ennis'. The sender was with the Army Veterinary Corps at the Western Front:

> 'GERMHUN KULTUR'
> We are very busy in our camp, we have nearly 2,000 horses with us at present and the number keeps changing each day, some coming in from the front line and others going out cured or dead. The weather is getting very cold now, especially at night, but we are very well provided for as regards clothing and grub ... I dare say you gather from the papers at home a good idea of Germhun Kultur. Here is another sample: Some prisoners were brought in here last week, and on being searched by our fellows, one was found to have in his haversack, wrapped up in a handkerchief a lady's hand, with five rings on the fingers.' Nuff said! I'll have a lot to tell you when I see you again, as I am taking notes.[17]

One young Clare man, James Power from Quilty, who was an able seaman on board the cruiser *Hermes*, had a very lucky escape when the *Hermes* was torpedoed and sunk by a German submarine in the Straits of Dover in November, 1914. The ship was about 9 miles from Calais when it was hit. Of the 367 hands aboard, about 40 were killed. James Power stated that he remembered some of the survivors in the water singing 'It's a long way to Tipperary', while waiting to be rescued.[18]

National Volunteers Parade

Meanwhile, at home in Clare, a large turnout of the National Volunteers was organised at the end of October. The purpose of the turnout was to re-affirm support for John Redmond's takeover of the National Volunteers and his policies of supporting the British war effort. The commander in chief of the National Volunteers, Col Maurice Moore, accompanied by Capt. Hemphill and Willie Redmond, MP, toured the county to assess the strength of and to boost the morale of the National Volunteers. They travelled by car from Dublin and stayed overnight with Mr E.E. Lysaght, the organiser of the National Volunteers for Clare, at Raheen Manor, near Tuamgraney. The men reviewed parades of Volunteers at Tuamgraney and Killaloe, where there were huge and enthusiastic turnouts. The local Catholic clergy, such as V. Revd Canon Flannery, PP, VG of Killaloe, and Revd Fr Quin, PP of O'Callaghan's Mills, presented Redmond with addresses of welcome, supporting the Home Rule Party, expressing full confidence in the leadership of John Redmond, MP, and support for his war policy.

The major review of Volunteers from Ennis and its environs took place in Ennis on Sunday after midday Mass. Between 600 and 700 Volunteers turned out. The weather on the day was very wet and was blamed for the relatively low turnout, but this excuse may have been used to mask the decline in enthusiasm for the National Volunteers after the war began. It seems that many feared that the National Volunteers would be conscripted into the British Army. This fear of recruitment was mentioned in the *Saturday Record* of 7 November 1914 as a factor in the 'fall-off' in National Volunteers. The activities of the Irish Volunteers in organising within the county may also have been a factor in this relatively small turnout.

The National Volunteers paraded from the O'Connell monument, which was draped with banners with slogans such as 'To God and Country True', to the Fair Green, Ennis. There were groups from Kilrush, Ennis, Clare Castle, Corofin, Doora, Miltown, Newmarket-on-Fergus, Lahinch, Kilmaley, Inch and Manus. They were accompanied by brass bands from Kilrush and Newmarket-on-Fergus, as well as the Ennis Fife and Drum Band. The colours were presented by Mrs Lysaght and speeches were made by Col Moore, Capt. Hemphill, and Willie Redmond, MP. In his address, Redmond emphatically declared that no member of the Volunteers would be forced to join the British Army.

Significantly, Dr Fogarty, Bishop of Killaloe, and several local clergy were on the reviewing stand, along with many local politicians and some unionists. The presence of the bishop indicated his public support for John Redmond and his war policies at this time. Indeed, it seems that Dr Fogarty played an active part in ensuring that many of the Clare Volunteers stayed loyal to John Redmond when the movement split in September. Earlier, Mr E.E. Lysaght wrote to Capt. Hemphill that 'he was afraid of the split, especially in West Clare'. Mr Michael O'Shea, a solicitor from Kilrush, also informed Hemphill that 'the Volunteer enthusiasm in West Clare was dormant'. It seems that membership of the Kilrush corps of National Volunteers fell by half from seventy-two to thirty-six by 4 November.

Just before the county review by Col Maurice Moore in October, Dr Fogarty warned Redmond, 'Ennistymon and Carron have unanimously refused to come to the review, in the other battalions there is a division more or less, the parade will be an accurate account of this division. McNamara and nearly all in Ennis are now right and will be there'. The turnout of between 600 and 700 must have been disappointing for the National Volunteers.[19]

One man who was active in West Clare in opposition to the war was Art O'Donnell from Tullycrine. Shortly after the war broke out he distributed anti-recruitment leaflets at a Killadysart sports meeting, at dances, football matches and wherever a crowd was gathered for any purpose in the district. According to Art O'Donnell there was a strong body of National Volunteers at Killadysart, who were organised by John O'Connell Bianconi. However, he stated that after the first month in which all men were exhorted to join the National Volunteers and parade in defence of their country, their activities practically ceased. The leaflets distributed by Art O'Donnell and others in West Clare may have had a big influence in the decline of the National Volunteers in the district. The anti-war pamphlet included the following passage:

What will England do?
She will recruit Irishmen to fight the Germans for her.
She will then, when finished with them,
Fling them back to the workhouses of Ireland
Reeking with foul, filthy diseases.[20]

War Pictures

Besides the war news in the local and national press, the people of Clare also had an opportunity to see images of the war in the local cinema at Ennis. In October war pictures under the title 'BRAVE BELGIUM' were shown at the Picture Palace in the town hall. This was promoted as a 'fine selection of war pictures, including the entry of the Germans into Brussels.' These silent movies with captions, though no doubt carefully selected and censored, brought images of the horrors of war to the local people. The people were reminded of the destruction of the great Catholic University of Louvain, which had a long association with the Irish Catholic Church since Reformation times. These propagandist images may have encouraged some young men of Clare to enlist. Jeffery states, 'though he stopped short of explicitly encouraging Irishmen to enlist, the primate of Ireland, Cardinal Logue denounced the barbarism of the Germans in burning Rheims cathedral'.[21]

Some time later there was also a concert in the Town Hall, Ennis, which was held in aid of the Belgian Relief Fund, with songs and recitals. In addition there was a series of 'excellent' war pictures, including scenes in the trenches. The second half of the concert was opened with the now world-famous marching song: 'It's a Long Way to Tipperary'.

> It's a long way to Tipperary
> It's a long way to go.
> It's a long way to Tipperary,
> To the sweetest girl I know!
> Goodbye Picadilly,
> Farewell Leicester Square.
> It's a long, long way to Tipperary,
> But my heart's right there.[22]

The burning of Rheims
Cathedral in August 1914.
(Courtesy of Wikipedia Commons)

Ruins of the Irish Nuns' Abbey at Ypres. (Courtesy of Australian National Archives)

The Cloth Hall, Ypres. (Courtesy of www.archives.gov.can)

One prominent businessman in Clare, Mr H.R. Glynn, JP of Kilrush, responded very enthusiastically to the crisis in Europe and offered whatever services he could to the Irish and British authorities. He sent a cheque for £10 to John Redmond for the Volunteer fund on 5 August and he wrote to Mr Augustin Birrel, the Chief Secretary in Dublin, offering his services, 'I met you in London some time ago … I will be glad to assist you in any way. Already about 100 men have left the town of Kilrush for the war.' On the same date in late August he wrote to the admiral in charge of the British naval depot at Queenstown, 'offering our services to you'.

About a month later, Glynn was appointed as deputy lieutenant of County Clare. In November he responded to an appeal by the British Prime Minister, Mr Asquith, to 'The British Cause' in the *The Times* of London. He wrote to the secretary of the Central Committee as follows:

> Re the appeal, "The British Cause" in *The Times* of 21 November, I beg to say that it will give me great pleasure to act as local hon. sec of the Central Committee for National Patriotic Organisations. I will do everything in my power to assist you in every way, and, if you approve of it, I will come to London to take instructions … I am the largest employer of labour in Clare, I am on the Finance Committee and Chairman of the Railway Committee of Clare County Council and I am a member of the Reform Club SW, Your obedient servant, Henry R. Glynn.

Glynn also wrote to Sir Michael O'Loghlen, HML for County Clare offering his services: 'If I can be of assistance to you in any way please send me a line'.[23]

Many members of the RIC voluntarily enlisted around this time as the local newspapers noted their departure. In November the *Saturday Record* noted that Constables J. Mannion, T. Love and ? Brogan of Bodyke had enlisted. While in December a much larger group joined the ranks of the army, including: District Inspector Connolly, Kilrush: District Inspector Rodwell, Sixmilebridge: Constables J. O'Neill, Carron; R. Barrett, Corofin, C. Ahern, New Hall: P.J. Callaghan, Whitegate: A.C. Johnstone, Kilrush: R. Howlett, Quin: M. Tierney and Jas Reilly, Ballynacally. The newspaper article noted that nationally more than 200 RIC men had joined the Irish Guards regiment.[24]

'He had burned several times to enlist. Tales of great movements shook the land. They might not be distinctly Homeric, but there seemed to be much glory in them,'[25] Stephen Crane, *The Red Badge of Courage*.

Practical and helpful, as ever, the ladies of Clare, through the agency of the Clare Needlework Guild, organised a collection in aid of the sick and wounded soldiers. The membership was mainly drawn from the Protestant gentry class, headed by Lady Inchiquin and Lady Dunboyne, with familiar county names such as Studdert, Stackpoole, Maunsell, MacDonnell, Butler, Burton, Blood, Hickman, Mahon, Molony, Fitzgerald, O'Brien, Ball, Vere O'Brien, Ivers and Henn, and some Catholic ladies such as Ms Wilson Lynch of Belvoir and Lady O'Loghlen of Drumconora.[26]

Lady Inchiquin and Mrs Hickman also collected funds for a motor ambulance as a gift from Kilnasoolagh parish and succeeded in collecting £400 for this purpose. These motor ambulances were badly wanted at the front to bring wounded soldiers from the trenches to the hospitals at the base, as many had died during the hours they had to wait before they could be moved or during the long journey by the ordinary horse-drawn ambulance wagons.

Lt Henry Spaight, Royal Army Medical Corps, from Tulla described in graphic detail in several letters to the *Clare Journal* in December 1914 and January 1915, the difficulties of driving motor ambulances over roads with huge craters near the front lines, and the dangers of driving by night if the sky was illuminated by flares, the crew being at risk from snipers and bombs.[27]

Roll of Honour

'For king and country'
Approximately fifty-eight Clare men died this year, most of them fell on the Western Front in Belgium and France; they were mainly professional soldiers and reservists, who were called up on the outbreak of war. The majority of them are buried in Flanders, some lie in unmarked graves, while seven were lost at sea. The most prominent victims from Clare included Capt. Alexander Vandeleur, Life Guards, of Cahercon and Kilrush and Lt R.E. Parker, Royal Horse Artillery, of Ballyvalley, Killaloe. They died 'for king and country'.[28]

3

PROPAGANDA, THE WESTERN FRONT AND GALLIPOLI

The war, which many had predicted, and hoped, would be over by Christmas 1914, intensified in 1915 and became a war of attrition, with huge losses on both sides and a voracious demand for new recruits. Following the first call up of reserves for the British Expeditionary Force under Sir John French, there was a demand for a new larger army. Conscription was introduced in Britain, but not extended to Ireland, largely due to the resistance of John Redmond and the Home Rule Party, which still held the balance of power in the British Parliament at Westminster, until the formation of a national coalition government on 25 May 1915.

However, a huge publicity campaign began in the press and elsewhere promoting voluntary enlistment. Recruitment in Clare was hindered by the growing opposition of the local hierarchy and some local clergy towards the war, especially that of Bishop O'Dwyer and Bishop Fogarty. Besides the war on the Western Front, which for the British Army was mainly fought in Belgium, a second war front was opened by the British in 1915 at Gallipoli at the entrance to the Dardennelles in Turkey. This second front was to prove a military disaster for the British and was later abandoned after huge losses.

Pope Benedict XV appealed for peace several times during the year, but was ignored by the belligerents. In February he blamed the war on the rejection of God's authority by modern society, secularism and socialism. 'There was', he said, 'a campaign to banish the Church from education. False principles were promulgated that all men ought to be equal in society. This belief only fomented class hatred, and a weakening of the bonds between superior and inferior classes in society. We have called down upon ourselves the just wrath of God.' The Pope called for special prayers for peace on Passion Sunday. The Blessed Sacrament was to be exposed after Mass till evening, followed by the rosary and benediction and the song 'Tantum Ergo'.[1]

Perhaps taking his cue from the Pope, Bishop Fogarty issued his Lenten pastoral in February in which he blamed mankind's wickedness for the war. He seemed to welcome the war as a purifying purgative for the evils of modern society. Under the heading, 'NO GOD BUT MAMMON', Fogarty wrote:

> The war is a divine retribution for the world's apostasy from God. It is another deluge let loose on the world for a state of depravity unexampled in the history of mankind. Happily, its purifying waters may wash the earth of the accumulated corruption that encumbered it ... Civil governments have shown contempt for the religious and the spiritual, they have an assured policy to secularise society from top to bottom, to loose the bonds of marriage and to secularise education. They have created a deadly ooze of infidelity, scepticism, coarse sensuality, race suicide and socialistic confusion.[2]

In May Fogarty urged his flock to follow the king's example and abstain from alcohol, except for medicinal purposes, but, Fogarty, a lifelong teetotaller, denounced higher liquor taxes. Later in the year Fogarty launched an appeal on behalf of Catholic Poland, which he said had also suffered at the hands of the Prussians.

However, Fogarty's support for John Redmond's policy was undermined by political developments in England during May 1915. When the new coalition government was formed in May, Sir Edward Carson, leader of the Unionist Party, became a minister, while John Redmond turned down the offer of a ministry. The presence of Carson in the government deeply offended Fogarty, who had been a strong supporter of the Home Rule Party and of the National Volunteers. Fogarty wrote a letter to John Redmond on 3 June denouncing the new cabinet, calling it:

> ... a horrible scandal and an intolerable outrage on Irish sentiment. The English have got all they wanted from Ireland ... such is our reward for our profuse loyalism and recruiting ... The people are full of indignation, but yet are powerless ... there is nothing to choose between Carsonism and Kaiserism and of the two the latter is the lesser evil ... And it almost makes me cry to think of the Irish Brigades fighting not for Ireland, but for Carson and what he stands for, Orange Ascendancy. Home Rule is dead and buried and Ireland is without a national party or a national press.

Redmond sent the letter to the Prime Minister, Mr Asquith. However, the bishop kept his opinions private for the moment.[3]

In his Lenten pastoral Pope Benedict XV appealed for peace and he repeated this plea earnestly to the belligerents on the first anniversary of the war. Bishop O'Dwyer of Limerick publicly requested John Redmond to listen to the Pope's appeal and to use his influence on the British to weigh in on the side of peace. O'Dwyer also warned Redmond that Ireland faced economic ruin because of the growing burden of the war debt, which would necessitate a huge tax bill when the war ended. Redmond's reply was published in the newspapers, including the *Saturday Record* of 14 August:

Dear Lord Bishop,

... to the best of my judgement, the course of action you suggest to me would not be calculated to promote the cause of peace. Nor do I think that I would be justified in endeavouring to bring pressure to bear upon the British government to enter into any negotiations for peace at a time when the German Powers, who have been the aggressors in this war, show no signs of any disposition to repair the wrongs they have inflicted upon Belgium and our other allies.

Yours, J. E. Redmond.

The call to arms.
(Courtesy of Wikimedia Commons)

This reply from Redmond infuriated O'Dwyer, who became more outspoken against the immorality of the war and more opposed to recruitment. His ecclesiastical friend, Bishop Fogarty did not, however, come out publicly against the war and recruitment for some time yet.

While Bishop Fogarty and the Irish Catholic hierarchy seemed to justify the war, without directly urging young men to enlist, the local newspapers, especially the *Saturday Record*, published several letters from Catholic clergymen appealing for Irishmen to join the British forces. A Tipperary priest wrote that 'it was the duty of Irishmen to fight, or else ... Ireland would suffer the same fate as Belgium'. A Dublin priest urged Irishmen to enlist and 'kill the savage Huns!' Another priest highlighted the Turkish atrocities against the Armenians.

Finally, at Christmas, Canon O'Leary, Parish Priest of Dingle, wrote that the country was in danger of 'being overrun by Huns and Turks, intolerable savages! There was', he said, 'a need for men of heroic courage to defend our country and to crush the enemy.'[4]

The main focus of the government in Ireland was the vigorous promotion of recruitment through propaganda among the Catholic, nationalist majority of Ireland. This campaign was mainly done through advertising in the national and local newspapers. These advertisements were mainly carried in the two 'unionist' local papers, the *Clare Journal* and the *Saturday Record*. There were fewer advertisements in the more nationalistic *Clare Champion*. The advertisements appealed to the patriotic duty and the fighting spirit of the Irishmen to emulate heroes such as Sgt Michael O'Leary who won a Victoria Cross; they were urged to fight for

Irish First World War propaganda, original published by David Allen and Sons, Dublin, *c.* 1915. (Courtesy of Wikimedia Commons)

Catholic Belgium, its priests, nuns and people; it was their 'duty' to join the Irish Brigade; women were encouraged to persuade their 'best boy' to join up; clerks and shop assistants were encouraged to emulate the brave young men in khaki; and appeals were made to the pride of young men, insinuating that they would be, 'slackers', 'shirkers' and perhaps cowards if they did not join up.[5]

Lt D.D. Sheehan MP, founder and former president of the Irish Land and Labour Association, which had several branches in County Clare, toured the county in April and made an appeal 'to his friends among the workers of Limerick and Clare to join his regiment, the 9th Battalion Royal Munster Fusiliers'. There was also a personal appeal from King George V, addressed 'to my people'. Many nationalists in Clare and elsewhere took umbrage at the suggestion that they were the king's people. Ironically, almost all the advertisements ended with the old Fenian slogan: 'God save Ireland!'

Besides the vigorous advertising campaign, the local newspapers, especially the *Saturday Record* and the *Clare Journal*, promoted recruitment by frequently referring to the 'bravery and gallantry' of the soldiers, especially those from Clare who were honoured for heroic deeds at the battlefront. The bravery of officers and men was honoured by the presentation of medals, such as the MC, given to officers and the DCM, given to NCOs and soldiers. Claremen who were promoted for 'gallantry in war', especially the officers, were also mentioned in the press.

Early in the year there was considerable alarm and a major scare in West Clare with fears of a German invasion. The alarm was sparked off by notices delivered to all residents of coastal areas by the RIC, advising people what to do if the Germans invaded.

The advice, especially to those living in coastal areas, was to leave their homesteads and to remove all their stock, farming implements, horses, bicycles, and motorcycles, if any, to certain indicated places, where their safety would be arranged by the authorities. In West Clare, Ennis was the designated place, while in East Clare the people were told to proceed to Killaloe and Ballina.

These precautionary notices in the event of a German invasion caused considerable fright. In Kilkee the people were told to take the Kilrush Road for Ennis after first destroying all foodstuffs, burying all spades and shovels, and destroying all motorcycles and bicycles. Publicans were directed to spill all their stocks of whiskey, porter, brandy etc. on the road; and farmers along the coast were instructed to drive their horses, sheep, cattle, in fact all their stock, before them on the road to Ennis. According to the newspaper report the people, especially the elderly, were in a terrible state of excitement and fear. The local parish priest, Fr Glynn, did his best at first Mass on Sunday morning to reassure the people and calm their fears that a German invasion was not imminent and said that an invasion was as likely to happen as that 'if the sky fell we would catch larks'. The newspaper concluded: 'even so, some ignorant old people are in a bad way'.[6]

John Redmond and other members of the Home Rule Party, while encouraging voluntary enlistment, repeatedly insisted that conscription would not be imposed on Ireland.

Letters from the 'front' were published in the press appealing for more men. Cpl M. Murphy, an Ennis man serving with the Royal Munster Fusiliers, appealed to 'slackers' at home – 'I am sure that there are some slackers in Ennis. It is about time that these fellows woke up and did their bit!'

An anonymous writer to the *Saturday Record* of 27 February sarcastically criticised the Sinn Féin Volunteers of Carrigaholt:

Whose pro-German mouthings have for some time past disgusted every decent Irishman in West Clare … Did you ever hear of The Yellow Dragoons raised in Carrigaholt by Lord Clare? … Do you know that in Carrigaholt Castle lived and died the ancestors of Marshal McMahon, President of France? … Rest easy you degenerate sons of heroic sires … Rest easy in your beds my gallant warriors of the Home Defence Service with the timber guns … Your hearths and homes and farms are being saved for you by the Watch Dogs of the North Sea and the 'gentlemen' and the 'corner-boys', who are spilling their blood freely in your defence on the battlefields of Europe!

Early in the year the *Saturday Record* carried an article under a sub-heading, 'ENNIS MEN FOR THE FRONT': 'About a score of recruits and reserves left Ennis station to join various regiments. One family in old Mill Street now has 4 sons serving with the colours, and 3 other families in the same neighbourhood had each sent 2 sons to the front.' On 29 March the *Limerick Leader* reported that over 200 recruits left the town of Kilrush by train. They were seen off by an enormous crowd of wellwishers.[7]

The highest profile recruit in Clare at this time was Willie Redmond, MP for East Clare. Redmond was commissioned in the Royal Irish Regiment in February. He wrote to Councillor P.J. Linnane, JP, an old friend from Ennis, to tell the people of Ennis and Clare that he had enlisted and the letter was published in the *Clare Journal* of 27 March:

> The future freedom and welfare of the Irish people depended on the part Ireland played in the war. Belgium was invaded and the Belgian people were massacred and their homes and churches destroyed. A niece of my own – a nun has been a victim – driven from her convent by shot and shell … if we do not strike a blow for Belgium then our name would be disgraced! … I believe the men of East Clare will approve of my action.

Another local politician who joined up was Dan O'Brien, a member of Ennis Rural District Council, from Clare Abbey. When Dr A.J. Hickey joined the Royal Army Medical Corps a public meeting was held in Kilmihil, chaired by the parish priest, Fr D. Hayes; a resolution was passed 'expressing regret at his departure, while commending his pluck and sacrifice.' The *Clare Journal* report noted that Dr Hickey was the second son of Dr P.C. Hickey, JP of Kilkee, to 'take a Clareman's part against the enemy of civilisation'.[8]

Emigration

While many men felt that it was their duty to join the British forces and take the 'king's shilling', whatever their motives, many others were reluctant to join the colours. One headline in the *Clare Journal* early in June highlighted emigration, suggesting an exodus from West Clare. These headlines were accompanied by warnings to those who intended to emigrate to America that there was a high rate of unemployment there. One sub-heading stated that the motive for emigration was fear of conscription:

AN EXODUS FROM WEST CLARE
FEAR OF CONSCRIPTION
For the past week or two there has been a steady exodus of young Clare people, mostly able sturdy youths of the agricultural class, for America, and the number that have left and are still going is attracting much public comment ... Queenstown having been closed to emigrants since the beginning of the war, they have to travel to Dublin ... For the past week nearly 300 have left North Wall Dublin, about 50 of these from County Clare ... and it was noticeable that most of them came from West Clare, and some from the most extreme part of the county ... It is freely stated that the 'rush to emigrate' was attributed to statements made in certain quarters that a policy of conscription was about to be adopted by the present coalition government ... Another batch of emigrants packed the Ennis station today.

About six months later this avenue of avoiding conscription through emigration to America was virtually closed off. In an article headed 'THE WHITE FEATHERS', the *Clare Journal* reported that twenty young men from Clare had been sent home from Liverpool. They were from the Tulla, Kilnamona and Inagh districts. These 'would-be' emigrants to America were made to feel unwelcome in Liverpool and were assaulted there. They received a sarcastic 'welcome home' to Clare from the *Clare Journal*! The White Star Line followed the Cunard Shipping Line's example in refusing to book men of military age for emigration to America. Also, further restrictions were put on the issuing of passports.

The treatment of the Irish emigrants at Liverpool outraged Bishop O'Dwyer, who publicly rebuked John Redmond, who had rashly stated in an interview with the Press Association that 'it was very cowardly of them to try and emigrate'. In a public letter O'Dwyer savaged Redmond for his remarks and failure to defend the would-be emigrants:

The treatment of the poor Irish emigrants at Liverpool is enough to make any Irishman's blood boil with anger and indignation! They do not want to be forced into the English army and sent to fight English battles in some part of the world ... these poor Connaught peasants ... Not one Irish man stands up for them ... Why should they die for England? ... Yet the poor fellows who do not see the advantage of dying for such a cause are to be insulted as 'shirkers' and 'cowards' … and the men whom they have raised to power and influence have not one word to say on their behalf.

This letter caused a sensation as it was published in the *Cork Examiner* of 11 November 1915 and in the *Limerick Chronicle* at the same time, and copies of it were found by the RIC in seventeen counties. They were distributed at chapel gates by members of the Irish Volunteers and Sinn Féin. Bishop Fogarty wrote privately to O'Dwyer in support of his letter. He stated: '… it is past time that some one would tell the truth though few beside yourself have the courage to do so. By the way, the whole body of people have rallied to you and your letter to the emigrants. It has opened their eyes … John Redmond … deserves a rebuke, which you have now given him with deadly force'. Fogarty also corresponded with Fr Hagan at the Irish College in Rome and suggested that recruitment had fallen off considerably at this time: 'Recruitment is unpopular, because no-one is to be spared for recruiting and they don't want to die in the present cause.'

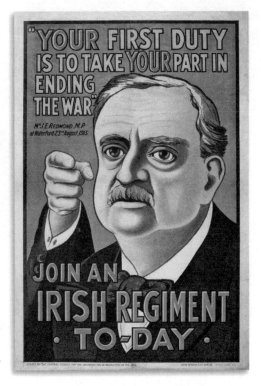

John Redmond urges recruitment.
(Courtesy of National Library of Ireland)

The Ennis Brian Boru branch of Sinn Féin also passed a resolution condemning 'the threats meted out to brother Irishmen by a Liverpool rabble'.

Such public attacks on John Redmond by O'Dwyer must have seriously damaged the recruitment cause in the region as O'Dwyer's letter was widely circulated in Clare. However, Dr Thomas O'Dea, Bishop of Galway, Kilmacduagh and Kilfenora declined to join O'Dwyer in publicly condemning the war and recruitment at this time, preferring ecclesiastical consensus on the war.[9]

'Slackers' and 'Shirkers'

The Irish Guards and the Royal Munster Fusiliers regiments toured County Clare during the year, urging men to enlist for king and country. This was a traditional method of encouraging men to enlist. The Irish Guards toured in April, while

The band of the Munster Fusiliers at
Ennis in 1915. (Courtesy of Sean Spellissy)

the Munsters toured in June, August and
November. The regimental bands played
many national airs, such as 'The Wearing
of the Green', 'God Save Ireland', and 'Let
Erin Remember', to give the impression that
the regiments were more Irish than British.
The band of the Royal Munster Fusiliers
got a huge reception in June at Ennis railway station and paraded to a mass meeting in
O'Connell Square, chaired by Mr P. Kennelly,
JP, chairman of Ennis UDC and other local
notables. Mr Kennelly said that there was a
good deal of misunderstanding and a good
deal of private intimidation with respect to
enlistment. He did not say who was responsible for the intimidation, but hinted that it
was members of the Irish Volunteers. He said
those who volunteered were doing their
duty and 'played a man's part'.

4 Questions to Clerks and and Shop Assistants

*If you are between 19 and 38 years of
age are you really satisfied with what
you are doing today?*

*Do you feel happy as you walk along
the streets and see brave Irishmen in
khaki, who are going to fight for Ireland
while you stay at home in comfort?*

*Do you realise that gallant Irish
soldiers are risking everything on the
continent to save you, your children
and your womenfolk?*

*Will you tell your employer today that
you are going to join an Irish regiment?*

Ask him to keep your position
open for you – tell him that you
are going to fight for Ireland.
He'll do the right thing by you –
all patriotic employers are helping
their men to join.

TELL HIM NOW AND
JOIN AN IRISH
REGIMENT TO-DAY.

Clare Journal, 8 April 1915.

Mr Kennelly said that while many had responded to the call, there were classes around them, who were not represented as they should be. He particularly alluded to the farming class, 'few of whose sons had gone to the front'. He also referred to the number of recruits that might be found among the young shop assistants in the county. Again, the fate of 'gallant little Belgium', with priests murdered, churches and convents burnt and women outraged etc. was mentioned to encourage recruitment.

Lt Dan O'Brien of the Royal Irish Regiment then spoke passionately, calling for men 'to do their duty' and enlist. The rural district councillor and former chairman of Ennis RDC said that he always had the greatest electoral support in the labouring crowd and in the democratic classes. But, he found that there were only two sections, the labouring classes and the aristocratic class who were fighting, and there was something lacking. They wanted something between these two classes. Capt. Larry Roche appealed 'in the name of God, of Ireland, as a Catholic, an Irishman, and as a nationalist' for young men to enlist and defeat the murderous Huns. He said that 100 Claremen were needed to enlist and serve under Irish officers.

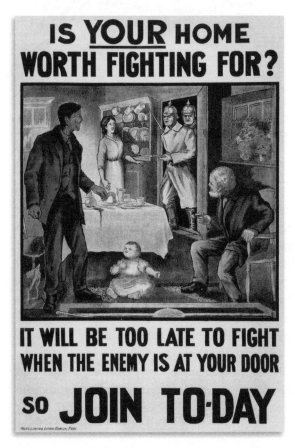

Recruitment poster by Hely's Dublin, *c.* 1915. (Courtesy of Wikimedia Commons)

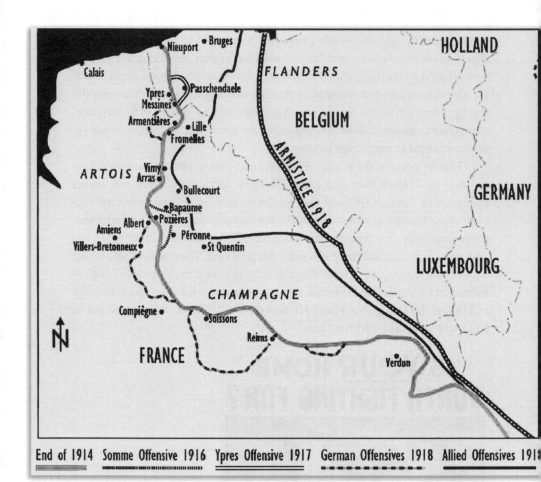

The Western Front between 1914 and 1918. (Map from the Peadar McNamara collection)

That afternoon the band members were entertained to tea by the ladies of the County Clare Belgian Refugees Committee at the Ordnance House. That evening the band played some more national airs followed by some more speeches urging recruitment. Lt Hall warned that if the Huns were victorious then Ireland's churches and convents would be desecrated like those in Belgium; her priests would be murdered and her nuns, women and children would be 'outraged'. Ireland, he said, had responded to the call, but, he said that the farmer class and the shop assistants were not represented among the ranks as they ought to be. The recruitment evening concluded with a fireworks display.

In the meantime, the propaganda campaign was subtly pursued by letters and poems in the papers. Revd R. Ross Lewin, a Protestant from Fortfergus, who was minister at Spanish Point, wrote a poem that was published in the *Clare Journal* in June:

The Lament of Dromindhuth

Why leave all the fighting to others,
who hold neither land nor demesne?
Not thus is the old Banner County
Under Brian they drove out the Dane.

Shall the homes that we love by the Shannon,
And the freedom these islands have won,
be left at the mercy tomorrow
of the villainous barbarous Hun?

No, no old black Dromin in horror,
Will utter these words of reproof,
There were men in the days now departed,
Who lived beneath old Dromindhuth.

There were men by the glades Gurtnacurra,
Liscormack and banks of Rusheen,
And Dysart, sweet village by Fergus,
By Coolteenagown and Coolmeen.

There were men like the grand Hugh O'Donnell,
There were men like the brave Owen Roe,
But slackers and shirkers from battle,
Ne'er did old black Dromin know.

R.R.L.

Note, Dromindhuth or Little Black Mountain, is near Kildysart and the other names are in the immediate vicinity.

'From Somewhere in France'

One letter published in the *Clare Journal* of 13 May was written by Bombardier John O'Donoghue of the 61st Battery Royal Field Artillery from the frontline in France addressed to his mother in Clare Castle. He described the cruelty of the Germans who, he said, had no respect for the dead, even bombing cemeteries and soldiers burying their dead comrades:

> One of the cruellest incidents of the war happened yesterday. One of our gunners was sent back from the firing line to bring our letters from the supply depot. On his way back he was killed by a shrapnel shell. I was one of a party sent to bury him and we had to take him to a cemetery near a big town. Just as we were approaching the gate four big shells came tearing through the air and burst right in the burial ground sending tombstones flying into the air. A civilian and his horse were killed and several of our men were wounded. I dropped flat on the ground with several others and this probably saved us from the flying fragments of shell. We had hardly recovered from this shock when I could hear another salvo of shells coming through the air. At this time I had hold of the stretcher with another man and was trying to get under cover with the poor corpse when crash came the shells. This time I thought I must get hit as fragments flew all round us. But God spoke before the Germans. He was protecting the bearers of the dead.
>
> They continued to shell the graveyard and we had to postpone the burial until nightfall. We were all sent back to our lines, except six men left behind as a burial party, and amongst those was the dead man's "best pal", as we say in the army, who remained to pay a last token of respect to his old pal. Well at six o'clock, pm, they took the body to the cemetery and were putting the last sod on the grave when they heard the buzzing sound that there was no mistaking. They all dropped flat, except the dead man's pal, who ran to take shelter under the wall, but he was too late. The shells burst, a piece struck him and he was dead. Today we buried them side by side with his friend – "pals" in death as in life. Such tragic incidents happen out here every day.
>
> Churches and convents are everywhere levelled to the ground. I am proud to see by the papers that our countrymen are doing their share at this critical time. The more that give a hand, the sooner the war will be over. I would like you to have a Mass said for me by the friars and ask everyone to pray for the poor soldiers who are facing death every moment and giving their lives for the cause of liberty and justice.

This 'cruelty' from the Germans was also highlighted in a Report of the French Commission of Inquiry into the conduct of the Germans in France, which was published in the British press and copied by the local press in an article headed 'KULTUR':

> Murder and rape and torture in which have been spared neither age nor sex have marked the progress of the German army … bestial atrocities … the work of devils in human form … The blood of our martyred allies calls to us for vengeance. Let every man who is fit and of military age answer the call in the firing line … Let us see to it that our reply is worthy of a great nation in arms for a splendid cause.

Another newspaper article cited a report in a journal called *The Architect* in the issue of 25 February, which described the Romanesque abbey of Hastiere near Dinant in Belgium, where 'the Huns murdered the abbot'. Such publicity was blatantly propagandist in tone and was widely published to assist recruitment into the British Army.

However, other letters to the press may have helped to boost the morale of the people at home who would be re-assured that the spiritual welfare of men was been helped by brave Catholic chaplains, who also faced death at the front. Bowman wrote, 'Many officers in the Irish regiments at least in the beginning of the war requested that their units be allocated Catholic chaplains. The Catholic chaplain could accompany his men right up to the firing line, whereas the Anglican chaplain was not officially permitted to go beyond base camp. This rule was relaxed in 1916, but the troops continued to label Anglican clergymen as 'cowards'.[10]

The Last Blessing of the Munsters at Rue de Bois, 9 May 1915, by Fortunio Matania. (Courtesy of Wikimedia Commons)

Fr Gwynn, SJ

One of the Catholic chaplains was Fr J. Gwynn, SJ. A chaplain with the Irish Guards, he sent a letter to a friend, Dr Garry, Trinaderry House, Barefield, which was published in the *Clare Journal* of 13 May 1915, describing his experiences as a chaplain at the front line. Fr Gwynn was wounded by a bomb blast and by gas from the shell. His account highlights the dangers to which the Catholic chaplains were exposed. Fr Gwynn's letter also shows the importance of meeting the spiritual needs of the Catholic soldiers, and indeed soldiers of all religions, when they were facing death on a daily basis. The presence of the chaplains and the availability of the sacraments of Confession, Holy Communion and Extreme Unction at the front line and in no man's land were of great comfort to the soldiers, who were about to go over the top into no-man's land, and presumably to their families in Ireland.

… On the day the Irish Guards took the brickstacks and trenches at Cuinchy, I knew there was going to be an attack and there would be casualties, so I stayed near … I am writing this in a little cellar under a graveyard. It is about 150 yards from the German lines … our furniture consists of a bundle of straw in the corner, where I sleep at night. Everyone here has a cellar or dugout as the Germans are constantly shelling us. As I write they are sending over big shells known as 'Jack Johnsons ' or 'Black Marias'. They are firing all sorts of shells today, little fizz bags that come with a rush, give no warning, and don't do much damage, unless there is a direct hit; then ordinary shrapnel bursting in the air and scattering some 300 bullets over 50 or 60 square yards; high explosive shrapnel, which burst with terrific force and cover a much larger area; percussion shells, from 5.9 inch to 8 inch, which simply blow a house into the air. As I write this there are big fellows screaming over my head with terrific force 40 or 50 yards away.

When in the trenches I see any wounded man immediately he's hit and give him the last sacraments. Then I hear the Confessions of the men in the trenches or their dug-outs. I can tell you it is easy to have contrition when the air is simply alive with bullets and shrapnel. At any moment if a shell dropped it would be all over for priest and penitent. Then a day we get a rest and we go back a mile or so from the firing line.

This morning I say Mass in the field for the battalion … We have to have Mass in the field as the Irish Guards are nearly all Catholics and we are at present the strongest battalion in the Guards Brigade. The men then sing their hymns at Mass and it is fine to hear nearly a thousand men singing out in the open at the top of their voices. You have no idea what a splendid battalion the Irish Guards are. You have Sgt Mike O'Leary (VC) with you, I often had a chat with him … but you know there are plenty of men in the Irish Guards who have done as bravely as Mike O'Leary and there is never a word about it.

Pray for me, if anything happens pray for me too, I often think they will get me … At breakfast I was called to assist a wounded Coldstream Guards soldier, it was a wet bleak, muddy morning and when I got to the place I found the poor fellow lying out in the open at the back of our trenches in a very exposed spot, the Germans were not more than 70 yards away. I crawled out flat to him and he was still alive and I gave him the Last Sacraments. He was absolutely unconscious. I crawled back again, the Germans had one shot at me, but missed badly … I was very glad to get back.

I was going back down the Coldstream Guards advanced trench, when an Irish Guardsman, all perspiring and muddy, came after me shouting that one our men named Ryan had been wounded and wanted to see me. I found that the poor fellow had been shot through the lung and was badly wounded. I heard his Confession, gave him Extreme Unction and saw him off to hospital. When I gave him Extreme Unction it was extraordinary how cheerful he got.

I had to go off then to bury a poor Irish Guardsman named Murrin, who had been shot during the day. Going a mile seems very simple to you at home, but here it means dodging bullets, a shell bursting now and again – when you hear a shell coming all you have to do is to lie flat on the ground, be it wet muddy or dry, and not mind your clothes and wait until it bursts – if you get down quickly enough you may escape, unless it falls directly on top of you. Wednesday, just finished Mass and some hundreds of the Guardsmen were at it … While we were at Mass a shell passed over us and burst a short dis-tance beyond. The men did not stir … I am sending you the brass noses of two German shells which burst quite near me … This morning I saw Ryan, the Irish Guardsman who was shot through the lung – he had a narrow escape … He said to me: "You can tell the Germans, your reverence that they are not done with Joe Ryan yet!"…

A soldier named 'Mack' wrote an anonymous letter from 'somewhere in France' to his former teacher in West Clare describing the awful conditions in the trenches during the battle of Hooge. What was surprising about this letter was that it shows that the author was highly critical of the strategy of trench war-fare; he questioned the tactics of the army leadership and wondered if the huge sacrifices made by the soldiers were worth it. The censors in the army, or those controlling the media in Ireland, must not have noticed this letter, which was published in the *Saturday Record* of 11 September 1915. It would not have encouraged recruitment and it is surprising that the letter was published in the *Saturday Record*, which was very supportive of the war effort:

… Well in that particular advance on Hooge, one regiment went too far ahead and the enemy caught it on its front and both sides, with the result that the fine body of men, numbering 1,000, had to retire, losing roughly about 800 men. This was somebody's fault, but that somebody could not be brought to account for it, as he was among the dead himself. See what a little mistake or carelessness can do.

Now the thing is over, thank God; the new trenches are being held, but when you look around and see the number of lives that were lost for the sake of gaining about 900 yards of ground, you ask yourself was it worth it. As far as all the poor fellows who have been killed are concerned, it does not matter to them. I hope they are happy, but how many hundreds of wives, fathers, brothers, mothers, brothers and sisters are mourning the loss of the men who have been cut down in the prime of manhood, and the many hundreds of homes in Ireland, England, Scotland and Wales that are silently bearing pain today?

… We are doing our best to bury them at night time, but we are not given a chance, and the Germans keep continually firing at us. I have been through it all, and I say this from my heart, that if there is a hell, the worst department of that 'shop' around here is around Ypres. The smell is terrible; we are all deaf, bothered, stupid, to put the whole thing into a nutshell for you. I was lucky; I've had two very narrow escapes. I have tried to tell you about the Hooge affair. It will just give you an idea of what driving them out of France and Belgium means. I have so much to tell you. I do not know where to commence and I am in an awful hurry. Will you kindly let me know when you receive this letter?

Your old friend, "Mack"

Pte O'Leary of the Connaught Rangers, who was recuperating from wounds at Le Havre, sent a letter to a friend in Ennis, which was published in the local press:

I am now out of hospital and am at the base of operations, but I don't know whether I will be at the front or not, as there is a bullet still in my side and the muscles are badly injured. I am out of hospital since before Christmas and I met a lot of chaps from Ennis going up to the front. They are leaving in thousands from here every day for the front. Let me know if Jack [a brother] was killed, as a chap of the Leinsters told me he was killed on Xmas Eve. He was in the Maxim gun section. I would be glad if you send a paper, we don't get any here. This war is fearful slaughter and I hope it will be over soon.

Dr Meagher, Royal Army Medical Corps, sent a letter from 'somewhere in France' to Revd Fr Meagher, CC Killaloe. Though he was optimistic of final victory, the scene he describes is rather depressing.

> You might like to hear from me. I am precluded by the censor from giving my exact location. My address is the Field Ambulance 7th Infantry.
>
> I am right in the thick of it now in charge of the stretcherbearers and located at a wayside inn about 700 or 800 yards behind our trenches. We take out the wounded every night, picking them out at a fixed point behind the trenches. This we do at dusk when there is only casual sniping. At present we are bombarding the Germans, some 400 guns being engaged in the work. The inn where I now write lies in a battery of five guns not more than 500 yards away. As you may imagine the din is indescribable. Of course this fire attracts the attention of the Germans to us, which they send in the shape of shells.
>
> … As to the progress of the war you can form a better opinion than we can. We are only a very small part of the line and we can see very little of what is going on elsewhere.
>
> Anyhow we are making progress and it will be slow, but I think there will be no doubt about the issue. We cannot hope for any respite now. The allies have now begun to put the pressure on, to continue with unrelenting crescendo until the Germans go under. I expect to be well employed and continuously so for months.
>
> This poor country shows its great wounds like the dead Caesar pleading for revenge. You see old women – who have seen and known God knows what outrages – strolling around deserted houses stupefied, mumbling and shaking their heads. The pretty villages are felled … the whole country is bleeding … If that is the case here, what must it be in Belgium? I cannot give you any continuous description of things under the present circumstances … the noise, the turmoil and the interruptions make that impossible …
>
> I sleep at present in my everyday clothes, booted and helmeted, ready for the fray. It is gloriously exciting – but when you see the slain, who die young, its miserable – damnable!
>
> The play is the tragedy, man …

Meanwhile, the recruitment campaign at home was vigorously promoted in the towns of Clare such as Kilrush. Here there was a large meeting in the town square, with patriotic speeches by Sir Michael O'Loghlen HML and others. These meetings were colourful occasions with flags and banners and the band playing national airs. There were emotional appeals to the fighting spirit of the young men of West Clare to 'do their duty' and fight for the honour of Ireland.[11]

A Viceregal Tour

Later in the year, towards the end of August, the Viceroy, Lord Wimborne, toured County Clare on a recruitment campaign, visiting Ennis, Kilrush, Kilkee, Miltown Malbay, Lahinch and Ennistymon. He and his wife came by train to Ennis and then went on a motorcade tour. Everywhere he went, the viceroy was given a loyal reception and a warm Irish welcome.

Kilrush was en fete for the occasion, gaily decorated with union jacks and bunting. One streamer on the platform in the square had the words : 'Down with the Huns!'; the principal streets of the town were planted with trees and shrubs for the occasion; the Kilrush Brass and Reed Band played 'God save the king' a couple of times, as well as national and some martial airs to entertain the aristocratic visitors and the huge crowd. The chairman of Kilrush UDC, Mr Culligan, welcomed Baron Wimborne to Kilrush and said that he was pleased to announce that 'our town, though small in number, has subscribed over 400 of her sons to the colours, though some have fallen in battle.' Mr Culligan also promoted the interests of Kilrush and district by suggesting that Kilrush and the Shannon Estuary would make an ideal naval base for the British fleet during and after the war.

Lord Wimborne in reply referred to the Irish Brigades in France: 'just like the Clare men of Lord Clare's Dragoons who fought at Fontenoy in olden times. It may well be that the Irish Brigades of today, who are fighting in Flanders, may help the French to win a new Fontenoy over a different enemy.' The meeting concluded with the band playing 'A nation once again'. Afterwards the viceregal party had lunch with Mr H.R. Glynn, DL. Among the guests were Miss Glynn, V. Revd Canon, McInerney PP, VG; the rector, Revd Canon Armstrong, and Mrs Armstrong; Mr W.J Glynn, JP, and Mrs Glynn and Mrs W. de Courcy.

Young Man

Is anyone proud of you?

Is your mother proud of you?

Is your sister proud of you?

Is your sweetheart proud of you?

Is Ireland proud of you?

Join an Irish regiment

TO-DAY

Clare Journal, 2 September 1915.

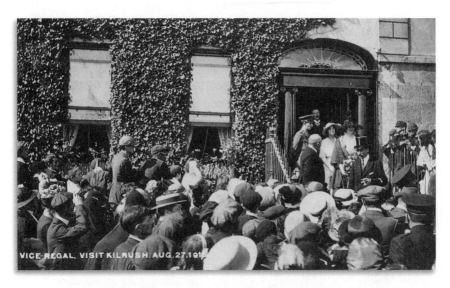

Lord Wimborne at Kilrush House, from *Irish Life* magazine.
(Courtesy of Glynn papers, per Paul O'Brien)

At Kilkee the visitors were given a royal reception, with the local band playing 'Rule Britannia' as well as some national airs. They proceeded to Moore Hall, where they were received by Canon Glynn, PP, and the chairman of the Kilkee Town Commissioners. Lord and Lady Wimborne walked along the West End before they departed.

After leaving Kilkee the distinguished party motored through Doonbeg and the parish of Kilmurry to Quilty where they were received by Fr John Glynn, PP. There was a short meeting attended by a large crowd.

At Miltown Malbay the viceroy was welcomed by Revd Canon Hannon, PP, and was informed that 'a considerable number of men from the west had enlisted', some from Miltown, and he met Capt. Tottenham from Mountcallan, who had lost an arm at Gallipoli.

There was a brief stop at Lahinch, where Lord Wimborne spoke to Dr C.H. Blood and Revd R. Ross Lewin. At the Temperance Hall Ennistymon, Lord Wimborne was told that Ennistymon, since the start of the year, 'had sent an average of ten young men each month to the colours.'

The tour concluded at Ennis, where Sir Michael O'Loghlen, HML for County Clare, and other 'worthies' attended his farewell from Clare.

Shortly after his visit, Lord Wimborne sent a letter of thanks to O'Loghlen, thanking him and the people of Clare for the cordial reception given to him and to his wife. He said that he was pleased to see Guards of Honour provided by the National Volunteers and to hear the national anthem played by the local town bands. In reply, Sir Michael O'Loghlen stated that the provision of

Guards of Honour by the National Volunteers and the playing of the national anthem by the local bands 'may be taken as showing the unity of our empire against the enemies of civilisation, who now menace the safety of our land'.[12]

At a meeting of Ennis Urban Council in July 1915 the council voted against conscription. Mr MacNamara said that Ennis had done its fair share, that 450 men had left the town of Ennis and its environs ... other towns had done as well, Kilrush, he said, had been 'weeded out'... conscription would not suit the county, it had done more than its duty. Mr P.J. Linnane said that many men who wished to enlist were rejected because they had one or two teeth out. These men were not wanted to eat the Germans, but to shoot them, he exclaimed. 'These men were now walking around the town of Ennis instead of fighting the Germans.'[13]

Lord Wimborne at Kilkee.
(Courtesy of Glynn papers, per Paul O'Brien)

The recruiting campaigns bore some fruit when the *Saturday Record* noted that six RIC men joined the Irish Guards. The constables were from the Corofin and Tulla stations. Furthermore, five members of the Ennis postal staff also joined the colours. These were men in secure state positions, who did not need to enlist and they were guaranteed jobs when and if they returned home.

Earlier in the year the recruiting agents in Clare got a boost when Jack Fox from Newmarket-on-Fergus enlisted. He was 'a well-known and popular Gael', who was a member of the Clare senior hurling team that won the All-Ireland title in 1914. Jack Fox had played in the right half back position in that team. The newspaper report stated that 'he got a hearty send-off on Tuesday'. His enlistment in the Irish Guards, it was hoped, might have inspired other Gaels to join up as well.

Jack Fox was born in 1892. He worked on Lord Inchiquin's estate at Dromoland and may have been inspired by the pro-war atmosphere in Dromoland at the time to enlist in 1915, when he was aged about 23. It must be remembered that Lord and Lady Inchiquin were very active in promoting recruitment and in helping war charities in Clare. In fact Lord Inchiquin's half-brother, the Hon. Desmond O'Brien, enlisted in the RAF in 1914; and his son and heir, the Hon. Donough O'Brien, joined the army in 1916. Even the children were exposed to war propaganda. At a Christmas party in Dromoland Castle in 1916 for the Church of Ireland children of Kilnasoolagh parish, 'Father Christmas' delivered the following message in a scroll:

Jack Fox in 1914.
(Courtesy of John Power)

> Have courage!
> To those who nobly fight
> Victory and peace shall come
> But Shirkers shall have nought
> But misery as their doom!

Jack Fox was a well-built, athletic figure over 6 feet tall. He served on the Western Front and fought at the Battle of the Somme in 1916. He was injured by shrapnel during that battle and was taken back to a Dublin hospital to recuperate. Apparently, some shrapnel remained in his body until his death.

Of course one consequence of his decision to join the British Army in July 1915 was that he was automatically banned from the GAA, because Rule 21, barred members of the RIC, British Army and Royal Navy from joining the GAA. The GAA ban may also have been a significant factor which discouraged many Gaels in nationalist circles, especially in rural areas of the county, from joining the British forces during the war. Jack Fox could no longer play for his club or county after he enlisted and for the duration of the war. This may have been a painful breach for him. However, after he was de-mobilised in 1919, he was again eligible to join the GAA and he did.

He resumed his inter-county career when he played in the Munster semi-final against Limerick in May 1919 at the Showgrounds, Ennis, which Limerick won by 6-6 to 4-1. That was his last senior championship game with Clare, though he did play for Clare in a senior challenge game against Kerry in April 1924.

Jack Fox also resumed his career with Newmarket-on-Fergus and he played in three more county finals, winning two more county senior hurling championship medals in the mid-twenties. He was a member of the losing side against Ennis Dalcassians in 1924, but he was on the winning teams against Tulla in 1925 and against O'Callaghan's Mills in 1926. He retired from senior hurling with his club in 1926 at the age of 34.

During the 1960s he, as a hurling hero of the first Clare All-Ireland win-

ning team, used to proudly lead the parade of Newmarket-on-Fergus hurlers around the pitch before county hurling finals. Jack Fox died in June 1967, the last survivor of the 1914 team.

According to his grandson, he said little or nothing about his wartime experiences. However, he did tell a story about how he was rescued after he was injured by a fellow soldier named Martin Faulkner. Martin Faulkner brought the injured Jack Fox to safety. In fact, Martin Faulkner was a well-known Itinerant, who tramped the roads of Clare and many other parts of Ireland for many years after the war up to his death in the mid-1970s.[14]

Martin Faulkner in 1975. (Courtesy of Francis Power)

A novel way of encouraging recruitment was demonstrated when an Ennis man was prosecuted for being drunk and disorderly. The judge, Mr McElroy, RM, gave the defendant, Michael Walsh, a choice of two months in jail or else the Probation Act if he enlisted. Mr McElroy, RM, said that Walsh was of no use in Ennis and that he might join the army. When asked by his solicitor, Mr Hunt, whether he would enlist if the case was adjourned for a month, Walsh replied, to the amusement of the court audience, "I will surr, begor I will surr".[15]

Opposition to Recruitment

However, other forces were at work in Clare to frustrate the recruitment campaign. Mr Ernest Blythe, a member of the Irish Republican Brotherhood and an organiser for the Irish Volunteers, was arrested in Ennistymon. He was ordered out of the county and country under the Defence of the Realm Act (DORA). According to the report, Mr Blythe had been busy in Clare for some weeks, having made Ennis his HQ. He was subject to very rigid police surveillance, with plain-clothed policemen detailed to keep him under observation at all times in his trips around the county. He was endeavouring to organise a corps of the Irish Volunteers, but, according to the report in the *Saturday Record*, his efforts in Ennis at any rate, 'had borne little fruit'. He had in fact reviewed the Ennis corps of the National Volunteers and was endeavouring to subvert their allegiance to John Redmond, until they discovered his true identity.[16]

Michael Brennan of Meelick reveals in his memoirs how he and others helped to organise Irish Volunteer companies throughout East Clare after the split with Redmond. He first started in Meelick and Oatfield, his native parish. In order to increase their numbers and publicise their cause, they used to hold parades after Sunday Masses and on popular social occasions such as hurling matches and tug-o'-war tournaments. Through these means they set up Irish Volunteer companies all over east and mid-Clare in parishes such as Clonlara, Cratloe, Newmarket-on-Fergus, Clare Castle, Crusheen, Ennis, Feakle, O'Callaghan's Mills, Ogonelloe, Scariff, Sixmilebridge and Tulla. They sang 'A Soldier's Song' over the hills of Clare. They did, however, encounter some strong vocal opposition on occasions from the wives of men serving in the British forces, 'separation women', whom he referred to as 'viragoes'.[17]

John O'Brien from Ennis was charged under DORA with covering up recruitment posters. He was given the benefit of the Probation Act. Later in the year an illiterate Kilrush man called Peter Casey was fined one shilling for covering up a recruitment poster in Kilrush. In July, Mr Sean O'Muirthile, a Gaelic League organiser in Clare, was prosecuted under DORA for refusing to fill out a residency form at a Lisdoonvarna hotel. He was fined the substantial sum of £2 plus 16 shillings costs.[18]

At a court case in Kilrush, James MacDonnell, a farmer, was prosecuted for assaulting a soldier in a pub in Kilrush. The defendant stated that there was a feeling that it was all the 'scruff of Kilrush that were in the army and that only for the rowdies there would not be an army at all!'[19]

Miss Adelaide Palmer from Dublin sought damages of £7 for being thrown off her bicycle and flung into a bog hole in Rahona. She was employed at Carrigaholt as a technical instructor. She volunteered as a nurse at the beginning of the war and immediately became unpopular and was denounced as 'a recruiting agent'. She said that the authorities at the Irish College at Carrigaholt called her 'a security agent'.[20]

A New Department of Recruitment

Towards the end of the year, because of the war of attrition and the huge casualties on the Western Front, the need for more recruits was urgent. The civil and military authorities decided to organise recruitment in a more professional manner. They established a new recruitment structure in the county. Lt Abrahall, son of the Church of Ireland minister at Drumcliffe, Ennis, was appointed recruiting officer for the county, with the Ennis barracks as his HQ. New recruits were requested to call to Sgt Connolly's offices at Military Road, Ennis. Mr Michael O'Halloran of Tulla was chosen as recruiting organiser for East Clare. Col Sir Charles Barrington, recruiting organiser for Limerick and Clare, also appointed Mr C.E. Glynn of Kilrush recruiting organiser for West Clare, including Ennis.

Mr C.E. Glynn was appointed with the temporary rank, pay and allowances of a lieutenant, with an outfit allowance of £20. He did not, however, wish to be based in Ennis and he requested that Kilrush be made a Recruitment Office for West Clare. After his appointment C.E. Glynn stated that 'he called on some of the principal shopkeepers in Ennis and Kildysart … and I am glad to say that all promised to assist me in recruiting and to do what they could to encourage farmers to join up'. One of the local newspapers commented: 'Owing to his intimate connections with the area, his efforts should prove fruitful.' Between the middle of November 1915 and the end of the year, Glynn was quite active in promoting recruitment. He canvassed all the leading people of West Clare for support and he made his family car available to officers to carry out a recruiting campaign in West Clare in November after Capt. Browning of the Recruitment Office, Limerick, requested the use of Mr Glynn's car 'for the use by four officers on a recruitment tour from Kilrush to Kilmihil and from Kilkee to Carrigaholt and Cross on Tuesday 9th and Wednesday 10th November'.[21]

Earlier in the year, his brother, H.R. Glynn, was in touch with the Department of Recruitment in Ireland. Sir W. Grey-Wilson wrote to him thanking him for cooperating with Sir Michael O'Loghlen HML 'in framing a plan for spreading the truth about the war, about its causes and consequences on Co. Clare.' H.R. Glynn also wrote to John Redmond advising him that 'a large number of our men have volunteered'; he also sought Redmond's opinion on the war and prospects about the state of things in twelve months time – 'businessmen have to look ahead!'

In March H.R. Glynn, an astute businessman, wrote to Mr E.C. Blanchflower, secretary to the vice-admiral commanding at Queenstown (Cobh), tendering for business, 'we can supply coal, flour, oil or provisions to any vessels patrolling the west coast. At Cappa pier we can take up to 1,100 tons'. He added, '80 men who used to work for us, some of them occasionally, are serving with the forces and more than 200 have gone from Kilrush.'

Mr Glynn also wrote to the director of contracts at the admiralty in London seeking business, 'Sir, add my name to the list of firms tendering for the supply of flour, coal and provisions for the navy. Cappa pier can accommodate vessels of up to 1,000 tons ... larger vessels at Scattery Roads. More than 100 men who worked in our employment are now serving with the colours and about 300 Kilrush men, out of a population of 3,600 have enlisted up to the present.'

In March H.R. Glynn wrote to the Chancellor of the Exchequer, The Hon. David Lloyd George MP, 'Sir, I read with great pleasure your reply to the deputation on the drinks question and trust you will stop or limit the sale of drink during the war ... the population of this town in the west coast of Ireland before the war was 3,600. Over 260 men are now serving in the army and navy and during the past week, fifty volunteered.'

Also in March of this year H.R. Glynn wrote to Maj. Ivers, Mount Ivers, Sixmilebridge, seeking special concessions with regard to his workforce at Kilrush, effectively a veto on the recruitment of skilled mill workers.

> As flour and Indian meal millers, will you kindly allow us to bring the following matter under your notice with respect to men from our employment wishing to join the colours. Up to the present more than 85 men who have worked with us are now serving with the colours and it is our wish to encourage all who possibly can to join. At the same time our mills can only be worked with the assistance of several skilled men, most of whom it takes several years to train, and if these skilled men leave us we shall not be able to replace them. Under the circumstances, we would be very much obliged if you would kindly give instructions to the Kilrush Recruiting Officer, not to take on any men without at least getting our permission.[22]

Belgian Refugees

In January 1915 the first Belgian refugees arrived in County Clare. Some of them were accommodated in the old army barracks at Clare Castle, while others were given accommodation by Lord Inchiquin at Castlefergus, Newmarket-on-Fergus, and at the Ordnance Survey House, Ennis. Ethel, Lady O'Brien, wife of Lord Inchiquin, played a major role in the county in looking after the Belgian refugees. For her work with the Belgian refugees and her generosity, Lady Inchiquin received a medal from the Queen of Belgium at the end of the war.

The presence of these Belgian refugees, who came from the Flemish part of the country near Antwerp, was used by the authorities for propaganda purposes. In interviews, they spoke of the horrors they had experienced at the hands of the 'merciless Huns', the foul deeds, massacres and 'outrages' committed by the Germans were told by those who had first-hand experience. These opinions were supplemented by letters from the front and by other sources, which spoke of the events such as the destruction of Louvain, an 83-year-old priest hoisted on a cannon gun, priests shot, and 'horrifying revelations by a Belgian nun', etc. The propaganda machine was well oiled. The 'brave Belgian Catholics' were getting good notice in the newspapers, which helped promote recruitment among the Catholic men of Clare.[23]

While the Belgian refugees were being welcomed to County Clare, their 'enemies' living in the county were arrested and interned. Two Germans working in Lahinch and one working in Ennis were arrested. Mr Esch, manager of the Golf Links Hotel and Mr Franz Bitzen a waiter at the same hotel, both German citizens, were picked up. In Ennis Josef Fehrenbach, a jeweller's

Clare Castle army barracks. (Courtesy of John Power)

assistant working in Ennis was also arrested as an enemy alien and sent to the Curragh for the duration of the war. Mr Joseph Maurer a leading jeweller and Mr Clement Dilger, watchmaker, both of whom had lived in Ennis for more than twenty-five years, were also interned.[24]

Distress in Clare

The war had an obvious economic impact upon the economy of Clare. It was certainly benefitting the farmers. The wives of men who were serving in the forces were receiving separation allowances, while their widows were granted pensions. However, the poor

> Is Ireland to share Belgium's fate?
>
> Read what the Germans have done to the
>
> Churches, Priests, women and children of Belgium,
>
> Men of Ireland
>
> The sanctity of your Churches, the safety of your homes, the honour of your women can only be secured by
>
> Defeating the Germans in Belgium

Clare Journal, 25 February 1915.

were being affected by high prices of food and fuel. Trade and business was also adversely affected. Many people were in great distress. The labourers working for Clare County Council sought higher wages to meet their basic needs, but this demand was rejected by the council. A public meeting was held at the Town Hall, Ennis, for the relief of the poor of Ennis, in view of 'the high price of food and fuel'.

This meeting resulted in the formation of a Committee for the Relief of Distress caused by the war. Mr James O'Regan, JP, chairman of Clare County Council, presided and there was a mixture of Catholic and Protestants on the committee: The Hon. Mrs Blood; Mrs Vere O'Brien; Mrs Hickman; Mrs Bulger; Col O'Callaghan Westropp; F.N. Studdert, DL; V. Revd Canon Hannon, PP; V. Revd Canon Bourke, PP; Councillor M. Considine; and C.W. Healy, JP; with Mr Wilson Lynch, JP, and Mr A.E. Wallace as honorary secretaries.

Various sub-committees reported from Kilkee, Clare Castle, Miltown Malbay, Doonagore and Killaloe. There were twenty-six families in Kilkee, with over 100 people in 'acute distress due to a fall off in tourism'. From Miltown Malbay it was reported that 'acute distress prevailed', with at least forty men unemployed. In Quilty it was stated that 'a considerable number of young men had joined the army or navy and that this was a major loss to the fishing crews, resulting in a poor fishing season'. The poor people of Killaloe were reported to be 'really destitute, owing to the absence of tourists'. Reports from Lahinch and Lisdoonvarna also indicated 'distress'. It is noticeable that there were no sub-committee reports for the following areas: Ennis, Kilrush, Ennistymon, Newmarket-on-Fergus and Sixmilebridge. This may have been due to the fact that many unemployed young men from these towns had enlisted in the army or navy.

Canon Bourke, the local parish priest, reported that 'in Clare Castle there were twenty-nine families in distress, fourteen carters and fifteen dockers. Their incomes had fallen due to the decline in imports of coal to the port due to the war. Many of the poor were now heavily indebted to the shop-keepers'. The committee voted a sum of £50 to the local sub-committee for distribution to the poor. Col O'Callaghan stated that the coal merchants and importers could not get supplies of coal from England because the Clyde Shipping Company's ships were committed to government contracts for the war. Canon Burke said that Mr Patrick Power, one of the coal importers, had done all he could to secure ships to import coal. He said that he had even brought coal by rail to Clare Castle. The committee resolved to write to the Board of Trade to secure shipping for Clare Castle. These representations to the Board of Trade must have been successful, as about five months later, Mr Power advertised that he had four cargoes of 'best Whitehaven and Lancashire coal' for sale at the port of Clare Castle, totalling 1,400 tons.[25]

The shopkeepers of Ennis and other towns in Clare were also experiencing an economic recession caused by the war. In response they decided to end a long-standing practice of giving 'Christmas boxes' to their loyal customers. A spokesman stated in November that Christmas boxes were being withdrawn, 'these bribes are ruinous and they only encourage dishonesty to the trade.' Another report stated that the war has upset trade and that 'Christmas boxes' would not be given. Traders who breached the rule would be fined £20. This policy applied to traders in Ennis, Killaloe, Kilrush and other towns. A third report stated that the master bakers and flour merchants have decided not to give 'Christmas boxes' this year under a penalty of £20![26]

Bishop Fogarty took the opportunity while consecrating a new altar at Crusheen church in July to make some comments about the state of the economy after a year of war. Probably influenced by the opinions of his friend, Bishop O'Dwyer of Limerick, he advised people to be cautious about their expenditure, as he believed that the terrible war would be succeeded by times of great distress and poverty. 'That was the opinion of economic experts. Money had already lost half of its value. They say it is God's will to bring us back again to the simple life, that this war and the consequences of it are intended in the hands of God to burn up and turn to ashes all the luxury and sensuality and extravagance that has begun to overrun the whole of Europe, and that the result would be that they would all be put back again to the simple life, where men of virtue would have an opportunity of living ... It would be well for them to look ahead and if money was plentiful in a year which was a good one for the farmers and everybody else, they ought to be careful and not waste it, not knowing what was before them'.[27]

Weather and Farming

Though there was a general perception that the farmers were doing well from the war economy, farming conditions in the county were not ideal for growth during many months of the year. The end of year review of the weather at Carrigoran by A.B. (A. Busker) in the *Clare Journal* of 3 January 1916, noted that the year 1915 had seen extremes of rainfall and temperatures. Exceptionally high levels of rainfall in January and February, following the very heavy rains of December, produced 'unprecedented levels of flooding in the fields'. The weather improved in March, drying up the land rather quickly, and to the satisfaction of all agriculturalists, bringing tillage lands 'into a very desirable state for cultivation'.

However, the following three months, April-June, were unusually dry and sunny, with rainfall amounts being less than half the average. 'This produced a state of dryness and everything parched up'. The weather in July was one of the wettest, gloomiest and coldest on record. It was, according to meteorologists the wettest July in thirty-four years, with rain recorded at Carrigoran for twenty-nine days of the month. The harvest months of August-October had near normal weather in terms of rainfall. There was a period of beautifully fine and hot weather during mid-September and mid-October. The rain in early November was exceptionally high, with more than an inch each day on 11 and 12 November. That was followed by a long dry, but cold spell, with frost on fourteen days.

Overall, the weather made it a difficult year for farming. However, despite the adverse conditions, the yields of hay, potatoes and cereals were 'surprisingly above normal and better than expected'. There was an increase in tillage farming in the county and in crop yields. This increase may have been a natural response to increased prices for cereals and to Tillage Acts requiring more tillage cultivation.

A report in the *Clare Journal* of 20 December 1915 stated that the average yield of the potato crop in Ireland this year was 6.2 tons per statute acre, compared with an average yield of 5.9 tons in 1914, and a ten-year average of 5.2 tons. There were 16,500 acres of Clare under potatoes, compared with 15,878 in 1914, (a 3.9 per cent increase). The potato harvest was up from 84,500 tons in 1914 to 95,567 tons in 1915, (a 13.5 per cent increase).

Cereals fell short of the harvest of 1914, partly due to the weather, which was too dry in the early season and too wet during most of the later period of growth. However, the harvesting weather was 'extremely favourable'. The acreage and production of tillage in 1914 and 1915 is shown in the following tables:

Table 1

Acreage under tillage in County Clare 1914–1915

Year	Wheat	Oats	Barley	Potatoes	Total
1914	619	10,710	857	15,878	28,064
1915	2,099	10,481	785	16,500	29,865

Table 2

Crop yields in tons 1914–1915

Year	Wheat	Oats	Barley	Potatoes	Total
1914	622	10,656	792	84,500	96,570
1915	2,149	10,307	700	95,567	108,723

Because of the war and increased prices, there was a great increase in the acreage and tonnage of wheat and potatoes, while the area under oats and barley declined slightly that year. The total area of arable farming in County Clare increased from 28,064 acres to 29,865 acres (+6.4 per cent). The total tonnage of cereal crops and potatoes increased from 96,570 tons to 108,723 tons, an increase of 12,162 tons (+12.5 per cent).

According to An Foras Taluntais, the extent of suitable land for tillage in County Clare is approximately 30 per cent of the county. County Clare has 777,347 acres and 30 per cent of that would amount to 234,094 acres. So, by that yardstick, the extent of tillage in 1915 fell far short of the maximum potential of tillage land in the county, as only 12.7 per cent of the suitable tillage land was being used then. This figure must be tempered by the fact that the quality of the tillage land varied so much. Much of the tillage land of the county was relatively poor as the following table shows:

Table 3

Tillage suitability classes for County Clare

Per centage of county

Class 1	Class 2	Class 3	Class 4	Total
Nil	3.1	5.1	21.9	30

In fact about 73 per cent of the land deemed suitable for tillage is of fourth class – that is of the poorest quality. If we combine the first-, second- and third-class land suitable for tillage we can estimate that 8.2 per cent of the county would make 'moderate to very good' tillage land. That would amount to about 19,195 acres. Judging by these figures, it would seem that all of the best and most suitable land of the county was in fact being used for tillage in 1915. Actually that figure was exceeded by more than 10,000 acres, so much of the least suitable land for tillage was also being tilled. Moreover, these figures do not take the cooler, duller, wetter climate of County Clare into account, by comparison with the drier, warmer, and sunnier climate of the east and south-east of Ireland, the tillage heartland of Ireland.[28]

War Charities

Given the level of distress because of the war there were many fundraising ventures for soldiers, sailors, and especially the wounded and for prisoners. Fundraising for charitable causes were traditionally carried out by middle- and upper-class ladies and in County Clare, usually Protestant women.

Collections were arranged for prisoners of war held by the Germans, organised by Miss Maunsell, Island McGrath; Miss Norah Stackpoole of Edenvale held a collection for sandbags for the front; Miss Gelston of Stamer Park raised funds for the 10th Royal Irish Regiment; Miss Geraldine Mahon of Corbally, Quin, appealed for eggs for wounded soldiers and sailors in Dublin hospitals; Miss Violet MacNamara of Ennistymon, raised funds for the Red Cross; Miss Studdert organised a concert in the Town Hall Ennis which raised £20 for the Blue Cross, a charity for wounded horses; Ethel, Lady Inchiquin of Dromoland and Ms Willis, Bindon Street, Ennis, promoted the Queen's Appeal, a charity for unemployed women and girls in great distress as well as shop girls; Mrs MacDonnell of New Hall set up a fund for wounded soldiers; Mrs Cullinan, Bindon Street, Ennis collected fresh fruit and vegetables for sailors; Mrs F.N. Studdert held a collection at the County Agricultural Show for prisoners; several fundraising efforts were made on behalf of Belgian refugees; the County Clare Lawn Tennis Club held a jumble sale for the relief of wounded Royal Munster Fusiliers; a collection was held to raise funds for cigarettes and tobacco for Clare prisoners in Germany; Christmas treats for the children of sailors and soldiers were organised by Miss Burton, Clifden, Corofin and by Miss Lane Joynt, Carnelly; and the Clare Needlework Guild sent socks and other items to Clare prisoners; Miss Bruce and other ladies of Kilkee put on an operetta to raise funds for the prisoners. Besides these collections, there were several church gate collections for Catholic Belgium and Catholic Poland, organised by the Catholic Church.[29]

Prisoners of War

There were many Clare prisoners of war by the end of 1915, indeed some had been captured as early as 27 August 1914 after the first encounter with the Germans in Belgium. Some of them sent letters back home via the Red Cross and some of them described the difficult conditions that they endured. One prisoner of war, Colour-Sgt Maj. John Browne, son of Mrs Browne, the Turnpike, Ennis, who was a prisoner in Limburg, Germany, wrote a letter to his mother appealing for help. The letter was published in the *Saturday Record* in January under the heading 'ENNIS PRISONERS IN GERMANY':

Clothing Badly Wanted
Find out if there is any soldiers' society formed in Ennis for the benefit of soldiers serving. If so, I would like you to inform whoever is head of it that there are several men here belonging to the town of Ennis, who are badly in need of some clothing. Shirts, socks etc. would be a great God-send to them.
    Another communication says that there are 474 of the Munster Fusiliers imprisoned as prisoners of war, and of these only about 80 have great coats, and the majority have only cotton shirts and no socks. One good lady in Wales, Mrs Gower, has already sent out 200 parcels to them.

The *Clare Journal* editor suggested that a prisoners' relief organisation should be set up in Clare.
    A second letter from Colour-Sgt Maj. John Browne, which was sent to Lt Col Brasier Creagh, County Cork, was published in the *Clare Journal* in March 1915 under the heading 'CAPTURED MUNSTERS CALL FOR CLOTHING':

The Munsters, who at Mons and in the dreadful opening battle of the early stages of the war were overwhelmed by vast numbers of Germans, now ask of those who live at home in comfort to help them in their necessaries. Many, if not most of them are interned at Limburg [Lahn] and in that camp they have to bear the rigours of an extremely cold climate, their sufferings being accentuated by sparse feeding. They are in need of some warm clothing as is shown by the following letter:

'Limburg (Lahn), Germany
24 -1-'15
Sir- on behalf of the NCOs and men of the RMF, who are prisoners of war here with me, I take the liberty of asking your assistance in obtaining some comforts for the men. It is five months since we were taken prisoners, and since then what warm shirts and socks the men had are worn out.

The shirts have been replaced by the German authorities, but, of course, we cannot expect anything better than cotton ones. Socks are not issued and out of the 400 odd I have here, only about 40 of them have socks. The men have to work all day and at present the weather is very cold and the men feel it terribly. It would be a great God-send if the men at present under your command would put their heads together and send us a couple of hundred pairs of socks. They could be forwarded to me made up in parcels of 10lbs. I have a card from Mrs O'Shea, saying that two sacks of underclothing were on their way to me, so that she might be able to supply a warm shirt for each man. All the Irish Catholics are here. It was a great blessing to get here as we are in a good barracks, and alright, except for under-clothing. All the men are in the best of health and spirits.

J. Browne, C.S.M.

2nd Royal Munster Fusiliers

But help was already at hand in County Clare, as Miss Maunsell, of The Island, (Island McGrath), Clare Castle, and Mrs McElroy, wife of the resident magistrate, the Barracks, Clare Castle, appealed for flannel shirts, woollen underclothing or flannelette garments, socks etc., or money to purchase materials for making garments for the prisoners of war in Germany who were of the Munster Fusiliers Regiment and for those about to be sent to the front, 'where this regiment has been earning undying fame'.

Miss Maunsell, who had been busy in prisoner relief since August 1914, took the opportunity of thanking all of her friends who had so kindly assisted her with time and money at her weekly working party at Clare Castle barracks. 'It was', she said, 'a great pleasure to be able to send off regularly large parcels of comforts to the Munsters, Irish Guards, Leinsters and the Navy, for which very grateful letters had been received'. She and some other young women had organised collections at Clare Castle fairs of May and November, as well as a collection in the parish of Clare Castle and Ballyea, which raised £5 10s.

Mr H.R. Glynn, DL, of Kilrush received the following letter from John Stafford, a Kilrush prisoner in Limburg Germany, in March 1915:

Dear Mr. Glynn,

I take this, the first opportunity I have got, of hastening to thank you for the valuable and very useful parcel which you were so kind to send to me. I received it alright on the 5th of this month and I shared it out among the other six Kilrush men who are here, they were all delighted. I hope you will not think it too much of me taking advantage of your kind offer to send on more tobacco when I want it, but should you be sending cigarettes please send Woodbines, as they are preferable above all other brands. Having no

money of course it is impossible to obtain the things we are used to in Ireland. Even if we had money, we could not get many of them here, therefore do not take it ill of me asking you to supply a small tin of cocoa, milk, sugar, butter, or jam or marmalade. A cake would be an extraordinary luxury, as also would be a supply of cheese. Should you be pleased yourself to send on another parcel you can please yourself as to the contents in addition to the things I have suggested, resting assured that whatever arrives will be appreciated and again thanking you heartily for the last parcel. I remain,
Yours sincerely, John Stafford.

In July a Prisoner Relief Committee was established in Kilrush after Mr Nagle, an urban councillor, received 'a very pathetic letter from a Kilrush man describing the in-human treatment meted out to him and his comrades by the Huns'. Mr Murphy, the town clerk, and Mr Thomas Lillis, urban councillor, acted as hon. secretaries, with Mr Nagle as hon. treasurer. The committee urged the people of Kilrush to respond generously to the call for help and to show that the prisoners from their native town were not forgotten.

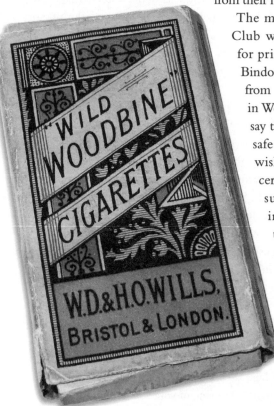

Woodbine cigarette packet. (Courtesy of John Power)

The members of Ennis Lawn Tennis Club were also active in fundraising for prisoners of war. Mrs Cullinan of Bindon Street, Ennis, received a letter from Pte R. McKenna, from a prison in Westphalia: 'I am very pleased to say that I received your parcel quite safe and in good condition, and I wish to say I thank you very sincerely for your kindness in sending such useful articles. Trusting in God that I will be able to thank you personally some day'. Letters were also received from other prisoners, including Bombardier H. Walton, L-Cpl Hegarty and Pte Jack Cronin, in Limburg; L-Cpl H. Yeoman in Westphalia, and Pte O. Withers in Hanover. The parcels were organised by Mrs Gower, 'who took a deep personal interest in the Munsters'.

Mrs Gelston, of Stamer Park, Ennis, wife of the Chief Inspector of the RIC, along with Mrs Cullinan of Bindon Street, Ennis also organised a jumble sale in Ennis, which raised £12 10s. This money was forwarded to Lady Hamilton for the 7th Royal Munster Fusiliers and the Connaught Rangers at the Dardanelles.

Mrs F.N. Studdert wrote to the paper expressing thanks to all those who subscribed to the Prisoners of War collection at the County Clare Agricultural Show held on 15 August. She said that she had received 243 letters and post-cards from Royal Munster Fusiliers prisoners, expressing their gratitude to the people of Clare. 'Many of them were pathetic in their inability to express their feelings of gratitude and many of them wrote that the people at home had no idea how much these parcels meant to them.'

Another source of comfort for the prisoners was the Clare Needlework Guild. Mrs G. de Laval Willis, honorary secretary, acknowledged the receipt of £5 from Mrs F.N. Studdert, part of the proceeds of a raffle; also thirty-five pairs of socks; £1 from Col Tottenham, Mountcallan, and shirts and socks from Mrs Maunsell, The Island, Clare Castle.

It seems that all of these fundraising committees were run by members of the Protestant community. However, in December, Mrs Roughan and the Ennis Ladies Auxiliary of the AOH organised a concert in the Picture Palace (Town Hall), Ennis, courtesy of the H&M Cinema Co., in aid of the County Clare Prisoners of War in Germany, for which a 'very handsome sum was realised'. Besides songs from various local singers, some cinematic views were shown, including scenes from Egypt and 'topical films'. A 'capital' war picture, *For the Empire*, was then shown, as well as other pictures. This was the only instance noted in the newspapers, where a collection was organised by the Catholic lady auxiliaries of the AOH for war relief.

Besides these local fundraising committees for the prisoners, a County Clare Prisoners of War Aid Fund Committee was established during the year with the Hon. Mrs Blood as president, Revd T. Abrahall, the Rectory, Ennis as honorary treasurer, Mrs F.N. Studdert as honorary secretary. Other members of the committee included Mrs Marcus Keane; Mrs MacDonnell; Mrs Arthur Greene; Mrs G. de L. Willis; Mrs Moynihan; Miss Parkinson; V. Revd Canon O'Dea, Administrator of Ennis; Sir Michael O'Loghlen, HML for County Clare; Col Tottenham; J.F. Gelston, Chief Inspector; and F.N. Studdert. Apart from Sir Michael O'Loghlen and Canon O'Dea, who were Catholics, it would seem that all the others were Protestants.

The County Clare Committee published a list of fifty prisoners from Clare in their December appeal for funds. Forty-two of them were from the Munster Regiment; three from the Royal Irish Regiment; two each from the Leinster Regiment and the Royal Dublin Fusiliers; and one each from the Connaught Rangers, the Gordon Highlanders, the South Lancashire Regiment, the King's Own Royal Lancashire, and the Royal Army Medical Corps.[30]

The Sinking of the *Lusitania*

Early in the year, as part of their war campaign, the German authorities had issued a general warning that all shipping entering UK waters was at risk of being attacked. They would not guarantee that even neutral or civilian ships would be safe from attack by submarines:

> Travellers intending to embark on the Atlantic voyage are reminded that a state of war exists between Germany and her allies and Great Britain and her allies; that the zone of war includes the waters adjacent to the British Isles; that in accordance with formal notice given by the German Imperial Government, vessels flying the flag of Great Britain, or any of her allies, are liable to destruction in these waters and that travellers sailing in the war zone on the ships of Great Britain, or her allies, do so at their own risk.
> Imperial German Embassy
> Washington DC, 22 April 1915

Despite the warning, many people did not take that threat seriously, never imagining that the Germans would attack a passenger ship sailing between New York and Liverpool. However, that complacency was soon shattered. On 7 May the transatlantic liner *Lusitania* was nearing the end of its journey from New York to Liverpool. The ship was about 10 miles away from Queenstown (now Cobh), when she was hit by two torpedoes fired from a German submarine U20, and sank within eighteen minutes, with massive loss of life. The shock of this sinking was almost as sensational as the sinking of the *Titanic* a few years earlier. It brought the horror and the danger of war closer to home. A few days after the sinking of the *Lusitania* there were several reported sightings of submarines off the coast of Clare in places such as Kilcredane Bay.

There were 1,257 passengers and 702 crew-members aboard the *Lusitania*, which regularly plied between New York and Liverpool. In fact she was on her 202nd Atlantic crossing. One thousand one hundred and ninety eight people perished in that indiscriminate attack by the German submarine, of whom forty-nine were Irish people, while only 761 were saved. The majority of the victims were buried in Ireland. Incidentally, bodies of *Lusitania* victims were washed up on the Clare coast in late July at places such as Loop Head, Liscannor, Doonbeg and Baltard.

There were at least two Clare victims of that appalling tragedy. Dr Joseph Garry, aged 25, from Shanahea, Kildysart, had recently qualified and was working aboard the *Lusitania* as an assistant surgeon. He was the son of Patrick Garry, Esq., a Justice of the Peace, and a member of Clare County Council, and Mary Garry. The second victim was 20-year-old Michael Galvin of Derryshane, Kilmurry McMahon. He had spent a few years in New York and was returning home to Clare. His body was never found.

Apparently, Dr Garry had been working for some time on the ship and had intended to leave after this last voyage. He was going to visit his family and then join the Royal Army Medical Corps, to assist in the typhus epidemic in Serbia. His body was never recovered either. The sinking of the *Lusitania* helped to turn public opinion in Ireland against Germany and was widely used for propaganda purposes.

Propaganda poster, 1915. (Courtesy of southdublinlibraries.ie)

One Clare woman, Miss Jane Hogan, from Derreen, Mullagh, Miltown Malbay, was fortunate to survive the sinking. She had been twenty years in America and was returning home. When the ship was hit a gentleman put a lifebelt on her and she fell into the sea. She spent about five hours in the cold water before being rescued and brought to the hospital in Queenstown. While in the water she was badly bruised, being hit by flotsam in the water. She witnessed six of her female comrades clinging to each other before they were drowned. Though she lost all of her belongings, she was lucky that all her money had been stitched into her corset. 'How good Almighty God has been to me, when I consider how all my comrades were lost', she said.[31]

The Gallipoli Campaign: 'Heroism and Slaughter'

In an attempt to end the stalemate on the Western Front and to defeat the Germans and their Turkish allies, the British began a new campaign in Gallipoli, Turkey, to capture the Dardanelles Straits and supply Russia from the Mediterranean Sea. This campaign turned out to be a military disaster for the British Army, with high levels of mortality. Thousands of Irish soldiers from regiments such as the Munster Fusiliers and Dublin Fusiliers were killed, among them many soldiers from Clare. Some of their stories and experiences were recorded through letters sent home.

News about the war was heavily censored in the media, and the War Office tried to ensure that negative reports should not be published, which might discourage recruitment or might lower the morale of the people at home. Some letters from the front line were published, but these were usually carefully filtered to show the gallantry, the courage, the bravery and the heroism of the fighting Irish regiments, and the barbarity of the enemy, whether Germans or Turks.

Nevertheless, despite the censorship, glorification, and propaganda, these letters give us some idea of the horrors of war. The following letter was written by an Ennis man, Drummer Hassett of the Royal Munster Fusiliers, describing his experience in the Dardanelles, and was published in the *Saturday Record*. There is a strong propagandist tone in the letter:

> Publish what I send you about a scrap which some of the Munsters have had. It was printed here in one of the papers in Malta, being sent from the battlefield. The battalion have done their duty, and also the Dublin Fusiliers. We landed together and we were the first two Irish regiments to land at Seddul Bahr – the 1st Battalion Munsters and the 1st Royal Dublin Fusiliers. We cleared the way with the English regiments behind us. We lost heavily, both regiments, but we captured the Turkish positions at the point of the bayonet. It was splendid to see them charging that night, every man with a brave dash in him. I did not take any part in the attack that night, owing to getting wounded the very first day before I landed; but I must say the two Irish regiments were put in the very hottest part of the landing, but every man did his duty, as every Irishman does when put to the test. Myself and my brother are wounded. He is gone to England and I am here in Malta, but I am going back again to get a piece of my own back from the Turk. I belong, as you know to Ennis.

The excerpt the private sends from the Maltese paper is as follows:

A very stirring tale is related of a most heroic fight between a handful of Munsters – there were 19 of them all told – and a company of Turks. The Munsters were watching a bombardment by one of the warships, when they were suddenly surprised by the Turks in the rear. They saw that the odds against them were tremendous, but they were determined to put up a good fight. They fought like demons, using the bayonet with great effect directly any Turk came near them, and very often charging with the bayonet and firing at the same time. In this way they kept the Turks at bay until assistance came, when it was found that no less than 70 Turks had been killed. The number of wounded was not known. The Munsters lost 11 men killed and four wounded.[32]

Another Ennis soldier, Cpl M. Murphy of the 1st Battalion Royal Munster Fusiliers, also wrote about his experience of war in the Dardanelles in a letter to a friend in Ennis, which was also published in the local press. This letter gives a graphic account of the landing and the sufferings and terrible conditions endured by the Munsters in Gallipoli. The letter ended with an admonitory tone to the 'slackers' of Ennis to do their duty and enlist. The newspaper article had subtitles such as ENNIS MEN WHO DID THEIR DUTY, and AN APPEAL TO 'SLACKERS' AT HOME:

My dear old chum, I hope this scribble will find you and father and mother and all at home in the best of health. As you will see by the address I am in hospital here. I contracted a disease in the … Dardanelles, which went very nearly having me, but thank God, I am over the worst of it now, but it will take me a long time yet, before I am fit, as there are not 16 ozs of flesh on my body and I am still very weak. I am now allowed out of bed for two hours in the evening and taken on a verandah on a deck chair by the nurses, where I can look down on the blue Mediterranean Sea. The nurses here are very nice, they are all ladies out of England who volunteered to nurse their soldiers, of whom they are very proud.

We landed at Gallipoli on the 15th April on a Sunday morning, which I will never forget, it was terrible. The Munsters and Dubliners were the first to land and we were met by a terrible fire from the shore and from a fort called Seddal Bahr. We lost heavily going ashore and it was one man out of every two who was lucky to get ashore without getting a hit. It was a terrible sight to see your chums struggling in the water after being hit. I was one of the lucky ones to get ashore without getting a scratch … I may say I was one of the first twenty men to land on that uninviting shore. The Dublins were just as badly off as we were, but we stuck to that shore all day and many acts of bravery were done by our men, which if it were seen, would gain many a man a VC. It was often given for less. There were several men saved from the sea badly wounded, who would never have got ashore.

We stuck to that shore all day – only a handful of us compared to the enemy. There was a terrible fire kept up from our gallant navy. All that day we were under fire from maxims, rifles and pom poms. And all that night we held it against the Turks and Germans, who made several attempts to drive us into the sea. But they had to meet the Irishmen, the cream of the British army, and they found out to their cost, that we had come to stay. Next morning, when we saw our dead and wounded, it made us only more determined to avenge them, and when the order was given, to fix bayonets and advance, it was done with a cheer. We advanced up on a village and met the Turks, but they could not face our bayonets. So, after several charges – but at a terrible loss – we took the village and fort and trenches and several prisoners. The Turks lost heavily that morning, but we had got a better footing. Still, there were some snipers concealed in the village, who were picking off our fellows. It was while surrounding the houses with six more that I got hit. I got a bullet through the shoulder, which put me out of action for the day. It is not painful when you get hit first – it is afterwards you feel it. I went on board a hospital ship where I was dressed and taken care of.

When I was fit I rejoined my comrades in the trenches, they were two miles from the shore, but there was a good many of the old faces gone. Still, those left were very cheerful. I was in the firing line for nearly three months and was in some very tight corners, but someone's prayers were heard as I had some very narrow escapes. I fought alongside several Ennis men, a good many of whom went to await the Roll of Honour, but they died fighting and got a soldier's grave which is not forgotten by their more fortunate comrades. We are very well looked after in the line of food, as we get fresh bread every day and fresh meat. When we come back from the firing line for a few days rest, we get an opportunity of having a swim in the sea, which is very refreshing after being in the trenches without a wash or a shave for a week. We get shelled every day, but the Turks very seldom do much damage.

I hope I will be spared to visit my old town again and to see all the comrades of my youth, when I will be able to give a good account of my experiences on active service. I got the old 'Record' from home this morning and was delighted to see by it that they held a big recruiting meeting in Ennis, where I am sure there are some 'slackers' yet. It is about time these fellows woke up and did their bit and not let the enemy on the fair shores of Erin. Let them come out here and meet and beat them in their own land. These are the fellows who will do all the shooting when the war is over and not the men who went through it and helped the nation to victory'.[33]

Capt. Poole Hickman

A third, and indeed the most comprehensive and most realistic account of the campaign in Gallipoli was given by Capt. H.Poole Hickman, who was killed the day after he wrote the account. He described the campaign between 6 and 14 August 1915. He was in command of D Company of the 7th Royal Dublin Fusiliers. He was tragically killed on 15 August 1915. He described how they landed and advanced from Suvla Bay as follows:

We left Mitylene at 2 pm on Friday 6th of August and arrived here at 4 am on Saturday morning. We carried our rations with us – a sandwich for the voyage and two days iron rations consisting of a tin of bully beef, tea, sugar, biscuits and Oxo tablets. From 2 o'clock in the morning onwards we could see the flashing of the big guns and hear the rattle of musketry, the first indications to us that we were within the war zone. Our first two boats, consisting of A and C companies, started landing at 5.30 am, but did not get ashore without mishap, as a shrapnel struck the boat, killing one man and wounding eleven. Among the wounded was one of our officers Second Lieut. Harvey. We landed a short while later, but escaped without being hit, and then around 8 am we commenced a general advance. It was allotted to us and to another Irish regiment to take a hill about three and a half miles from where we landed. We had not advanced 100 yards when we were greeted with a perfect hail of shrapnel, and shrapnel is not a pleasant thing. You hear a whistle through the air, then a burst and everything within a space of 200 yards by 100 yards from where the shrapnel burst is liable to be hit. The wounds inflicted are dreadful, deep, big, irregular gashes, faces battered out of recognition, limbs torn away.

We got some protection under cover of a hill and steadily continued our advance in a line parallel to the enemy's position. We had to change direction and advance in a direct line on a position on a small neck of land, and the crossing of this neck was awe-inspiring, but ghastly. The enemy guns had got the range to a yard and a tornado of high explosives and shrapnel swept the place. Your only chance was to start immediately after a burst and run as fast as you could across the place as there was some cover at the other side. We lost heavily at this particular place and from then on commenced the serious business. The enemy were strongly entrenched on a line of hills about two miles from the neck of land. The right of the attack had to get over a bare sandy sweep, but there was some cover for the left. The heat was intense and the going very heavy. We advanced in long lines with two paces between each man and about eight such lines altogether at the start. Of course, by the time we got to the hill, the supports and reserves had caught up with the firing line.

Meanwhile, we presented an open target to the enemy, but though we advanced through a regular hail of bullets and shrapnel, our casualties were not heavy. Maj. Harrison was in charge of the first line and was marvellously good. About 3 o'clock in the afternoon we were within 600 yards of the hill, which was fairly high, a network of trenches and sides covered with furze and thorny scrub, which afforded cover from view. When we got to the foot of the hill A and D Companies led by Maj. Anderson, were in the first line, about a platoon of each, with some Inniskillings and a few stragglers.

They took the hill at the point of the bayonet, the Turks fleeing in all directions. It was a magnificent performance and we have been personally congratulated on it, and we called the hill Fort Dublin. Our casualties were over 100, including Maj. Tippet shot dead and Lieut Julian, who has I hear, since died. D Company lost 22 injured altogether and only one killed outright, though I am afraid some of the others will not recover. It was just dusk when we took the hill and then we had to go and get water for the men, who were parched with the thirst. This was a long job and we had to go back two miles to a well. Meanwhile, we had established ourselves on the trenches on the hill and at 1.30 am I ate a biscuit, the first food I ate since breakfast the previous morning. The enemy counter-attacked during the night, but they were easily driven off.

All Sunday morning and afternoon a furious fight was going on on the ridge to our right, where our forces had the advantage. Meanwhile, shrapnel and high explosives were spoiling our day's rest, and the place was full of snipers. These snipers are the very devil, as if you put up your hand at all, bullets whizz past you. They are up trees, hidden in furze, and in every conceivable hiding place and it is very hard to spot them. We captured some, including a woman and a man draped in green to resemble the tree he was in and shot several more. On Monday there was a tremendous fight for the hill on our left by an English division. The brigade on our right ran out of ammunition and D Company was called upon to supply them. I sent 40 men under Captain Tobin, to bring up 20,000 rounds to the supports and took 80 men myself to get 40,000 rounds, which were further away to the same place, but with orders from the colonel to come back immediately as our side of the hill was very weakly held. When I got up I found that Tobin and 12 of his party had gone further up as the ammunition was urgently needed. I dumped down the ammunition with the supports and came back to the hill as ordered. Meanwhile, Tobin and his party had got into the firing line and one of my best sergeants, Edward Miller, was killed. He died gallantly and his name has been sent forward for recognition.

The next few days were uneventful save that we got no sleep, as we had to stand to arms about six times each night; and the incessant din of howitzers and heavy guns allowed no rest whatsoever. Finally, on Thursday night, or rather on Friday morning at 1.30 am, we were relieved, and were not sorry to leave a hill, which none of us will ever forget, and the taking of which will add lustre to the records of the Dublin Fusiliers. D Company's casualties amounted to 40 out of 188 men landed on Saturday morning. I forgot to say that we discarded our packs at the landing (and have never seen them again), and all this time we never had our boots off, a shave, or a wash, and even the dirtiest water was greedily drunk on the hill where the sun's rays beat pitilessly down all day long and where the rotting corpses of the Turks created a damnably offensive smell. This is one of the worst features here – unburied bodies and flies. But the details are more gruesome than my pen can depict. Well, we marched out at 1.30 on Friday morning, a bedraggled and want of sleep tired body, and marched seven miles back to a rest camp. Several of the men walked back part of the way in their sleep, and when we arrived at 4.30 on Friday morning, everyone threw himself down where he was and fell asleep. But our hopes of a rest were short-lived, as we were ordered out again at four the next day, and here we are now, on the side of a hill, waiting to go forward again and attack. Meanwhile, it is soothing for us to know that we have achieved something, which has got us the praise of all the staff and big men here, but I dare say, you will hear more about it in despatches from the front.[34]

Capt. Hickman was killed the very next day on 15 August 1915. He was the second son of Francis William Gore-Hickman, DL of Kilmore, Knock, Kilmurry McMahon. He was 35 years old. A well-known sportsman, he played rugby for Trinity College and was later captain of Wanderers Football Club. He was called to the bar in 1909 and was secretary of the Munster Circuit. He was also a freemason, having been enrolled in Lodge 60, Ennis, Co. Clare He enlisted in September 1914, joining the 'Pals' battalion. Two of his brothers also joined the 7th battalion of the Dublin Fusiliers, the 'Pals' battalion. Capt. Hickman was killed in action leading a bayonet charge on a ridge at Kiretch Tepe. He was well out in front, leading his men forward, shouting: 'On Dublins!' before he was cut down by Turkish fire. The famous D Company of the Dublin Fusiliers was practically wiped out in the Dardanelles.[35]

The conduct of the Irish soldiers at Gallipoli was 'a story of heroism and slaughter'. The Munster and Dublin regiments arrived at Suvla Bay in August 1915 and displayed enormous courage when making a landing on the treacherous beaches, which were stoutly defended by the Turkish Army. The landings have been described as being one of the most terrible days's fighting of the war. One eyewitness was Lt Commander Josiah Wedgewood, a British MP, who was present on the steamer *River Clyde*, which was run aground at the landing. His description, published in the *Westminster Gazette*, testifies to the bravery of the Irish soldiers:

I never noticed the grounding, for the horror in the water and on the beach. Five rows of five boats, each loaded with men were going alongside us. One moment it had been early morning in a peaceful country, and the next, while the boats were just twenty yards from the shore, the blue sea around each boat was turning red. Of all those brave men, two thirds died, and hardly a dozen reached the shelter of the five foot sand dunes. Then they charged from the wooden horse. From the new large ports on the lower deck they ran along gangways to the bows, and then moved three lighters to a spit of rock. Twenty slippery yards over the rocks and there was shelter. I think theirs was more terrible. In the first rush none got alive to land and they repeated these rushes all day. There was no room on the rocks, there was no room on the lighters and boats, they were so covered with the dead and wounded.

It was the Munsters that charged first, with a sprig of shamrock on their caps, then the Dubliners, then the Worcesters, and then the Hampshires. Lying on the beach, on the rocks, on the lighters, they cried on the mother of God. Even when I looked ashore, I saw five Munsters. They at some moment had got ashore. They had been told to cut off the wire entanglements. They had left the shelter of the bunk, charged fifteen yards to the wire and there they lay in a row at two yards interval. One could hardly believe them dead. All the time the great shells kept hitting the shivering ship and doing slaughter in the packed holds. These shells were fired from Asia, but it was the maxims and pom poms in Seddul Bahr and on the amphitheatre that kept our heads down below the bulwarks and boiler plate.

When the village of Seddul Bahr was cleared, it was found that there were no wounded survivors of the Munsters and Dublins. Two German officers were found and killed. These fiends, it appears had instigated the things done to the dying Irishmen, and we never afterwards found similar Turkish atrocities.[36]

'The Turk' Gormley

One Ennis soldier, Pte Gormley, who also served in the Dardanelles, described in detail how he killed a Turk with a bayonet after a desperate hand-to-hand struggle. For this action he was re-christened with the nickname 'The Turk' when he returned to Ennis after the war:

I happened to get wounded while up in the Dardennelles. My wound is pro-gressing favourably. We had a very warm time of it up in Gallipoli, most of my regiment being knocked over. The hospital is situated down on the seashore, so we are in quite a healthy spot, with plenty of sea breezes etc. We are getting well treated, so I have no cause to complain. I have one consolation in knowing that I killed my opponent.

I was coming from the firing line with a wounded comrade. I brought him to the nearest dressing station, about four miles from Aki Baba. Returning again to the firing line, I had to pass a battery of howitzers on my right, when the major of the battery called me asked me if I was returning to the firing line. I told him I was so he told me to look out for snipers. I went about 150 yards from the battery. I stood against a tree to have a drink, when I heard some noises. I got closer to the tree, where I could see the bayonet and part of a rifle of a Turk protruding from a tree. Unfortunately, I did not have my rifle with me, having left it in the trenches. I made a grab for his rifle and he fired, wounding me in the right hand. I made a grab with my left hand and caught hold of his rifle. I then forced the rifle upwards. He tried to wrench the rifle from me, but I held on. I watched for my opportunity and kicked him in the groin. He then dropped, letting go of the rifle. With his struggles I gave him another kick, this time in the jaw. This knocked him unconscious for a time. I then pointed the bayonet at his stomach and putting my weight on the butt drove the point home.

During the affair the major of the battery heard the report, on which he came up with four men and asked me if I were very much hurt. He bandaged my hand up with my field dressing, there being a constant flow of blood. He congratulated me, and took my name, number and regiment. When I said it was the Munsters, he said he thought so. So that is the only one I can account for. I can tell you it is no picnic up there. I regret to say Jack Regan was killed by my side on 2nd May and Pat Frawley and young Burley.[37]

Pte Armstrong of the 7th Battalion, Dublin Fusiliers, from Kilrush, son of the local Church of Ireland minister, Canon Armstrong, sent a letter home describing the very difficult conditions, especially the shortage of water and the dangers from snipers in the Dardanelles:

We took a hill just before dark. The Turks did not wait for the bayonet, but cleared when we got near their trenches, leaving their slippers, etc. behind. We had a very stiff time of it for about nine days, getting practically no sleep, as the Turks used to threaten us with attacks every night, sometimes coming very near the trenches.

We had to clear out a lot of unexploded shrapnel shells, which the Turks had stored up in a dug-out running along with them, while snipers were landing bullets rather too near us to be comfortable. However, we captured all the shells, without any casualties.

We had to get our water supply under fire, and the only way to escape the bullets was to keep on the move. I have trotted a couple of miles over and over again, with water bottles, while the snipers were potting for all they were worth, often getting half a dozen bullets running a few feet in front of me. Then they would sometimes turn shrapnel on the wells and cause a good many casualties. However, thank God, I have not had a bullet in me yet, although I have had a few narrow shaves ...

I am here (Valetta Hospital, Malta), recovering from dysentery. We are very well cared for – nice porridge for breakfast, with an egg, bread and butter and ripping tea. Chicken etc., nicely boiled for dinner, then tea and supper. The hospital seems like a palace after Gallipoli.[38]

The Gallipoli campaign turned out to be an unmitigated disaster for the Allied forces. The British-led attempt to defeat the Turks and to open a supply route to Russia via the Black Sea was a costly failure, partly due to incompetence in the high command and to the very strong Turkish defences. The bravery of the Allied soldiers could not be faulted. The British withdrew their forces from Gallipoli on 9 January 1916 after ten months of slaughter, which began on 25 April 1915. About 70,000 British troops were killed in the Dardanelles on the Gallipoli Peninsula, including 2,017 men from the 10th Division, among

On the beach at Gallipoli. (Courtesy of Great War photos.com)

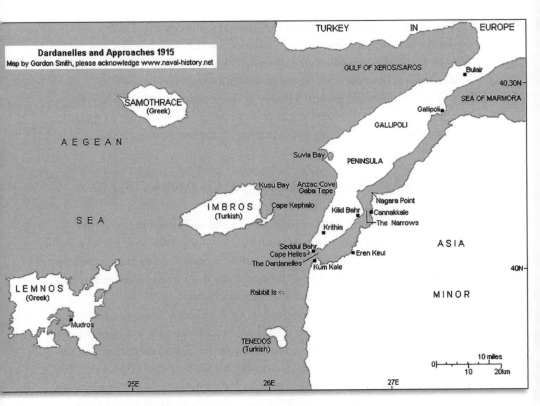

Map of Gallipoli. (Courtesy of Gordon Smith, www.navalarchive.net)

them at least forty-eight Clare men, mainly from the Munster, Inniskilling and Dublin regiments, who met their baptism of fire in August 1915, and whose bones are resting on the beachheads of Gallipoli. Besides the dead, more than 150 Clare men were wounded here.[39]

Among those wounded at Gallipoli was Capt. Robin Tottenham of Mountcallan, County Clare. He was badly wounded on 25 April within six hours of arrival at the battle scene. His right arm was amputated above the elbow. After treatment in a London hospital, Capt. Tottenham drove himself home to Clare to recuperate. He learned to shoot with one arm and shot his first snipe on 19 January 1916! His severe wounds did not deter him from action and he went to France on 16 March 1916 as an ADC to Maj. Gen. Hickie, commander of the 16th Irish Division and served for the rest of the war.[40]

Maj. Brian Mahon, commander of the 29th Brigade, wrote:

Never in history did Irishmen face death with greater courage and endurance than they did in Gallipoli and Serbia in the summer and winter of 1915 …

The four plagues of Gallipoli were flies, thirst, dirt and enteritis ... For a week the battalion held the line that was captured ... water was very short and had to be fetched from a considerable distance ... by day the Turkish snipers made this impossible, so the men lay hot and thirsty and tormented by flies ... to add to the horror the unburied bodies of those who had fallen in the previous fighting, lay in inaccessible gullies in the midst of scrub, began to spread around the foul, sweet, sickly odour of decay ... the real trouble was thirst.[41]

The Clare MPs and the War: Maj. Willie Redmond, MP

While Willie Redmond, MP, was true to his word and joined the army to fight for Ireland in France, he did not see much action during this year. He seems to have been used by the British Army for public relations and to assist recruiting throughout Ireland. In November he visited the front line in France. He gave an account of his experiences to the Press Association.

On 18 November he met the Sir Henry Rawlinson, commander of the 4th Army Corps, and Maj. Gen. Holland. He addressed a battalion of the Munster Fusiliers and was 'cheered lustily as they marched away to the strains of 'O'Donnell Abu'. On the following day he went to the HQ of the 2nd Army under Gen. Plummer, where he met and addressed the 2nd Battalion of the Leinster Regiment, after which he was given 'a most enthusiastic reception'. Here he also met some Catholic chaplains, who spoke highly in praise of the men. Then he went to the Divisional HQ, where he met Gen. Dore, a Wexfordman. He was brought along the trenches within 80 yards of the German lines and he heard the continuous roar of the big guns. While he was there he wrote that one of his constituents, a Clareman, was killed instantly by a bullet.

After this, he met members of the 2nd Battalion Royal Irish Rifles, with Fr Gill, their chaplain, leading them into the trenches. Again, Willie Redmond was given a 'warm welcome' and was 'heartily cheered' when he reminded them that the men were from the north and south of Ireland. He was told that the men from the north and south were the best of friends. On 29 November he met men of the Royal Irish Rifles and Royal Dublin Fusiliers and after addressing them, 'received a hearty greeting'.

He brought a message from Sir John French, congratulating the Royal Irish Regiment 'for gallantry in the field' and he told them of how proud Sir John French was to be their colonel. Then Gen. Hull brought him to the most dangerous part of the firing line, after traversing almost 2 miles of communications trenches. There he saw men of the Dublin Fusiliers and the Ulster men of the Royal Irish Rifles 'fighting side by side in the trenches'. After this, on

21 November, he met the Irish Guards Division commanded by Lord Cavan. Here he also met the Prince of Wales and Lord Claud Hamilton. He noted that the prince seemed to be 'in first-rate health and spirits and was leading the same life as any other young subalterns'.

Willie Redmond stated that the King of Belgium had graciously expressed a desire to meet him. He was moved by the occasion, 'I shall never forget my visit to the king – his kindness, his courtesy and his sympathy, and how generously he spoke of the little that Ireland had been able to do to help him. I confess that my emotions were stirred by this interview, more perhaps than ever before.'

The following day, Redmond returned to London on a troopship carrying 1,400 officers and men home on leave. Throughout the visit he had received 'the greatest courtesy'.[42]

Col Arthur Lynch, MP,

Col Arthur Lynch, who had enthusiastically endorsed the war and spoke of raising an Irish Brigade to fight alongside France against the Germans, did not join the British Army at this time; instead he gave lectures about warfare. Because of his fluent French and his wide connections, he aided communication between English and French leaders. Considering his past, it would have been difficult for Lynch to join the British Army at this time as his treason during the Boer War was not easily forgotten or forgiven.

Towards the end of May 1915 he had passed through Ennis to give a series of lectures to his West Clare constituents on topics such as modern warfare, which he had witnessed as an observer on the Western Front, by courtesy of the French military authorities.

He spoke at venues in Ennistymon, Miltown Malbay, Lahinch and Kilfenora. He also addressed a meeting of Kilrush UDC. According to the *Clare Journal*, Lynch returned to England 'having made many friends by his eloquence and magnetic personality. After the meeting in Kilfenora he was cheered enthusiastically after his lecture, with the words of the song, 'He's a jolly good fellow' ringing in his ears.

One of his supporters, Mr C.E. Egan BA from Lahinch, sent a letter to the *Clare Journal* on 9 September to inform his constituents that:

> The brilliant member for West Clare was gradually recovering from his injuries suffered in a train crash. The gallant Colonel's versatility stood him in good stead on the occasion. His rapid recovery from severe personal injury showed the FIGHTING soldier, and his immediate attention to the helpless, while he himself was dazed and in pain, showed the medical man at his

best … These thoughts evidently pervaded the minds of the crowd at the late Miltown Malbay Races, for the Honourable Member's arrival on the course was greeted with uproarious cheering, for the Milesian Irish dearly love a MAN … Colonel Lynch hopes to carry out in the near future the lecture tour which the railway accident compelled him to abandon. [43]

A War of Words

Another war broke out towards the end of the year. This time it was a war of words over the publication of a book by Col Lynch. He published a book entitled *Ireland: Vital Hour* in August 1915 and it proved to be a controversial, indeed notorious publication in which he outlined his liberal views on politics, education and religion and the role of the clergy in Irish politics. This book did enormous damage to his political career in County Clare, as it made powerful local enemies for him in the Catholic Church and in the *Clare Champion*.

Among the controversial topics discussed in the book was the role of the clergy in politics. In Chapter V he wrote the following:

> I am resolutely opposed to priests in politics when the parish priest throws into the scale his sacerdotal emblems, and when he speaks ex cathedra and dictatorially on subjects wherein he has no special intelligence and where his religion, if truly invoked, would cover him with confusion.
>
> Certainly the priests have great influence in politics in Ireland, they have undue influence, and it must be the task of Irish nationalists to emancipate themselves from that undue influence, if ever they mean to lift the country out of the slough of despond, where it has lain so long.
>
> These questions must be tackled resolutely. This is not the way of popularity, but it is the way of the salvation of Ireland. Irishmen should face the issue with courage for it requires more courage sometimes to acknowledge a truth than to shout war cries to the approval of the mob. [44]

Naturally, such comments, which may have had a popular audience in Protestant England or in anti-clerical France at this time, were not popular in Catholic, nationalist Ireland. Lynch's popularity rapidly evaporated when the contents of his book became known to his constituents in West Clare and they must have been concerned and alarmed when the book was condemned in the national and local press. A damning indictment of the book was published in both the *Clare Champion* and in the *Clare Journal* in late November by Fr James Monahan, Administrator of Crusheen, who wrote the following letter to the papers:

15 November 1915
Dear Sir,

Will you kindly allow me space in your valuable journal to tender my apologies to the nationalist electors of West Clare for having proposed at a nationalist convention in Kilrush, Mr Arthur Lynch as an MP for one of the most Catholic and nationalist constituencies in Ireland.

At the time I believed Mr Lynch to be an honest nationalist and would voice the cause of West Clare, with ability and fearlessness in the British House of Commons, and that he would be loyal to the Irish leader and the Irish Party. I have been sadly disillusioned.

His greatest effort in the House of Commons is to ask a question. And his loyalty to his leader and party is well known in West Clare, where he has been whispering their various drawbacks.

To have been the sponsor for such a representative is indeed cause for regret, but to have supported at convention a man who is the author of a book in which our Church, the pope and the priesthood of Ireland have been defamed, will be a source of regret to me for the remainder of my life.

There is one art in which he excels, and that is the art of libelling, slandering, and vilifying the Catholic Church, the pope and the people of Ireland. With deep regret for having assisted to foist on the sterling nationalists of West Clare, the glorifier of Cromwell, Queen Elizabeth, of Luther, and Pitt and Castlereagh and the vilifier of the Catholic Church, the pope and the immortal Daniel O'Connell.

Yours, Faithfully,
James Monahan, Adm.

This sensational letter sparked off a war of words between Col Arthur Lynch, MP, and Fr Monahan, and others, which was waged in several editions of the local papers between 18 November and 25 December 1915 and indeed into the New Year. Col Lynch denied these charges and alleged that Fr Monahan had not read the book and had misquoted him and taken his words out of context. He asserted that he had not glorified Cromwell and other English rulers, nor had he vilified O'Connell, the pope or the Catholic Church. He ended his defence with confidence: 'I am not in the least daunted, for I know that the great majority of the staunch men who elected me have full confidence in my intentions. I have a duty to them and to Ireland; I will do my duty up to the hilt'.

Several others, some under nom de plumes, also took part in the literary battle, which became more bitter as it developed. Fr Monahan's final commentary on 20 December denounced the 'anti-Irish, anti-Catholic calumniating book ... by his vilification of the Catholic Church, the pope, the priesthood of Ireland and Daniel O'Connell, and by his glorification of Cromwell and Pitt and Castlereagh, he has secured for his book a ready and lucrative market among the enemies of Ireland'.[45]

The *Clare Champion* also attacked Lynch over the 'notorious' book and regretted his election as a candidate in West Clare in 1909:

> We believed at the time of Mr Lynch's selection at the Kilrush convention that the delegates were making a mistake. They knew little of the political character or antecedents of the Australian man from the mining camp at Ballarat. They selected him because of his incursion into the South African (Boer) War, which had nothing to do with Irish politics. They selected him as Fr Monahan proposed him and because they believed him to be a fighting nationalist.
>
> At that time we believed that an honest fisherman from West Clare would have been a more creditable member, loyal to the leader and to the party, would understand the realities of Irish life and certainly he would never attack the Catholic Church, for fidelity to which our forefathers sacrificed everything and faced the cruel sword of Cromwell and all the penal statutes of Elizabeth and the rest.

Col Arthur Lynch,
MP in 1915.
(Photo from Ireland:
Vital Hour)

However, Mr Lynch was selected, it was luckless and unfortunate, he has shown poor gratitude to the trusting electors of West Clare.[46]

Finally, Mr Egan, one of Lynch's main supporters in Clare wrote to the *Clare Journal* 'calling for a truce during the festive season in the somewhat painful controversy' on the subject of 'Ireland: Vital Hour'. The *Clare Journal* also rallied to Lynch's defence, stating that 'the gallant member for West Clare had arranged to meet his constituents during the Christmas recess, but serious illness in his household had compelled him to postpone his visit'.[47]

Col Arthur Lynch had enjoyed some popularity during his lecture tour of Clare in May 1915, but he did serious damage to his reputation in Ireland and to his prospects of re-election as MP for West Clare when he published his controversial book, *Ireland: Vital Hour*. With the publication of this book he managed to alienate two very powerful forces in County Clare at this time, the nationalist newspaper, the *Clare Champion*, and the Catholic Church. In the opinion of many influential Clare people Col Arthur Lynch, MP, was no longer 'a jolly good fellow'.

'Some Gallant Clare Men'

Several Claremen were the recipients of military awards. Two Clare officers were given medals of honour for bravery in battle. Capt. George W. Stacpoole of Eden Vale was given the Distinguished Service Order (DSO) and Lt Robert Hallam Studdert, Hazelwood, Quin, of the Royal Field Artillery was awarded the MC for 'heroic conduct and distinguished service in the field of battle'. Sgt Maj. T. Corry, from Labasheeda, a member of the Irish Guards, was awarded the DCM for 'gallantry and courage under fire'. Sgt Thomas J. Lee, RFA of Mullagh, West Clare was awarded the DCM and promoted to a lieutenancy for 'gallant conduct in the field'. First Class Staff Sgt Maj. Michael McNamara of Market Street, Ennis, was presented with a bronze medal by the French Government for 'an act of courage and devotion to duty on the battlefield'. The French Foreign Minister made the presentation. Sgt McNamara was one of four brothers serving in the army, two in the ASC, one in the Guards and one in the RGA.

The *Saturday Record* highlighted the bravery of Sgt Tom Corry of Labasheeda:

He was mentioned in Sir John French's despatches, but it was not his first distinction, as he was similarly honoured some time ago – a unique record for a young man … The heroism of Irish regiments has been one of the most

CLARE CASUALTIES.

The following names appear in the last casualties lists. Some of the cases were reported unofficially lately.

KILLED.

J Keane, Kilrush, The Munsters
Act-sergt. Muldoon, Feakle, „

DIED OF WOUNDS.

M Hartigan, Ennis, R.E., „

WOUNDED.

C' Guilfoyle, Ennis, Leinsters
P Bailey, „ „
P Blood, Ennistymon, Munsters
Sergeant T Crowe, Corofin, „
S Culligan, Kilrush, „
T Devers, „ „
J Dinan, Scariff, „
P Dillon, Ennistymon, „
J Downes, Kilrush, „
Loe-Corpl P Griffey, Ennis „
P Guilfoyle „ „
P Hehir „ „
J Kelly „ „
J McDonucH, Kilrush „
J McMahon „ „
Loe-Corpl T McMahon, Ennis „
S McNamara, Kilrush „
P Meehan, Ennis „
Loe Opl J Murphy, Ennistymon „
P O'Brien „ „
D O'Halloran, Corofin „
M Reidy, Sixmilebridge „
Corp T Russell, Ennis „
M Shannon, „ „
J Stapleton, Kilkee „
T Sullivan, Castleconnell „
R Walsh, Kilrush „

SHELL SHOCK.

Sergt Kelleher, Ennistymon „

MISSING.

W Rochford, Ennis „

Clare casualties, from the *Saturday Record*, 28 October 1916.

stirring features of the Great War and Tom Corry must have risked almost certain death in the firing line to win his renown and to worthily uphold the unparalleled bravery of Irishmen. The DCM comes next to the Victoria Cross for bravery. He has been in the war since the commencement – fighting for liberty against the hellish Huns – and he has emerged from many terrible engagements uninjured, but glorious … a fine type of Irishman and

Catholic, highly intelligent and chivalrous to the utmost, but withal most gentle and unassuming, is it any wonder that Providence has been so kind to him … It is earnestly hoped that when the Kaiser's fate is forever sealed, he may soon reappear crowned with fresh laurels in that little village by the Shannon, where a hero's welcome awaits him.

Another 'gallant Clareman' was Sgt Thomas J. Lee, of Mullagh, who was awarded the DCM and was promoted to the rank of lieutenant for his acts of 'bravery in the field of battle'. He was in the army at the outbreak of the war, attached to the Royal Field Artillery, and was sent to France in August. He escaped unscathed until 29 November, when he was wounded in the arms and legs at Ypres. After he recovered from his injuries he was sent to the Dardanelles and being attached to the Australian contingent as a signaller, was among the first parties to land on the Gallipoli Peninsula. On the fourth day after landing he was cut off from his comrades, but he kept in contact with them by field telephone. After he was ordered to withdraw, he was making his way back to the British lines, when he observed a wounded Australian, about ninety to 100 yards from the line. 'Without giving a thought to his own safety, he rescued the fallen comrade and carried him on his back to safety, being wounded in the leg, the shoulder and

Sgt Tom Corry, DCM, third from right, with members of the
1st Battalion Irish Guards. (Courtesy of Cormac O'Comhrai)

Capt. Robert H. Cullinan of Bindon Street, Ennis, RMF, who died
for king and country at Gallipoli on 8 August 1915.
(Courtesy of Peadar McNamara Collection)

in the lung by Turkish fire while doing so, but they reached the safety of the
trenches. After recovering from his wounds, again, Lt Thomas Lee, DCM,
was sent back to the Dardanelles.[48]

Telegrams from the War Office

As the carnage continued in several theatres of war on land and at sea, anxious
families worried and prayed each day for the safety of their relatives – fathers,
sons and brothers. The postman might bring a welcome letter from the field of
war. But a telegram from the War Office only meant the worst possible news,
and that was news of the death of their loved one. The telegram was usually
followed by a letter written by an officer of the regiment in which the soldier
was serving, by the chaplain attached to the regiment, or by a friend of the dead
soldier. Examples of such letters included the following addressed by Lance Cpl
Musgrave to Mr John and Mrs Augusta Carroll of Edenvale offering his sympathies on the death of their son, 24-year-old L-Cpl William Carroll of the 5th
Lancers, Royal Irish Regiment, who was killed on 2 May 1915, at Ypres. His
mother, Mrs Augusta Carroll was a Presbyterian who had been born in Germany,
but had lived in Edenvale for many years, having married and settled locally.
She may have had divided loyalties and her son may have been fighting against
his and her own relations in Germany.

Dear Mrs Carroll,

… It was on Sunday, 2 May, and we were preparing to be relieved from our trenches where we were reserved. At about 5.30 in the evening the enemy made an attack with poisonous gases, which no doubt you have heard about. Our infantry were overcome by the fumes and we were ordered to advance to take their places. As we were advancing the shells fell very thick and our squadron happened to take the brunt of the fire. Will was knocked over by one shell and was trying to rise when another shell came and killed him on the spot. A married private with him was also killed, another died later and several were badly wounded.

It was impossible to get a message from him, but I know that he had your photo with him. It is impossible to tell the name of the place, but I can tell you it is where all the fighting has been going on for several months, and where thousands of our brave men have fallen. You have the knowledge that he did not suffer much, if at all. Our losses that day were four killed and about twenty wounded.

Another Clareman, Pte Pat McMahon from Ennis, of the Royal Munster Fusiliers, was also killed that week and his wife received a letter from his commanding officer, Capt. Filgate, who took great pride in the gallantry of the men and honour of the regiment in the field of battle:

I deeply sympathise with you in your great loss. It may be a little consolation to you to know that the regiment was the only one in the brigade to reach the German trenches, and behaved in a gallant manner. We are all proud of the many gallant officers and men that fell and they succeeded in adding to the honour and name of the regiment, which I know always came first with them.[49]

Pte Thomas Davis

One unfortunate young Clareman was court-martialled and shot by the British Army on 2 July 1915. Twenty-one-year-old Pte Thomas Davis, a member of the 1st Battalion Royal Munster Fusiliers, married with one son, from Ennis, was executed for allegedly deserting his post during the Dardanelles campaign in Gallipoli. He was the son of a shoemaker from Kerry, who had moved to Ennis and resided in a one-room cottage along with a wife and six children in The Turnpike area. Poverty was their lot and young Tommy Davis enlisted along with one of his brothers, Francis. After surviving the first landing at Gallipoli, in which there were huge casualties, Pte

Davis was accused of being absent from his sentry duty post on 20 June 1915. Despite the fact that he, like many others, was suffering from dysentery, he was found guilty of 'deserting his post' and Pte Davis was shot at dawn (5 a.m.) on 2 July 1915 at Gully Beach on the Gallipoli Peninsula. He was posthumously pardoned in 2006.[50]

Pte Davis was one of about 138 people from Clare who died that year because of the war on the Western Front, at Gallipoli and at sea. Their bodies lie in France, Belgium, Gallipoli, Greece, and at sea.[51]

'... *Dulce et decorum est, pro patria mori.*'

Wilfred Owen (1917)[52]

4

RECRUITMENT AND REBELLION

The question of recruitment became more urgent as British losses continued to mount with a war of attrition on the Western Front, and the War Office was planning a major offensive after the disaster of Gallipoli. This turned out to be the notorius Battle of the Somme, with horrific losses. Early in the New Year the recruiting committees established in East and West Clare towards the end of 1915 began their work in earnest. The committees were set up in response to a new recruitment campaign initiated by the Department of Recruitment in Ireland and the Lord Lieutenent, Lord Wimborne, in which significant locals were to be prominent in the campaign. Conscription was introduced in England, Scotland and Wales for all men between the ages of 18 and 45, but Irishmen in Ireland were exempted, thanks to the determined efforts of John Redmond and the Home Rule Party. The Easter Rising of 1916 had a significant impact upon Irish attitudes towards England and the Great War and recruitment slowed down considerably. The Roll of Honour grew longer each year.

The West Clare Recruitment Committee was established at a meeting in Kilrush in early March 1916. This meeting was chaired by J.K. Kett, JP, Kilkee, chairman of Clare County Council. The attendance included: B. Culligan, JP, chairman of Kilrush Urban District Council; W.C. Doherty, chairman of Kilrush Board of Guardians; M. Mescall, chairman of Kilrush Rural District Council (RDC); M. Leyden, JP, chairman of Ennistymon RDC; M. Griffin, JP, chairman of Kildysart RDC; and C.E. Glynn, controller of recruiting for West Clare, who organised the meeting.[1]

The committee resolved to promote recruitment by setting up sub-committees in the following areas: Kilrush, Kilkee, Cooraclare, Mullagh, Kilshanny, Miltown Malbay, Ennistymon, Kildysart, Kilmihil and Carrigaholt, with important local people involved such as Catholic and Protestant clergy, deputy lieutenants, JPs, town and rural councillors, bank managers, doctors, solicitors, members of the AOH and business people.

Speaking at this meeting Mr Hurley, a government official from Ennistymon, said that over 200 men from Ennistymon had joined the colours, but there were some yet around the district who had not enlisted. Mr O'Dwyer, also from Ennistymon, corroborated what Mr Hurley had stated: 'The town had done very well and I do not think that there were many more left, but in the outlying districts there were men available and they would do all in their power to get them to enlist.'

Significantly, Mr C.E. Glynn persuaded many parish priests of West Clare, including Canon McInerney, Kilrush; Revd P. Glynn, Kilkee; Revd Fr Hehir, Cooraclare; Revd J. Glynn, Mullagh; Revd McGurran, Kilshanny; Canon Hannon, Miltown Malbay; Revd Cassidy, Ennistymon; Revd P. Barrett, Knock and Killimer; and Revd D. Vaughan, Doonbeg; to head the committees in each parish, as well as several curates. Of all these 'notables', the Catholic clergy would probably have had the most powerful persuasive influence over their flock in the matter of recruitment. The Department of Recruitment in Ireland had encouraged all the local recruitment committees 'to use priests where you can get them'.[2]

Though the majority of the Catholic clergy in West Clare seemed to be promoting recruitment, some clerical voices were raised in opposition to the war. McCarthy mentions that only four Catholic priests in County Clare, all curates, spoke out openly against recruitment before the Easter Rising: Fr John O'Dea, CC Bodyke; Fr Culligan, CC Carrigaholt; Fr Marcus McGrath, CC Clare Castle and Ballyea, and Fr Maher of Killaloe and Garranboy. Fr John O'Dea advised his parishioners at a Sunday Mass in Bodyke 'to resist conscription by every means in their power instead of being

---

4 QUESTIONS TO THE WOMEN OF IRELAND

You have read what the Germans have done in Belgium. Have you thought what they would do if they invaded Ireland?

Do you realise that the safety of your homes and children, the sanctity of your Churches depend on our defeating the Germans in Belgium?

Do you realise that the one word 'Go' from you may send another man to fight for Ireland?

When the war is over and your husband or your son is asked 'What did you do in the Great War?' is he to hang his head because you would not let him go?

Women of Ireland do your duty!

Let your men enlist in an Irish Regiment TODAY.

GOD SAVE THE KING
GOD SAVE IRELAND

Clare Journal, 25 February 1915.

led like sheep to the slaughter.' Fr Marcus McGrath told his flock that 'they should not believe all the stories about German atrocities in Belgium'. *De Wiel* states that in 1914 only twenty-four out of a total of about 3,000 Catholic priests in Ireland openly condemned the war, and that the role of the parish priest was crucial.[3]

These recruitment sub-committees were for men only, but the ladies of Clare also wanted to play a role in the recruitment campaign. Shortly after the establishment of the West Clare Recruitment Committee the ladies of West Clare held a meeting in Kilrush to promote recruitment in that district. This meeting was held in the Market House, Kilrush. The meeting was chaired by Ms Florence Glynn, with Ms M. Hennessy as hon. secretary. A total of twenty-eight 'respectable women' attended the meeting which was addressed by Mr C.E. Glynn, director of recruiting, and by Mr Johnstone from Limerick. All the ladies resolved to promote recruitment in their districts, to encourage young men from West Clare to take their place in

TO THE YOUNG WOMEN OF IRELAND

Is your Best Boy wearing Khaki? If not, don't you think he should be?

If he does not think that you and your country are worth fighting for – do you think he is worthy of you?

Don't pity the girl who is alone – her young man is probably a soldier – fighting for her and her country – and for you.

If your young man neglects his duty to Ireland, the time may come when he will neglect you.

Think it over –
then ask your young man to
Join an Irish Regiment to-day
Ireland will appreciate your help

Clare Journal, 1 April 1915.

the Irish regiments to join their comrades 'who are fighting gallantly to defend our country and the defenceless women and children who are left behind'. The meeting unanimously resolved to do what they could to encourage recruiting and to look after the interests of the soldiers.[4]

An East Clare Ladies Recruitment Committee was established at a meeting in Ennis courthouse. Lady Inchiquin was elected president and Mrs Willis became hon. secretary. Sub-committees were established in the following districts: Ballyvaughan, Lisdoonvarna, Dromore, Sixmilebridge, Scarriff, Tuamgraney, Tulla, Killaloe, O'Callaghan's Mills and Lahinch. More than sixty women attended the meeting, representing many long-established families in Clare, with a mixture of Protestant and Catholic ladies, though mainly Protestant.[5]

A 'highly representative meeting' of the East Clare Recruitment Committee was held at the courthouse, Ennis in March. It was chaired by Sir Michael O'Loghlen of Drumconora, Barefield, HML for County Clare; with Lord Inchiquin as vice-chairman and M.V. O'Halloran, JP, as secretary. About thirty gentlemen attended and they decided to seek the support of local councillors to encourage recruitment in rural areas. There was strong criticism of the farming community, who were said 'not to be pulling their weight' in the national crisis.

Col O'Callaghan Westropp said that Ennis had contributed magnificently, 'this town alone had sent about 800 recruits, which was almost a battalion', but, he said, 'for some reason, the farmers' sons were holding back. That was a fact that no one could deny'. The colonel sought the revival of the old Clare Militia, which had been disbanded about ten years previously, of which he had been colonel, to boost recruitment. Capt. R.J. Stacpoole, DL, of Eden Vale offered the use of his services to travel by motor car around the county to assist in the recruitment campaign.

Mr George McElroy, the resident magistrate for County Clare, complimented the good work by Lt Abrahall and Sgt Connolly. He said that the committee should send local county and rural district councillors to canvass the community. These would be 'known and trusted men', who with the assistance of the clergy, would create 'a healthy public opinion among the farmers'. Mr C.E. Glynn, Recruiting Organiser for West Clare said that he had met all of the parish priests and that every priest he met was 'willing to give assistance'.

Mr McElroy, RM, who lived in the old barracks at Clare Castle, also suggested using the soldiers who were home on leave to assist in recruiting: 'Whenever a soldier came home on furlough (leave), to Clare Castle he brought back two or three recruits with him!'

Councillor P.J. Linnane, Ennis UDC, said that 'Ennis had done its duty by sending more than 800 men, but the farmers of Clare did not realise the gravity of the situation. There were', he said, 'terrible scares about conscription, but the farmers had it in their heads that the war would be won without them, however, if their homesteads were in danger they would look upon it differently!'[6]

At a specially convened meeting of Clare County Council held in April, a County Clare Recruitment Committee, led by Lord Inchiquin, with members including G. McElroy, Resident Magistrate (RM); Dr E. Frost, JP; Col Sir Charles Barrington, of Glenstal, Limerick, the recruitment officer for Clare and Limerick; C.E. Glynn; M.V. O'Halloran, JP; P. Kennelly, JP; J. O'Regan; F.N. Studdert, DL, secretary to Clare County Council, and Mr T. Lynch, sought a resolution of support from Clare County Council in favour of voluntary recruitment. Lord Inchiquin read a letter from Viceroy Lord Wimborne, seeking co-operation from the rural district, urban and county councils for the recruitment campaign.

Lord Inchiquin, in addressing the council, said that the Home Rule Party and the clergy of all denominations were in favour of recruitment, and in fact, he thought that the people of the entire county were in favour of it. But he said that the farmers had done very little, while the people of the towns had done well in joining the army and navy. The Clare Recruitment Committee wanted the sympathy and support of the councillors and wanted them to canvass potential recruits in their electoral areas.

Dr Edmund Frost, speaking about the Newmarket-on-Fergus district, said that seventy or eighty young men had enlisted, and with the exception of Mr McMahon of Knocknagun, they were all from the labouring classes. He stressed that it was proper and opportune that the farmers should come forward.

One councillor, Mr Bart Crowley, from the Knockerra district, rejected the allegations that the farming class were 'slackers'. He thought that the resolution, if carried, 'would be a stepping stone towards conscription'. He said that sixty or seventy young men from his rural area

Sir Lucius O'Brien, the Right Hon. 15th Baron Inchiquin in his coronation robes, 1902. (Courtesy of the Hon. Grania R. O'Brien)

around Knockerra had enlisted in the army, but because they joined in the towns, they were included as urban recruits.

A motion to form a central committee comprising members of the county council and the recruitment committee to promote recruitment voluntarily was passed by thirteen votes to six. One of those who voted against the motion, Mr Bart Crowley, said that 'he did not want to be a recruiting sergeant for the British Army!'

Eight months later, another resolution was passed by Clare County Council after a heated debate in the council chamber. This resolution unanimously protested against conscription in Ireland.[7]

'Freedom Begets Loyalty'

Early in January the *Clare Champion* had an editorial, which reflected the opinion of its proprietor and editor on the war and Ireland's role in it. It still supported the policy promoted by John Redmond and the Home Rule Party, though there were reservations about the question of Ulster exclusion from Home Rule. The editor rejected the old Fenian policy and by using the phrase 'freedom begets loyalty' was still accepting Redmond's policy of support for the war:

… Ireland's position is that having got Home Rule, England's difficulty is no longer Ireland's opportunity.' The Home Rule Act is now on the statute books and the majority of Irish people have accepted that as a guarantee of England's good faith. The only cause for concern is the fact that an amending bill has been promised to Ulster, and a small minority of our people believe, or affect to believe, that this renders Home Rule uncertain. The vast majority of people, however, accept Home Rule as an Act of Irish settlement and they have shown in the present crisis that freedom begets loyalty …[8]

Col Arthur Lynch returned to Clare early in the New Year, partly to redeem his reputation among the nationalists of the county and to support the cause of voluntary recruitment. He was, however, given a frosty reception by his constituents. An editorial comment in the *Clare Champion* of 12 February 1916 stated about his visit, 'Never in political history has an Irish MP received such an icy reception by a body of representative constituents.' His coming was not announced in the press. He arrived at Ennis and proceeded to Ennistymon by rail and though he notified some of his supporters of his visit, no one turned out to meet him. The *Clare Champion* editor commented, 'He looked a lonely and desolate figure and the chilling nature of his reception must have brought home to him how much he had offended and annoyed nationalist opinion by his unnatural and unworthy literary effort, which some wags in the west re-christened, *Ireland: Fatal Hour*.'

Dr Fogarty's Lenten pastoral was issued in February and he made no comment whatsoever about the war, or recruitment. But, perhaps influenced by the frightful mortality of the war, he devoted the entire pastoral letter to the neglected condition of graveyards in the diocese. The *Clare Journal* may have been disappointed with his seeming lack of enthusiasm for the war, but they compensated for this by taking selected quotes from the Lenten pastorals issued by other members of the Irish hierarchy, who were pro-war with sub-headings such as 'justice of the allied cause', 'unwarranted German aggression', 'cruelties and excesses of the Prussians', the 'desecration of Catholic churches in Belgium, France and Poland', and 'the Armenian massacre'. The *Clare Journal* published a speech by Revd John Mullan, Provincial of the Passionist Order at Mount Argus, Dublin, appealing for Irish men to volunteer 'to fight for Ireland and their co-religionists in Belgium'.[9]

Recruitment in West Clare

Mr C.E. Glynn, Kilrush, controller of recruitment in West Clare, was tireless and enthusiastic in his efforts to promote recruitment in the area. He claimed to have persuaded more than a hundred recruits to enlist since he was appointed in November. However, he complained about the lack of a recruiting office in

Kilrush, which was three-and-a-half hours' journey by rail from Ennis and which did not have a recruiting sergeant. C.E. Glynn wrote to the Lord Lieutenant, Baron Wimborne seeking a roving commission in the army. In his letter Glynn states that he met Baron Wimborne at Limerick and at the coursing meeting at Clounanna,

> since my appointment over 100 recruits have been accepted … but I find I am greatly handicapped in recruiting … the recruitment office is three and a half hours railway journey to Ennis … When I ask a man to join it is awkward and unpleasant when he replies to me 'why are you not in uniform yourself?'… It is hard to expect men to throw up their employment and go to Ennis and find that they are rejected, as happened in several cases.

But he was advised that his civilian status gave him more freedom and flexibility and that he would be more useful as a civilian with his wide contacts than as a commissioned officer.

C.E. Glynn wrote to Capt. Kelly at the Recruitment Office in Dublin to complain:

> Up to now the whole of West Clare has been neglected … it is hard to get recruits without a recruitment sergeant in the district since last September and no recruitment office … I hope you will take steps to have paid recruiters as suggested appointed immediately in the following towns of West Clare, Kilkee, Kilrush, Doonbeg, Miltown Malbay, Ennistymon, Kildysart, Knock, Carrigaholt, etc.
>
> On Saturday I called on a great many influential people in Ennis, Ballycorick, Ballynacally, and Kildysart, including some of the leading ladies, businessmen, JP's, county councillors, district councillors etc. and most of them promised to assist me and act on the proposed local committees and to do everything in their power to forward recruiting. I hope to have seen all the principal people within a fortnight.
>
> May I have your permission to insert a short notice in the local papers for people who are desirous of helping in recruitment? It is advisable to hold recruiting meetings at different venues with a band in attendance and send down some good speakers. If John Redmond could be induced to visit and to address a meeting in Kilrush or Ennis, it would have a splendid effect.

Mr Glynn secured two paid recruiting agents, one civilian and one military, in each of the market towns of West Clare, to be paid 14*s* per week and 2*s* 6*d* for each successful recruitment. However, Mr Glynn suggested that 'the recruiting agents were not to be badly wounded and they were warned that they must not talk about the horrors of the war,' in case they discouraged potential recruits.

He claimed to have travelled more than 2,000 miles since his appointment, without receiving a penny in expenses. The West Clare Recruiting Committee recommended that the following people be employed as paid recruiters: Thomas Shannon, Ennistymon; Michael Bohannon, Kildysart; J. Cunningham, Kilrush; William Frost and Francis Keane, Kilkee.

At a meeting in February, Kilrush Urban District Council unanimously passed the following motion:

> That we, the members of Kilrush Urban Council, have read with much inter-est the manifesto issued by Mr John Redmond to the Irish people, that we desire to express our unanimous approval and appreciation of his efforts to bring the war to a successful termination, and we feel it is the duty of every Irish man and woman to do their best to assist him in every way by encour-aging young men eligible for military service to come forward voluntarily at once and take their place in the Irish regiments, which are gallantly fighting in defence of our empire.

This resolution was actually drafted by Mr C.E. Glynn, who asked the chair-man of Kilrush UDC, J. Ryan, to propose it and the vice-chairman, B. Culligan to second the proposal. Mr Glynn also met the chairman of Ennis UDC and persuaded him to have a similar resolution proposed at Ennis Urban Council. A letter from John Redmond urging the Kilrush Board of Guardians to sup-port recruitment was read out at a meeting of that board, seeking their support. Mr Carmody proposed a motion that the Kilrush Board of Guardians unani-mously support the motion. However, two members dissented. Mr O'Brien stated that the Irish were slaughtered at Suvla Bay in Gallipoli. Another member, Mr Lillis, also objected to the motion, stating, 'this is England's war not Ireland's war'. After a heated exchange between the chairman, Mr W.C. Doherty, JP, and the two objectors, the motion was passed by twenty-six votes to two.

Meanwhile, Clare County Council passed another motion supporting vol-untary enlistment, but rejecting conscription. Mr C.E. Glynn was instrumental in persuading Mr J. Kett, of Kilkee, chairman of Clare County Council, to call a special meeting of the council to facilitate an address by a delegation from the County Clare Recruitment Committee, led by Lord Inchiquin. However, not all of the councillors were enthusiastic about recruitment, for instance, mem-bers of Kildysart Rural District Council refused to allow the letter from John Redmond to be read at their statutory meeting in March.

Lord Pirrie, chairman of Harland and Wolff, Belfast, a friend of H.R. Glynn, congratulated him for the successful meeting of Clare County Council, 'I am glad such a successful meeting was held under your direction and that County Clare shows such a good fighting spirit'.

Early in February C.E. Glynn advised Mr Dinneen of the Department of Recruiting:

> I am sending you a copy of a circular which we are sending out to all the parish priests in the district as well as several others ... We are endeavouring to get all the local boards to pass resolutions in favour of Mr Redmond's policy and manifesto ... I hope the names of the men eligible for military service will not be published in the Clare papers at present, or at least until the time is ripe for same.

It seems from Mr Glynn's letter that the Department of Recruitment proposed to publish a list of all men of military age in the local papers. Presumably, the purpose of this tactic was that by highlighting their names there would be public pressure on them to sign up. Fortunately for many young men, the time for the publication of such a list was 'not ripe'.

Mr Dineen at the HQ of the Department of Recruitment complimented Mr Glynn for involving the clergy, which he said, 'was a step in the right direction, and if you succeed, it will be all plain sailing in future as regards recruiting.' Mr C.E. Glynn got the public bodies of West Clare, such as boards of guardians as well as rural and urban councils, to pass resolutions in favour of voluntary recruitment. Capt. Kelly of the Department of Recruiting, Dublin, thought it was 'a capital idea to involve the public boards in the area to get their support'.

Mr C.E. Glynn complained to Capt. Kelly of the Department of Recruitment in Ireland about the fact that many West Clare men were persuaded, by high wages and other inducements, to travel to England and Wales to work in munitions factories and in mines. He condemned this 'leakage', which was damaging to recruitment in West Clare:

> I wish to draw your attention to the fact that the following men have signed forms for

---

5 REASONS WHY IRISHMEN SHOULD JOIN THE ARMY

The country is engaged in a just war.

We were pledged to defend the sacred rights and liberties of Belgium.

Had we not struck a blow for Belgium, our name would have been disgraced among the nations of the world.

If the Germans come to Ireland and we should be at their mercy – what that mercy is likely to be can be judged by Germany's treatment of Belgium.

During the war thousands of Irish soldiers have upheld the reputation of Ireland as one of the great fighting races of the world. Never have Irish soldiers shown greater devotion, more splendid heroism, than they have displayed on the battlefields of Belgium.

More MEN are wanted NOW!

Enlist to-day,

Join your gallant countrymen in Belgium

GOD SAVE THE KING

GOD SAVE IRELAND

Clare Journal, 11 March.

Some unknown recruits at Kilrush House, *c.* 1915.
(Courtesy of Glynn papers, per Paul O'Brien)

Mr Blackhall, Clerk of Petty Sessions, Kilrush, and are leaving for England and Wales: Mark Coughlan, c. 20 years old; Dan Foley, about 35/40 years old; and Tom Kelly, 25 years old, all of whom left on 16 March. The following men have now signed to leave today or Monday for South Wales – Ed O'Brien, c. 22 years; John Grogan, c. 25 years, Michael Downes, c. 40; James Bourke, c. 23 years and J. Kiely, c. 20 years old. If all the men are taken out of this country by the English Labour Exchanges it will be difficult to get recruits in Ireland. Very high wages and other inducements are offered to encourage men to go.

He wrote to Barrington at this time also to complain about the 'leakage'. 'I hear a great many men are at present leaving West Clare for England, where they have been offered very high wages and other inducements to work for railway companies and in mines, and that will prevent recruiting in the district. The Clerk of the Petty Sessions at Kilrush is filling up the forms and is sending these men away'. There was an implied suggestion in this assertion that if the men were unemployed in West Clare, then they might be more inclined to enlist, because of their poverty.

Mr C.E. Glynn arranged a huge public recruitment meeting at Kilrush in February, 'which was attended by a large and enthusiastic crowd'. At this meeting it seems that eleven men decided to enlist and a further fifteen men 'agreed to think about it'.[10]

The well-known nationalist Tom Kettle MP, sent a letter to the Irish people calling upon farmers' sons to enlist and fight for Ireland. He wrote that there are masses of unemployed and under-employed labourers in Ireland. John Redmond issued an appeal to the farmers of Ireland to join up and help to sustain the three Irish divisions. Later in the year the viceroy, Lord Wimborne, appealed to the farmers to enlist and fight for Ireland. These letters were published in the *Clare Journal* of 24 and 28 February and 2 March and in the *Saturday Record* of 28 October and 18 November 1916.

Besides the major propaganda and advertising campaigns seeking recruits for the British Army, anonymous poems were occasionally published in the local press urging conscription, such as the following:

Onward to battle, ye brave men of Erin
Fill up the gaps till victory be won
Let each do his part till the final destruction
Of Belgium's despoiler, the race of the Hun.
They may boast of the 'Kultur' their proud domination,
Their Kaiser may rave about his 'place in the sun',
But here is our answer, it can't be mistaken,
It lies in the bayonet that's fixed in our gun.
Then shoulder to shoulder, young men of Erin,
Come forward and join, for there's work to be done,
Far better we died on the Altar of Freedom,
Than live on as slaves of the bloodthirsty Hun.
Rally, then, you men of Clare, ready to do or dare,
Think of the honour the Munsters have won,
Sons of old Brian Boru your country appeals to you,
On then for Ireland and stick to your gun.
'CLARE'

Other letters to the local press attacked those who would not join as being cowardly. The editor of the *Clare Journal* thought that one letter, written anonymously by 'Jack', allegedly a private of the Leinster Regiment at Kilworth Camp, to his 'old folks' at home in Newmarket-on-Fergus, 'breathes a fine spirit, worthy of imitation':

Dear Old Folks ... I was very sorry to hear of Patrick McMahon's noble death, for after all, there is something noble and grand in dying such a death.

What can be nobler than to die in defence of our homes, our loved ones at home? And to know that one is helping even in the smallest way from Belgium's and Servia's fate is consoling, even though we are living a life of comparative discomfort; the little sacrifice is worth it.

To me it seems degrading and shameful that so many Irish boys can close their ears to the call. They must be devoid of every spark of manly courage, and to think that they are the descendants of the noble warriors whose deeds were daring and self-sacrificing for faith and home, and which has made Irish history the most soul-stirring reading in the world, is absolutely appalling.

… With my love to all, I remain, always, your devoted son and brother, Jack'.[11]

The Irish Volunteers

The crime rate in Clare had greatly decreased because of the war. Addressing the Grand Jury at the Ennis Quarter Sessions, Judge Bodkin KC said that County Clare was at one with crimeless Ireland. There were only three cases before the court, none of any special character, two cases of larceny and one of burglary. The low level of crime may have been related to the enlistment of hundreds of young unemployed men from the towns of Clare.

Judge Bodkin said that in the great crisis 'Clare had done its duty, and no towns in any part of Ireland in proportion to their population had more distinguished themselves than Ennis and Kilrush. They had sent many brave soldiers to the front, men who had done their duty fearlessly to uphold the traditions of the Irish race as the finest and cleanest fighters in the world'.[12]

Meanwhile, the Irish Volunteers, also known as the Sinn Féin Volunteers, were busy organising throughout the county. One of the most audacious acts of the Irish Volunteers was to hold an illegal meeting of their county executive in the boardroom of the Ennis Union Workhouse in Ennis. A group of about thirty men from various parts of the county marched into the building in the afternoon of 29 January and took over the building for about an hour. Among those who occupied the building was Fr Charles Culligan, CC of Carrigaholt, who chaired the meeting.

In January the Inch branch of the Irish Volunteers decided to make a house-to-house collection to raise funds for equipment for the corps. The activities of the Irish Volunteers in trying to expand their membership caused tension between themselves and those supporting the National Volunteers. For instance, the members of the Manus National Volunteers sent a letter to the *Saturday Record* to state publicly that they had no connection whatsoever with the attempt made to form a branch of the Irish Volunteers in the Clare Castle district. And they strongly 'condemned the actions of two parties, who once belonged to the corps for trying to hold a meeting, and cause dissension in this peaceable district'.

In East Clare, the Irish Volunteers were drilling and playing their own war games in preparation for a different conflict, perhaps as a prelude to the Easter Rising. Three Brennan brothers and other farmers' sons from the Meelick district were arrested in January by a party of RIC from Killaloe. They were bound to the peace for twelve months on sureties of £20 each. This did not deter them as three months later 'Capt.' Michael Brennan was arrested under DORA for drilling illegally and shooting on Glenomra Mountain. Michael Brennan was not shooting grouse on the hills of Clare – he was training for war! He was sentenced to three months' hard labour. As Mr Justice Sharman stated at the trial, 'It was a very serious thing to have armed men marching around the country roads of Clare'.[13]

County Inspector Gelston, who had been twenty-six years in the RIC and three years in Clare, while giving testimony to the Inquiry into the 1916 Easter Rising, described the rise of Sinn Féin in the county since 1914. He stated that the first branch of the National Volunteers was formed in March 1914.

There were four branches with a membership of about 400. When the split occurred in September 1914, the majority of about 300 seceded from Mr Redmond's party and became the Sinn Féin party.

A Sinn Féin branch was organised in the county by Thomas O'Loughlin of Carron, but nothing was done until May 1915, when a paid organiser, Mr Ernest Blythe, came to the county and made himself very active. He went on creating branches until July 1915, when he came to be looked upon as a danger and a deportation order was served upon him ... When Blythe left the county the movement stood still until a man named O'Hurley, a Gaelic teacher and organiser, became very active, with the result that by the beginning of this year [1916] there were ten branches with a membership of over 400 in the county. They drilled and some of them wore uniforms and practised shooting with miniature rifles ... In the whole county they had about 35 rifles. They were not well armed, but they had plenty of shotguns and miniature rifles. These branches became more or less aggressive in some parts of the county and people got afraid of them.

One Volunteer leader in East Clare, Michael Brennan, publicly told the Irish Volunteers before a route march at Meelick on St Patrick's Day to arm themselves. He said that 'it was a matter of self-defence for Irishmen'. He said that 'if an attempt was made to seize their arms then they should use them, shoot anybody who attempted to seize their arms, it was self-defence and not murder ... If their weapons were taken, then he said that the next thing would

Commandant Michael Brennan, East Clare
Brigade IRA. (Courtesy of NLI)

be conscription.' Mr Brennan was sentenced to three months' imprisonment with hard labour for this seditious speech. At his trial, Michael Brennan refused to recant; instead he defiantly repeated the statement in court before Mr McElroy, RM.

Mr Gelston said that some of the younger priests had Sinn Féin tendencies, but the older men, as a rule, did not, and parish priests had spoken against the move-ment in some areas. There were quite a number of sedi-tious sermons or remarks from priests. One young priest told the people in January 'to arm themselves and if they could not get rifles then to get shot-guns, which were very useful in the hands of Irishmen. If they couldn't get shotguns, he told them to get revolvers. If they failed to get revolvers then they should arm themselves with pikes that the blacksmiths could make them. If pikes were not available then they should get a hatchet or a slasher'.[14]

This sermon was not reported to headquarters. Neither was the priest arrested for this seditious speech. The RIC probably thought it prudent not to arrest a Catholic priest at this time. It would have been highly publicised and controversial and might have had a very negative impact upon recruitment by giving 'fuel' to the Irish Volunteers.

Easter Rising 1916

The Easter Rising occurred in Dublin at the end of April but County Clare was relatively quiet during the week. The editor of the *Clare Journal* wrote:

It is highly satisfactory to state … that County Clare has not witnessed a soli-tary outbreak or disturbance of any kind. Today, practically normal conditions prevail, but it was very evident that during last week there was a considerable atmosphere of unrest and suppressed excitement, which found however, no actual vent; and the news of the surrender of the leaders of the Dublin rebellion on Saturday, which spread like wildfire, had a powerful effect of bringing home to possibly disaffected circles, limited and without influence as they may be, an idea and appreciation of the realities of the situation.

Our Kilrush correspondent writes, 'up to the time of writing, I am glad to say that things remain in the usual state of peace in West Clare; a young man named Art O'Donnell from the Tullycrine district, an ex-teacher, was arrested in Kilrush'. He had, according to the western correspondent of the *Clare Journal*, 'turned up in Kilrush on Saturday, dressed in a Volunteer uniform, with a revolver and ammunition and was arrested'.[15]

The resident magistrate in Clare, Mr George McElroy, RM, spoke of the admirable conduct of the people of Clare during the Dublin crisis. He said that there were no disturbances of any kind in Clare and they should thank the National Volunteers of Ennis, Kildysart and other places for helping to keep law and order. In June Mr T. Lynch, Capt. of O'Callaghan's Mills National Volunteers, had a letter from Gen. Leland, HQ, Irish command, commending the patriotic activities of the O'Callaghan's Mills National Volunteers in offering their services to the military authorities during the recent disturbances in the county. Sir Richard Neville Chamberlain, Inspector General of the RIC, also sent a letter in appreciation of the prompt manner in which the Volunteers took over guard duty at O'Callaghan's Mills. However, about a week after this notice in the paper, Mr Dan Minogue of O'Callaghan's Mills denied that he offered his services to the authorities at Kilkishen during the Easter crisis.[16]

County Inspector Gelston testified at the inquiry into the Easter Rising. He stated, 'at the time of the rising there was considerable activity. Organisers were moving about and the Sinn Féiners were evidently anticipating something. On Easter Monday many of the Sinn Féiners met along the banks of the Shannon, evidently anticipating the landing of arms from the Kerry side of the river.' (Inspector Gelston's testimony was corroborated by Michael Brennan's memoir in which he describes how he mobilised about a hundred men from Meelick and Oatfield, Cratloe and Newmarket-on-Fergus. They marched to Bunratty and waited all day in the rain for orders to join the rebellion, but the orders never came.) Inspector Gelston attributed the fact that there was no rising in Clare to the failure to land arms in Kerry.

The Sinn Féin movement was very small, but it grew rapidly at the end of 1915 and the beginning of 1916. We had a record of over 400 Sinn Féiners in the county, but of course there were a great many sympathisers, who did not openly join, but showed themselves in sympathy with the Sinn Féin movement. My own opinion is that if they had had a rising in Clare we would have had a great many more than 400 – we would have probably had three times that number.

The older clergy, as a rule, the parish priests in a number of cases have spoken against the Sinn Féin movement. They assisted to the extent of denouncing the rising from the pulpit. In one case a parish priest addressed the Sinn Féiners and asked them to give up their rifles to us. That was the only case in which rifles were given up to us.[17]

Early in May, Lord Inchiquin of Dromoland sent a letter to his son in England, the Hon. Donough O'Brien, giving his opinion on the Rising. He described the county as being 'very quiet':

County Clare has been very quiet all through, the reason being that the Sinn Féiners in this county are very much scattered about, and consequently couldn't organise themselves, and so have been very quiet, though three or four of them have been arrested ... we haven't had an *Irish Times* for 10 days, and the *Clare Journal*, though it arrives, says very little more than the official telegrams. Private motorcars have been stopped, and all petrol has been commandeered, so we had to drive to church last Sunday in the Victoria.

A notice has just come from the police saying that certain ports are open to traffic to England, but all passengers must have identity certificates, and must state their business for crossing. All this is like the government! 'Shutting the door after the horse is out of the stable', as all the trouble is over now. They seem to have had a hot time in Dublin, from the little we know of it, but I fancy it is very nearly cleared up now. The whole of the rest of Ireland has been very quiet, only one or two small outbreaks here and there, that were easily suppressed'.

Lord Inchiquin's observations on the state of Clare during the rising were corroborated by Judge Bodkin at the Ennis Quarter Sessions on Wednesday 1 June. Judge Bodkin QC was presented with white gloves, as there were no indictable cases before the court. During the recent troubles he noted that 'County Clare remained perfectly peaceable, with not a single disturbance. Clare was', he said, 'an example to the rest of Ireland'.[18]

The *Clare Champion* editor of 5 May also gave his opinion on the Easter Rising. The newspaper was still loyal to John Redmond's policy and tactics: 'It is not for us as journalists to pass judgement ... we appeal to the authorities to be merciful to the misguided masses drawn into this conflict. We congratulate our own county on its magnificent and unanimous loyalty to Mr Redmond. Clare men, the bravest of them all, kept the peace, they have had their reward. Home Rule has not been destroyed, and the Irish leader assures us that it is indestructible'.

However, Ennis Urban Council, largely Redmondite in its composition, unanimously passed a resolution condemning the Easter Rising:

> That we, the members of Ennis Urban Council, while sympathising with the families of those who have fallen on both sides in the combat in the metropolis of Ireland, deeply deplore this awful bloodshed, and on behalf of those whom we have the honour to represent, we disassociate ourselves and deeply detest the actions of those on whose shoulders lies the responsibility for so many innocent victims being cut down in the prime of manhood … We repose full confidence in John Redmond, the wise and noble leader of the Home Rule party.

The members of Kilrush Urban Council also adopted a resolution on 1 May condemning 'the recent deplorable outrages in Dublin as detrimental to the real political and industrial interests and calling on nationalist Irishmen to support John Redmond's constitutional policy.'

'A Sea Change'

Within a week or two of the Easter Rising, the mood of the country began to change as the leaders of the Rising were court-martialled and sentenced to death. The 'blood sacrifice' idea, promoted by men such as Pearse and Connolly, began to take root and sprout.

About a week later, after some of the leaders of the Easter Rising had been court-martialled, sentenced to death and shot, the members of Ennis Rural District Council met and passed a resolution 'condemning the actions of the British government in shooting our brave and patriotic Irishmen, who took part in the recent Irish rebellion'.

Also, a meeting of the Ennis District of the AOH passed a resolution 'deeply regretting that the government found it necessary to shoot our countrymen after they had surrendered and we strongly appeal to them not to shoot any more prisoners and to deal leniently with our fellow countrymen who participated in the recent rebellion.' A sea-change in the political mood of the county was occurring as the condemned leaders were becoming martyrs.

At the end of May, Clare County Council passed a resolution, which included the following: '… We hereby place on record our abhorrence of the drastic punishment meted out to the patriotic, but misguided leaders of the late attempt to set up an Irish Republic.'[19]

Bishop Fogarty, speaking at Quin about two weeks after the Rising, refused to denounce the 'unhappy young men who were responsible for that awful tragedy'. He bewailed and lamented their 'mad adventure', but, he said:

Whatever their faults or responsibility may be – and let God be their merciful judge – this much must be said to their credit, that they died bravely and unselfishly for what they believed – foolishly indeed – was the cause of Ireland. Let their spirits rest in peace for the present in the silence of eternity.

Fortunately – and we should thank God for it – our diocese has been spared from any part in these unhappy troubles. I caution the people to exercise patience and self-control in a crisis, which is very provoking to Irish feeling.

The government, I am sure, did not mean to be cruel or provocative, but from the beginning of this lamentable occurrence, every step they have taken is calculated to exacerbate Irish sentiment most bitterly.

Sir Edward Carson has been the root cause of the trouble. He it was who schooled our unfortunate country into ideas and practices of rebellion. He has been allowed to go free; he has been honoured with a seat in cabinet, while the young Irishmen, who were goaded into the madness of insurrection by insulting taunts, have been treated unmercifully. The shooting of surrendered prisoners must be stopped. Blood enough has been spilt to satisfy the most bloodthirsty passion for vengeance.

The wholesale arrest and deportation of young Irishmen is causing great disquiet and must be stopped. Decent young men in this neighbourhood have been arrested and carried away, who, as far as we can make out, had never thought of or had sympathy for rebellion.

About a month later, Bishop Fogarty, speaking at Ruan, said: 'If the actions of these brave but misguided youths, who gave their lives for what they believed to be was the cause of Ireland, had the effect of stirring up of the national spirit and stemming the tide of saxonism, then their blood was not shed in vain'.[19]

Meanwhile, in private letters to Bishop O'Dwyer, Dr Fogarty expressed his horror at the executions and said that the public were outraged by them. He also attacked the hypocrisy of the British and the slavish mentality of the Home Rule, MPs, and local councillors:

Most people don't want rebellion, but the brutal shooting and deportation of these young irregulars after surrender has filled the country with indignation and raised such an anti-English feeling as I never saw before ... What brazen hypocrites the English are, and what slaves our so called Members.'

(31 July 1916)

Poor Casement, may God grant him eternal rest. I do not think that Ireland understood his real worth. His cruel death is neither an honour nor a blessing to the 'mother of small nationalities'...

(7 September 1916)

Whatever your own views may be about the merits or unwisdom of the Dublin rebellion, you are not going to cast stones on the dead bodies of Irish patriots to placate the English parliament ...

(10 September 1916)

I could not say a harsh word about these poor Dublin fellows. I admire them, for their motives were the highest and their bravery unprecedented ... It would, I fear, be a very risky thing for a bishop to openly approve of the rebellion ...

(12 September 1916)

I feel that it is a great privilege to stand with the dead bodies of Maxwell's victims and vindicate their memory ... One of the most disgusting things in our recent public life is the way our public bodies, co. councils, urban councils etc., have all rushed up with sickening resolutions undermining the rebels. The national door of Ireland is 'half-closed'... You have your critics among the sober birds, but the great body of the people, especially the young, male and female, are in boundless admiration of you ...

(17 September 1916)[20]

Naturally, the pro-war newspapers in Clare, denounced the rebellion. The *Saturday Record* editor showed little sympathy for the rebels in Dublin, describing their surrender as being 'like rats caught in a trap'. The *Clare Journal* referred to the rebels as 'misguided fools and dupes of a dangerous pro-German element, which had sought to disrupt our country in this great crisis.' The *Saturday Record* stated that:

the insurrection, whether it was premature or otherwise, was deeply involved with German intrigue, 'the gallant allies'. What 'allies' for the brave but misguided young Irish dupes and tools – the wreckers of poor Belgium, the violators of her nuns, the murderers of her priests, and the burners of her cathedrals and churches!

... Already, three of the signatories of the republican proclamation have paid with their lives for their acts of amazing madness ...The forces who rallied to the green flag of the republic, fought with splendid bravery and reckless enthusiasm, and we feel they should be acquitted of individual blame for the acts of murder and robbery, which will forever make Irish men blush with shame at an ill-fated effort at achieving separation from Britain.

> The Citizen Army of ill omen, with its attendant mobs of ill-conditioned and vicious followers … was only too ready to join in the insurrection, and it was these mobs which on the opening day of the insurrection, started on their old game of looting and pillage.

The *Saturday Record* editorial distinguished between the leaders and men of the Irish Republican Brotherhood, who fought 'with splendid bravery and reckless enthusiasm' by contrast with the forces of the Citizen Army led by James Connolly, 'of ill omen, with mobs of ill-conditioned and vicious followers … looting and pillaging … '. Clearly, there was an anti-socialist tone in this description, with memories of the Dublin 'lock out' in 1913.

The *Clare Journal* was denounced by the *Clare Champion* as a unionist paper for using the sub-heading; 'EXIT CASEMENT!' to describe the execution of Roger Casement, who, the *Clare Champion* writer said, 'would be remembered by Irish history as a patriot! His death was a tragedy, what a contrast to Carson and other traitors!' The *Saturday Record*, just like the *Irish Independent*, also seemed to be calling for the execution of James Connolly, judging by

Sackville (O'Connell)
Street, Dublin after
the Easter Rising.
(Courtesy of
Wikimedia Commons)

the following paragraph: 'Connolly still lies in Dublin Castle Hospital mending slowly from his wounds. His leg has been fractured below the knee joint. His ward of the castle has been guarded by half a dozen men with fixed bayonets. In the grounds of the castle are many graves, where have been buried soldiers and civilians killed during the fighting'.[21]

In the weeks following the Easter Rising, many Sinn Féin activists and others were arrested throughout Clare and some, such as Michael Brennan of Meelick and Art O'Donnell of Tullycrine, were deported to England. Others who were deported around this time included the following Claremen: H.J. Hunt and W. Hunt, Corofin; W. Byrne, Cloyne South, Ennistymon; Martin Crowe, Corofin; Denis Healy, Bodyke; Eamon Waldron, Gaelic teacher, Ennistymon; Pat Comer, Gaelic teacher, Killaloe; M.J. Shannon, Quin, formerly of Fountain, Thomas Kierse, Corofin, and Colman O'Loughlin, a prominent Irish Volunteer and Sinn Féin leader from Carron, who had been one of the four signatories, along with Pearse, MacDonagh and O'Rahilly, of the document in which the Irish Volunteers were set up in September 1914. One county councillor, Denis Healy of Bodyke was also arrested. The paper noted that the young men were sent from Ennis to Limerick, that there was 'no excitement over the arrests and only a few people watched their departure from the station'. The men were deported to England. The *Saturday Record* noted sarcastically that all those who had been arrested were farmers' sons!

A military flying column of about seventy to eighty men of the Leinster regiment camped in the Fair Green, Ennis and carried out searches for arms in Corofin and Crusheen. They had previously been in the Newmarket-on-Fergus area. The government ordered that all weapons should be handed up to the authorities but only two shotguns were handed up and no arrests were made. It seems that the two illegally-held shotguns were handed in after the parish priest in Carrigaholt persuaded the owners to hand them over to the police. About 150 extra police were brought to Ennis from counties Longford, Fermanagh and Down and they were billeted around the town. Eventually Martial Law was introduced which banned all public meetings, parades, sports meetings, fairs etc. All legally held shotguns and other guns were temporarily confiscated by the authorities.[22]

'A Terrible Beauty is Born'

Over the following months and for the rest of the year the Sinn Féin rebellion and its consequences transformed the political landscape in the county. A new charity was born when the Irish National Aid Association was founded to collect funds for the Irish Volunteers dependants' funds. Collections were held after Masses on Sundays in many places throughout the county, such as at Barefield, Kildysart, Kilchreest, Clondegad and Liscannor.

Charity of a different kind was promoted through an appeal by Sir Michael O'Loghlen, HML for County Clare, and Mr Thomas O'Gorman, DL, of Cahercalla, who initiated the fund from the Banner County to relieve the distress, with which the poor of Dublin, and thousands of deserving working men are faced with as a result of, what the *Saturday Record* of 20 May, called 'the insane outbreak of Black Week'.

The activities of the recruiting committees for the British Army seemed to have been greatly hampered and recruitment dropped off very sharply after the Rising. Mr C.E. Glynn was advised by Capt. R. Kelly, Department of Recruitment, Dublin, 'much has happened since your letter of 24 April … civilian recruitment was temporarily suspended'. Col Barrington wrote to C.E. Glynn: 'I am sorry, but I can do nothing at the moment due to the general upset.' Capt. Kelly also wrote to Mr Glynn on 8 May: 'I congratulate you on all you have done and are doing; I agree that it was of the utmost importance that you have been able to commit the local leading men and the clergy to loyal work.' In another letter written in early June, Capt. Kelly thanked C.E. Glynn in connection with 'your timely efforts on behalf of recruiting, which I am sure, had an important influence during the disturbed time'. C.E. Glynn also made some representations about Art O'Donnell, the young republican from Tullycrine, who was arrested in Kilrush during the Easter Rising; 'I have written to the provost marshal about young O'Donnell and I hope the result will be that the wishes of yourself and your friends will be met'.

The Battle of the Somme, 1916.
(Photo by Geoffrey Mallins,
courtesy of Wikimedia Commons)

H.R. Glynn, DL, wrote to David Lloyd George, who had recently succeed Asquith as prime minister: 'As an employer of labour in this county I beg to state that it will give me the greatest pleasure if I can be of assistance to you in any way and wishing you every success'. Early in July Glynn wrote to Mr Birrel, the Chief Secretary of Ireland, 'Dear Mr Birrel, owing to the action of some men in the north of Ireland it is an anxious time, but you can rely on the Irish people and I trust in the interests of Ireland and the empire you will retain the wise policy of friendship towards Ireland this and every year … if I can be of assistance to you at any time do let me know.' In October of that year Glynn contacted the Ministry of Munitions in Ireland, seeking information about munition contracts, as he was interested in investments in this work, 'as there was money in it'. Glynn did not open a munitions factory in Kilrush, but he secured a contract to supply flour to the British Army.[23]

Following some changes to the Home Rule Bill in Westminster, with more guarantees to unionists, an editorial of the *Clare Champion* in July signalled a sea change in the political allegiance of this paper away from allegiance to John Redmond's policy and the Home Rule Party towards the new Sinn Féin party:

> Strange things happen, saddest of all Mr Asquith's desertion of the Irish race. Now he is the betrayer of the living and dead. There is many a whitening bone in Flanders today, silent gruesome, but eloquent testimony of how Ireland kept the pact. These men were deceived, these men, even in death, have been betrayed. We feel sore in Ireland just now; we feel and rightly feel that we have been very dishonourably duped and callously betrayed, the British cabinet dishonestly and guiltily broke faith, a terrible act of treachery and deception.

Col Arthur Lynch, MP, also denounced the Rising, but he did not break away from the Home Rule Party. Addressing a public meeting at Miltown Malbay in July, he condemned the executions, 'These cold-blooded shootings were the worst action that a British government perpetrated for a long time … Those executed will take their place in the gallery of Irish heroes and martyrs beside Emmet and Tone … We should put in a stronger claim for Home Rule, the spirit of Home Rule must be enlarged.' However, in May 1917 Lynch deplored the Rising, describing it as a 'reckless scheme that miscarried'.[24]

Meanwhile, the Great War continued and men were fighting and dying on the Western Front and indeed several other fronts. One Clareman, Lt Col C.J. O'Gorman, Royal Army Medical Corps, DSO, brother of T.A. O'Gorman, DL, of Cahercalla, was with the British forces in a campaign against the Germans in East Africa under the command of Gen. Smuts. He wrote to his brother:

On the 11 March we had a big fight on the borders of German East Africa, when we beat the Germans towards their own railway, Tangamanschi. After taking this town I had to make arrangements to have all our sick and wounded transported to the base. The rains may stop active operations, but as soon as they are over, the pace will go on, as General Smuts is splendid. We had 186 wounded on the 11th. Fighting started at 12 noon and went on all the afternoon and most of the night. All the work had to fall on one field ambulance until the morning of the 12th, when I got a second field ambulance to assist. The field ambulance that did all the work was the one that I came out in command of from India in October 1914. Some of my field ambulance I cannot move from want of transport, so I am carrying on with what I have, but will be pleased when they get their transport, as it is a very unhealthy country, and lots go sick as well as the wounded. You will see more accounts of the war now that General Smuts has got a move on. The great thing about General Smuts is that he says nothing and does a lot ...[25]

There was little mention of recruitment during the year, especially after the Easter Rebellion. However, the *Clare Journal* of 4 December proclaimed that Councillor P. Kennelly, chairman of Ennis Urban Council, had enlisted after two years of promoting recruitment and encouraging others to enlist. He said that it was his 'duty to enlist, following Willie Redmond's example'. Also, the *Saturday Record* of 26 February noted with pride that four members of the Ennis Post Office staff joined the army telegraph section in February.

Prisoners of War at Limburg

By now, there were many Irish prisoners incarcerated in German, Turkish and Austro-Hungarian prisons, but the majority were held in German prisoner-of-war camps. In the middle of February eight Clare prisoners in Limburg, Germany sent letters of thanks to the ladies from the Prisoners Association of Clare for sending them very welcome parcels of food and other products. Most of the prisoners were from the Royal Munster Fusiliers. The food parcels included products such as half a pound of tea and sugar; tins of meat, salmon and beans; a dozen cigarettes; soup, cheese, bread; soap; golden syrup; mustard and biscuits. Meanwhile, a Kilrush man, Mr William Poole of Cappa, a captain in the Mercantile Marine Company enjoyed the hospitality of the Austro-Hungarians after his ship was torpedoed in the Mediterranean. He was reported to be 'in splendid health'.

One Irish prisoner, Pte Patrick Burke, who served about three years as a prisoner in Germany told a harrowing tale of his experiences as a prisoner of war and how Sir Roger Casement tried to recruit him and other Irish prisoners to form an Irish Brigade to fight against the British in the Easter Rising.

He was already a soldier in the British Army when the war broke out and was in the Second Munster Division. He was sent to France as part of the British Expeditionary Force and took part in the first Battle of Mons. However, during the army's tactical retreat the Munsters were surrounded by the Germans at Etreux and were forced to surrender because their position was hopeless, when their ammunition ran out and when casualties were high.

First they were kept in an old mill. One loaf of bread, weighing about 2lbs, was divided among each group of thirteen men. They were also given a bucket of cold coffee without milk or sugar, again to be divided among thirteen prisoners. For 'dinner' they got a bowl of thin, watery vegetable soup, without any more bread. They slept without mattresses on the cold floor of the old mill and there was no fire or any heat in the building. They were beaten regularly by the prison guards.

After twelve days they were ordered to march for a day and that night were kept in a Belgian church and given some watery soup. On the next they marched again for a day without food. Even the wounded prisoners had to march if able, or else were carried by their comrades. Then they were put on to four wagons of a train and given a pound of black bread each, which was to last for the four days' journey.

While on the train journey they were shouted at and abused by the German civilians, who called them '*Schweinhunds!*' and made gestures of cutting their throats. The wounded received no attention for these four days on the train.

When they arrived at Sowenlager they were put into a field. The wounded were placed on a 'sop of straw'. When it rained they were put into a tent, but there was only standing room. Some of 'the poor chaps who were wounded had to lie down in the mud and water, while others stood up to their ankles in mud'.

While in this camp they were put to work in constructing their own accommodation. They spent six months cutting and transporting timber from a wood, which they called 'Siberia'. Each pair of able-bodied men had to carry six 20-foot planks for a distance of about 2 miles. They worked about twelve hours a day, from dawn to dusk. After their work they were fed a 'drink of soup and a mouthful of black bread each'.

Some of the men, 'dying for a fag', used to gather up the waste coffee thrown out of the cookhouse. They dried it and used to put it into their pipes. Others gathered withered leaves and cut strips of newspaper to make 'cigarettes'.

Then in November, some German officers came and sought detailed information from the prisoners. After this all the Irish prisoners were put into a

separate group and not put to work for a few weeks. They were then transferred to another prison at Limburg, where they were told that there were
some Irish ladies who would take care of them. At Limburg they were treated
much better for a while. They were given knives, forks and spoons for the first
time. Each man was given a fresh shirt and a 2lb loaf of bread.

The men soon discovered the reasons for the sudden improvement in their
prison regime. About a month after their arrival at Limburg they were visited
by Sir Roger Casement, though they only found this out afterwards. Sir Roger
tried to persuade them to join an Irish Brigade to fight with the Germans
against the British. They were also given propaganda leaflets highlighting the
history of British misrule in Ireland. They were told that England was losing
the war and that Germany would win. Despite all these efforts to turn them
from their allegiance to Britain, most of the prisoners did not wish to join;
some who did were beaten up and almost killed by their fellow prisoners.

On his second visit to the prison camp Casement offered each man a 'bribe'
of £10 if he would join the Irish Brigade. He also told them that they would be
joining about 10,000 Americans who would also fight for Germany. However,
as there were no volunteers to join the Irish Brigade, they noticed that their
rations were cut to 'a small cut of bread and black coffee without milk or sugar'.
Dinner consisted of vegetables or broad beans and there were no potatoes.

On the occasion of his third and final visit to Limburg prison one of the pris-
oners threw an old boot at Casement and struck him in the forehead. Sir Roger
Casement did not return again as he clearly failed in his mission to form an Irish
Brigade amongst the Irish prisoners of war to fight for Germany against Britain.

Their conditions deteriorated again and the men were put to work on the
prison farm, sorting potatoes. If they were caught concealing even a small potato
they would be punished by being put into solitary confinement for three days
without any food! Or else they were put into a 'hot press' for a few hours. (A hot
press was a small container in which prisoners were left four hours at a time, in
cramped conditions and with no food or water.) Some of the men gathered up
the potato skins that were discarded by the cooks. Other men were put to work
in factories or in mines, where they were treated like slaves.

Pte Burke stated that the food parcels sent from Ireland, irregularly at first,
were a godsend. The men eagerly gathered around hoping that their name
would be called out. Sometimes parcels were tampered with and straw or
mouldy bread was put in the parcels.

One factor that raised their spirits and did most to help them endure the
harsh conditions of prison life was the occasional visits of an Irish priest,
Fr Crotty, and a Belgian Christian Brother, who brought some religious consolation, 'only for them all of us would be dead'. Fr Crotty 'kept their spirits up
and was always cheerful and most helpful.'

Then, in July 1916, Pat Burke and about thirty other prisoners were taken to Mannheim, where they were examined by German and Swiss doctors. Eventually, Pte Burke was sent to Switzerland, where he was examined by doctors. After about a week he was informed that he was being sent home to Ireland. Before that he was sent to recuperate at a place called Chateau D'Oey near Bern. He left Switzerland on 11 September, reached London on 15 September and arrived back in Ennis on 18 September.

The newspaper reported that he was in poor health. 'He was a well set-up young man, who looked very well despite the treatment he received. He was rapidly regaining his old health and spirits, but at times showed signs of the strain which he underwent in his soul-trying experiences.'

Pte Burke's recollections of the visits of Sir Roger Casement have been corroborated in several publications. Apparently Casement arrived at Limburg on 4 December 1914 as part of his mission to form an Irish Brigade from among the Irish prisoners of war at the camp to fight in the forthcoming rising being planned by the Military Council of the Irish Republican Brotherhood. He addressed an audience of NCOs and ordinary rank and file, most of whom had been in the British Army for years before the war. However, he found them to be hostile to his mission. He told them that the German Government had made a promise of Irish independence, but he could not shake their loyalty to the British Army. A corporal named Robinson described how Casement was struck and pushed by the prisoners, after which he walked out of the camp. They greeted him with cries of 'three cheers for Redmond!' and they taunted him with questions such as 'How much are the Germans paying you?' He visited the camp on at least three occasions between 4 and 9 December, but his overall mission was a failure, as he only managed to persuade about 50 men to join 'Casement's Brigade'. He observed to one friend that he might be able to bribe them: 'These men are mercenaries, pure and simple!' The Irish prisoners were not moved by Casement's republicanism and they insulted him.[26]

The rejection by the vast majority of prisoners of Sir Roger Casement's overtures to form an Irish Brigade among the prisoners to fight for an Irish republic was also reflected in the general attitude of soldiers at the front towards the 1916 uprising. The phrase, 'gallant allies in Europe' (that is, the Germans), in the 1916 Proclamation annoyed and disgusted the soldiers who faced the 'Huns' in mortal combat in the trenches. Tom Kettle, MP, wrote that 'the Sinn Féin nightmare upset him a little'. John Lucy, a sergeant with the 2nd Royal Irish Rifles, noted, 'my fellow soldiers had no great sympathy with the rebels, but got fed up when they heard of the executions of the leaders.' Fr Henry Gill, chaplain to the 2nd Royal Irish Rifles, wrote that 'on the whole, the event created very little comment.'

The Germans when they heard of the rebellion tried to discourage the Irish troops in the British Army by putting up placards denouncing the English suppression of the rising. However, the Irish soldiers were, apparently, not impressed by the German propaganda. The 8th Royal Munster Fusiliers captured a placard erected by the Germans, which read, 'Irishmen! Heavy uproar in Ireland, English guns are firing at your wives and children!' The placard was later presented to King George. The 7th Leinster regiment played 'Rule Brittania' in response to the placards. The 9th Royal Munster Fusiliers hung an effigy of Sir Roger Casement in no man's land.[27]

'From Somewhere in France'

Late in November Willie Redmond, MP, sent a letter to his friend in Ennis, Councillor P.J. Linnane, JP, expressing his downhearted opinion on the Easter Rising, which he regarded as 'foolish and uncalled for'.

Headquarters
16th Division
B.E.F.
23.11.'16
My dear PJ,
I have been intending to write to you for a long time, but as you will understand, it is not easy out here as there is a great deal to do. I am keeping very well so far thank God and I sincerely hope you, Mrs. Linnane and your family are the same. I wonder will I ever see you in Ennis anymore. It is nearly 25 years since we met now and I must say in all that time no one was so good as yourself and whether we meet or not I shall always have the warmest regard for you.

I had not the heart to write to you about the Rising. It seemed to me so foolish and uncalled for, just when Home Rule was absolutely certain. You would think the worst enemies of Ireland could not have planned a worse stroke to injure us in all ways. Long ago I could have understood anything but now when we have won so much and were at the threshold of victory it seemed to me to be madness to set up a rebellion which could only end one way.

I need not tell you I came here to help what I thought was best for the country. I still believe the Irish part in the war makes our own chance of Home Rule certain … I have seen a great deal and the more I see the better pleased I am that Ireland is against the Germans in this war. I would be sorry to see Ireland at the tender mercy of the men who ruined poor little Belgium.

The Irish troops here have won a great name for themselves by their bravery and work. I did my six months work commanding a company in the trenches and now I am attached to headquarters and still visit the troops in the trenches and give what help I can. I need not say I feel being away from home, but I do not like leaving the men. I will stick to them as long as I can. I have been a year here now, all but a few weeks. I had one or two letters from the Bishop (Dr Fogarty), but from no one else in Clare in all the time. With my very best to you and Mrs Linnane and hoping you will have every good for yourself and your family.

I am as ever,

Your sincere friend,

William Redmond[28]

Councillor P.J. Linnane, artist unknown. (Courtesy of Dr Michael Linnane)

Maj. Willie Redmond, MP, had several letters from the front published in the press. Between 17 August 1916 and 19 April 1917 he contributed a series of articles dealing with various aspects of life in the Western Front, which were published anonymously in the *Daily Chronicle*. These articles were later published after his death in a book called *Trench Pictures from France*. He also wrote a couple of letters to Dr Fogarty, and to Mr P.J., Linnane, Ennis, describing his experience of trench warfare and these letters were published in the local newspapers:

My Dear Lord, just a line to let you know that I am all well, for which I may certainly thank God … Our first spell in the trenches was for 12 days and in that time we had no change of clothing, just stayed as we were all the time. The shelling was terrific and the division suffered some losses. The day before we came out the enemy began to celebrate the Kaiser's birthday and we were shelled without ceasing for 24 hours … The men of our division behaved very well and received good reports, so the general says. Our men are very attentive to their chaplains and flock into the churches in the little French villages. I was in one place where amidst ruin all around a big crucifix stood untouched. The destruction and suffering I have encountered, even in a short time is truly appalling. I am sure we have your prayers. With my best wishes to you, Canon O'Dea, and all who care to hear of me.

Yours Sincerely,

Willie Redmond.

Later in the year, Willie Redmond sent another letter to Linnane in Ennis, in which he wrote about more of his war experiences: 'The 16th Irish Division never lost a trench; this is due to the moral superiority of our men, and the gallant conduct of the troops. The division needs re-enforcement. All who love Ireland should unite to keep the 16th Irish Division at Loos after the hard-fought battles of Guillemont and Givinchy'.

In the book, *Trench Pictures from France*, Willie Redmond wrote about life in the British Army on the Western Front, including the role of the Catholic clergy and religion:

It is a strange scene in this church at night. Entering it all is dark save for the few flickering candles on the altar before which the priest kneels to say the prayers. It is only when the men join in that one becomes aware that the church is really full; and it is solemn and appealing beyond words to describe – when up from the darkness rises the great chorus of hundreds of voices in prayer – the darkness seems to add impressiveness to the prayers, whilst from the outside are heard the rumble and roar of the guns, which not so very far away, are dealing out death and agony to the comrades of the men who are praying ...

The day and night before a battalion goes to the trenches the chaplains are busy in the churches, for the men throng to Confession, and it is a wonderful and most faith-inspiring sight to see them in hundreds approaching the altar before marching off to danger and in many cases to death itself ...

Nothing is more noticeable than the way the Catholic soldier holds by his beads. The rosary beads seem always to be treasured, and every soldier at mass seems to have them. Prayer books are often missing, but the rosary, as a rule, never is. Of all the symbols of his faith, the soldier's rosary is foremost. The rosary beads are usually placed around the dead man's neck before he is wrapped in his blanket for burial ...

When the turn in the trenches is over and the men resume their rosary in the darkened church in the evenings, there are always some absent, ones who were there the week before. For this very reason perhaps – because of the comrades who will never kneel by them again – the men pray all the more fervently and with ever increasing earnestness say, 'May the souls of the faithful departed through the mercy of God rest in peace'...

Mass has been said in the very trenches and the writer has attended Mass in many a ruined church and in many a shell-wrecked shelter. And ever, as always, the men are the same, devoted and earnest, the more wretched their surroundings, the more eager they are.

With all the evil that has followed in its train, it is good to find at least one beneficial result from the war. It has led to the revival of religion in a most remarkable way ...[29]

Pte John Power from Clare Castle, a dental student at the Royal College of Surgeons in Dublin, who had enlisted in the 10th Battalion ('Pals' Division) of the Royal Dublin Fusiliers, sent a couple of letters home to his family. His first letter, part of which is missing, posted from 'somewhere in France' was written to his mother just before he entered the war zone. In the second letter he wrote to his sister Mary, describing his life and needs in the trenches. Religion was clearly important to him at the front. His mood seemed cheerful, despite the horrors he was witnessing in battle:

J. Power, 26017, "C" company, 10th Service Batt., R.D.F., B.E.F., France
Tuesday 22/8/'16
Dear mother,
I'm delighted I had an opportunity of saying good-bye to you before I left, I'm only sorry I hadn't a chance of doing so with father (especially) and the rest. I've done so often in spirit. I don't think I'd be allowed to tell you where I am, but we're well within sound of the guns, and expect to be going into the trenches shortly. I feel absolutely in the best of form (T.G.) and had Confession and Communion just before I left. There was a rumour that we were going to stop where Tim (his brother in the Royal Army Medical Corps) is, but we passed through. I was terribly disappointed not to see him and I've lost his address …

27/10/1916
My dear Mary,
I was never as thankful for anything as I was for your last parcel. We had just come out of the trenches when I received it; I didn't half start on it. I got through alright this time again, thank God. I wrote to Tim, and had an answer. His ears seem to be troubling him again, I will leave it to your own discretion whether you tell mother or not. We did a lot of roaming about lately, but we are settled down now somewhat.

It's very cold here at present, so I wish you'd send me some warm socks. I'm very glad to hear father and mother and you all are well at home. It's a great tonic to me to know it. We're in tents at present, and when the rain comes it's mud, mud everywhere. Mud and jam will be my two pet aversions when I get back.

I'm sure you will smile (taking good care you didn't let me see you), if you saw me before I started this letter, sitting by the camp fire (i.e. the candle) stitching in buttons that absolutely refuse to stay in.

All the boys here are in good spirits. When you see them you know we are winning. I don't believe they'd stop at anything. We had (in my battalion), a good many casualties this time compared with the last. We've got a very good chaplain who gives us Communion and General Absolution if we haven't time for Confession, before we go in the trenches.

Are you going back to [the Dominican Convent in] Cabra? I expect you've had your holidays and hope you enjoyed them. I've gone one better this time in having them on the continent! I hope Frank is in good health. He might drop me a line and let me know some news. I would love to hear from him. I trust that father, mother, Bunny, George, and Joe are well. I heard from Christy, he's a great little chap. I must finish now, expecting to hear from you soon.
From your loving brother,
John.

Six months after his death, his sister Mary received a letter from Joseph P. Carroll, who had soldiered with John Power in Flanders:

Dear Miss Power,
It will be a little surprise to you to receive the contents of this envelope. I was one of your dear brother's 'mates' in the Dubliners and lived with him all through our soldiering days, so I may claim to say to you that he was one of my best chums. My brother also (he was killed on Feb 7) was in the same section and was commander of section 5 to which Jack belonged. We have just received my brother's personal effects from France and amongst them was the enclosed wallet, which I presume Jack wished to return to you and I am carrying out his wish.

With it may I offer you my sincere sympathy. Words are such poor means of expression in circumstances like this and knowing full well what it means in France (I was wounded, November 13, the same day poor Jack was killed). I do hope that your people will feel that he is better off. Please understand that I do not wish to re-open the sad event, but I am sure you will be glad to have this token of remembrance. May he rest in peace.
Yours Sincerely, Joseph P. Carroll.[30]

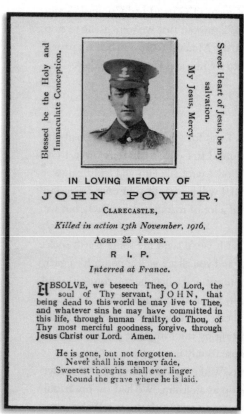

Memorial Card. (Courtesy of Ada Power)

A 1916 War Diary

Extracts from the war diary of the Hon. Donough E. O'Brien, 2nd Lieutenant. Kings Rifles Brigade, 1916:

Thursday 26 October – Rained all day, reported to camp adjutant, allotted quarters, no. 11 camp, which consisted of minute canvas and wood shack, holding two, which I shared with MacGregor; bed, table and work stand made of packing cases.

Friday 27 October – Posted to 1st Batt., went up to Central Training Camp, [CTC] for lectures on bombing, skirmishing and patrolling, poured with rain all afternoon, night frightfully cold.

Monday 30 October – Went for a ten mile route march, column counting about 5,000 men, drenching rain the whole time, three and a half hours, everyone wet through to the skin.

Thursday 2 November – Rained all day, attended most excellent lecture on spirit of bayonet fighting, also gas and work to be done in trenches by company and platoon officers, went to watch boxing competitions.

Monday 6 November – Was orderly officer, spent day, except during duty, censoring letters, generally between 300 to 500 letters, rained all night.

Wednesday 8 November – Rained most of the day … in the afternoon paid out my detail, 1st Batt., dined with Blake and Rowley at KRR [King's Rifle Regiment], officer's mess, worst storm of thunder, lightning rain and hail I have ever seen.

Sunday 12 November – Took RC church parade and attended my first service in RC church. Went to opera (Faust) in the evening in the Grande Theatre du Havre, this is my first opera.

Monday 13 November – On musketry all day, 30 yards range. In evening went to excellent concert given for the soldiers in Woodbine Hut [Miss Vera Askwell].

Thursday 16 November – I was orderly officer, bitterly cold day, had to wash in water with ice on it in the morning.

Wednesday 22 November – Threw live bombs, rained very hard during the night.

Thursday 23 November – C.T.S. went through gas and saw demonstrations of phosphorous and smoke bombs, day fine, but heavy showers.

Saturday 2 December – Musketry, 30 yards range all morning, billiards, Leake brought over draughts. Dinner in Havre at Hotel Moderne …

Friday 8 December – A large draft was suddenly called for and about 500 men were sent up to the line this evening. I spent practically the whole day censoring letters.

Tuesday 12 December – I received orders to join my unit and conduct a draft of King's Rifle Regt. (to the front).

Wednesday 13 December – We marched down to Havre and left at 11.30 pm; roads very bad and we were heavily laden; we drew three days rations and iron rations, detrained at Rouen.

Thursday 14 December – I took the men to a rest camp at Rouen. Had a very good bath and excellent lunch at the Officers' Club. Entrained at 2.30 pm, men travelled in ordinary luggage vans, 30 per van.[31]

This was the last entry in the diary. The diary is useful for a number of reasons. It gives a very good insight into the work of junior officers behind the front lines, drilling, inspecting the men, getting experience of trench work, gas warfare, route marching, bayonet fighting etc. Besides all this, there were duties as orderly officer in paying the men's wages, taking them on Sunday parade to church or chapel, and censoring their letters. It seems that the men were requested or advised to send letters home after they received instructions to go up to the front lines.

Of course there was also rest and recreation, which largely took place at Le Havre, where among other activities he saw an opera and had dinner on several occasions with other officer friends. There was also a concert for the men and visits to cinemas, a boxing tournament, games of cards and board games such as draughts, as well as billiards. The men would have also played sports such as soccer, rugby and cricket.

He frequently commented upon the weather, which was quite wet, cold and wintry, between the last week of October and mid-December. It must be remembered that the soldiers had to fight in these wintry conditions.

Wounded.

Sec.-Lieut. the Hon. D. E. F. O'Brien, Rifle Brigade, wounded, is the son and heir of Lord Iuchiquin.—(Lafayette.)

Lt the Hon. Donogh O'Brien in 1917. (Courtesy of the Hon. Grania R. O'Brien)

Freeman of Limerick

In September Bishop O'Dwyer, as a
tribute to his outstanding contribution to nationalism, was made a
Freeman of the City of Limerick.
During his acceptance speech, about
which he consulted Bishop Fogarty,
Bishop O'Dwyer publicly declared
his support for the Sinn Féin policies,
stating, 'I will now state my alterna-
tive to the Party (the Home Rule
Party) who trust the Liberals ... in
my judgement, Sinn Féin is the true
principle, and alliance with English
politicians is the alliance of the lamb
with the wolf; and is it is at this point
precisely that I differ from present
political leaders [John Redmond],
and believe that they have led and are
leading the National Cause to disas-

Bishop Edward Thomas O'Dwyer.
(Courtesy of limerickdioceseheritage.org)

ter.' Dr Fogarty wrote to his friend, congratulating him on his speech and
stating that it was widely read and appreciated. 'The great body of people,
especially the young, male and female, are in boundless admiration of you.'
Bishop O'Dwyer's outspoken support for Sinn Féin damaged both the party
of John Redmond and his policy of support for the war. Naturally, it did not
encourage recruitment in the region.[32]

In November a large advertisement called upon the men of Clare to enlist:
'Men of Clare ... join your county regiment, the 5th Royal Munster Fusiliers ...
recruits must be over five feet in height ... train at the Curragh and by the
summer of 1917 you will fight shoulder to shoulder with the gallant heroes
from the hills and valleys of Clare, who stormed Guillemont and Givinchy
last September and added fresh laurels to the banner of the Royal Munster
Fusiliers ... '[33] What was ironic about that advertisement was that the 'gallant
heroes' were mainly not from the hills and valleys of Clare, but were largely the
labouring classes from the towns of Clare!

The advertisement also did not state that 244 officers and 4,090 men of the
16th Irish Division were either killed, wounded or missing in action following the Battle of the Somme; as Johnstone observed, 'for the disastrous loss
of the finest manhood of Britain and Ireland, there was only a small gain of
ground to show'.[34]

By this time, mainly because of the Easter Rising and the high level of mortality in the battlefields, recruitment in Ireland was minimal, as Harris wrote, 'By October 1916 it was abundantly clear to both senior officers and leading politicians that Irish recruiting was almost at a standstill'.[35] There is no reason to believe that it was any better in County Clare.

The war continued to have an impact on the economy. Daylight Saving Time was introduced and Dr Fogarty announced that the hours for Masses and the angelus would be at the new 'summer time'.

Agricultural land values as reflected in rentals were still rising. For instance, an auction of meadowing for letting at Lissane near Clare Castle showed a huge price increase, with prices of between £6 and £8 10s per acre on the O'Grady Roche estate. This significant increase reflected the prospering farming economy.

The Weather

The weather during this year, as measured at Carrigoran, created a difficult farming environment:

> The rainfall at 44 inches was 3 inches above average, with rainy days being 17 days above average. There was much unseasonable and adverse weather throughout the year. The frequent rains, with cold, sunless weather of spring, being followed by phenomenally low temperatures and many sunless, gloomy days of May and June created an almost unprecedented record for the first six months of the year. A period of fine seasonable weather, with high temperatures from mid-July to August 10th, a practically rainless period, gave us a fortunate hay-making season, though it was too dry for other crops. Following on this, as if to complete a bad record, we have had during the last three months of the year, for this locality, an almost unparalleled rainfall, with violent gales, with 8 inches of rain in October [during the harvesting of the main potato crop]. There were frosts and fog in December of most unusual severity, with frost on 20 days.
>
> Such bad weather was not conducive to a good harvest, which had adverse effects on the price of food. The bad harvest for the second year in a row, accompanied by the sinking of British merchant ships by German submarines, led to a scarcity of food in Britain. The poor experienced more hardship when the price of a loaf of bread jumped by 50 per cent from 2d to 3d a loaf.[36]

Sport and Leisure

In November, cinemagoers in Ennis got an opportunity to see some scenes from the Battle of the Somme. This cinematic projection was shown for one day only. There was also an exhibition of war relics, which were put on display as a fundraising measure for Royal Munster Fusiliers prisoners of war.[37]

Martial law was lifted in Clare after three months and some social and sporting life continued in the county. The following sports events took place; the County Clare Agricultural Show, the West Clare Show, Labasheeda Regatta, Tubber Sports, the County Clare Horticultural Show, Ennis Races at Clare Abbey, Quilty Races, New Quay Regatta, Scariff Sports, Ballynacally Sports and Kilrush Races. The team sports of cricket and hockey, usually associated with the Protestants of Clare, were abandoned during the war, mainly because most of the gentry were in the services.[38]

'Some Gallant Clare Men'

The following officers and soldiers were mentioned in despatches and received awards for gallantry and heroism in warfare: Lt Col C.O'Gorman, Cahercalla, Ennis, Royal Army Medical Corps, was awarded a DSO; Maj. F.C. Sampson, MB, Royal Army Medical Corps of Moynoe House Scariff was awarded the DSO; Lt Col John O'Brien Minogue, Scariff, of the West Yorkshire Regt., received the Third Order of St Michael and St George (a Russian award); Sgt Michael Butler, Ennis, of the Royal Munster Fusiliers, received the DCM for bravery; Lance Cpl J.A. Hynes, a clerk of Ennis Post Office, was awarded the DCM for bravery at the Battle of the Somme; Lt Hugh Murrough Vere O'Brien of Ballyallia, was awarded the DSO for gallantry; Gunner James T. Sullivan, Royal Field Artillery, from Clare Castle received the DCM for devotion to duty and conspicuous gallantry while repairing telegraph wires under shellfire; Cpl T. McMahon of the Royal Munster Fusiliers, from Ennis, was awarded the Cross of St George, second class for bravery; Capt. Michael Fitzgerald, Royal Navy, from Roughan, Corofin, was awarded the MC for gallantry with the 19th Bengal Lancers, and Cpl John O'Shea, Royal Engineers, Rangoon, Burma, from Lack West, Kilmihil, was decorated with the DCM.[39]

Roll of Honour

The Roll of Honour that year included Pte John McDonnell of Kilrush, who died of wounds after fighting for more than twelve months in France and

Flanders. He actually took part in eighteen engagements with the Germans, being injured in the last battle. Among the battles he took part in were: Festurbebt, Le Basse, Neuve Chapelle, Lerig, Loos, Guinchy, Richburg, Vimy, Hulloch, Vermeilles, the Brickfields, Ypres, Arras, Contelmaison, Guillemont, Ginchy, Combles, and Espinol. He was seriously wounded in Espinol and died in Cardiff Hospital. He left a widow and child as well as a mother and sisters. His remains were brought back to Kilrush for burial in Shanakyle.[40] That year at least 147 Clare people died because of the Great War, mainly in France and Belgium, while three died at sea.[41]

To My Daughter Betty, the Gift of God

… So here, while the mad guns curse overhead,
And tired men sigh with mud for couch and floor,
Know that we fools, now with the foolish dead,
Died not for flag, nor king, nor emperor,
But for a dream born in a herdsman's shed
And for the secret scripture of the poor.

Tom Kettle, MP
September 1916

THE SPIRIT
OF 1916

'Sinn Féin arose and struck the English rust from the soul of Ireland.'

Bishop Fogarty

The war entered its third year, with no end in sight and the frightful mortality rates continued. There was growing concern about a food shortage in Britain and Ireland due to the war and the bad weather, which led the authorities to sponsor a major advertising campaign to promote tillage farming instead of pastoral farming. The spectre of food shortages and the promotion of compulsory tillage by the government – also encouraged by Bishop Fogarty in his pastoral letter – fomented a wave of cattle drives and illegal tillage on large ranches throughout the county.

The mood of the people turned more against the war and the Home Rule Party, and more in favour of the policies of Sinn Féin. The *Clare Champion* and bishops such as Dr O'Dwyer and Dr Fogarty began to publicly oppose the war and the policies of John Redmond and the Home Rule party. The 'Soldier's Song' began to replace 'A Nation Once Again' and the popular British Army marching song, 'It's a long way to Tipperary' also went out of fashion. This was seen during the East Clare by-election of Eamon de Valera in 1917, following the death in France of Maj. Willie Redmond, MP, for the constituency of East Clare. Naturally, levels of recruitment continued to decline. Apart from 'political' crimes, such as drilling openly with arms, and the cattle drives, for which many republicans were arrested under DORA, there were very few indictable petty crimes in the county.

Early in the New Year, before the growing season started, the British authorities encouraged farmers to grow more tillage under a new compulsory

Tillage Act. Farmers were obliged to till 10 per cent of their land. Compulsory tillage had been decreed because there was a necessity to have more home-grown food. Great emphasis was put upon the growing of crops such as wheat, oats and potatoes. These, they argued, were the cheapest, the best and the most easily procured foods in Ireland. It was argued that 1 acre under oats or potatoes would supply more food than many acres under grassland. It was claimed that 1lb of oatmeal was equal in food value to 3lb of beef. As an incentive, farmers were promised a guaranteed market at fixed prices for these products. More tillage would require more men, give more work, produce more food and provide more prosperity for Irish farmers. Ironically, there was no reference at this time to the reluctance of the farmers to enlist! They had other more important duties.[1]

Bishop Fogarty issued his Lenten pastoral letter in February and that year he returned to the theme of war, but, perhaps to the disappointment of many Sinn Féin supporters in Clare and elsewhere, he did not condemn the war. 'It was', he said, 'the most dreadful visitation of divine wrath that has ever befallen humanity. Everything about this war is a portend, a terrible instrument in the hand of God chastening a world that has largely disowned its creator. But it is not only a purge, it is gradually revealing itself as a curative agency of Providential good purging gross social evils like a purifying fire.' He welcomed as Providential the Compulsory Tillage Act, which would put people back on the land and end the 'life-less' cattle ranches. He referred to the ruthless and tyrannical manner in which the Irish people were driven from the lands they cultivated by rapacious evictors. He hoped the young men and women would not disdain to work on the land in the wholesome clay, which if it stains their hands will not be the dirty stain of the city slums! He warned that the danger of famine was grave and he urged that surplus grain and potatoes be kept in Ireland until June.[2]

WHY GRASSLAND MUST BE BROKEN

To furnish the most food, for the poorest people in the shortest time.

Quantity: an acre of merely average land will produce: 1 ton of oats, or 1 ton of potatoes. An acre of the finest fattening land will not produce more than 5cwt. of beef (live weight containing hides, bones and all).

Food Value: an acre of oats will feed for a week 100 people.

An acre of potatoes will feed 220 people.

An acre of beef will feed 8 people.

Time: to grow oats takes 5 months;

to grow potatoes takes 4–6 months;

to rear fattening beef takes 2–3 years;

to grow beef takes 2 years!

Deptartment of Agriculture and Technical Instruction, *Clare Journal*, 15 February 1917.

A few months later, Bishop Fogarty addressed an audience in Birr, reminding them of his pastoral letter, saying:

This universal war … came only because man has become unnatural in his devices and has defied Heaven … as a sign of this witness the cry of the suffragettes. While they might be otherwise bonafide, the idea of educated bejewelled ladies attacking policemen and being dragged along the street in a manner which one was accustomed to associate with the most abandoned of women, was a clear indication of how wrong Ireland was going.

The world was in a terrible state and no one could tell when the war would end. The present was no time for running around spending money at cinematic exhibitions and such like. It was no time for wasting money. A drunken man was now an unthinkable anomaly … for before twelve months we may be faced with famine, at least a bread famine. Women in particular, ought not to be wasteful of money, it is sacrilegious to spend the money wrongly … above all, women should never enter a public house! The present was a time for patience and charity. The employer should understand that the working-man could not live now on anything but a very substantial wage. He could not possibly exist on 14 or 15 shillings a week. The present was a time for sharing burthens. I hope for an early close of the war, it has caused great suffering here, but I am told it is greater in England than in Ireland.

Dr Fogarty, becoming almost puritanical or Calvinistic in tone, also denounced the influences of 'frivolity, fancy costumes and hedonism'. He welcomed the 'restriction on excursion trains'; he hoped that the 'demoralising picture houses' would be closed down, as well as the 'detestable clubs in the towns', all of which 'were promoting scandals'.[3]

Besides commenting on the war and its economic and social impacts, the bishop, later in the year, reacted against Summer Time this year. He instructed his clergy to ignore the new Summer Time Act and to leave the hours of Sunday masses to be regulated by Greenwich Mean Time. The new Summer Time Act was, he said, wholly inapplicable to the circumstances of the country. Some parts of the diocese, he said, would be almost two hours ahead of the great clock set up by nature for the guidance and regulation of human life, namely, the sun in the heavens. He told his clergy to say the Masses at the old time, 'God's time'.[4]

Though Bishop Fogarty did not publicly condemn the war yet, an editorial in the *Clare Champion* of 14 April strongly called for an end to the war: 'What is the object of prolonging the war? Has not the slaughtering been sufficient to satiate the most bloodthirsty? Are not the maimed and crippled sufficient appeals to the cause of humanity? Has not the greatest treasure been spent, sufficient to realise the utopian dreams of our greatest reformers? Is it not time to rescue the world from the horrors into which secret diplomacy has lured it?

Two weeks later, on 28 April, the *Clare Champion* denounced the 'bad faith' of England in Mr Asquith's proposed Amending Act to the Home Rule Bill, allowing for the exclusion of six counties. The editor declared that partition would never be undone. 'Asquith and Lloyd George were traitors to Ireland; enemies of the Irish people … no Irish person could trust them.' The editor was clearly indicating to John Redmond that the *Clare Champion* was no longer supporting his Home Rule Party or his policies.

A surprise intervention on the issue of partition was made by Dr T.S. Berry, Church of Ireland Bishop of Killaloe at the Killaloe Diocesan Synod, as reported in the *Saturday Record* of 11 August. The bishop stated, 'I would to God that we could feel that the most terrible war in history was nearing its close, but of this there were, at present, no signs. We must pray for the dawn of peace and the reuniting of the nations … As to the partition of Ireland, I believe that every Irishman who loved his country said "may no such partition take place"'.

On 28 July, near the third anniversary of the outbreak of the war, the *Clare Champion* editor wrote; 'We are nearing the end of the third year of war, the most wicked crime ever committed against the human race'. Such comments in the local nationalist paper did not encourage recruitment for the British Army at a time when the need for recruits was desperate because of the terrible losses due to the war of attrition on the Western Front at battle sites such as Ypres and on the Somme.

Dr O'Dwyer, Bishop of Limerick, became more vocal against the war and recruitment. In his Lenten pastoral letter of February of this year he launched a strong attack on Britain's continuance of the war. He said that Britain had rejected the peace talks proposed by Germany and that England was the real cause of the war.

The pastoral letter must have had a huge impact, not alone in the diocese of Limerick, but throughout Ireland, and certainly in the diocese of Killaloe, according to Bishop Fogarty. Bishop Fogarty wrote a private letter to Bishop O'Dwyer congratulating him on his pastoral and agreeing with him that 'England was the real cause of the war … your pastoral has created a furore of delight amongst the people. They are all scrambling, especially the young, to get a copy of it. They are sick and tired of falsehood, hypocrisy and cowardice with which the papers drench them …'[5]

Cattle Drives

Perhaps inspired by advertising in the local press urging more tillage with slogans such as: 'Why grassland must be broken', cattle drives became common in Clare during 1917. The men who drove the cattle from the large ranches of Clare may also have been spurred into this illegal activity by the words of Bishop Fogarty in his pastoral letter in which he attacked the 'lifeless' ranches. There may also have been other reasons such as 'land hunger' and ancient disputes over land holdings behind the new agrarian conflict.

Whatever the reasons, large groups of small tenant farmers and labourers invaded the cattle ranches. They drove the cattle off the lands and began to plough up large areas to grow crops such as oats and potatoes as soon as possible. This agrarian revolution apparently started in north Clare and, in a manner reminiscent of the old Land War, spread throughout the county during the spring of 1917. The Irish Volunteers took a prominent role in this land agitation. Sinn Féin men and women turned out in large numbers, sometimes hundreds of people, almost whole communities, armed only with hurleys and sticks to drive the cattle from the graziers' farms, and then the men ploughed up the land. County Clare was becoming ungovernable as the people brazenly defied the RIC and openly ignored the law. An editorial in the *Clare Champion* of 20 January 1917 was sympathetic to the broad aims of the cattle drives from the non-residential grazing farms: 'A large portion of the ranches is still being left to the bullocks. Yes, for generations the bullock has taken the place of the tiller of the soil of north Clare. The awakening is extraordinary …'

The testimony of leading IRA volunteers in the county recorded in the 1930s and '40s clearly indicated that the local Irish Volunteers or Sinn Féin leaders were very active in the agitation. While some recorded that the landowners would be compensated, others were interested in the acquisition and division of the large ranches and the remains of the old landed estates in the county and tried to ensure that the local Sinn Féin members would get preference in any land division:

> The lands were ploughed and put under oats by people who had taken lots, mostly small farmers, whose holdings were unsuited to tillage. Most of the ploughing was done by Irish Volunteers, and, while this was going on the police took their names. It was made clear to the authorities that there was no question of confiscation of the seized lands and that the people who had taken lots or tillage would pay reasonable compensation to the owners.
>
> (Andrew O'Donoghue)

> We took an active part in the campaign in the agitation for the acquisition of ranches … we tried to ensure that our members would get preference …
>
> (Joseph Barrett)

Cattle were driven from the lands of Dr Howard, Drumclife and Tom Crowe, Loughavilla. Both holdings were non-residential and the owners were well-known imperialists who used the lands entirely for grazing.

(Peter O'Loughlin)

In many districts large tracts of land had been cleared of tenants in order to make ranches for the landlord class, who were mostly absentees and who used the lands solely or grazing purposes. The descendants and friends of the evicted tenants never gave up the idea of recovering the farms from which they had been ejected and a continuous agitation was carried out to get the ranches divided …

(Thomas MacNamara)

Cattle drives became very popular and all over the county Volunteers took part in them as organised units …

(Michael Brennan)

Fr William O'Kennedy, St Flannan's College, Ennis, a well-known Sinn Féin supporter, expressed concern that cattle drives were being organised against 'comparatively small farms and non-ranchers' and he warned against undesirable elements joining the cattle drives 'for private grudges, personal spleen, jealousy or greed'. These 'irresponsible individuals', he said, would try to shelter under the wings of Sinn Féin. However, Bishop Fogarty did not seem unduly concerned with the phenomenon, claiming that 'cattle driving and ploughing up the grasslands had 'no political significance, it was', he said, 'a social trouble'.[6]

The authorities were keeping a close eye on the Catholic clergy at this time and Catholic RIC men, who were attending Masses reported 'seditious' sermons to their superiors, which were brought to the attention of the highest authorities in the chief secretary's office in Dublin and files were kept on such clergymen. Fr Maher of Garranboy and Killaloe allegedly made a seditious sermon in 1917. Another prominent Sinn Féin priest at this time was Fr Charles Culligan, CC. He had been curate in Carrigaholt and was part of the group of Sinn Féiners who occupied the boardroom of the Ennis Workhouse on 29 January 1916. He was subsequently transferred to the parish of Silvermines in Tipperary, but that did not silence him, or curtail his activities as the following police reports testify:

While attending divine service at Ballinclough chapel Rev Fr C Culligan addressed the audience and said:
"I want to speak to you about the grave times we are passing through at present. In a couple of months or less we may be unable to buy anything except

by food tickets. Germany threatens to sink every ship in sight, and there is not enough food in England to support her for a fortnight. She is on the brink of starvation.

So till all ye can and I do not mean so to be tilling for the British army, but to till it for yourselves, if you can keep it, if is not taken from ye, which is doubtful.

Some time ago some people went around to these parts of the county collecting for the Red Cross societies and eggs for the wounded soldiers. These people now are not giving an acre of land to people who need it for tillage purposes, because they don't care about ye and will grind ye if they can!

It shames me to see people living under those whose ancestors were from the rottenest country in the world. I would like to say a lot more, but maybe I have said enough. Anyway, till all ye can and keep it for yourselves if ye can, because ye have nothing to get from outside sources.'

The local sergeant, Sgt Daughton reported to the authorities, 'This clergyman is an extreme Sinn Féiner and he is endeavouring to foster and develop Sinn Féinism in Silvermines and its parish'.

In a second report, Fr Culligan was reported as saying the following at a sermon in Silvermines:

Anyone who takes an interest in the policy of Sinn Féin might like to get this paper, *Nationality*, it costs only a penny, you can order it locally, Mr Griffith is the editor … he organised Sinn Féin in this county seven years ago …

Ye are on the verge of starvation, or very soon will be. Some people with hundreds, in some cases, thousands of acres of land were very anxious to get men for the army when the war started. Now these people to avoid tilling want to let it out on conacre … that would be only improving the land under such a system. They want exorbitant prices for it. If ye don't get it at a better term then don't take it, they will have to till it themselves then. They will have to employ labour and I should like to tell you that this is a time when labourers ought to combine for a better wage. A weekly wage of 10/- or 12/- is scandalous. How is a labourer on such a wage to support a family, pay the rent and keep a cow?[7]

The Sinn Féin party was anxious that its local leaders were not to be seen to be prominent in the cattle drives, though they probably organised them. The Sinn Féin leadership at national level were also anxious to ensure that the party should not be tainted by allegations of communism, though the cattle drives in north Clare, which sparked off the phenomenon, actually predated the February Revolution in Russia. It must be remembered that the communists under Lenin did not seize power until October 1917. The Bolsheviks confiscated the landed estates from the aristocracy in Russia and divided their estates amongst the peasantry. This was not the case in County Clare. Bishop Fogarty and the Catholic Church strongly condemned socialism and atheistic communism and respected the rights of property owners. But property had its duties as well as its rights and the needs of the people were paramount when there was a danger of a serious food shortage in Ireland at the time. There was little sympathy for the landlords or for the extensive graziers on 'the lifeless ranches' of County Clare. The Catholic Church did not condemn the cattle drives as immoral, as long as compensation was paid.

Immorality

Bishop Fogarty seemed to be more concerned about other forms of immorality, which he believed were causing greater scandals in the county. Early in January Councillor P.J. Linnane of Ennis UDC condemned at a meeting of the council what he said were 'immoral' pictures at the cinema in Ennis. He said that the pictures were promoting adultery; 'they were not suitable for young women.' A week later, Bishop Fogarty, taking his cue from Mr Linnane, launched a tirade against the local cinema in a letter to the editor of the *Saturday Record*:

Dear Sir,

I hope the people of Ennis will note well the revelations made by Mr P.J. Linnane at the last meeting of the Ennis Urban Council, about the pictures shown at the Town Hall. Every man in Ennis should be grateful to that worthy gentleman for drawing public attention to this scandal.

We now know how foul the stuff in which our young people are being fed in that Hell shop. Our duty is clear and unmistakeable; it is to shun the place as infected by a plague.

It is said it brings £200 to the rates, but it takes double that amount out of the town, and from the very class who can least afford it. But are we for any price however great, sunk to the level of those vile wretches who live on white slavery?

It is suggested to have the films censored by a local committee. It is hopeless. I doubt if there are decent films enough to last a week.

These films are not made in Ireland for the Irish mind, they are made in England and America for a people steeped in sensuality. We may check them or a week or two. But, Satan will bide his time, gradually thickening the dose until our palate will relish the worst he can serve.

No, the sooner this source of corruption leaves our town the better for Ennis. It should never have come here. The Town Hall is no place for it. I ask the people to shun its doors. No girls especially should enter them. Let us shun its doors and they will soon close.

I am, yours sincerely,

M Fogarty,

Bishop of Killaloe[8]

Other forms of social life such as drinking did not seem to cause much concern at this time. At a sitting of the local court, District Inspector Townshend objected to the granting of a licence for another public house in Ennis. He said that the population of the town was about 5,200 and there were already 112 pubs in the town. However, trade may have been bad as there were few reports of drunkenness in the town.

At the Ennis petty sessions court in January Mr George McElroy, RM, said that there was only one case of drunkenness in the town. This, he said, spoke well of the morals of Ennis. Addressing the Clare grand jury, Judge Bodkin KC, congratulated them on the state of the county, for the entire calendar of the court consisted only of the larceny of a goat! He offered condolences to the Grand Jurors – respectable farmers – 'for wasting their valuable time, like using a steam roller to crack a nut!' Later, at Kilrush quarter sessions court, Judge Bodkin was presented with a set of white gloves by Mr William Healy, clerk of the commission and peace. It was a symbol of the peaceful state of West Clare, as there were no indictable cases before the court. There was, it seems, little or no petty crime in the county around this time.[9]

This virtually crime-free phenomenon may be explained by the fact that a huge proportion of the previously unemployed labouring classes of the towns in Clare seemed to have enlisted in the armed forces of the Crown. This meant that probably most of the previously unemployed young men of the community had found steady employment and the 'separation money' given to the wives of serving soldiers and sailors was significant as well. For instance, Mr P. Kelly, from The Glen, Kilrush, wrote a letter to the *Clare Journal* in January in which he

---

INCREASED SEPARATION ALLOWANCES

For soldier's wives and children

Corporal, Sergeant, or Private

Wife	12/6	to	15/-
wife & 1 child	17/6	to	20/-
wife& 2 children	21/-	to	23/6
wife & 3 children	23/-	to	25/6

with an addition of 2/- for each subsequent child.

Each motherless child 5/-.

Allowances for other dependants:

Full particulars at any Post Office

God save the King

God Save The King.

Saturday Record, 18 January 1917.

said that 'in response to His Majesty's call, 500 boys of Kilrush are now in the battle front hammering the barbaric and savage German Kaiser's hordes.' He had two brothers, six cousins and other relatives fighting in the battlefields of France 'and the government are nobly treating their dependants in Kilrush'.[10]

There was, however, still much hardship in the county due to the war. A concert was organised by Miss Maunsell of Island McGrath in the Boy's National School at Clare Castle, with songs 'comical, sentimental and patriotic, pianoforte solos, recitations and step dancing.' A sum of £11 9s was raised, including 'a very generous donation of £2 given by Mr Patrick Power, to be divided among the poor of the village'. Of the sum collected, £1 was voted to the Clare Needlework Guild, £1 to the Royal Munster Fusilier's Prisoners of War Fund, and the balance of £9 9s was given to the poor, 'many who deserve better, suffering severely from the hardships of high prices of food and the lack of employment'.[11]

While the army and navy were desperately seeking more volunteers, one young man was discharged from the army because of his age. Patrick Leahy from Kilkee enlisted when he was only 15 years old! When his mother, Mrs Bridget Leahy, found out she was tried to get him discharged, but the War Office were reluctant to release the enthusiastic young man. She sought the assistance of the local MP, Col Arthur Lynch, and, following his representations, the War Office sent the boy home.

Another Clare youth who volunteered to fight was an Ennis boy named Luke Coote, who enlisted in the Royal Munster Fusiliers when he was 16. On 16 June 1917 he was shot in the arms, stomach and chest, just after the Battle of Messines Ridge in France. By then he had been promoted to the rank of corporal. When he had recovered from these very serious injuries he returned to Ireland. Later, he used his military experience to support Michael Collins in the War of Independence.[12]

The Death of Willie Redmond, MP

Maj. Willie Redmond, MP, was not so lucky, as he was killed at the Battle of Messines Ridge on 7 June 1917. Bishop Fogarty, in a letter to John Redmond, MP, leader of the Home Rule Party, seemed to have become disillusioned with the war: 'This accursed war has claimed one of its expiating victims, our brave and beloved member, your dear brother Willie'.[13]

Willie Redmond, MP, had joined the Royal Irish Regiment in January 1916 and was commissioned as a captain. He was one of five Irish MPs who actually served in the British forces during the war, two of whom came from County Clare. He was first elected to parliament in 1883 and had been elected for various constituencies including Wexford, where he was born, and North Fermanagh. He was imprisoned along with Charles Stewart Parnell in Kilmainham Jail in 1880-81. When the Home Rule Party split over Parnell's affair with Mrs O'Shea, he stood by Parnell and was chosen and elected as a 'Parnellite' candidate for East Clare, even though Parnell was dead, in 1892. The election of 1895 was also bitterly contested, but he was re-elected for East Clare. Since that election he had been returned unopposed for the East Clare constituency. Thus, he had been an MP for the East Clare constituency for twenty-five years. At the age of 54 he was deemed to be too old for actual service in the field and served in an administrative and promotional capacity in the regiment, touring the country and encouraging young men to enlist and join Irish regiments.[14]

While on active service, he occasionally addressed the House of Commons, urging the British to keep their promise with regard to Home Rule for Ireland. He also wrote regular columns on his wartime experiences for a British newspaper, the *Daily Chronicle*. Perhaps his finest hour in parliament was his last one, in which he delivered his 'Cheerio' speech in March 1916. His last speech made a profound impression on all sides of the House of Commons and indeed throughout the country. In what the *Manchester Guardian* described as 'a masterpiece of simple eloquence, he made another heartfelt, yet helpless appeal to the government in the name of Irishmen in the trenches to solve the Irish question'. He addressed the House of Commons dressed in his military uniform. He had just come back from the frontline in France and described in glowing terms the gallantry of the Irish men from all parts of the country in the trenches of France and Belgium. He highlighted the comradeship among the troops from all parts of Ireland in the Irish regiments. He finished his speech, ironically prophesising his own death, with a plea to the British to grant self-government to Ireland:

> In the name of God, we, who are about to die, perhaps, ask you to do that which largely induced us to leave our homes; to do that which our mothers and fathers taught us to long for; to do that which is all we desire, make our country happy and contented, and enable us, when we meet the Canadians, the Australians and the New Zealanders side by side in the common cause and the common field, to say to them: "our country, just as yours, has self-government within the empire".[15]

Maj. Redmond wrote one more letter to his friend, Councillor P.J. Linnane, JP. In this letter he expressed the hope that he might see his friend again and that he was having a difficult time. The letter was written on 26 May 1917, just twelve days before he was killed:

D.H.Q,
16 Div,
B.E.F.
Dear PJ,
I got your letter as to John Coffey. I need not say I should be glad to do as
you wish, but I fear I have absolutely no power or means of doing so. I hope
you and your family are well and that I may meet you some day again. I often
think of our many days together. I am having a by no means easy time but
I am still convinced Ireland should take her side in the war – especially now
with America in.
With every good wish,
Yours very truly,
Willie Redmond,
26-5-'17[16]

One commentator wrote, 'Major Willie Redmond, MP, was a leader and was
not prepared to ask other men to do what he would not do himself'. He had
frequently requested to be sent to the front line to join the rest of his bat-
talion in action as they 'went over the top'. His wish was finally granted.
On 7 March 1917 at 3.10 a.m., he led the men of B company Royal Irish
Regiment, 16th Irish Division, over the top at Passchendaele in the Battle of
Messines, near Ypres. He allegedly went over the top shouting: 'Up the County
Clare!' He was wounded about twenty minutes afterwards in the leg and in the
wrist and he died about three hours later. A subaltern in his company described
Redmond's demeanour on the day of his death: 'Major Redmond exhibited
the dash and exuberance of a schoolboy on the morning of his death. He had a
joke and a smile for every man, and as we flew over the parapets to the shouts
of "Up the County Clare!", Maj. Willie showed us a clean pair of heels'.[17]

In the introduction to *Trench Pictures from France*, E.M. Smith-Dampier
described how Willie Redmond was determined to share the danger with the
ordinary soldiers. According to Smith-Dampier, the only criticism ever heard
against Willie Redmond, one of the most popular officers in the regiment, was
that 'he could not bring himself to be hard enough with the men':

Here was a man who felt he would die, who nevertheless never swerved for
a moment from the determination to face death ... Others who knew him
are agreed that Willie Redmond foresaw his death. More than that, he may
be said to have sought it. He refused to be content with any sort of post,
however honourable, which kept him behind the firing line. Not only was
he determined to share danger with the men, not only did his religion lift
him above all fear of the end, but he was convinced that his blood would

prove a sacrament of unity to his own countrymen and lift up their hearts to a higher place.

The end was near at hand. When the great push came on in June 1917, he was in permanent HQ at the village of Lucre … Fr Kelly, chaplain to the forces wrote in a letter to Monsignor Ryan:

> During the three nights previous to the battle he and I slept in the same cellar under the chapel at the hospice, and I can assure you that he felt absolutely miserable at the idea of being left behind. He had used every influence with the general to get over the top with the men, and he had little hope of succeeding. He spoke in the most feeling manner of what awaited the poor fellows and longed to share their sufferings and their fate. However, he was not to be denied, and to his extreme delight, was given leave to charge with his old battalion of the Royal Irish Regiment. He put on his equipment in Fr O'Connell's room and was simply bubbling over with joy … when the men saw him they gave a cheer.
>
> May God have mercy on his soul! No purer-hearted man, no braver soldier ever died in the battlefields. He was absolutely convinced he was dying for Ireland … In my humble opinion, Willie Redmond deserves the admiration of every man capable of admiring sanctity in a Catholic, valour in a soldier, and the most unselfish love of country in a patriot.[18]

Tom Johnstone gives a different view of the motivation behind Willie Redmond's determination to go over the top, suggesting a baser motive, implying that Redmond wanted to prove that he was not a coward by going over the top: 'At the battles of Guillemont and Ginchy Gen. Hickey had insisted that Redmond remain at divisional HQ, considering him too old at 56. Following this, Redmond had received letters (anonymous) accusing him of cowardice. Nevertheless, Redmond was deeply hurt. For this reason he requested Hickey to allow him to join his battalion for the Messines attack. At first Hickey remained obdurate, but Redmond implored so insistently that at last the general gave way'.[19]

There were messages of sympathy from Pope Benedict XV and from King George V, among many others, and the French Government posthumously awarded him the Legion of Honour. Bishop Fogarty wrote a letter of sympathy to John Redmond, MP, brother of Willie Redmond. The letter was published in the *Freeman's Journal* and in the *Saturday Record* of 16 June:

Dear Mr Redmond,
Alas what I long dreaded has come at last. This accursed war has claimed as one of its expiating victims our brave and beloved member, your dear brother

Willie. I feel for you greatly, I could see in our many talks of over twelve years how strongly devoted were he and you to one another. It will be some particle of consolation to you to know that his death is deplored and lamented by almost everyone in Clare, even by those who differed politically from him and you. As for myself, I not only esteemed him, but was fondly attached to him. I lament and mourn his sad death more than I could tell you. May God grant him eternal rest. He was fit to go. His life in the trenches, as it was everywhere else, was religious, manly and Catholic. We shall not see his like in Clare again and perhaps do not deserve it. I beg you to accept the expression of my profoundest sympathy and sorrow.

Yours sincerely,

M. Fogarty, Bishop of Killaloe

Dr Fogarty, who was on his diocesan visitation at the time, regretted that he could not say a memorial Mass in memory of Willie Redmond at Ennis Cathedral on Monday 18 June. He stated that if it were possible he would say the Mass himself, but unfortunately, he could not be available.

Expressions of sympathy were also recorded at Clare County Council, Ennis Urban Council, the AOH, the Ennis Labourers, the Ennis Brian Boru corps of the Irish National Volunteers, the Ennis Foresters and the Ennis Board of Guardians. On 17 June an empty coffin was paraded through the streets of Ennis, with a guard of honour provided by the Ennis Volunteers, while the O'Connell monument was draped in black. Councillor P.J. Linnane, JP, delivered an oration in memory of his great friend at the memorial Mass the next day.

One man, though he did not share Willie Redmond's political philosophy, wrote generously about Willie Redmond after his death; Edward Lysaght of Raheen said, 'Though I have not been able to see eye to eye with the policy which led him to join the British army, I recognise none the less that his death was a noble one and his life honestly given for Ireland's sake'. In Limerick, Bishop O'Dwyer allowed a novena of prayers to be offered for the soul of Maj. Willie Redmond.[20]

However, not everybody in Clare was willing to express sympathy on the death of Willie Redmond. Indeed, his death caused some controversy both in the Catholic Church and in the Ennis Board of Guardians. At the meeting of the board of guardians a vote of sympathy was proposed, and seconded, but it caused a heated debate, when one member, Mr Hegarty, objected. He 'heatedly' declared that 'Mr Redmond was not an Irishman – ever since he joined the Wexford Militia – since then, he was never a friend of Ireland'. Furthermore, he declared that Willie Redmond 'never did anything for the Irish farmers'.

This outburst led to an animated discussion and uproar, which turned the meeting into a 'bear garden', with Mr Kerin making a vehement protest against

Mr Hegarty's attack on 'their dead chief'. He declared that Willie Redmond was a patriot who had been incarcerated in Kilmainham Jail along with Parnell in 1881. After many heated exchanges the room was 'a regular bedlam' as Mr Hegarty and Mr Kerin exchanged mutual insults. Mr Kerin accused Mr Hegarty of having taken the Oath of Allegiance for ambitious motives, while Willie Redmond, he said, took it for patriotic motives, for his love of Ireland. Mr Hegarty and Mr Kerin threatened each other, but order was eventually restored by the chairman, Mr Considine.

Then Mr Kerin launched a tirade against two unnamed clergy, who, he said, had refused to pray for the soul of Willie Redmond:

I am very sorry to have to say it the Catholic clergymen of two parishes adjoining closely this town refused to offer up a prayer on the altar of their God for the soul of poor Willie Redmond. That certainly was a deplorable scandal before God, while the murderer who would be executed for his offence would be prayed for, or the man who would commit suicide and even the hangman who executed the murderer would be prayed for. But for the soul of poor Willie Redmond, no prayer was offered up from the altar of God by those two clergymen. May God forgive them for their act. Even Cardinal Logue, no friend of the Home Rule party, paid tribute to Willie Redmond, that he was an Irishman worthy of his steel.

After further acrimonious debate and bitter personal insults, order was eventually restored and Mr Glynn proposed a vote of condolence to the widow and family of Willie Redmond. This motion was unanimously adopted, after further 'animated discussion'.[21]

There may have been some foundation to the allegations by Mr Kerin that some Catholic clergymen of neighbouring parishes had refused to say a Mass for the soul of Willie Redmond. Speaking at a Sunday Mass in Clare Castle, by permission of Canon Bourke, PP, Fr Marcus McGrath, CC, publicly defended his honour against what he described as 'a mean and malignant attempt to defame me before the county':

You will all know to what I refer. When I came here on Sunday last to celebrate Mass a notice was handed in asking me to request the prayers of the congregation for the late Major Redmond. Major Redmond's death was a matter of public knowledge. It was as quite well known to me, and, if all were known, as deeply regretted by me as by the individual who wrote the notice, and it struck me as curious that in a matter which was so public, and which didn't affect Clare Castle more than any other parish, any individual should dictate to me what my priestly duties were on that sad occasion.

It was in these circumstances exactly that I omitted to make the public announcement, and by permission of the canon (Bourke), I am here today to explain my position and my action and to offer Holy Mass and to ask the prayers of the congregation for the soul of Major Redmond, making sure that I do not do so at the request of any person, whose claim to dictate to me, I repudiate.

Refuse to pray for the soul of Major Redmond! Such is the vile calumny that has gone forth. I can tell you in all sincerity that at both of my Masses on that day I gave him a special memento that God would have mercy on his soul. Refuse to pray for his soul! I never refused to pray for anyone, living or dead, and least of all would I refuse to pray for the soul of him, who, though one may differ from him in politics, was a good Catholic, a brave soldier, who had the courage of his convictions, and when the bugle sounded went over the parapet and gave his life for the cause he thought was right. He was no shirker and paid the penalty. His body lies on a foreign land. May God have mercy on his soul.

This then is the vile calumny that has created such commotion during the week and has brought my name on every lip as the name of one who refused to pray for a departed soul. This is the calumny that has been used to decoy and to bring out at midnight a number of men to insult their priest. This then is the calumny that has even reached the board of guardians for discussion. But I tell the people of this parish and the leaders of the midnight raiders and the man who had the impertinence to speak on behalf of prayers for anyone, and those who have criticised my position without knowing the true facts of the case, that I have done nothing of which I am ashamed, and which I would not do again 100 times in the same circumstances … Imagine this guardian, praying for forgiveness for those priests – this defender of religion![22]

Reading through the reports of the meeting of the board of guardians and the sermon at Clare Castle Catholic church published in the *Clare Champion*, one can detect the underlying tension and bitterness at parish level between the supporters of the Home Rule Party and the National Volunteers, led by John Redmond, and the supporters of the Irish Volunteers and the Sinn Féin party, led by de Valera, which was rising in popularity in the year after the Easter Rising. Both of these parties were zealously seeking the popular mandate at this time.

Fr McGrath was not a follower of John Redmond at this time. Indeed, on the contrary, he was elected president of the Sinn Féin club in Ballyea on Sunday 18 September 1917. It must be remembered that Fr McGrath was one of only four curates in County Clare, who publicly opposed John Redmond's policy of support for recruitment to the British Army during 1914 and 1915. Fr McGrath had told the congregation at Mass in Clare Castle on Sunday

4 October 1914 that 'they should not believe all the stories of German atrocities in Belgium'. However, three weeks later, Fr McGrath was on the reviewing stand alongside Bishop Fogarty and others at the National Volunteer parade in Ennis on Sunday 25 October 1914, which supported John Redmond's policy on the war. Fr McGrath must have, like Bishop Fogarty and other clergy, turned against Redmond's policy during 1915 and 1916.

It is also clear from his vigorous defence that Fr McGrath, while he may have privately prayed for the soul of Maj. Redmond, did not do so publicly at the Mass on Sunday 10 June in Clare Castle. By his own admission he took this action to teach a certain person (presumably a political opponent) a lesson, for having the temerity to dictate to

Fr Marcus McGrath CC, Clare Castle & Ballyea. (Original courtesy of the late Mrs K. McAllister. Copied by John Power)

him whom he should pray for. One presumes that Fr McGrath may have been instructed by either his parish priest, or perhaps even Bishop Fogarty, to limit the damage to the Church because of this controversy by offering public prayers for Willie Redmond's soul at the Mass on the following Sunday, while proclaiming publicly that he would not be dictated to by any parishioner.[23]

Following the death of Maj. Willie Redmond a committee was established to erect a memorial in his honour at Wexford, his native county. A national subscription was invited and committees established in various counties to collect funds. In County Clare fundraising was mainly in parishes such as Quin, Newmarket-on-Fergus and Clare Castle, where the Home Rule Party vote was strongest. A significant sum of £37 2s 0d was collected in the Clare Castle district alone. The names of the individual subscribers were given, along with their donations. This generous sum included 2 guineas from the parish priest, Canon P. Bourke and 5 guineas from the Clare Castle Land and Labour Association. Significantly, and perhaps not unexpectedly, the curate, Fr Marcus McGrath, CC, did not contribute to the collection, which was publicly acknowledged in a local paper.[24]

The East Clare By-Election of 1917

The death of Willie Redmond, MP, necessitated a by-election for the East Clare constituency. Shortly after the death was announced a meeting of Sinn Féin sympathisers took place in Ennis to secure the return of a Sinn Féin candidate as opposed to a member of the Home Rule Party. The meeting took place in the Clare Hotel at which the following attended – Revd A. Clancy, PP, Revd J. O'Donoghue, Revd M. Crowe, Revd T. Molloy and Revd W. O'Kennedy, (president of St Flannan's College, Ennis). Besides the clergy the following also attended: Messrs Sean McNamara, Con Kearney, M. Nugent, P.C. Casey, M. O'Brien, M. Hegarty, A. Brennan, J. Barrett, J. Spellissy, M. Quin, RDC, D. Bugler, J. Crowe, T. McGrath, P. Brody, T. Considine, J. Spellissey and M. McInerney. The meeting, after some discussion on the merits of various candidates, unanimously agreed that Peadar Clancy of Cranny should be the candidate in the forthcoming election. Peadar Clancy fought during the Easter Rising; he had been sentenced to death and was currently serving a ten-year sentence of penal servitude. After selecting their candidate, the members formed a provisional election committee and appointed three men as joint secretaries – Revd M. Crowe, CC, and Messrs M. O'Brien and S. McNamara. The provisional committee then decided to summon a convention at the Old Ground Hotel, Ennis, on Thursday 14 June at 12 noon (old time), to select a Sinn Féin candidate and to form an election committee.

More than 200 delegates attended the Sinn Féin Convention in the Old Ground Hotel. Revd A. Clancy, PP, acted as chairman, while Revd M. Crowe, CC, acted as secretary. Mr Sean Milroy of the central executive of Sinn Féin addressed the meeting, after which nominations for the vacancy took place. Five candidates were proposed and seconded. After a full discussion, the names of four of the candidates were withdrawn in favour of Professor Eamon de Valera, Dublin, who was one of the commandants during Easter Week and had been sentenced to death, but this had been commuted to penal servitude for life. As can be seen from the lists of those attending the Sinn Féin meetings, the Catholic clergy took a prominent part in the Sinn Féin organisation. Acting as chairmen or secretaries, they would have been a very influential voice for moderation among the other delegates.[25]

According to Michael Brennan, de Valera was not a compromise candidate. Brennan stated that he, himself, was 'on the run' and was approached after a meeting of Volunteers and Sinn Féin members in Ennis to stand for the constituency. Brennan declined the offer and suggested de Valera. Brennan's brother Paddy wrote to another brother, Austen, that all the older men and the clergy wanted Eoin McNeill to stand for election. There was, apparently, a majority at the convention in favour of McNeill. However, Austen Brennan stated, after an adjournment, that if McNeill were selected by the convention that the Volunteers would not support him and they would put up de Valera to oppose both McNeill and the Home Rule Party candidate, Patrick Lynch.[26]

A Soldier's Song

The combination of the death of Willie Redmond, MP, the 1916 Rising, the influence of bishops such as Bishop O'Dwyer, and the feeling of betrayal by Mr Asquith towards Ireland, brought about the conversion of the *Clare Champion* proprietors to the policies of Sinn Féin. In the issue of 30 June the editorial described Mr Patrick Lynch as 'a crown prosecutor, who had never once advocated the cause of nationalism or Irish Independence'. On the other, hand the *Clare Champion* editor, with the support of the proprietors, the Galvin family, became enthusiastic supporters of de Valera. He was described as a man who appealed to the voters of East Clare to show their horror and detestation of the manner in which the English Government shot the leaders of the Dublin Rebellion. The *Clare Champion* described the 'affecting scenes the wild enthusiasm and the tremendous reception given to de Valera when he arrived in Ennis' before the election. The words of 'A Soldier's Song' were boldly printed on the front page and his visit was comprehensively covered.

A SOLDIER'S SONG

We'll sing a song, a soldier's song
With cheering, rousing chorus
As round our blazing fires we throng
The starry heavens o'er us.
Impatient for the coming fight
And as we wait the morning's light
Here in the silence of the night
We'll sing a soldier's song.

(Chorus)
Soldiers are we
Whose lives are pledged to Ireland.
Some have come
From a land beyond the wave
Sworn to be free
No more our ancient sire land
Shall shelter the despot or the slave.

Tonight we man the gap of danger
In Erin's cause, come woe or weal
'Mid cannons roar and rifles peal
We'll chant a soldier's song.

It should be noted that 'A Soldier's Song' was written by Peadar Kearney in 1907. It was adopted by the Irish Volunteers as their marching song. It was translated into Irish by Liam O'Rinn in 1923 and 'Amhrán na bhFiann' became the Irish National Anthem in 1926.

The paper noted that 'a frenzied effort was being made to frighten the voters of Clare into the belief that de Valera is a desperado and an anarchist out for revolution, bloodshed and strife'. There seems to have been some truth in these allegations as one parish priest, Fr Slattery, PP of Quin, had urged the people to vote for Mr Patrick Lynch, KC, the Home Rule candidate, or else, he said, 'they would face red ruin and revolution'. Another Catholic clergyman, Fr Hayes from Feakle, denounced Sinn Féin as having 'a policy of socialism, bloodshed and anarchy which struck at the root of authority'. He appealed to his congregation to 'save our country and our religion from a great danger by returning Mr Lynch, and not a foreigner, by an overwhelming majority at the head of the poll'. Fr P. Gaynor noted that 'separation women' put up fierce opposition to Sinn Féin.

Eamon de Valera, *c.* 1916. (Courtesy of National Library of Ireland)

However, one prominent national priest, Fr James Clancy, PP of Kilballyowen, spoke out publicly on de Valera's behalf and in a letter to the *Clare Champion* of 30 June launched a powerful attack upon Mr Lynch: 'There are two candidates for the honour of representing East Clare, Mr De Valera, with the shadow of an English prison still upon him and Mr P. Lynch, KC, with the hallmark of Dublin Castle. One has worn England's chains, the other has worn England's livery ... Is Mr Lynch a nationalist, if so he has managed to conceal it very well? Can his most devoted partisan point to a single word or act of his on behalf of Ireland? ...' Meanwhile, the *Clare Journal* observed that the contest would be an historic one between Commandant de Valera, who represented the spirit of 1916, and Mr Lynch, of old Clare stock, representing constitutional methods, which won so much for Ireland.

According to police reports, just before the election leaflets were circulated throughout the county, warning voters that the choice was between de Valera and conscription! One leaflet asked the question: 'Who will you follow, the men who fought for you in Dublin, or the men who would have sent you to meet German guns?'[27]

On his journey to Clare before the election, Mr de Valera paid a courtesy visit to Dr O'Dwyer, Bishop of Limerick, who by then had become a strong supporter of Sinn Féin. With this ecclesiastical blessing from the most nationalistic of bishops, along with his republican pedigree, Mr de Valera won the election by a huge margin, defeating Mr Lynch by a margin of 5,010 votes to 2,035.

After the election victory de Valera made triumphal tours of the county as the people rejoiced. Sinn Féin branches sprouted up all over the county, especially in the rural parishes. They were set up in places such as Ballynacally, Kilmihil, Coore, Knockerra, Kilmaley, Carron, Inagh, Kilrush, Ennis, Clare Castle, Ballyea, Kilshanny, Tulla, Quin, Kildysart, Inch, Newmarket-on-Fergus, Killimer, Kilbane, Ballycorick, Inch, Cloonanaha and Cratloe. Besides these, many branches of Cumann na mBan and Connradh na Gaeilge were established in the county. There were mass meetings held in towns and republican flags appeared all over the county.[28]

Dr Fogarty, who, according to Gaynor, 'kept strict silence during the election', now openly declared his sympathy for Sinn Féin and sent a congratulatory message to the newly elected Sinn Féin MP. In this letter, addressed to Mr T.V. Honan, Bishop Fogarty regretted that he could not come to a public meeting to celebrate de Valera's election. There were loud cheers for Bishop Fogarty at the meeting when the secretary to the meeting, Revd W. O'Kennedy, of St Flannan's College read out the bishop's letter:

Dear Mr Honan,
I join with you and the people of the county in giving a warm welcome to the brave and honourable representative of East Clare, Eamon de Valera.

He stands for the honest policy of Irish independence, which should have behind it, and please God, will soon have behind it, the whole manhood of Ireland, both north and south.

Had we that acknowledged right of every nationality, and were we free from all intermeddling in our national affairs by English cabinets, who have made such a mess of their own big business, the country would not now be convulsed by the horrors of Mountjoy Prison and the death of poor Thomas Ashe, to whose persecuted soul may the good God show eternal mercy.

At this moment not one but several young men from Clare are undergoing the same infamous torture in the same degrading dungeon. And for what crime? Have they wronged or injured any man, or menaced public peace in any way? No, but they have been openly drilling, with no thought of injury or insult to any man. And for so doing they are arrested – some of them I am told mere lads of 17 years old – and thrust into prison and degraded to the level of jailbirds; and because their manly spirit preferred death to degradation of that kind, we have the hunger strike and forcible feeding with all its disgusting episodes. The whole proceeding is, I presume to say, a disgrace to civilised government.

Public order is impossible in a community where young people are tyrannised over as they are now in Clare by petty officials because they had the audacity to elect Eamon de Valera as their sterling representative.

Wishing your meeting and your efforts for Irish freedom every success and the blessing of God.
I am, yours sincerely,

Michael Fogarty, Bishop of Killaloe.

Dr Fogarty's letter to Mr T.V. Honan was published in the *Clare Champion* of 6 October, 1917.[29]

Bishop O'Dwyer died on 19 August 1917 and his great friend Bishop Fogarty gave the eulogy at his memorial Mass about a month later. Bishop O'Dwyer had been the moral leader of the Irish opposition to the war and now it seems that the role was falling upon Dr Fogarty. He gave a powerful panegyric about Dr O'Dwyer, which included the following:

For the crisis is soon to come which will test to the core the stuff that Irishmen are made of. When brave and heroic Irishmen were being shot down in Dublin with unmerciful brutality, when poor Irish emigrants were being kicked and spat upon in the streets of Liverpool, when the whole country was being raided of its manhood and dragooned into terror, the one man in the land who had the courage to raise his voice in Christian protest and challenge the march of tyranny was the Bishop of Limerick.

Then Bishop Fogarty published a leaflet entitled, *The Sinn Féin Banner of Irish Independence*, a letter from the Bishop of Killaloe, which had the following, 'We had almost ceased to be Irish until Sinn Féin arose and struck the English rust from the soul of Ireland. Unfortunately that rust had eaten deep and spoiled many a good Irish heart.' Bishop Fogarty later sent a letter to Edward Lysaght of Raheen in which he expressed his fear 'that Home Rule would only be a sham'.

Though he openly supported Sinn Féin after 6 October 1917, there is evidence that Dr Fogarty was moving towards supporting Sinn Féin policies, including abstention from Westminster, as early as May 1917. In a letter to Bishop O'Dwyer he stated:

... The older folks, especially the older clergy, are not prepared to contemplate abstention yet. The (Home Rule) party is contemptible. The country would gladly give an independent party a new flag. The best course for Plunkett [Count Plunkett, father of the 1916 patriot, Joseph Plunkett], and Sinn Féin would be to form such a party, and having got it, then retire from the House of Commons, if they didn't get what they wanted ...[30]

Some of the members of Clare Castle GAA club were so enthusiastic for de Valera and Sinn Féin, that they organised a GAA sports meeting in aid of the de Valera election fund! Obviously, they ignored the GAA rule that the organisation was supposed to be non-political! Not everybody in this parish was happy with this support, however. When a republican flag was placed on the

CLARE CASTLE
G.A.A.

SPORTS,

IN AID OF THE

DE VALERA ELECTION FUND
WILL BE HELD

ON SUNDAY, 7th OCTOBER.

EVENTS :—

Boys' Race under 16 years.
100 Yards (open)
220 „   „
440 „   „
440 „ (Confined to Parish).
1 Mile (open).
Bag Race.
Relay Race (Confined to Hurling and Football Teams).
2 Mile Cycle Race.
3 Mile Cycle Race.
Ladies Cycle Race (novices).
Long and High Jumps (open).
Ass Race.

ENTRIES CLOSE 2nd OCT.

VALUABLE PRIZES GIVEN.

ADMISSION - - - 6d.

Advertisement for Clare Castle GAA Sports Meeting from *Clare Journal*, 28 September 1917.

belfry of the chapel in Clare Castle, the parish priest, Canon Bourke, ordered it to be removed, and it was later burned by supporters of John Redmond's party. Local republicans also put a flag on the chimney of the home of the local chairman of the Home Rule party, and, cheekily, put another flag on the chimney of the local RIC barracks.

On Christmas night that December, the premises occupied by the Eamon O'Daly Sinn Féin Club at Clare Castle were broken into around midnight. Some tables and chairs were taken and thrown into the River Fergus. The local branch of the Home Rule Party condemned the action.

Early in June republican flags were flown from the Kilmurry McMahon, Coolmeen, and Labasheeda parish churches, as well as from the chimneys of the Cranny, Coolmen and the Six Crosses National Schools, and from the dispensary of Six Crosses. The newspaper noted that the flags were flying for more than a week. This suggests that the priests of these parishes did not object to the placing of republican flags over the churches and over the schools, of which they were managers.[31]

Meanwhile, the republicans of Clare became more active, drilling, getting more arms and carrying out manoeuvres. They were harassed by the authorities, who arrested and court-martialled some of the leaders, such as the Brennans of Meelick, Art O'Donnell of Tullycrine, and Hugh Hunt of Corofin. Some of these men were among the first republicans to go on hunger strike. On 10 November the *Clare Champion* published a letter from the Clare republican prisoners who were on hunger strike at Mountjoy, which included a list of the sixteen men involved stated that they had been forcibly fed at least thirteen times between 20 and 30 September.[32]

Naturally, in these political circumstances it was difficult to promote a recruitment campaign for the Great War. With very poor timing, which shows how insensitive and incompetent the British authorities were, and how little they understood the Irish, a new recruitment campaign was begun during the middle of the East Clare by-election. A recruiting party of the Royal Munster Fusiliers toured the county seeking recruits. Unsurprisingly, there were few, if any, recruits on this occasion.

The Roll of Honour continued to expand as many 'gallant heroes' met their deaths mainly on the Western Front. The *Clare Journal* and the *Saturday Record* noted the deaths and injuries in each issue, while the *Clare Champion* only mentioned more prominent victims. The *Clare Champion* also subtly showed its opposition to the war by publishing the total weekly casualty lists of officers, rank and file and ratings killed, wounded and missing in action for the entire British Army and navy. For instance, the issue of 14 July showed 4,714, killed and 19,188 wounded, missing or taken prisoner. After the death of Willie Redmond, MP, only the *Saturday Record* really promoted the war and continued to give extensive coverage to the different theatres of war. Bishop Fogarty grew more disillusioned with the war. He declared: 'The world is sick of this accursed war! It is a useless massacre!'[33]

A Battle for Equality

While women in Britain and other countries were taking on many positions previously held by men due to the war, another battle was taking place in the courts for the right of females to be appointed to the position of petty sessions court clerk. Miss Georgiana Frost of Sixmilebridge sought the right to be appointed to the vacancy at Sixmilebridge and Newmarket-on-Fergus Petty Sessions Courts. She had been assisting her father in his duties as a petty sessions court clerk in these courts for three or four years. After his retirement she sought the appointment on Tuesday 13 July 1915. There was no other candidate for the position. She was proposed by Lord Inchiquin, seconded by Mr W.W.A. Fitzgerald and unanimously elected by the assembled Justices of the Peace.

Mr McElroy, RM, the chairman said then that 'her election was unprecedented and an historic occasion, as she was the first lady to be appointed to the position of petty sessions court clerk in Ireland'. He said that 'great credit was due to the chivalry of the magistrates of Clare, the first in Ireland to set such an example'.

However, there were legal objections and the case was taken to the High Court Dublin, where Mr Justice Barton ruled that Miss Frost 'was incapable on account of her sex of holding the position'. He said that an Act of Parliament was required to allow women to do this work. Miss Frost took the case to the Court of Appeal, but it failed there too. She eventually won her case after an appeal to the House of Lords in April 1920 and the passage of an Act of Parliament. She retired in 1922 after her historic breakthrough as the first female petty sessions court clerk in the UK.[34]

'From Somewhere in France'

While some short letters from the Western Front were published in the local press over the previous couple of years, an Ennis priest, Fr Moran, who was a chaplain with the British Army in France, gave a comprehensive description of the horrors of trench warfare in 1917. The letter, dated 14 March, which was addressed to Councillor P.J. Linnane, JP, was published in both the *Clare Champion* and the *Saturday Record*.

B.E.F., France,
14 March 1917
My Dear Mr Linnane,
I must sincerely apologise for not writing to you before now, but really,
I haven't had much time at my disposal, and I don't like writing to a man of
your calibre without a little previous reflection, not indeed that I have had
much now, but yet, I have a clear two hours to myself, which haven't been the
same since 11th of January ...

Before touching on the state of affairs out here I must give expression to
that which is nearest and dearest to my soul, viz., that our own dear country
will before long enjoy the fruits of a fight, or better still, the differences that
have been rife between the two countries for well-nigh 700 years. No doubt
the Irish have been driven to desperate measures from time to time owing
to a hard-hearted, prejudiced and un-sympathetic government. But, ethically
speaking, good gives rise to evil at times, and so evil gives rise to good. Let us
hope that the final good of our dear old country – at present on the threshold
of achievement – will soon be a reality. I may tell you that the Irish out here
are anxiously and patiently looking forward 'to the brighter days to come' for
their dear land, as are we all.

And now, a word about 'the state of things in Denmark', or more correctly,
France. I must tell you that I have to be very careful about what I consign
to paper, as I am the official censor of letters for the RAMC [Royal Army
Medical Corps], to which I am attached, and some of the letters are re-cen-
sured at the base. Hence, the unit censor has to keep well within the line!

The division that I came with came to France under the worst possible
conditions – we had intense frost and snow for four weeks – the coldest
weather experienced by the natives for twenty-two years; then came a thaw,
which lasted for two days, followed by a downpour, which has enveloped
us in oceans of mud. To give you a faint idea of the ground during the frost,
I need only tell you that it used to take two men to open a grave, one grave
about four feet deep. At present it does not take long to open a grave, as you
can imagine, when I say in many places we have been up to our chests in
mud and water, and very glad to have such places when the big shells are
bursting round us. We have no regular trenches where we have been since
we went into action – nothing but a series of shell holes. The whole sector
that we are in is nothing but a ploughed garden, ploughed by shells – both
German and English. Our division has been very unfortunate, indeed, as we
have been put into the worst sector of the whole British front. You have read
in the papers of the recent retirement of the Germans, so there goes!

To be candid, their seeming retreat has been anything but good for us.
We have been lured into seas of mud, roads etc. that are utterly impassable.

The result is while we are repairing or renovating the roads, they shell us fearfully – simply waves of shells swelling over us, some with effect and some without. The rear-guard fighting as you know is most difficult; hence the German morale is affected when we get up to them fast enough.

The villages they have vacated are no gains to us in a certain sense. They blow up everything as they retreat and mine almost everything. Just a few examples of the devilry the Germans practice, the dug-outs they leave are all mined, so that when you go downstairs and step on the last step, up goes the whole place. This is quite common. In one dug-out they left a piano. A crowd of our lads rushed in and started to play, the keys were connected to a mine, so you know the result. Another case, they left a fountain pen and pencil in a dug-out on a sideboard; naturally, they were picked up. There was a detonator in each so a few chaps had their hands blown off. In another dug-out they left a fire ready to be set ablaze – but under the paper and bits of wood were several small bombs.

The whole of France in occupation is just one big ploughed garden; nothing so desolate could be imagined; whole villages razed to the ground; in what was once was a prosperous village, nothing now remains to show that it was a village, except the church bell thrown on the ditch. I officiated in a ruined church some time ago, 600 present. I am told since that the ruined church is absolutely blotted out with shells.

I was giving Holy Communion a few days ago to a number of chaps near the trenches. I had everything nicely laid out on top of a few shell boxes, and had actually begun to give Holy Communion, when a huge shell landed within ten yards from us. The force of the explosion was terrific. We ourselves got quite a shaking and of course we were covered all over with mud. This is only one little incident. I should be in the other world many a time out here, I am sure, were it not for the prayers of my kin and friends at home and abroad. I shall tell you of the many miraculous escapes I have had when I get my first leave.

The French people we have met here are a very poor specimen. They are of the peasant type and no such thing among them as generosity. I have been refused a cup of water in a French house. But, of course, there is something to be said for them – armies going through their houses every day and asking for their out-houses for sleeping quarters etc. Sanitation in the French villages is awful, and religion in these parts is at a very low ebb – four or five people turn up to Mass out of a possible 400, or so the old cure [priest] told me.

I started this letter a few days ago. This is St Patrick's Eve and you'll be glad to know that I got my shamrock three days ago. I've been writing it in fits and starts according as I was free. Hence, you will not be surprised at the want of logic that prevails. I just write down things in any order as they strike me and

I think will be of interest to you. The scenes from day to day are indescribable. Just think of the following things. Thousands of dead and dying horses here and there mutilated in all shapes and forms; dead and dying men, lying overground for three months. I have buried men in no man's land, who have been there for weeks and months, some there since last November. You find a head here and there – God knows where the rest of the man is. I pulled a chap out of a shell hole a few days ago and in his hand was a pipe and tobacco. He was killed while filling his pipe. Men are killed under all circumstances of time and place, for instance, in their dug-outs, in bed, at breakfast, when sitting down for a bit of food etc.

The German dug-outs are marvellous, some fitted with electric light, telephones etc. I am writing this in what was a German dug-out a few weeks ago. Some of them are about 70 feet under the earth; this one is about 40 feet only.

Another terrible trouble here is the rats, every place lined with them. They follow the ration wagon everywhere. They are a huge size and are as used to us – they walk over you in bed. And now, another word about the progress of the war. It is certainly a war of artillery and artillery will win it and not Peace Conferences. The British artillery is in some respects superior to the Germans, and for the one shell they send over to us, we send back twenty. At times, when the heavy guns begin to work the whole earth shakes for miles around. A fly could hardly live in the earth so intense is the fire. If the British keep on with the output of shells as they have been doing, I feel certain the Germans will have to keep on the move. According as the Germans retreat, they take maps and distances of the roads and dug-outs they have left behind. The result is that they shell all the roads that they think we use and all the crossroads. Of course we do the same, and always with different results. When they think troops are being relieved, or rations going up to the lines, they shell like the very mischief.

Sniping is another part of the gruesome game. Do you know I've been burying chaps for nine days in a bit of a garden, and a German sniper was only about twenty yards from me all the time? He saw me all right, but, seeing me doing my job, saved me. I never saw him, but visited his dug-out after our fellows got him. We too have our snipers, who are every bit as good as the Germans. The best shot in the Gordon Highlanders is an Irish chap. As far as I see we are not by any means near the end of the war, but I am quite confident of the result.

The weather today is very nice after a small frost, but the roads and gardens are something frightful with mud. I haven't seen a blade of grass for ages and of course there is no cultivation of any kind going on here. It is a terrible thing to consider, in our supposed enlightened age of progress and science, that we can't settle our differences in some other way than by shedding so much blood and cutting off the flower of all the nations engaged in this seemingly interminable war. To wake up these fine spring mornings amid the roar and crashing of shells (when we should be all as brothers) is something inconceivable to any ordinary intellect. But when people are abandoned by God then they can blame themselves and so it is at present. Nations for some years have disowned God and now He is leaving them to reflect and scourging them with a war that has been unexampled in the history of the world ... the pity is that it should form part of the scheme of Providence to punish the innocent with the guilty; but it is inevitable and God's ways are not our ways ...

This reads like a sermon, but I am soliloquising as I sit by a few bits of green wood, which I picked myself, trying to make a bit of fire. We do many things of this nature here and thank God to be spared for it.

I have just got the paper from home. I have been astounded at some of the things which I read therein. I am sorry to see that Clare people are contributing to keeping alive the idea that we, Irish people, are unfit for self-government.

I was very glad to see the resolution you put forward in regard to Lloyd George's proposals, re spirits and beer in Ireland. If it were to be enforced it would certainly spell ruin for many thousands in Ireland.

It is now 11.20 St Patrick's Eve (I've had scores of interruptions while consigning these few ideas to paper) and I must finish whether I like it or not as my candle is on the point of winding up a well-spent career. The big guns are roaring just now all round us. You can't possibly keep a light on when they get going properly – all lights are extinguished by the commission. Had I time, I would write you for weeks, but I hope to get ten days leave in the near future, with the help of God, and then I'll be able to say many things that time doesn't now permit me to write.

With all good wishes to self and all family,

Yours very sincerely,

M Moran, CF[35]

Fr Moran's description of the 'scorched earth' policy carried out by the Germans is corroborated by Ernst Junger, a German officer, who described the destruction carried out by the Germans when they made a tactical retreat in 1917. This policy also demoralised the German soldiers:

As far back as the Siegfried Line every village was reduced to rubble, every tree chopped down, every road undermined, every well poisoned, every basement blown up or booby-trapped, every rail rolled up, everything burnable burned; in a word we were turning the country that our enemies would occupy into a wasteland ... the scenes were bad for the men's morale ... utter destruction does more harm than good to the destroyer and dishonours the soldier.[36]

The Weather

Undoubtedly, there was a growing food crisis in the country because of the war and there were fears of another famine. A summary of the weather at Carrigoran for this year, as reported in the *Saturday Record* of 19 January 1918 suggests that it was not conducive to good farming, with a very cold, dry spell in the early growing season up to April, and with exceptionally heavy rain in August and October, during the harvesting season:

> The rainfall of 1917 has been about four inches below the average for this locality, and this has been the first occasion since 1905 in which any notable deficiency has been recorded. But, owing to the unusual distribution of the rainfall, the disadvantages of the shortage have not been felt to any appreciable extent, as it was during the winter, or first four months of the year that the great variation occurred. The rainfall for these four months only amounted to about half of the normal at this time.
>
> Comment on the nature of rainfall during the end of summer and autumn months, would be almost needless, as the deluge of rain during that period will remain an unpleasant recollection for years to come; the rainfall for August being of an almost unprecedented character throughout the country.
>
> [Although the total rainfall for the month of August was recorded at 8.74 inches, this seems to have been concentrated in the middle and latter half of the month, as a report in the *Saturday Record* of 11 August commented favourably on the 'spell of fine weather at Kilkee, which has had the effect of inducing a very large number of visitors to this peerless watering place, and most of the lodges are now in occupation, while all the hotels are crowded. The bathing places about the bay are patronised by hundreds daily, at all hours, and the scene is everywhere gay and animated. The large crowds were entertained nightly with theatricals and concerts, followed by dances in the new Concert Hall.']
>
> It may, however, be of interest to note that December 1916 and the first four months of 1917 furnish a most unusual record of severe and prolonged frosts, as during these months frost was recorded on 97 nights, ranging from one or two degrees, to 17 degrees on different occasions, with 15 degrees of frost recorded on the night of April 1st. In January, frost was registered on 25 nights, and in February on 21 nights. These unusual frosty periods continued with the almost unbroken prevalence of fierce NE and SE winds, bring the winter of 1916-1917 well to the fore amongst record cold winters, and I should say, this might surely be classed as 'one of the old fashioned winters, which many people infer are almost extinct.' The consequences of the very bad weather this year were realised in the winter and spring of 1917 and 1918, because food stocks were lower than normal.

Distress

The war continued to have a huge economic impact in the county. Emigration had almost ceased, and the papers noted that the numbers emigrating in 1916 was the lowest on record. There was a sense of shock when the *Clare Journal* ceased publication on 30 April 1917. The reason given was that there was a scarcity of newsprint. Perhaps sales and revenue were also declining because of the war. But the loss of this venerable newspaper, which was established in 1778, was still a shock and a big loss to journalism in the county. Its sister publication, the *Saturday Record*, also owned by the Knox family, and the *Clare Champion*, owned by the Galvin family, continued to be published. However, the shortage of newsprint meant that the papers were greatly reduced in size, down to four pages by 1918.

Early in the year the *Clare Champion* of 31 March announced that the Food Controller's regulations regarding bread came into operation. 'The new loaf will be of a darker colour and less palatable than the present and must contain not less than 81 per cent flour, with an admixture of rice, barley, maize, oats or beans to 6 per cent, a further 10 per cent is admissible.'

One anonymous correspondent wrote to the *Saturday Record* of 24 November to complain about the high cost of food:

> The Food Controller's Act having fixed a price on all articles of food, I cannot understand how shopkeepers should be permitted to add to these prices with impunity.
>
> A scare about flour took hold of the people last week and to add to the panic, the shopkeepers said "it won't be had at all", and at the same time tacked on 5s. advance on the Food Controller's fixed price. Best tea has been fixed at 4s. in the pound, shopkeepers are now charging 5s and 5s 6d in the lb.
>
> Potatoes had been sold freely at the Miltown market for 5d per stone. The police visited the butter merchants on Monday to see that they did not exceed the Food Controller's price. I wish they visited the shopkeeper. The shopkeeper, ingeniously, to avoid prosecution, put all the account in one item – sugar, tea, etc. It is not easy then to see where the deception comes in.
>
> Any person aggrieved has only to complain to the police. I am sure they will do their duty impartially. No doubt, but the police are more in touch with the shopkeeper than the labourer or farmer.
>
> Yours, Fair Play.

The *Saturday Record* painted a depressing economic picture at the end of 1917, with great scarcity, which was barely raised by the spirit of Christmas:

> The Christmas of 1917 will long be remembered by householders for the difficulties which confronted them in securing their supplies to celebrate the great festival in the time-honoured way.
>
> Every article, whether of luxury or direct necessity, was scarce to be had. Sugar was almost an unknown quantity, tea was to be had with only less difficulty; hams were not to be had at any price, and so the stories of house-keepers go.
>
> Those traders, who were fortunate enough to have normal supplies in these days, were able to do a very fine business, money being evidently, no bar when the required article was to be had. Though the heavy hand of war was over all, the inextinguishable spirit of Christmas, the greatest festival of the Christian world, was still living, and in Ennis, its great traditions were observ-able as fully as possible under depressing conditions.
>
> Christmas morning was bright and clear and the day remained very fine and so did St Stephen's Day, with the exception of a light drizzle in the morning. Large numbers of pleasure seekers travelled to Limerick for the annual holiday fixture, which was one of the most successful yet held over this popular course.
>
> Business in Kilrush was fairly good under the circumstances of the times of stress. On Saturday things were lively and the town had large crowds from the rural districts, but it was nothing like the volume of business done in pre war times. The arrival of a couple of companies of military in the early part of the week caused an agreeable stir. Their reception by the vast bulk of the inhabitants was quite cordial, and there was nothing to complain of their behaviour, as they became quite friendly with the people – officers and men. They passed through after four days stay in Moore Street. The Christmas period was quietly observed.[37]

'Some Gallant Clare Men'

The following Clare officers and soldiers received various distinctions for bravery in the war: Cpl Jack Barrett, from Barnageeha, serving in the French Army, was posthumously awarded the Croix de Guerre for bravery; Sgt John Joe O'Shea of the Royal Munster Fusiliers, from Miltown Malbay, was awarded the DCM; 2nd Lt Burke, of Kilrush received the MC; Capt. R. Hassard Stacpoole of Eden Vale was awarded the MC for 'conspicuous gallantry and devotion to duty'; Pte John Dwan of Scariff, Royal Munster

Fusiliers, received the DCM; Capt. A. Hickey, MD, of the Royal Army Medical Corps, received an MC for distinguished service; Pte Michael Canny of Ennistymon, got a DCM; Sgt P. McKnight, of Killaloe, received a DCM; Dr J. Mescall, Royal Army Medical Corps, received a silver badge for medical services; Sgt C. Kelly, Kildysart, was awarded the DCM; L-Cpl T. McMahon, Royal Munster Fusiliers, got the MSM and the Russian Cross of St George, second class; Pte T. Devers of Kilrush, Royal Munster Fusiliers, received the DCM. (Pte Devers had been sixteen months in France, had been wounded four times, and took part in the Battle of the Somme, and he was one of five brothers serving in the British forces.)[38]

Roll of Honour

Among the Clare officers killed in action that year was Maj. George MacNamara, of the Wiltshire Regiment, who was the third and youngest son of Mr and Mrs H.V. MacNamara, DL, of Ennistymon House. He was born in 1890, entered Sandhurst to pursue a military career and was gazetted as cadet in 1910. He was sent to the front in France in October 1914 and, about a fortnight later, he was severely wounded and invalided home. He was engaged on home service from February 1915 until June 1916. He then went back to the front and joined his old regiment, which he commanded for about two months. He was subsequently posted to a unit of the North Staffordshire Regiment as acting major and second in command when he was killed. The general of his division wrote:

He met his death at the conclusion of a most recent successful enter-prise carried out by the battalion,

KILLED IN ACTION.

The late Lieutenant Daniel Joseph O'Brien, R.M.F., son of Mrs. O'Brien, Clare Abbey, Clarecastle, who was killed in action in Flanders on the 10th inst. The late Lieutenant O'Brien served a term of three months' imprisonment under the Coercion Act, 1902. While not yet 20 years old, he was member of the Clare County Council, Chairman of the Ennis District Council, member of the Committee of Management of the Clare Co. Infirmary and also held the position of clerk to the National Health Insurance Committee.

Obituary notice for Lt Dan O'Brien, found among the Linnane papers.

and for the success of which he was largely instrumental. I deplore exceedingly the loss of this most valuable officer, in whom I had the most complete confidence, and who was loved and respected in his battalion.

Just before he was killed his name was mentioned in the list of those mentioned in the despatches by Field Marshal Sir Douglas Haig.[39]

One well-known Clare victim of the war was Lt Dan O'Brien of Clare Abbey, Clare Castle, who was killed in action at Passchendale in Flanders on 10 November. Inspired by the example of Willie Redmond, MP, he joined as a private in the Royal Irish Regiment, from which he later exchanged for the Royal Munster Fusiliers. He was commissioned as an officer early in the year. Councillor Dan O'Brien was in fact the third member of Ennis Urban District Council to join the forces. Mr John Joe Connolly, a former soldier who had served in the Boer War joined the Royal Irish Rifles in September 1914; and Mr P.E. Kenneally, a former chairman of the council, joined in December 1916.

His regimental officer, Lt Col H.R.A. Ireland, sent a letter of sympathy to his mother:

Dear Mrs O'Brien – it is my painful duty to inform you of the news of the death of your son, Daniel O'Brien. He was killed in action fighting at the head of his men at about 7 a.m. on 10th November. He was seen to have conducted himself with the greatest gallantry throughout the action, and when he was killed he was at our furthest objective. He was shot dead and suffered no pain. The regiment and myself feel the loss of a brave officer ...

Another officer, Lt Corry O'Callaghan of the 2nd Battalion, Royal Munsters Fusiliers, also wrote to Mrs O'Brien:

... He died a very gallant death, leading his men and encouraging them on. No soldier could wish for a better death. I have known Dan well since he joined this battalion, as we were in the same company, and he was a universal favourite with his brother officers and with the men. We have suffered very heavy casualties amongst officers and those of us who are still with the battalion will always cherish the memory of those grand lads who have fallen ...

Tributes to Lt Dan O' Brien were published in the local newspapers.

Dan O'Brien was well known in the public life of County Clare. He was a member of the Ennis Rural District Council and a member of Clare County Council for a number of years. He first came to prominence in the county as a 19-year-old in 1902, when he was one of eleven 'respectable farmers' from

Clare Castle incarcerated for three months over an alleged 'conspiracy to intimidate' following the formation of a branch of the United Irish League at Clare Castle. He was for some years a member of the magisterial bench in Clare, and was a member of the management committee of the Clare County Infirmary. Mr G. McElroy, RM, wrote of him that as a magistrate 'he was particularly sympathetic towards the working men in his district ... the only fault, if that was a fault, it inclined to the side of virtue with him, was that he was too inclined to leniency.' Mr P.J. Linnane, JP, said: 'He was always sympathetic to the working man and was always fair in his judgements at the petty [court] sessions.' At a special meeting of the Clare Castle Land and Labour Association, the chairman, Mr Edward Russell, spoke 'in feeling terms of the late Mr Dan O'Brien and of the good he did for the labourers, not only of Clare Castle, but of the whole county'.[40]

Another Clareman who died in France and achieved distinction this year was John (Jack) Joseph Barrett, who was born in 1890. Jack Barrett was a member of the Barrett family from Barnageeha, in the parish of Clare Castle and Ballyea, members of whom were prominent in Sinn Féin and in the War of Independence. Indeed, his brother Frank Barrett was commandant of the Mid-Clare Brigade of the IRA during the War of Independence and the Civil War. Perhaps because of his family's political allegiances, Jack Barrett, a railway official, did not join the British Army. Instead, he joined the French Foreign Legion on 10 September 1914 and, after training, was sent to Morocco. In September 1915 he transferred to the First Foreign Regiment and was promoted to the rank of corporal. He was sent to the Western Front on 18 November 1915 and was killed on 20 April 1917 at Auberive in the Marne. He was advancing at the head of his squad of riflemen during an assault on a heavily defended trench when he was killed. For his heroic actions, Cpl Jack Barrett was posthumously awarded the Croix de Guerre, with Silver Star.[41]

The death of the prominent Kilrush businessman, Mr H.R. Glynn, DL, a member of Clare County Council also took place around this time. After his death a resolution was passed in December 1917, calling for the co-option of his brother Mr C.E. Glynn, the recruiting officer for West Clare, to fill the vacancy and called upon all other candidates to withdraw their names. However, despite this resolution, Mr Glynn was defeated by Mr Denis McInerney of Kildysart, who was opposed to recruitment. His defeat was another indication of the rise of Sinn Féin and of the decline of the Home Rule party.[42]

An editorial in the *Clare Champion* at the end of the year reflected the growing disillusionment with the war and highlighted the profound political changes which had taken place in Ireland during this year, with the decline of the Home Rule Party and the rise of Sinn Féin following the death of Willie Redmond, MP, and the election of de Valera as MP for East Clare:

The year 1917 is drawing to a close. The history books will record it as a memorable one in Irish history. Not even the World War, of which the world has grown wearily tired, will overshadow the great happenings which have taken place in Ireland. For the first time in the history of their subjection, the Irish people have cast off their shackles and demand the freedom of the Gael.[43]

This year a total of at least 113 Clare people died because of the Great War, mainly on the Western Front, though some died in Mesopotamia and Salonika, while ten were lost at sea. Among those who drowned were three sailors from Clare Castle, A. Considine, R. Cole and J. McMahon, along with the captain, William McCready, who was married to a woman from Clare Castle, Delia Murphy, besides eight others aboard the merchant ship SS *Keeper*, carrying grain for Bannatyne's of Limerick, which was sunk by a German submarine off the coast of Antrim on 10 June 1917.[44]

A Soldier's Grave

Then in the lull of midnight, gentle arms
Lifted him slowly down the slopes of death
Lest he should hear again the mad alarms
Of battle, dying moans, and painful breath.

And where the earth was soft for flowers we made
A grave for him that he might better rest,
So spring shall come and leave it seet arrayed
And there the lark shall turn her dewy nest.

Francis Ledwidge

6

FROM CONSCRIPTION CRISIS TO ARMISTICE

'England has no moral right to introduce conscription in Ireland.'

Dr Fogarty

The shortage of voluntary recruits for the war, combined with a massive German onslaught on the Western Front, following the collapse of Russia in 1917, persuaded Lloyd George and the British Government to pass a Bill introducing conscription into Ireland. This, of course, was fiercely resisted by almost all sectors of society in Ireland, and Clare was no exception, uniting Home Rulers and Sinn Féiners, farmers, trade unionists and the Catholic Church in a mass campaign to resist any attempt to impose conscription. There was a general fear of another famine in Clare and many poor people were in great distress due to the high price of food and fuel. Sinn Féin became more active in the county and law and order was breaking down, with cattle drives and the ploughing up of fields on the large ranches. Clare was again put under martial law. The sinking of the mail boat, MV *Leinster* had a significant impact on the people of County Clare. The war finally ended in November of that year and a general election was held three weeks later, which ended in a success for Sinn Féin at the expense of the Home Rule Party, which was almost wiped out nationally. The weather was appalling in September, with adverse affects on the harvest. Finally, the dreadful 'Spanish Flu' epidemic affected the county towards the end of the year, resulting in many deaths. The Roll of Honour increased again this year, mainly due to the final German onslaught, which lasted from March until it petered out in July 1918.

In January Bishop Fogarty became totally opposed to the war and to conscription, and seemed to have been infected with socialist philosophy when he declared 'Not one of these young Irishmen will fire a shot under compulsion in this war of plutocrats!' Two months later he issued his Lenten pastoral prophesising a whole new order of society after the war ended:

> We are now living in days of transition ... Great empires are being dissolved ... political institutions are undergoing daily dissolution and principles are universally avowed, which if they run their course, must completely change and re-arrange the face of Europe and European society ... What the ultimate fate will be only God knows. That is God's secret, whose all-powerful hand is now shaking the world to the centre. But there can be little doubt that a whole new order of things awaits mankind, when the war has finished the work of destruction.[1]

At the end of January Dr Fogarty became more outspoken on the national issue and became more supportive of the Sinn Féin policies. He sent a letter to Mr E.E. Lysaght of Raheen, Tuamgraney, who had just resigned in protest from the National Convention at the lack of progress on the issue of Home Rule. The bishop also condemned the proposals at the convention:

> Can it be possible that they are contemplating above the heads of the people, another tragedy for Ireland in the shape of a sham Home Rule?
>
> Any form of Irish Government short of the authority sketched in your letter, will not satisfy Ireland, or bring peace to this country and would only intensify our present confusion. A country without control of its own trade would be like the Irish farmer in the past who could not get his daughter married without his landlord's permission.
>
> If the great advocate of 'self-determination' for all nationalities of the world has nothing for Ireland but feudal slavery of that kind, then he [Lloyd George] had better leave the Irish deputation at home. The country is sick of all of this huxtering when the path of national interests is so very clear to every honest mind.[2]

Fear of Famine

A New Tillage Order was issued by the Department of Agriculture and Technical Instruction, Dublin in February.[3] The phrase at the end of the advertisement stating 'bad weather may be ahead' unfortunately turned out to be an accurate prediction of what was to come in 1918. As we have seen, the weather of 1917 was very poor from an agricultural point of view, with unseasonably low rainfall and severe frosts in the early part of the year, followed by a deluge of rainfall during the summer and autumn, the peak harvesting season for hay, cereals and potatoes. Besides this, the German submarines were still sinking British merchant ships, trying to starve Britain into submission. Naturally, the harvests were poor and consequently food became scarcer and dearer. The bad weather, combined with bad harvests and scarcity of food may have contributed to the agrarian agitation of cattle driving and illegal ploughing in the springtime. There was, it seems, a genuine fear of famine in Ireland at the time.

However, the farmers could not anticipate, control or predict the weather for the year ahead. They could only hope and pray for the best as they prepared for the spring sowing. The *Saturday Record* of 23 February published an appeal from Cardinal Logue, Catholic Primate of Ireland, to farmers to cultivate every possible acre of land: 'we know from experience that, by a more extensive and careful tillage, we can not only produce food abundantly, to support our own people, but have a large surplus for export. Hence, in the season upon which we have entered, an effort should be made to cultivate every acre. It is our only security against want.' The Bishop of Kilmore also issued an appeal to farmers: 'the remedy against famine is in our own hands, for the country can pro-

duce more than enough to support ourselves, and I earnestly exhort the people to plant and sow the greatest amount of food crops they possibly can'.[4]

A NEW TILLAGE ORDER AND AN APPEAL

Extra 5 per cent on the larger holdings, full 15 per cent required of all others.

The Department have decided in view of the extreme need for further food production, to issue an Order, requiring an extra quantity of tillage on holdings of 200 arable acres and upwards. The extra quantity to be 5 per cent in addition to the 15 per cent over 1916 already required by the existing Order – or a total of 20 per cent on these holdings.

"Reasonable Effort" this year will not be enough. The full percentage will be required of everybody. Moreover, so urgent has become the need for more food that the Department appeal both to the occupiers of the larger holdings and to all others, down to the smallest cultivators, to till as much as possible over the amount actually required by the Tillage Order as bad weather may be ahead.

To accompany this great task not a day should be lost. The plough should be kept going every fine hour. Bad weather may be ahead.

Saturday Record, 9 February 1918.

Cattle Drives

Respect for law and order deteriorated rapidly in the early months of the year as cattle drives and other forms of agricultural agitation became widespread,

reminiscent of the Land War. It is significant that the agrarian agitation and outrages usually took place in the early part of the year before new lettings would
commence in March and before the growing season would begin in the spring.
Besides the land agitation the Irish Volunteers became more active and bolder in
parading and raiding for arms and attacking policemen. The county was becoming ungovernable as the security resources of the RIC were inadequate and
seemed powerless to deal with the widespread political and agrarian agitation.

There were cattle drives in East Clare at places such as O'Callaghan's Mills,
Feakle, Tulla and Broadford during February. There were also drives at Doolin,
the property of H.V. MacNamara, JP, DL, of Ennistymon. Here a crowd of
between 200 and 300 ploughed up the land 'without the slightest opposition from the police'. Lands were ploughed at Lemanagh, the property of
Lord Inchiquin, of Dromoland. More land was ploughed up at Ballymangan,
about 5 miles from Ennis on the estate of Mr Thomas Crowe, DL. A cattle
drive took place at Caherphuca, Crusheen. Cattle were driven off the lands
near New Quay belonging to Mr W.J. Corbett, JP, of Willbrook, along with
cattle on the lands of Mr P.L.K. Dobbin at Kilkishen, who had to move to
Kilkee for safety, as he was threatened and told, 'his lands were required by land-
less people'. At Caher in East Clare a large crowd drove the stock belonging to
Mrs O'Dwyer off her lands. This estate was the scene of evictions about twenty
years earlier. After the drive, negotiations took place with Mrs O'Dwyer, who
agreed to give certain lands to small farmers after 1 April.

Another significant cattle drive took place at Kilgorey. This farm, belonging to
Dr Sampson, JP, of Moynoe House, Scariff, had been the scene of several cattle
drives. On Wednesday 6 February a huge crowd of between 700 and 800 people
gathered at the farm and drove the stock off the land to his house in Scariff.
On the road to Scariff a party of between twelve and fourteen policemen were
met and the police were overpowered by the mob. Some of their bicycles were
smashed and their overcoats slashed. Later another group of three policemen
were assaulted and badly beaten and rifles were taken from two of them before
the third policeman fired a shot at the crowd, who dispersed. Near Killaloe
two more policemen were assaulted and their rifles taken. Trees had been felled
at Scariff to delay the police and another shot was fired by a police sergeant.
The telegraph wires to Tulla and Ennis were cut as well, and trees were felled to
block the roads and impede the movements of police and army. Trees were also
cut down on the Ennis to Kildysart road near Cragbrien and at New Hall.

There were 'exciting scenes' at Ennis following court cases where some men
from East Clare were found guilty of agrarian crime and sentenced to prison.
A huge escort of police, more than 100 strong, brought the prisoners to the Ennis
railway station for transport to Limerick Jail. The police were jeered at by a huge
crowd who cried 'how, how' (cattle drover's cries) at the police, who were also

pelted with stones. Later that evening the police cleared O'Connell Square and adjoining streets by a baton charge. Two days later, on Sunday, the town of Ennis was the scene of much police activity as more than 100 RIC men patrolled the streets on foot, on bicycles, sidecars and motor cars. They watched a farm on the Clare Road where a cattle drive was rumoured. Another large body of police were vigilant on farms north of the town. Meanwhile, a body of young men visited a farm at Claureen and drove some cattle off the land. After this they marched triumphantly through the town.[5]

At Toureen, Barefield, the proposed letting of some lands on conacre was interrupted when a crowd of more than 300 people assembled at the farm and interrupted proceedings. Printed notices of the letting were torn down. The property was registered as belonging to Dr Sampson of Scariff, but two young men called O'Neill from Miltown Malbay claimed ownership of the lands due to their relationship with the late Mr Francis Hynes, of Toureen, who was controversially hanged for murder in a celebrated case during the Land War. Fr Crowe, CC, acted as spokesman for the people and told the Department of Agriculture inspector, Mr Dorgan, 'that no bids would be made for the farm'. A large force of policemen arrived, but there were no disturbances. The letting of the farm did not proceed on this occasion.[6]

Memories of another more recent land dispute at Derrymore near Ennistymon were revived when two policemen, Constables Sullivan and Dennehy, who were guarding a family named Marrinan at a police hut in Derrymore were fired upon and wounded. The Marrinan family were Crown witnesses at the trial of two men, named Ryan and Hegarty, who were charged with the murder of a man named John Kildea, who was shot dead at the threshold of the Marrinan house in 1914. However, the jury disagreed on three occasions, once in Dublin and twice in Cork, and the two accused men were subsequently sent by the Crown to America.

On Sunday 24 February Michael Marrinan went to Mass as usual at Ennistymon and was accompanied by his two police escorts. After Mass the party was attacked by a gang of six masked men at as they were cycling up a steep hill about a mile-and-a-half from Ennistymon. The men shouted 'hands up' and demanded the weapons, at the same time knocking the policemen down. Some revolver shots were fired at the policemen and both constables were injured, Sullivan in the arm and Dennehy in the thigh. The masked men then cut the straps of the rifles, which were strung across their backs and seized them.[7]

Clearly, the motive for this attack was political, the acquisition of weapons, and not agrarian. This, from a police point of view, was more worrying as the Irish Volunteers were clearly behind this attack.

On the same day another cattle drive took place at Clare Castle on the McInerney farm at Manusmore. More than 200 acres of the farmland had been advertised for grazing in February on conacre in eleven divisions. A crowd of more than 300 men, one of whom was in a Volunteer uniform, drove 104 cattle and twenty-five sheep from the farm, which had been let on conacre (rented for eleven months), by Mrs McInerney, who was recently widowed. Three policemen were present but were unable to prevent the cattle drive. The cattle were then driven towards Castlefergus, where there was a temporary police barrack with three constables. When they were near the barrack, according to the police report, someone in the crowd allegedly shouted, 'Close in and kill them and take the barrack!' The RIC men after firing some warning shots into the air over the crowd then fired into the crowd and wounded three men, John Ryan, Pat O'Neill and James Liddy. After the shooting the crowd scattered. A large force of police arrived later, accompanied by a party of soldiers. The people denied that any such cry 'to kill the police' was made. Unfortunately, Mr John Ryan died from his wounds five days later.

Jim Reilly was a member of Sinn Féin and the IRA, who was then living in Clare Castle. He was one of six men arrested for the cattle drive at Manusmore. When they were arrested, they left the courthouse singing 'A Soldier's Song'. After four months in jail they were released without charge. Jim recalled that the motivation for the cattle drive was 'that the people were in dread of a famine and that they went to the people with land and asked them to till the land and grow vegetables'. He said 'that Captain Blood [of Ballykilty Manor, Quin] refused and all his cattle were driven off '. He also said that Sinn Féin organised a potato market in Ennis.

Jim Reilly's recollections, recorded more than fifty-nine years after the event, are significant as they suggest that the cattle drive was motivated for honourable reasons and that Capt. Blood had leased the lands at Manusmore. That explains why the cattle and sheep were being driven towards Castlefergus, which is on the road to Ballykilty Manor (Captain Blood's home). Jim also stated that the Sinn Féin club, which was below the main gate of Sutton's Coal Yard in Clare Castle, was visited by a party of Scotch Borderers, who wrecked the building and took away the roll book. Jim's reminiscences about the raid on the Sinn Féin club are corroborated by an article in the *Saturday Record* of 5 January, 1918, which states:

> On Christmas Night the premises occupied by the Sinn Féin club at Clare Castle were broken into at midnight and some tables and chairs taken away and flung into the river. The police are making enquiries, but there is no clue to the perpetrators of the act, which is condemned by the local followers of the Irish Party.

The paper also recorded in a separate article that 'a claim had been lodged with the secretary to Clare County Council by Mr James Reilly of Clare Castle, for damage done to his windows and dwelling house there a few nights ago.'

Incidentally, Jim Reilly's memory of a Scottish Regiment being in the district at the time was correct as the *Saturday Record* of 5 January 1918 also included the following:

> On December 26th the NCOs and men of the Scottish Rifles stationed at Ennis were entertained under the auspices of the YMCA at Harmony Row Ennis. After supper, various amusements were indulged in, including an impromptu concert in which some distinguished amateurs took part. The guests expressed their thorough appreciation and the singing of the National Anthem, ('God save the King'), brought a very enjoyable evening to a close.[8]

There is some evidence that some Sinn Féin members had orchestrated the cattle drive at Manusmore on Sunday 24 February for political purposes, as the *Clare Champion* of 19 January 1918 reported that a meeting of the Clare Castle Sinn Féin Club took place on Sunday 13 January, which was chaired by Fr Marcus McGrath, CC. At that meeting two members raised 'a matter of extreme public importance in connection with the grazing of lands on the eleven month's system in the Clare Castle district'. The 'matter of extreme public importance' may have arisen after an advertisement appeared in the *Clare Champion* of 12 January 1918, offering the sale of grazing at Manusmore in ten lots averaging 18.5 acres each for eleven months. After some considerable discussion it was decided to call a general meeting of the members for Sunday, 20 January 'to enter fully into the matter and consider what action may be taken … in this vital question'.

It is not clear whether all of these outrages were orchestrated by some central body or were spontaneous. Michael Brennan in his memoir of 1980 states: 'During the middle of January 1918 there was much agrarian discontent in Clare and we decided to cash in on it, Volunteers took part as organised units. They also prevented woods being cut down as props for trenches in France'.[9] There was, it seems, a significant link between the agricultural outrages and political agitation fomented by the Irish Volunteers. In several instances, as suggested by witness statements in court cases, the outrages took place under the auspices of the local Volunteers, though this may not have been sanctioned by HQ. In fact the following notice was published in the *Clare Champion* of 9 February:

> To the Irish Volunteers
> County Clare
> The laws of the Constitution of the Irish Volunteer Organisation do not permit of the use of our forces in Cattle-Driving. Commanders of every rank will note.
> P. Brennan G.O.C.
> Irish Volunteers
> Co. Clare

One woman, Mrs Kenneally of Calluragh, Ennistymon sued for damages of £70 for the malicious burning of a hayrick containing 7 tons of hay. Mrs Kenneally said that she 'was told by a respectable farmer's wife from Kilfenora that it was alleged in the district that she sold her hay to Mr H.V. MacNamara, DL, of Ennistymon House [a landlord and a controversial unionist] who had bought her hay for the British Army.' Mrs Kenneally denied this allegation.

In another court case in north Clare, several young men were charged with illegally ploughing lands on Mr H.V. MacNamara's lands at Killilagh. Sgt Cadogan testified in court that one man named Stephen Hillery was among the illegal party. 'Mr Hillery denied the right of the court to try him and said that he was a soldier of the Irish Republic'. Sgt Cadogan stated that he had earlier seen Mr Hillery drilling about forty other young men at Toomullen. He challenged Mr Hillery who declared that 'he was willing to die for his country'. Sgt Cadogan testified that on 26 February he saw over 500 men assemble on Mr MacNamara's lands at Killilagh. They had fifteen double ploughs, spades and sticks. They were headed by a band and carried republican flags. Mr Hillery was seen ploughing by Sgt Cadogan and was sentenced to two months imprisonment with hard labour, fined £20 and bound to the peace for twelve months. This was clearly a blatant public demonstration harnessing the political and agrarian agitation by illegally ploughing in broad daylight.

The Clare Sinn Féin executive committee met at Newmarket-on-Fergus on Sunday 3 March and issued a directive to the local *cumainn* on the 'land question'. The executive committee recognised that 'owing to the large monopolies and trusts of land, the vast prairies that raise but cattle and sheep, the utter neglect of the ranchers to till and produce food, and the seeming unwillingness of the Department to enforce the proper percentage of tillage, there exists amongst the labourers and small landholders, disquiet, distrust and anxiety. Men of all shades of political thought are affected and have joined together to end this unproductiveness of so much land'. However, the executive committee became aware that some cattle drives 'were indefensible and were not in accordance with the moral law.'

It would seem that the phrase, 'not in accordance with the moral law', reflected the influence of the Catholic clergy on Sinn Féin at this time. For instance at the meeting of the East Clare Sinn Féin Executive on Wednesday 24 January, at Ennis, a total of forty-nine delegates attended, representing thirty-two clubs in the district. Among these were seven clergymen: Fr O'Kennedy, president of St Flannan's College; Fr Crowe, Barefield; Fr Marcus McGrath, Clare Castle; Fr Neylon, Crusheen; Fr Roche, Inch; Fr Hewitt, Oatfield and Cratloe; and Fr Flynn, Kilmore. The Catholic clergy would have had a significant moderating influence upon the deliberations of the delegates.

In an attempt to control the activities and to prevent actions that might bring Sinn Féin into disrepute, the executive committee directed members of Sinn Féin clubs to take no action on the question of land, without having previously submitted their line of action to the Comhairle Ceanntair.[10]

There was also a genuine fear of famine in Ireland at the time. A *Clare Champion* editorial of 19 January reported that when the price of potatoes was twelve pence a stone and the price of turf was one penny a sod, members of Sinn Féin set up a potato market in Ennis and sold them at six pence a stone and took measures to provide cheap turf for the poor. On Thursday 17 January potatoes were purchased from more than 200 farmers and more than 550 stones of potatoes were distributed among the poor. They even distributed the potatoes to the 'separation women', though some Sinn Féin members protested at this. The potatoes were sent in to Ennis by the people of Newmarket-on-Fergus, Barefield, Carrahan and Doora. The Sinn Féin members also distributed cheap turf among the poor.

At the meeting of the East Clare Chomairle Cheanntair of Sinn Féin in Ennis on 16 January, Revd William O'Kennedy of St Flannan's College stated that they had fed more than 200 families in Ennis. He said that they had been doing it since before Christmas at a time of critical need in Clare. He said, 'A lot of big people in the county were fond of calling upon the workers and labourers in fine language, in tones of high patriotism to lay down their lives for John Bull. Within the past month one of those most prominent in recruitment work, a large farmer in a neighbouring parish, sent his potatoes over to feed John Bull and had them guarded by nine policemen between his house and the railway station! Since that event happened the poor people of Clare Castle had been canvassing the Ennis Food Committee to be given potatoes'. Other speakers, including Fr Hewitt, CC, and Fr Crowe, CC, called for measures to avert a famine. Mr Molony mentioned a case in Newmarket-on-Fergus where an attempt to send potatoes out of the country was stopped by the people.

In a letter to the *Clare Champion* of 2 September entitled, 'A plea on behalf of the poor', Mr F.J. McNamara of Sixmilebridge, stated that bacon, 'the poor person's meat', could not be purchased in any town or village of Clare for less than 2s a pound, which was way beyond the means of the poor families. Mr McNamara suggested that a co-operative scheme, similar to the potato scheme organised by Sinn Féin could bring down the price to 1s 3d per pound.

Besides the agrarian activities of cattle driving and illegal ploughing the Irish Volunteers became more active at this time. While the rural areas were being convulsed by illegal activities, one of the leading republican activists in the county, Michael Brennan of Meelick, was busy organising parades and meetings around the county. After a baton charge on Sunday 24 February, Michael Brennan led the Ennis Volunteers on a parade through the town of Ennis on the following

Tuesday night. About 200 Volunteers in military uniforms marched through the principal streets of Ennis in a military procession. At O'Connell Square they were addressed by 'Commandant' Michael Brennan, who called upon the Volunteers to continue their nightly parades. In the speech he was heard to say that 'they could only die once, and they could not die in a better cause!'

The next day, Michael Brennan, wearing the Volunteer uniform, was arrested at Ennis railway station, after getting off the train from West Clare. Mr Brennan was taken under heavy military escort to the Ennis RIC barracks as troops lined the streets of the town. He went on hunger strike the next morning, one of the first republicans in Ireland to use this powerful weapon.

That evening the Ennis Volunteers did not parade in Ennis as members of the local constabulary had warned the people during the day to keep off the streets at night because of the military curfew under Martial Law. The founder and deputy leader of Sinn Féin, Arthur Griffith, was due to hold a public meeting in Ennis Town Hall that evening, but the meeting was cancelled as the military had commandeered the building and the meeting was banned.[11]

Martial Law

As a result of all these mass movements and illegal activities, whether motivated by political or agricultural agitation, the British authorities introduced martial law in the county, as by the end of February much of the county had become virtually ungovernable. The following communiqué issued by the commander-in-chief of the British Army in Ireland was issued on Tuesday evening 26 February:

THE OUTBREAK OF LAWLESSNESS WHICH HAS OCCURRED IN COUNTY CLARE RENDERED IT NECESSARY ON SUNDAY TO SEND ADDITIONAL TROOPS INTO THE COUNTY TO ASSIST THE POLICE. THE COUNTY HAS BEEN DECLARED A SPECIAL MILITARY AREA, WITHIN THE MEANING OF THE REALM REGULATION 29B, AND ALL THE POWERS HEREBY CONFERRED ON THE COMMANDANT WILL BE ENFORCED SO LONG AS IT IS NECESSARY FOR THE RESTORATION OF ORDER.

Maj. Gen. Burnett, the new Competent Military Authority in Clare, issued an Order proclaiming 'Special Measures' for the preservation of law and order in Clare. Restrictions were placed on entry into the county and movements within the county. Drilling and wearing of uniforms was prohibited, along with all meetings, assemblies and processions. Censorship was established over written and printed matter. Another Order directed the closing of all licensed premises save between 9 a.m. and 8 p.m. in areas within one and a half miles radius of Scariff Post Office and within a similar radius of the post offices of Bodyke and Tuamgraney. All persons are also required to be within doors from 9 p.m. to 6 a.m. within the same areas, except those having permits.[12]

Besides the introduction of martial law, a huge burden of compensation claims was charged to the county rates. Compensation was sought for a variety of offences including, cattle being driven off the lands and going missing and being maimed, tree felling, ploughing up land, knocking down of walls, breaking windows, cutting telegraph wires, burning hay, destruction of policemen's bicycles and theft of valuables such as watches. The total claims by the end of February amounted to almost £9,500.[13]

DAY PASSES

To enter County Clare will be issued to persons desiring to enter the county, by the Military Commandant, Courthouse, Ennis. All applications to be made through the local police.

Official hours in COURTHOUSE

WEEK DAYS

9.30 am to 12.30 pm

2.30 pm to 4 pm

6 pm to 7 pm.

SUNDAYS

10.30 am to 12.30 pm

LOCAL PASSES:

To residents in the county will be issued by the District Inspector of the district where the person resides.[12]

Saturday Record, 3 March 1918.

The Conscription Crisis

Meanwhile, the ceasefire on the Eastern Front caused by the Bolshevik revolution in Russia during 1917, followed by the Treaty of Brest Litovsk in March 1918, which took communist Russia out of the war, gave an opportunity to the German High Command to concentrate almost all of their forces on the Western Front. They made one last desperate effort to win the war before large numbers of American troops began to pour into France. This massive German onslaught necessitated a huge demand for more Allied soldiers. Consequently, the British Government decided to introduce conscription into Ireland.

Naturally, this policy united almost all the people of Ireland, except the unionists, to vehemently oppose the new Bill. In April a mass petition opposing conscription was signed all over the country, including County Clare. The Catholic bishops of Ireland issued an anti-conscription pledge, which was drafted by Dr O'Dea, Bishop of Galway and seven others, 'To enforce conscription would be perfectly unwarrantable, with all the responsibility that attaches to our pastoral office, we feel bound to warn the government against entering upon a policy so disastrous to the public interest and to all order, public and private'. Because of martial law, banning public meetings, the anti-conscription pledge was signed in churches all over the county. In an impressive ceremony at the crowded cathedral in Ennis, Dr Fogarty was the first to sign the pledge after denouncing the policy of conscription in a passionate speech after Mass:

> Not since the foundation of this building had such a large congregation assembled within its walls and never did the people assemble in the church with such terrible issues before them. Ireland was now faced with one of the most unlawful and brutal exercises of tyranny known to history ... It was assumed that they were a nation of slaves and to have no voice in the disposal of their own lives ... This Act was oppressive and unjust and they called on the people to resist it by every means at their disposal ... If the people stood behind their leaders and behind Labour, no power on earth could conscript the people ... Should they attempt to enforce it, it would be the right of the people to resist ... They had their bishops, priests and a country united as it never was before, standing together under God against this most horrible, inhuman and atrocious act of tyranny, and whatsoever befell them in the struggle, let them bow their heads before God and face it like men and with unflinching hearts.

Dr Fogarty also thanked the labour leaders and trade unionists in Dublin for passing a resolution in favour of a national general strike on Tuesday 23 April. He also sent a letter to the Ennis Sinn Féin club in which he declared that 'England had no moral right to enforce conscription'.

Anti-conscription pledge:

> Denying the right of the British Government to enforce compulsory conscription in this country, we pledge ourselves solemnly to one another to resist conscription by the most effective means at our disposal.

After Bishop Fogarty signed, he was followed by seven other priests, including three Franciscan friars and Fr W. O'Kennedy, President of St Flannan's College. Then the adult male parishioners in the cathedral signed the solemn pledge.[14]

Conscription was also denounced by local councils such as Kilrush, Ennis, Tulla and Clare County Council. One peace commissioner, Mr Hugh Hennessy of Lissycasey, resigned his commission as a magistrate in protest against the proposed introduction of conscription into Ireland.

The national protest strike against conscription, organised by the Irish Council of Trade Unions, was well observed in Ennis on Tuesday 23 April, two days after the pledge was signed throughout the country.

All the business establishments, without exception, were closed and all the public offices, with the exception of the banks and Ennis Post Office, were also shut for the day. There was no public demonstration on the day due to the ban on parades and meetings because of martial law. Owing to the stoppage of the trains at midnight on Monday, no papers or mails arrived in Ennis, and except for telegraphic communications, Ennis was cut off from the world.

Col Arthur Lynch, MP, arrived in Clare in April and gave an interview to the *Clare Journal* in which he also denounced conscription, 'It was important in this great crisis of national affairs for all members of the Home Rule Party to show themselves solid with the people … The country is more unanimous than it has been for a great number of years.' He advised against any precipitate actions which might play into the hands of their enemies. He also cautioned against offending the Americans, 'the great trump card of the Irish people'. 'America', he said, 'would support Ireland in all her just and reasonable claims and it behoves us … to avoid doing anything that shows unfriendliness to America, or opposition to her actions in the war … '. Finally, he warned against rushing into any ill-considered acts of rebellion, which in the circumstances 'would be utterly hopeless …'[15]

Dr Fogarty, who seemed to be taking up the nationalist mantle of the late Bishop O'Dwyer, published a letter in the *Freeman's Journal* denouncing conscription. His tone became more militant. He wrote, 'the people are entitled to resist it, what form that resistance is to take in order to be effective is for the nation in its wisdom to decide.' He also wrote a letter to the Ennis Sinn Féin Club on 5 April condemning conscription. This letter was widely circulated in pamphlet form. Bishop Fogarty also gave a powerful concluding sermon at the golden jubilee of the Limerick Confraternity in June, denouncing conscription and condemning the war before a congregation attended by nine bishops and over 7,000 people:

> The war had taught a terrible lesson … it has been carried out with a horrible and shocking brutality … one of the greatest curses of modern European life is what we know as conscription … An attempt was made to foist this blood-stained horror on our country against its will … but she confronted this horrible thing with a heart of Christian fortitude, determined to die rather than submit to this tyranny.[16]

However, while the majority of Irish nationalists supported the anti-conscription campaign, a few loyalists and others were opposed to it. It took a brave and perhaps foolhardy person to publicly oppose the general consensus in the county. A police report for County Clare stated that 'nobody publicly supports the conscription proposal, as the scattered loyalists, while ready to submit to it themselves, can hardly be expected to make themselves unpopular by advocating it publicly. Fr Maguire, PP of Flagmount near Lough Graney, County Clare was rash enough to denounce the signing of the anti-conscription covenant on 21 April, so an attempt, fortuitously, unsuccessful, was made to burn the church three days later'.[17]

Cumann na mBan

The women of Clare also played a role in the anti-conscription campaign. A special day, the feast of St Columbcille, was set apart to give the women of Ireland an opportunity to demonstrate their opposition to conscription by signing an anti-conscription pledge. Because of Martial Law the meetings had to be conducted under the guise of religious gatherings, which were most useful for this political purpose, when Church and nation were united in a common cause.

The women of Ennis and district turned out in large numbers. They assembled at the cathedral at 1 p.m. after Mass and from there a procession was marshalled by the leading members of the Ennis Cumann na mBan under Mrs Roughan and Miss Begley. Led by the cathedral altar boys carrying a large crucifix, they marched through the main streets to the Franciscan church. The members of the Women's Sodality were in their own sections with separate banners. The women sang hymns and recited prayers. At the Franciscan church they offered prayers for the purpose of their procession and the women then returned to the cathedral for solemn Benediction of the Most Holy Sacrament by V. Revd Fr Hogan, Administrator.

There was also a large demonstration by the women of Miltown Malbay. After Mass, the women from all the surrounding districts marched in procession following a large green flag. They walked to St Joseph's Holy Well about a mile away. They sang sacred songs as they marched through the streets. The women were accompanied by two priests, Fr Enright, CC, and Fr Lalor, CC. At the holy well the rosary was recited, followed by the prayer of St Joseph and by the singing of hymns. On the return journey through the town of Miltown Malbay the women sang 'A Soldier's Song'.

In addition to their opposition to conscription, young women were also discouraged by members of Sinn Féin from courting British soldiers. One Ennis man, Paddy Reidy, a member of the Sinn Féin Club, was fined 21*s* at the Ennis Petty Sessions in January for assaulting his sixteen-year-old sister, who had been going out with a member of the Welsh Fusiliers. When he found her in College Road with a soldier he, allegedly, slapped her and knocked her to the ground.

Katie and Peg Barrett of Cragbrien, Mid-Clare Brigade Cumann na mBan.
(Courtesy of Peadar McNamara collection, per Prof. David Fitzpatrick)

Fr O'Kennedy, president of the Sinn Féin Club in Ennis, publicly denounced at a Sinn Féin meeting the 'savage' sentence imposed by the RM, Mr McElroy:

She was a slip of a thing, sixteen and a half years old. She had got out of her mother's control and, like too many Ennis girls, got a craze for running after soldiers. On one occasion he snatched her from the company of a Welsh Fusilier. Several times he followed her to the Watery Road and the College Road, where he found her in the company of other women, who were evidently not out for recreation.

He said that the 'Irishman loves the purity of the Irish woman'. He stressed that Paddy Reidy would not pay the fine for 'protecting the morals of his sister from becoming the playthings of Welshmen and Scotchmen and that he would go to Limerick Jail for a month to herd with criminals of every kind rather than pay the fine'.[18]

"ENGLAND HAS NO MORAL RIGHT TO ENFORCE CONSCRIPTION"
His Lordship Most Rev. Dr. Fogarty, Lord Bishop of Killaloe, has addressed the following letter to the Ennis Sinn Féin Club:

Ennis, 5 April 1918
Dear Mr Guinane,
I must thank you and the Sinn Féin Executive for the resolutions you have sent me, and which I highly value.

Sinn Féin needs no vindication from me or anyone else. We had almost ceased to be Irish until Sinn Féin arose and struck the English rust from the soul of Ireland. Unfortunately, that rust had eaten deep, and spoiled many a good Irish heart.

For one thing, I hope we are done forever with that mockery of a constitution: the English House of Commons.

The self-control maintained by the young people of Ireland, and especially of Clare, in spite of the callous provocations to which they are being subjected is beyond all praise. Everything truly Irish is being oppressed with a tyranny, both brutal and scandalous. Young men, the flower of the country, are being arrested wholesale, degraded, insulted, imprisoned, shot or bayoneted like poor Thomas Russell, of Carrigaholt, the killing of whom is, in all its circumstances, one of the most horrid and atrocious things I ever heard of. Were these things done in Belgium how the world would be made to ring with the cry of German atrocities.

But this policy of oppression and provocation will not succeed in its purpose, which is obvious enough to clear the ground by the extermination of national spirit for the 'English friendlies' of the 'sanity' Party, and, if possible, prepare the way for conscription – which, by the way, no government, in my opinion, has the moral right to inflict on any nation without that nation's clearly expressed consent.

Martial law has not shaken the hand of Clare, which still holds in firm grasp the Sinn Féin banner of Irish Independence, and will continue to hold it until that independence is fully realised. No scheme of federation, which leaves Ireland as a morsel swallowed in the British stomach will be accepted here.

I enclose, with my good wishes, a cheque for the support of the Clare prisoners.

I am, yours sincerely,

M. Fogarty

Closure of the Clare Champion

The *Clare Champion* gave prominence to Sinn Féin activities and propaganda, with 'seditious and subversive' articles, which annoyed the authorities. One provocative and cheeky small advertisement was placed in the edition of 2 February 1918, announcing a 'GRAND DANCE to be held at Rath on Sunday 3 February, in aid of the Rath Company of the I.R.A. Admission: Gents 2s. Ladies 1s.'

GRAND DANCE

To be held at RATH on SUNDAY, 3rd FEBRUARY, in aid of the Rath Company of the I.R.A.

Admission—Gents, ... 2s.
Ladies, ... 1s.

Advertisement for the IRA in the *Clare Champion*.

The editor of the *Clare Champion* refused on principle to comply with the censorship rules imposed by the British authorities and as a result the newspaper was closed down for about six months from 30 March until 28 September 1918 under DORA regulations. Part of the printing press was 'dismantled' by police and soldiers.

Now, there was only one local Clare newspaper left to inform the public of what was happening in the county, the 'unionist' *Saturday Record*. Of course, there were national papers circulating also, such as the *Irish Independent*, as well as some Limerick papers, which had some circulation in the county, perhaps in Ennis, Killaloe and Kilkee. This lack of a local publicity forum did not deter the republicans, in Sinn Féin and Cumann na mBan, who grew from strength to strength, despite arrests and harassments of leading republicans throughout the year. Because of the void in the local press the power and influence of the Catholic clergy probably became more prominent in the county at this time.

The banned newspaper, the *Clare Champion*, re-appeared on the streets again on 28 September 1918. In an editorial, Mr Sarsfield Maguire defiantly stated, 'We need not say that where we stood previous to our enforced silence we stand today. The best return is to give a clear and honest journal, which true to the motto, and having arisen to complete its tasks, will remain firm to the cause until our people become free men and victory is won'.[19]

'The German Plot'

One extraordinary event occurred early on 13 April, when a stranger landed mysteriously from a canvas canoe on Crab Island, near Doolin, County Clare, having been brought to Ireland on a German submarine. Sub-headings in the local paper referred to 'The Crab Island Visitor' or 'The Man in the Collapsible Boat'. The landing at Doolin sparked off a sequence of events leading to the internment of the Sinn Féin leadership under what became known as the 'German Plot'. The man was arrested and it was revealed in the House of Commons that he was Joseph Dowling, a former lance-corporal in the Connaught Rangers, who had been incarcerated in Limburg Prison, Germany, after being captured early in the war during the retreat from Mons in 1914. He was one of the fifty-two prisoners who had allegedly volunteered to join Sir Roger Casement's 'Irish Brigade'. L-Cpl Joseph Dowling was a native of Bantry and had apparently been in the RIC before the war. After interrogation in Ireland he was taken to the Tower of London, where he was put on trial. He was found guilty of treason and sentenced to death, but this was commuted to life imprisonment. He was released following representations from the Irish Government on 2 February 1924.

The arrest of Joseph Dowling in Doolin, along with the arrest of two Sinn Féiners in Dublin allegedly trying to contact a German submarine, provided 'moral proof' for the government that the Sinn Féin Party were plotting and co-operating with Germany to launch an armed uprising. These events spurred the authorities in Dublin Castle and the British Government in London to arrest and intern the Sinn Féin leaders. The 'German Plot' was used as a propaganda excuse to discredit the Sinn Party in America, suggesting that the Sinn Féiners were co-operating with the enemies of the USA as well as Britain, France and Belgium. One hundred and fifty members of Sinn Féin, including de Valera, were arrested on the night of 16-17 May and interned in England. It is widely believed that there was no substance to the allegations, but they were used by the British authorities for propaganda purposes to discredit Sinn Féin, especially in the USA.[20]

A New Recruitment Campaign

As the war slowly dragged on the military authorities in Ireland embarked on a new voluntary recruitment campaign, seeking 50,000 new Irish recruits to fill the gaps in the ranks. Large advertisements appeared in the papers, urging Claremen to enlist. Subtle differences in advertising referred to 'fighting alongside the American and French allies'. There was no mention of the fate of 'gallant little Belgium' on this occasion.

Selected letters were also published in the only local paper in circulation at the time, the *Saturday Record*, referring to the fate of Irish prisoners in Germany.

Mr Thomas Ryan, a member of Kilrush Urban Council, received a letter from a prisoner of war, Pte J. Manning from Kilrush, who had been imprisoned in Germany. It was selected for publication in the local paper in August, obviously for propaganda purposes:

Dear Mr Ryan – just a few lines to thank you for your kindness and generosity, referring to parcels sent by you early in 1915, which were distributed amongst the Kilrush men. I can say you were an exception. I think you were the only one who tried to help. I am now myself in Holland and I shall never forget my sufferings in Germany. They are an inhuman race of people. You can well believe that we were suffering severely that time I wrote to you for help; but a little after that our parcels started coming. Then we were not badly off, but the 'Gerrys' still kept beating us. But if I was to fight again in the morning, I would not take a square head prisoner, I would knife him. It is these people that has caused all the trouble in our land. God help Ireland if she should be under German rule, then we would be slaves. They would do

Postcard sent by a prisoner of war, Cpl T. Kelly, Royal Munster Fusiliers, to Miss Maunsell, Island Magrath, Clare Castle. The card was sent from a camp in Holland. It is dated 22 May 1918. (Courtesy of Brian Honan Collection)

the same with us as they have done with Belgium, Servia and Russia. I know what the German is, he is worse than the beast in the field. You would hardly believe that was true until you had seen it. So, dear Mr Ryan, I will close now, thanking you once more.

I remain, your sincere friend, J. Manning.[21]

Another former prisoner of war, J.F. O'Connor, a member of the Gordon Highlanders, wrote a letter of thanks to Mrs Isabel Studdert, honorary secretary of the County Clare Prisoners of War Committee, Bindon Street Ennis. The letter was posted on 31 May from Schevingen, Deplaan, Group No 5, Holland:

Madam, I am sure you will be pleased to hear from me, and that I am enjoying good health since my arrival here. I am having quite a good time, and find the people very nice, and ever ready to help us enjoy ourselves. I assure you my treatment here is a thousand times better than in Germany. I wish to thank you and all good friends in Clare for your kindness to me and other Clare prisoners in our very hard and trying times in Germany. I firmly believe were it not for the help of the Prisoners of War Fund, I would not have lived. Thank God those days of torture, starvation, hard marches in Russia with nothing to eat for days, bullying and prison life in Cologne in Germany are all over. Now that I am in a friendly country, I have the pleasure of enjoying my much longed-for freedom. Who knows, but I may be back soon again in France fighting those barbarous Huns, and getting a little of my own back. I hope this finds you in the best of health.

Again, thanking you for your kindness, which will live in my memory for years.

Yours, very sincerely, JF O'Connor.[22]

Another letter was published in the *Saturday Record*, allegedly written by an Irish priest in Paris to Mr P. Howard, honorary secretary, Maj. Willie Redmond Memorial Fund. The letter was sent to the paper by Mr Pat McInerney, a district councillor from Doora:

Dear Sir,

For many reasons, but above all being Irish, I admire the beautiful and heroic death of Major Wm Redmond. I hope it will be a good example to those who must join in the great struggle of war, if they wish Ireland to be free and a great nation.

Your, faithfully, L'Abbe Flynn PP.[23]

Capt. J.F.J. Fitzpatrick, assistant organiser of recruitment, appeared before Kilrush Urban District Council in June and appealed for volunteers to help the Allied cause. 'Volunteers', he said, 'would prevent conscription'. He was given a polite but courteous reception, but no resolution in favour of recruitment was passed this time. In a follow up letter to the *Saturday Record* in September, Capt. Fitzpatrick, describing himself as a Catholic, an Irishman and as a home ruler, emphasised the 'folly, the hopelessness and therefore the wickedness of active resistance to recruitment'. In October the local recruitment committee sent a delegation to address Clare County Council. They also got a polite hearing, but little support, and no resolution in favour of voluntary recruitment was passed on this occasion.[24]

In the middle of September, Lt Abraham, assistant organiser at the recruitment office, Ennis, wrote a letter to the *Saturday Record* suggesting the formation of a local committee to promote recruitment:

> Recruiting Office,
> Ennis, co. Clare,
> Sir,
> 12th September, 1918
>   May I be allowed to intrude upon your space to invite the assistance of the people of Clare in the campaign for the voluntary enlistment of the 50,000 recruits asked for by the Lord Lieutenant? For this task the support of public opinion is essential, and in connection with this out-station a local committee will be set up to advise upon the local organisation of publicity and the supply of information to prospective recruits. I shall be grateful if all who are prepared to join the committee, or to assist in any way, will communicate with me.
> Yours faithfully,
> L.A. Abraham, Lieut.,
> Assistant Organiser, I.R.C.

During October and early November Lt Abraham hired a car from M.F. Tierney of Abbey Street, Ennis and toured around the county meeting significant people as part of his work seeking more recruits. On 28 October he travelled to Kildysart, Lissycasey and district, a total of 45 miles. On 2 November he took a longer journey, travelling to Ruan, Corofin, Ballyvaughan, New Quay, Lisdoonvarna and Kilfenora, a total round trip of 68 miles. Finally, on 8 November, he took a journey to the districts of Crusheen, Carrahan, Quin and Newmarket-on-Fergus, a total of 34 miles. The rate for hiring the car was one shilling per mile, plus the cost of the petrol.[25]

Col Arthur Lynch, always sensitive about urging Irishmen to fight for the British Army, ever since his anti-British activities during the Boer War, where

Postcard sent by prisoner of war, Cpl T. Kelly, Royal Munster Fusiliers, from Clare Castle to Miss R. Scanlan, Main Street, Clare Castle. He had been a prisoner in Germany since the Battle of Etroux in August 1914. The card is dated 15 June 1916. (Courtesy of Brian Honan)

he was a 'colonel' of an Irish pro-Boer 'brigade', tried a new tack. He sought to set up an Irish Brigade of his own to fight alongside the 'gallant French and American allies in Europe'. Though, he said, that they had spurned his offer to form an Irish regiment in 1914, in June 1918 the British Government granted him a commission in the army as a colonel and he swallowed his pride and accepted it for a greater cause. He came to Ireland to raise a regiment. He proposed that they would fight under Irish officers and that they would form a distinctive Irish Brigade with Irish colours and fight alongside the American and French allies. This concession of a distinctive Irish Brigade was sought by John Redmond in 1914, but denied to him then. The French Prime Minister, Mr Clemenceau, sent a special message to Col Lynch, MP, who had lived in Paris for many years and had been a well-known journalist, as well as being a well-known Francophile: 'I am deeply touched by the evidence of personal friendship for France conveyed in your letter. I send you ardent vows for success in the new task which your patriotism has induced you to accept as well as the expression of my most cordial good wishes'.[26]

In July Col Lynch sent the following appeal to Col Theodore Roosevelt, who as President of America had sent a special appeal to the English Government to reprieve Arthur Lynch in 1903, requesting his help in persuading young Irishmen to fight for the Allies:

Send me a word of encouragement, or better still, my great and splendid friend, come yourself in all your power and prestige and help me win the souls of young Irishmen to the Allied cause ... When the Stars and Stripes was raised over the cause, when once Old Glory had blown out her folds, the emblem of liberty, a sign of protection to millions of Irish men, I had hoped that opposition to the Allied cause would cease. But the ancient wrongs and present resentment proved too strong ... We must win the souls of these young Irish men to the Allied cause.

In August Col Lynch agreed that many motives that appealed to him 'did not appeal to the hardy tillers of the soil in West Clare', yet he asserted that the war should be of as much concern to the tiller in Clare as to the inhabitants

Clare prisoners of war in a camp in Germany, May 1916. Sent by Cpl T. Kelly RMF to Miss Scanlan. (Courtesy of Brian Honan)

of the invaded countries. But, he warned that if the Germans were victorious 'there would be an end to the Irish question, there will be an end to Ireland, except as an outlying German province ... In the event of a German triumph there will be an enforcement of an indemnity which will 'bleed white' not only France, but England and Ireland as well.' Nationalist MPs such as Col Arthur Lynch and Capt. Stephen Gwynn toured the country, appearing at recruitment meetings in military uniform, but they got a cool reception, being shouted down by Sinn Féin speakers. According to a report in the *Daily News*, Col Lynch experienced 'considerable difficulties' at the hands of the War Office in Dublin, as they refused to allow him to spend any money for propaganda purposes. In Galway the MPs

Young Irishmen France and America are calling to you. **You have now the Chance** TO JOIN **An Irish Brigade,** Composed of Irishmen only, with Irish Officers, Irish Uniforms, Irish Colours, Irish Pipers—Irish everything. When attesting you have the opportunity of being attached to **LYNCH'S IRISH BRIGADE. DO SO NOW.**

Advertisement for Col Lynch's Brigade *Saturday Record*, 2 August 1918.

were refused permission to address a meeting of Galway County Council in August and the war ended on 11 November 1918 before he could realise the quixotic dream of raising Col Lynch's Irish Brigade.[27]

'From Somewhere in France'

Councillor P.J. Linnane, JP, received another letter from his friend, Fr M. Moran, from Tulassa, Ennis, who was a chaplain on the Western Front. The letter strongly attacked the Germans for their atrocities in Belgium, referring to them as 'Prussian beasts', 'Huns' and 'Prussian butchers'. This was rather intemperate language for a priest. Councillor Linnane released the letter to the *Saturday Record* for publication. It was published in two editions, the first called 'Somewhere in France' and the second entitled, 'The German horror in France'. The letter was timely from a propaganda point of view:

Dear PJ
... I am splendid myself, thank God, except that my right hand gets suddenly weak occasionally, but not to the extent of incapacitating me from my work. I am very lucky to be alive, and the best thanksgiving I can make to God for preserving my life is to stick to my post until His holy will is accomplished in this war...

I have been anxious many a time to send you some fairly graphic accounts of life and experiences out here, but want of time chiefly and physical disability (owing to my hand), have prevented me from doing so. However, both obstacles are now removed, and so I'll give you in brief my experiences for the week, which might prove interesting to you and your friends. I might say that no pen can possibly convey any idea of the grim realities we witness from week to week and day to day ...

I have been resting in the village of ... in France, from which the Germans have been driven out a couple of weeks ago ... they had to 'hop it' as the Lancashire people would say. They had been here since the beginning of the war ... The Germans mined the churches with intent to wipe them out ...

On entering the village after the Germans left you find men thrown on all sides and in the most abandoned attitudes of violent death. The same scene meets your eye on going round the side streets of the village. Here and there you find cellars containing dead, wounded and dying. In some instances you see cellars mined and blown in and so all inside are dead.

Here and there in the village you find a group of dead horses that have been killed by shells. Outside the village and in the open fields you find many horses and men who have been caught by machine gun fire.

The Germans try to get all the people to go back with them and when they refuse they have been severely dealt with. Some of the old people would rather die than leave the village ... the priest in this village refused to go, but he escaped to the next village and hid in a cave until the Germans were expelled from that village also ... Every single house was looted, anything they could not take was smashed to pieces ... everything treasured by the people was destroyed.

In the farmyards your horses and cows have long since been removed, your wells are all mined, poisoned or else blown up. Your orchards, greenhouses are all blown up, everything you hold dear in a home or a farm is destroyed. Your house is reduced to a heap of rubble ... Such is every house in the village I am resting in. Such is every village in France where the savage Hun has settled.

Even potato fields, orchards and vegetable plots have been mined ... Heavy fines were placed upon the villagers ... they had to be indoors by nine in summer and seven in winter ...

Many of the villagers had to be brought to hospital suffering from many complaints, including starvation after the Germans had left, and some had gone mad after the terrible times they had gone through ...

The first year in the village the Germans broke the church bells and took away all the brass fittings in the church ... a poor baker was shot for refusing to bake bread for the Germans ...

Now for the real hero, and saint of the village, the dear old cure [priest]. The Germans repeatedly asked him to leave the village under all sorts of threats but he refused. In all their dealings with him they were singularly harsh and diabolical. For refusing to salute a German corporal he was put into a dark room for ten days. During all this time he got very bad food and no meat. During all his persecutions he continually prayed for his enemies. For refusing to salute another officer he was spat upon and his biretta torn off his head. For hiding in a cellar and having a revolver to protect himself, he was sentenced to death, but he managed to escape. They took everything of value from his house and drank the altar wine in his presence.

The priest or cure of … a friend and neighbour of his was brutally murdered for giving some soup and milk to British soldiers. He was first struck in the back of the neck ten times, then stabbed in a dozen places and left unburied for two days. He was found later by some of the civilians about 200 yards from where he was killed having been dragged outside the village by those cruel butchers and allies of the devil. A bayonet was still stuck through his chest and an epitaph attached to the bayonet. I shan't desecrate paper by translating it for you. This noble priest died the death of a veritable martyr.

… The treatment meted out to the women and girls in those villages I dare not refer to except to say that the vast majority of them will have their names inscribed as 'Saints and Martyrs' in the annals of the Catholic Church here …

That was a very tragic affair, the sinking of the SS 'Leinster' mail boat. I have travelled on it many a time … May God comfort those stricken families who have suffered from such a wanton crime … I have collected £7. 5s. for the Chinese Mission from my men in addition to £2. 15s. from myself to make it an even £10, which you will kindly hand over to whoever is collecting in the town for it. I am asking the chaplain with me to collect for the Irish Martyrs' Fund, and we hope to send another £10 before the Holy Season of New Year comes in. Even amidst the din of war we must not forget the great work that is being done in Ireland for such noble causes.

I have scarcely any Irishmen with me at present … I heard some time ago that there were some aspersions cast upon our Irish soldiers in one of the Irish papers. It hasn't been my privilege since August or September of last year to have anything to do with Irish soldiers, but even if I hadn't that short experience, I make bold to say that their piety and bravery have been rarely equalled and seldom, if ever, surpassed. I say this with respect to the other brave fighting men of other nations out here. The writer of the letter should be out here and see the stuff the Irish are made of and then he wouldn't be showing his colossal ignorance, or making himself a veritable 'Hun' by writing such vile and cowardly stuff. The iniquitous press deserves to be boycotted by every decent Irishman.

When I suggested to some Irishmen on the advice of an officer that we should change from the old stable where we had Mass, Confessions and the rosary, to a safer place (for we were under machine gun fire), one of them said, 'Sure, Father, nothing will happen to us while we are praying and even so we couldn't die better than having the name of Mary on our lips'. Could anything be more eloquently put, or with greater sentiments of faith and piety?

We are moving now, so I trust this attempt will make up for not having written to you more frequently. I may not have an opportunity again for the next twelve months. The weather is very wet these days and fairly cold and notwithstanding this we have a fearful amount of flies, due mostly to dead horses and corpses … and also due to the insanitary conditions of the village after the Germans.

I almost forgot to tell you the most awful thing they perpetrated in the village. It is really almost too bad to confine to paper, but it will show you and others what is meant by the Prussian element in the German army. They did the same with carpeted rooms. Too terrible for words. They actually used the church as a latrine or a closet, while holy Mass was being celebrated.

This is the element that disgraces the entire German army … The Prussian element is like a cancer in an organism. It must be eradicated … It is not right to say 'that there is no good German except "a dead un"', as they say in Yorkshire.

There are some good German regiments, but most of the German army have the Prussian beast mixed up with them.

Their satanic majesties who have condoned these most unnatural crimes in the history of any war previously fought, must go down and be got rid of for all time … The names of the Prussians butchers who took no steps to prevent such crimes as I have outlined the murderers of helpless women and suckling babes should be carved out in bold relief in every civilised country, town and village to be held in everlasting execration …

I feel and speak very strongly, for you must remember I was (were it not for God's protection) dead many a time out here, and on 26th July this year there was a doubt whether I should have a right hand till the x ray photo relieved me of my worries. I know that shouldn't enter into what I say, but there it is. I can't get rid of it.

Yours, sincerely

M. Moran, CF[28]

Fr M. Moran from Tulassa, Ennis, was awarded the Military Cross (MC), for his bravery under fire. His citation read as follows: 'During operations lasting ten days, he displayed conspicuous gallantry and unselfish devotion to duty in attending to the wounded, often under heavy fire. On one occasion he was wounded and severely shaken by the explosion of a shell, but he continued to work with an undiminished zeal. He was a splendid example to all about him'.[29]

'Heroism at Guillemont and Ginchy'

As an inducement to promote recruitment there was a large article in the *Saturday Record* celebrating the anniversary of the heroic charge of the Irish Brigade at Guillemont and Ginchy during the Battle of the Somme in France. The paper printed a tribute from a 'distinguished' war correspondent Mr Philip Gibbs:

> Guillemont fell on Sunday, September 3rd to a charge which was one of the most astonishing features of the war, with pipes playing and flags flying the Irish Battalion swept on like a huge avalanche, right through the first, second and third German lines with an irresistible rush till the village as a whole was in their hands ... by Sunday night victory was overwhelming and complete.
>
> Then on the afternoon of 9 September came the order to attack the village of Ginchy. Amid wild hurrahs and cries of 'Up the Dubliners', and "Up the Munsters" they swept forward. In eight minutes they had reached the first objective in the village across the German lines, 600 yards, a wonderful record ... reckless of snipers and machine guns the Irish swept through the village seeking out Germans in concrete huts and cellars. They were Bavarians and fought savagely, but the Irish bayonet was too much for them. They were 600 yards ahead of the rest and both their left and right flanks were exposed ... THEY DID IT!
>
> The splendid success of the Irish Brigade from a military point of view, is their success of taking a hostile front of 900 yards in the depth of nearly a mile, with no supporting troops in either flank ... from a non-military point of view the greatness of the capture of Ginchy is the valour of these Irish boys, who were not cowed by the sight of death very close to them, and who went straight on to the winning post like Irish racehorses ... Shouting: 'Up the Dubs! ... Up the Micks!'
>
> And as they strode proudly along to the rest they had earned so well, and as the pipers played them out, now with a march of triumph, and now with a lament for the boys who would never march behind their flag again, each man felt sure in his heart that his countrymen at home would see to it that the dead would not be un-avenged, or the living be deserted by their brother Irishman. WILL THEY?[30]

This glorified version of the success of the Irish at the engagements of Guillemont and Ginchy in France bore little relationship to the actual reality of these battles. Tom Johnstone describes the scene at Ginchy:

> Up to their knees in mud … on a tour of duty of forty-eight hours … conditions were terrible … trench latrines were non-existent and diarrhoea was common in the cold, wet, slime and filth of trench life in Ypres … Rifles had to be carried all the time … on the journey up to the trenches the men were overburdened with kit, ammunition and entrenching equipment … there were dead bodies of humans and horses everywhere and rats were common … there was little rest for the men who were suffering from fatigue …[31]

There is not much evidence that many young men in County Clare were persuaded by appeals or by propaganda to volunteer and to join the services in 1918. The *Saturday Record*, however, noted one man who had enlisted – 'Mr M.F. Hassett had resigned his job as petty sessions clerk at Killaloe and had joined the army early in October'.[32]

Gaelic Sunday

Earlier in the year in July, because of the unrest in the country, the Dublin Castle authorities prohibited the holding of any public meeting, including sports events, without a special permit. This outraged the GAA and, as an act of defiance, the Central Council instructed all county boards to organise as many matches as possible on Sunday 4 August at 3 p.m. More than 1,800 games were organised throughout Ireland on this day, in a national protest, which they called 'Gaelic Sunday'. The GAA publicly challenged the government and when tens of thousands of Gaels, men, women and children, turned out to play and watch Gaelic games, the government was unable to do much about the massive public opposition to the unpopular law.

There was only one report of this public defiance in County Clare in the *Saturday Record*. The paper carried a report that visitors and locals celebrated 'Gaelic Sunday' at Kilkee: 'It was truly a Gaelic revival. Instead of the usual cricket, tennis, golf, etc., a splendid and keenly contested game of hurling was enjoyed on the strand. The competing teams were made up of visiting clergy, the Priests vs the Brothers. After a well-fought contest the former were declared winners by 11 goals 3 points to 3 goals 2 points. The enthusiasm of the hundreds of spectators as either side scored gave much evidence that the "game of the Gael" is, notwithstanding trying times, holding its own'.[33]

The SS *Leinster*

There was one other major tragedy of the war which had a significant effect upon Ireland and County Clare, and which almost delayed the peace – that was the sinking of the mail boat, the SS *Leinster*, without warning in what the *Saturday Record* noted as 'Another Hun Horror'. The *Leinster* sailed from Carlisle pier Kingstown, (now called Dún Laoghaire) County Dublin around 9 a.m. on 10 October 1918. She was bound for Holyhead in Wales. There were 705 passengers and a crew of seventy-six aboard the merchant ship. The majority of passengers were military personnel either going on or returning from leave. There were also 180 civilians aboard, men women and children.

Shortly before 10 a.m., about 16 miles from Dublin, the ship was hit by two torpedoes fired from a German submarine UB-123. There was a huge explosion and

"We have loved them in life, let us not forget them in death."—*St. Ambrose.*

In Loving Memory

OF

DILLIE & NORA DAVOREN,

Clareen House, Ennis,

Lost in S.S. *Leinster,*

On 10th October, 1918,

R. J. P.

O Immense Passion ! O Profound Wounds ! O Profusion of Blood ! O Sweetness above all Sweetness ! O Most Bitter Death ! grant them eternal rest. AMEN.—*400 days' Indulgence.*

Obituary Card for the Davoren sisters.
(Courtesy of the Peadar McNamara Collection)

the ship sank quickly before many of the passengers and crew could be saved. The sea was rough after some recent storms, which made it difficult for rescuing the passengers.

There were at least 529 casualties of that sinking. At least 115 out of 180 passengers died either from injuries caused by the explosion, or else by drowning or hypothermia. Among those who died were nine people associated with County Clare: Head Constable Ward, RIC, Ennis, (who had recently transferred from Portumna); Pte John Coyne, Raheen, Scarriff; two sisters, both of whom were nurses returning to duty, Nurse Nora Davoren and her sister Delia Davoren from Claureen House, Ennis; another couple of sisters, Ms Margaret O'Grady and her sister Ms B. O'Grady; from Newmarket-on-Fergus, also nurses; Miss Nellie Hogan, a nurse from Ralahine, Newmarket-on-Fergus; Mr Hynes, from Tulla and his daughter Ms Clare Hynes also from Tulla.

The sinking of the *Leinster* was condemned by public bodies in Clare, such as the Ennis Board of Guardians, and the Kilrush Board of Guardians, as a 'horrible and inhuman outrage'. Members of the Ennis Urban Council also unanimously condemned the sinking, 'another sorrowful example of German 'Kultur' and friendliness towards the people of this county, to whom they have professed to be our so-called "gallant allies"'.

However, there was some controversy at the monthly meeting of the management of the Clare Asylum, which was chaired by Revd A. Clancy, PP, a strong supporter of Sinn Féin. When one member, Mr Lynch, proposed a motion of sympathy with the victims and condemned the sinking 'as a cruel act on a defenceless people, a cowardly crime', the chairman, Fr Clancy, described it as 'an act of warfare on a vessel carrying troops and munitions.' Councillor P.J. Linnane described it as 'a cold-blooded, cowardly treacherous act by the Germans.' The motion was passed unanimously only when the chairman, Fr Clancy, included an addendum, 'and also condemning in the strongest possible manner the British Government for the murder of Thomas Russell at Carrigaholt.' (Thomas Russell was a teacher at the Irish College and a member of the Irish Volunteers, who died after being stabbed with a bayonet by a British soldier at Carrigaholt, while the British Army was endeavouring to clear a hall, where a banned Sinn Féin meeting was being held).[34]

The sinking of the SS *Leinster* almost jeopardised the peace talks to end the war. On 6 October the German Government requested United States President Woodrow Wilson to arrange an armistice to end the war. Four days later, on 6 October, President Wilson, obviously aware of the tragic loss of life after the sinking of the *Leinster*, sent a telegram to the Germans stating that there could be no peace talks as long as Germany was attacking passenger ships. Shortly afterwards, the Germans took heed of President Wilson's ultimatum. Admiral Scheer, chief of the German navy, signalled an order to all German U-boats on the high seas, to return from their patrols as soon as possible. They were ordered not to take any hostile actions against merchant ships. The U-boats were only allowed to attack warships in daylight.[35] Three weeks later, the Germans surrendered unconditionally on 11 November 1918. The Great War was finally over.

'All Quiet on the Western Front'[36]

The news of the termination of the war was received with much jubilation in the county. In Ennis there was a 'liberal display of bunting' in the local military headquarters. Many people in the town of Ennis displayed red badges and there was deep satisfaction that the war was finally over. The editorial in the *Clare Champion* of 16 November, questioned whether the peace in Europe would bring peace to Ireland:

> The war is over and peace is at hand. One must wonder if that peace will bring peace to Ireland. By all the principles of justice it should and if Irishmen assert themselves we believe it will. We speak for no party now; we plead for the Irish nation and its freedom ... We do not under-estimate the difficulties;

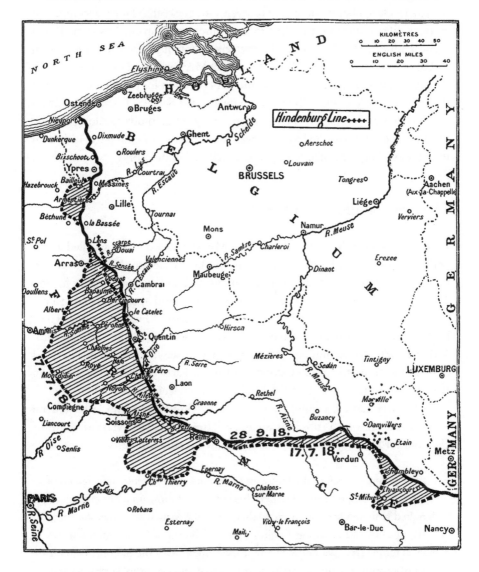

Map of the Western Front, 1918. (Courtesy of Peadar McNamara Collection)

we know how Ireland will be maligned and mis-represented and we can gauge the forces against us, but we believe that a united demand on the part of Ireland cannot be defeated or mis-represented at the peace conference. Can we not have unity on one particular issue?

Thanksgiving services were held in all the major churches around the county. A special inter-denominational (Protestant) Thanksgiving Service for victory for the Allied cause was held at the Church of Ireland, Bindon Street, Ennis on Sunday 17 December. A contingent of seventy-three Scottish Horse, accompanied by pipes, fifes and drums marched to the church, accompanied by some Royal Welsh Fusiliers. Members of the Presbyterian Church joined the congregation and the church was crowded. Revd T. Abrahall MA conducted the service, which consisted of hymns, readings and a sermon. A collection for the Red Cross raised the large sum of £17 6s 8d. 'It was', according to the *Saturday Record*, 'altogether a memorable service, characterised by deep feelings of gratitude to Almighty God, the only giver of victory, and to the brave men, thousands of whom had laid down their lives willingly that liberty might be established in the world'.

The General Election of 1918

Three weeks after the war ended, Prime Minister Lloyd George called a general election, which became known as 'the khaki election'. In his election propaganda he promised, among other things, 'to build a country fit for heroes'. There was no contest in Clare as no candidate stood against the Sinn Féin candidates, Eamon de Valera in East Clare and Brian O'Higgins in West Clare, both of whom had been arrested and held in prison since 'the German Plot'. Arthur Lynch, the incumbent MP for West Clare, wisely decided not to stand again in the county. Instead he stood as a Labour Party candidate for the South Battersea constituency in London, but he was not elected there either.

Dr Fogarty came out publicly in favour of Sinn Féin in the 1918 general election and he sent a subscription and a letter to Mr J. O'Mara, director of elections for Sinn Féin, publicly endorsing the Republican Party:

… The country is sick of the House of Commons with its plutocratic record of oppression, corruption and chicanery. Ireland, since it came under its influence a hundred years ago has wasted and withered like the Armenians under the Turks.

The policy of massaging English ministers by our 'expert statesmen' has had an ample trial. We know where it has landed us, in the national degradation of partition. The authors of that criminal and cowardly surrender will never be forgiven by Ireland.

I am not afraid of abstinence; it is only a logical and long called for protest against the pillage of our national rights under the infamous union. But in view of the insulting policy expounded by the prime minister as to the share reserved for Ireland under his world-wide reconstruction, no other course is open to us, if we have a particle of self-respect.

Irish representation in a House of Commons dominated by Mr Lloyd George and his anti-Irish coalition is a horrible imposture, which it is time to terminate. That unionist combine will work its shameless will on Ireland whether Irish members are present or not. Why then send them there to be spat upon as paupers, to come back to us with empty hands, or with a few crumbs from the English table garnished with rhetoric, but as always with the leprosy of anglicisation visibly represented on their person for the ruin of our national spirit.

Partition is to be defeated and liberty won not by talking to the dead ears of the House of Commons, but under God, where emancipation was won, landlordism broken, and conscription defeated, at home in Ireland by the determined will of the people. John Mitchell was right when he called for the withdrawal of the Irish Members fifty years ago, and time has fully verified the words he then used in speaking of this subject. 'That Parliament', he said, 'is a lie, an imposture, an outrage, a game in which our part and lot is disgrace and defeat for ever. To Ireland it is nothing besides a conduit of corruption, a workshop of coercion, a storehouse of starvation, a machinery of cheating, and a perpetual memento of slavery.'

I am,

Yours sincerely,

M Fogarty,

Bishop of Killaloe

Not alone did Bishop Fogarty publicly endorse Sinn Féin, he and many other Catholic clergy in Clare proposed and endorsed de Valera for re-election – in fact five parish priests and twenty curates supported de Valera's candidature. With such powerful ecclesiastical backing, combined with the support of the *Clare Champion*, the Home Rule Party did not stand a chance in Clare and did not put up any fight this time or propose any candidates. Incidentally, during the election Sinn Féin propaganda literature discredited the Home Rule party and asked the electorate: 'Will you vote for the faith of Tone, Davitt and Parnell? Or will you vote for that of Arthur Lynch, Stephen Gwynn, W. Archer, Redmond – all of the English army?'[37]

Earlier in the year, when the leader of the Irish Home Rule Party, John Redmond, died on 6 March in London, Bishop Fogarty, though he had long before this time abandoned his support for John Redmond's Home Rule Party in favour of Sinn Féin, was 'much affected' when he heard the news, and issued the following terse statement: 'I am sorry to hear of the death of this eminent Irishman, who has filled a very big part of our public life. I have no doubt future historians of Ireland will give his name the prominent place it deserves'.[38]

Weather and Harvests

Despite the Tillage Acts, the illegal ploughing activities, and the appeals from Dr Fogarty and other bishops earlier in the year to till as much as possible this year, the farmers of Ireland had a tough battle against the elements to save the autumn harvest.

The weather at Carrigoran in 1918 was very poor from an agricultural point of view.

> The total rainfall for the year was more than six inches in excess of our aver-
> age annual rain, and this may well be styled a "wet" year ... There was a great
> deficiency of rain in the first six months of the year ... with disastrous results
> to agriculture caused by the excessive rainfall this year. There was a great
> excess of rain in the second half of the year, especially during the months
> when hay and corn crops were harvested, thus causing almost unprecedented
> damage and loss to the crops.

The Carrigoran annual weather report was corroborated by contemporary accounts of bad weather in the autumn.

The weather had been very bad, so bad that in September prayers were offered for fine weather. Huge damage was done to hay and cereal crops all over the county, rivers burst their banks, there were destructive storms at seaside resorts and the houses of the poor people in the back lanes of Ennis were severely flooded. The *Saturday Record* of 28 September recorded that Bishop Fogarty offered prayers for fine weather and for the preservation of the harvest at first Mass on Sunday 22 September at the cathedral in Ennis:

> The prospect before the county could not have been worse. For some time
> portions of the county, especially in the low-lying districts have been more or
> less flooded from the heavy rains which have prevailed since the beginning
> of the month – but the torrential downpours of Friday night, Saturday and
> Sunday night have left far-reaching stretches of water on all sides, and already
> incalculable damage has been suffered.
> Hay has been washed away in places where it had already been made up,
> and in the low-lying lands along the lower Fergus towards the Shannon, has

been carried away by the rivers, which have become enormously swollen. Here and there half-submerged cocks of hay are like miniature islands in the surface of the waters.

Corn crops have also suffered disastrously and on Saturday, groups of men wading waist deep could be seen near Ennistymon endeavouring to save the stooks of corn on the lands along the swollen Inagh River.

The bank of the Shannon near the Cratloe district has given way and the countryside is under many feet of water. The same story comes from many localities along the Fergus and along the upper reaches as far as Ennistymon, by both sides of the West Clare Railway, which presented a spectacle of an inland sea.

But perhaps the most damage was done about Doora, where a large breach was made in the river bank, mid-way between the Metal Bridge and the Railway Bridge, fully 20 yards wide. Through this an enormous volume of water poured, inundating the country inside the bank. The water also poured into the tract of land on the Cappagh side, where there was another immense spread of water.

Along this tract there are many sufferers, amongst them, Mrs Corry, whose corn and green crops have been almost destroyed, also Mr McInerney, Mr Hogan and others. In the early hours of Sunday morning, thanks to willing hands, a number of cattle and sheep were brought out of danger, or many would have been lost in the rapidly rising waters, which still cover this side of the county. From some quarters come stories of the loss of cattle and sheep, but in most places all stock have been moved to higher ground in good time.

In Ennis on Sunday morning, the tide was so enormously high that all the lower levels of the town were flooded to a depth of from two to three feet, notably in Lower Mill Street, and the poorer inhabitants in the adjoining lanes off the quays were left in a miserable condition.

At Kilkee on Sunday, a tempestuous Spring tide broke over the sea front and all the men's bathing boxes belonging to the Benn Brothers, well known to visitors to this fashionable resort were dashed against the battlement and made matchwood of, involving the owners in huge losses. We are glad their patrons are taking steps to come to their assistance in this disastrous occurrence. At Lahinch a large sea demolished the remains of Reidy's Baths, once a landmark in this resort, and broke a number of windows along the front.

At Latoon the Fergus overflowed its banks and poured into the adjacent corcasses; about 30 acres of hay belonging to Mr Lynch were badly damaged and he also had about 7 acres of oats almost ruined. At Ballycorick the banks also gave way and much damage was done to hay and corn.

There were serious fears entertained for the potato crop, which is widely showing symptoms of rotting in the sodden ground. Altogether, the outlook is of the gravest nature.

Despite the prayers of Sunday 22 September, the bad weather continued. The *Saturday Record* of 5 October commented on the adverse weather at harvest time: 'The weather during the past week was adverse to harvesting operations.' In a letter to the paper Mr R.F. Hibbert of Woodpark, Scarriff noted that the rainfall for September had been 8.52ins, a record since 1894. The rainfall of July amounted to 4.69ins and that for August was 4.37ins. Mr Hibbert attacked the Compulsory Tillage Act by observing as follows, 'The futility of attempting to grow grain crops in such a climate, where the average rainfall is from forty to fifty inches, should be evident to the authorities'.[39]

Besides the bad weather the economic conditions in other areas of the county were still deteriorating. The only newspaper published in the county, the *Saturday Record*, announced a 50 per cent price increase from 1*d* to 1½*d*. Their justification was that the price of newsprint had become exorbitant. It must be remembered that the paper had been reduced in size to just four pages due to the shortages. The editor promised on 1 June 1918 that at the first opportunity they would return to the old price.

The Spanish Flu

Though the Great War had ended, more misery and deaths occurred due to the great influenza epidemic, which affected Ireland between June 1918 and March 1919. The outbreak of influenza was a worldwide epidemic, which apparently killed between 16 and 20 million people in the world at this time, perhaps more than were actually killed during the Great War itself. It was called the 'Spanish flu', as it was first reported in Spain. It arrived in Ireland in the late spring and early summer of 1918 and reappeared again in the early months of 1919. About 800,000 people were affected in Ireland, of whom about 20,000 died, a national mortality rate of around 2.5 per cent.

The second wave of the flu outbreak from mid-October to December 1918 had the most impact in Ireland. The provinces of Leinster and Ulster seem to have been most affected. Some counties escaped with a very low outbreak of the epidemic. County Clare, for example, had the lowest rate of infection and mortality in the country, with only 0.4 per cent mortality, whereas County Kildare had the highest with 3.9 per cent mortality. Nevertheless, the outbreak created a major health scare in the county, judging by the newspaper reports of the epidemic and some deaths in the county. According to Dr G. Peacocke of the Adelaide Hospital, Dublin, 'Death came with dramatic suddenness, often within 24 hours.' Many of its capricious victims were young people.[40]

The epidemic seems to have hit County Clare between the end of October and the end of December of that year. The weather at this time of the year was quite wet, with about 16 inches of rain during these three months as recorded at Carrigoran. The first mention of the virus was in the newspaper of 2 November, 'the outbreak in Ennis not as virulent as in other areas, yet it is of considerable severity. There is public alarm. The Mercy Convent has been closed, but the CBS and the Ennis National School are still open. There are two cases of death, a young lady, Miss McInerney, in Doora and Mr Frank Moloney, Victualler, Ennis. There is a big run on disinfectants … soldiers also affected … the virus resembles malarial fever.'

The next edition of 9 November indicated that the flu outbreak in Ennis had become more serious. The article referred to the 'scourge of influenza', 'the national school has been closed and the hospital is full. There are at least forty cases in town, only one death in hospital, but four deaths in the town. Some police affected … no necessity for alarm … avoid crowded places of assembly and disinfect.'

A week later the epidemic was still raging in the town:

This dreaded scourge continues to rage through the district, with violence, little if any abated, and again this week, some deaths have to be chronicled from its effects, the immediate cause in nearly all cases being pneumonia, following the influenza. In some cases the victims were only a few days ill. Among those who have succumbed are Mrs Hastings, mother of the parish clerk; Mr M. Torpey, a popular clerk in the West Clare Railway and Mr J. Cullinan, a well-known carpenter …

The hospital is now full to excess … Dr Coghlan, the Medical Officer, who has had a most strenuous time, day and night for some weeks, has at last been attacked and his work in the hospital has been undertaken by Drs MacClancy, Counihan and Duggan, and much valuable help is also being given by Mr Power, a medical student of Clare Castle.

All the national schools throughout the district within a wide radius of the town have been closed and reports from some country localities state that there have been some deaths from the scourge. We see it has considerably abated in Dublin.

By 23 November 'the scourge was still raging through the county, and though the worst effects seem to have passed in the town, still there have been several deaths from it, its principal resultant being pneumonia, chiefly of the septic type. On Thursday afternoon Constable Burke, a young man of splendid physical physique, a native, we believe, of County Mayo, succumbed to it at the County Infirmary. Constable Crowley, Corofin and Constable Burke, Quilty have also died from influenza, also Mr James Lillis, an enthusiastic and well-liked follower of the Mill Street Hounds. All the patients in the hospital are, we believe, doing well. Mr Denis O'Grady, Upper O'Connell St., a compositor at the *Clare Journal*, died after contracting a heavy cold, which developed into pneumonia.

On 30 November the paper reported:

> The epidemic still continues to claim its victims through the town and dis-
> trict and the hospital is still overcrowded with patients, the energies of doctors
> and nurses being taxed to their utmost by the constant demands upon them.
> There were over 200 cases in the institution on Wednesday and on the whole
> they are making steady progress. Among the victims this week is Mr O'Dea,
> of Barefield, for years foreman to Mrs McMahon, the Square and O'Connell
> St., Ennis … There are a number of cases in the county Infirmary and all are
> doing well … There were 37 cases in Clare Castle on Wednesday. There was
> one death in the village.

The Ennis Dramatic Club put on a special performance of *The Colleen Bawn* at
the Town Hall on Tuesday 3 December:

> The performance is in aid of the poor of Ennis, who are at present suffer-
> ing under one of the worst visitations which has befallen us for many years.
> In ordinary times the pain and misery of the present scourge of influenza
> would be severe, but in the abnormal conditions of the present day, its effects
> are accentuated by the difficulty of obtaining adequate food and fuel and nat-
> urally, the poor are among the worst sufferers. The gaunt spectre of death has,
> alas, too often been amongst us in recent days, and where his scythe has not
> fallen, there have been left the ravages of disease in various forms. The victims
> appeal for help in their distress is one that will not fall on deaf ears, and we are
> sure that the charitable of the district will nobly respond.

In addition to this, the local branch of St Vincent de Paul held flag days on
Saturday and Sunday, 7 and 8 December to help the suffering poor of Ennis.

A special meeting of the Ennis Urban Council took place at the Town Hall
to take measures to relieve the distress in the town. At the meeting it was
revealed that Bishop Fogarty had donated a sum of £30 to relieve the distress
and that the local clergy were coordinating relief efforts through the Society
of St Vincent de Paul. Earlier in the year, the *Clare Journal* of 2 February noted
that Bishop Fogarty was willed £1,000 by the late Mr Matt O'Dea of Ennis,
who also gave £100 to the poor of Ennis, per the St Vincent de Paul Society.
Mr O'Dea was a brother of the Bishop of Galway. Other significant donations
to the relief fund, which were publicly acknowledged and amounted to about
£74, included a sum of £10 from Mr Thomas A. O'Gorman, Cahercalla, while
Mr James O'Regan of Sixmilebridge promised to send two wagons of fire
blocks before Christmas.

On 7 December the epidemic was reported to be on the wane, as there were no fresh cases reported compared with past weeks. 'Among the deaths were those of Mr Patrick McGann of Market Street, Ennis and Constable Gilligan of Connolly.'

The newspaper, however, reported that influenza had appeared in West Clare and in Kilkee its effects were accentuated by the 'merciless boycott' to which the turf sellers of the district had subjected it, since the Town Commissioners had the 'temerity' to fix a controlled price for that fuel. One peculiarly painful case was referred to at a meeting of the Town Commissioners – the tragic death of a young boy who was suffering from pneumonia. It was reported that the nurse attending the young boy was unable to get any hot water to apply a poultice, due to the absence of turf.

The death of this young man in Kilkee provoked a man named M. Whyte of Ennis Road, Miltown Malbay to write a very angry letter to the newspaper, denouncing the turf cutters of Kilkee for their role in the death of the young man:

Could such an act of selfishness and niggardliness be perpetrated by any Hun or savages as to leave their own kith and kin destitute of a fire during these hard and cruel war days. The turf cutters of Kilkee should blush with shame to call themselves Sinn Féiners …The turf belonging to the turf cutters should be taken from them and placed in a circle in some Fair Green. A fire should be made and all the jaunters thrown into the centre of the fire. This indeed, would be punishment poor enough when taken into consideration the recent death and of the insurmountable hardship they have placed their fellow brethren in.

The newspaper of 21 December reported that the influenza was on the wane, 'It is pleasant to be able to state that the Spanish influenza, malarial fever, or whatever it was, is now on the wane in Kilrush and Kilkee and the district generally. There are no further cases now for some time, nor, after all, were there so many deaths either in West Clare. Of course, there have been some sad cases.'

Overall, County Clare got off lightly, by comparison with other parts of Ireland and some parts of County Clare escaped the deadly effects of the flu altogether. For instance, there were no reported deaths from flu in the villages of Ballyvaughan and Kildysart.

However, there were more deaths early in the New Year. One of the unfortunate cases was that of Lt Francis James Slattery of the Royal Engineers, from Fergus View, Darragh, who contracted the virus in London, while returning home after being in a prisoner of war camp for about nine months. His death occurred on 9 January 1919. His incarceration may have contributed to his death as he may have been in a weakened state after his prison experience.[41]

Prisoners and Belgian Refugees

Although hostilities ceased on 11 November, there was still much war-related business to be conducted, such as the care of and repatriation of prisoners of war and the winding up of various charitable committees. The Prisoners' of War Aid Fund Committee were quite active throughout the year up to the end of the war and long after it. They identified all the Clare men who were prisoners of war on the Western Front and endeavoured to look after their needs, sending them clothes, such as socks, mufflers and other garments, as well as monthly food parcels, including cigarettes.

The cost of providing these services to the prisoners amounted to almost £90 a month and the government did not give financial assistance. The various committees relied mainly on contributions from a relatively small group of people, principally of the Protestant community, judging by the list of names of the subscribers. They also organised fundraising events such as bazaars, jumble sales, church collections and golf competitions. The Clare Needlework Guild was one of many charities that also worked assiduously throughout the war years to help the cause.

Serving soldiers were not forgotten either; as early in March, Mrs Studdert of Bindon Street, Ennis, issued an appeal for shamrock for the Irish regiments. The shamrock had to be despatched by Sunday 3 March to arrive in time for St Patrick's Day.

It seems that Lady Inchiquin of Dromoland Castle was the overall co-ordinator of war relief charities in the county. She and many other ladies gave generously of their time and money to war relief. In August Lord Inchiquin of Dromoland, who was county director for the Red Cross, published a list of the total monies subscribed to the various war charities since the outbreak of the war. He wrote, 'The list will not compare well with what other counties in Ireland have done, but considering how very few people subscribe in this county, it shows how great has been their individual generosity, and I am sure grateful thanks are due to the "few", who have done so much.'

Table 4
Total money subscribed to all war charities since the beginning of the war

Clare Needlework Guild	£548 11s 4d
Sailors' and Soldiers' Association	£1,086 12s 6d
Irish War Hospital Supply	£736 0s 0d
Prisoners of War Fund	£1,459 13s 3d
Belgian Refugees, Ennis and Clare Castle	£920 0s 0d
Belgian Refugees Newmarket-on-Fergus	£1,475 1s 0d

Irish Counties War Hospital £221 10s 0d
Queen's Work for Women £200 0s 0d

Total. £6,646 8s 1d

There seems to have been some substance to Lord Inchiquin's remarks about the 'few who have contributed so much', as a table of Red Cross Contributions in Ireland for the years 1917-18 showed that the amount collected in County Clare was £285 in 1917 and £439 in 1918, a total of £724. This was by far the lowest county subscription in all of Ireland during these years.[42]

Christmas parcels were sent to all Clare prisoners of war in November. The parcels contained the following: 2lb Irish stew; 1½lb cooked dinner; 1lb bacon; 1lb oxtail soup; ½lb of onions; 1lb dripping; 1lb plum pudding; 1lb strawberry jam; 1lb Parkin cake; 1lb milk; 1lb sugar; ½lb of tea; 150 cigarettes or tobacco; chocolate; Christmas card and a sprig of holly from Ireland.

One ex-prisoner, Sgt Maj. Browne from Ennis, who had spent three-and-a-half years in German prisons, sent a letter to the County Clare Prisoners of War Aid Committee thanking them for their assistance over the years. Sgt Maj. Browne, who was released before the war ended because of his poor health, thanked them on behalf of all those prisoners, 'who were still in the hands of the vile Huns'. He thanked them profusely for their help, 'which had sustained the prisoners and enabled them to laugh at their captors. Were it not for that support, many of them would be sleeping the long sleep in German soil ... Trusting that the people of Clare will respond to the call for funds ... the charitable funds were a great comfort to their brave sons, whose sufferings are unimaginable ...'[43]

Ethel O'Brien, Lady Inchiquin.
(Courtesy of the Hon. Grania R. O'Brien)

In October of the following year (1919), at the final meeting of the Prisoners of War Aid Committee, held in the Court House, Ennis, Sir Michael O'Loghlen of Drumconora, HML, reported that the County Clare Prisoners of War Aid Committee had assisted a total of 110 Clare men who had been prisoners of war. Three of these men had died in Kut, another one died in a separate Turkish prison, one died of neglect in German captivity, one was missing and two prisoners died on their way home from captivity.

Sir Michael O'Loghlen also stated that 5,897 parcels of food, as well as seventeen parcels of clothing, 156 pairs of socks, seven mufflers, two footballs and 102 parcels of tobacco were sent to the prisoners in Germany. However, they stopped sending all non-food parcels as the Germans confiscated them. More than £2,301 0s 3d had been collected between November 1915 and December 1918.

On their return home, each of the ninety-four prisoners was given £1 and further cash advances were given to twenty of them while they waited for army severance pay. Mrs Studdert, honorary secretary of the committee, proposed that the County Clare Prisoners of War Aid Committee be wound up and that the balance of £322 17s 10d in their account should be given to the Sailors' and Soldiers' Families Association

Co. Clare Prisoners of War Aid Fund Committee.

At the last monthly meeting of the above, the Hon. Sec stated that 4246 L/C J. F. O'Connor, Gordon Highlanders, has been repatriated, to Holland, and that parcels had been sent since March to 11317 Pte. Peter Keane, Irish Guards, from this Committee.

The Jumble Sale at Sixmilebridge, held by Mrs. Loftus Studdert and Mr. Wilson Lynch, realised the sum of £31, and a hearty vote of thanks was accorded to the promoters

The following subscriptions were handed in :—

Per the Hon. Sec. :—		£	s	d
Miss Kerin, Ennistymon (Collection for March) ...	...	4	0	0
Mr M. Lynch, Magowna	...	0	10	0
R. J Stacpoole ...	....	5	8	0
Mrs Hibbert ...	...	2	0	0
The Misses Butler ...	...	5	8	0
Mrs Stopford Hickman	...	1	16	0
R. C Edwards ...	...	0	5	0
Lady FitzGerald ...	...	12	16	0
F. V. Westby ...	...	5	8	0
Miss L Macnamara (Corofin Collection) ...	...	1	6	0
Mr and Mrs F. N. Studdert ...	...	1	16	0
Mrs M H Ellis ...	...	2	2	0
R. G. E Ellis ...	...	1	1	0
Mrs McCard ...	...	1	0	0
Mrs A. B. McCard ...	...	1	0	0
Miss F. K. Knox ...	...	1	0	0
Miss Kerin (Ennistymon Collection ...	..	4	0	0
Per the Hon. Treas :—				
Right Hon Lord Leconfield ...		25	0	0
Col O'Callaghan-Westropp	...	1	0	0
Thos Westropp ...	...	1	0	0

The parcels sent out for the month amounted to £54 14s 0d.

Saturday Record, 18 May 1918

in County Clare. This proposal was unanimously agreed.[44]

Meanwhile, conditions in the Turkish prisons were particularly bad as they were poorly fed and mistreated by the prison guards. One Australian sailor, John Harrison Wheat, who was an able seaman in the Royal Australian Navy (Ran 7861) was captured and incarcerated in Bor Nigde Prison (where Sgt Fred Perry was held) for some time. He describes the conditions as being horrific, 'the climate was very hot and the food was so bad that we wouldn't give it to the dogs in Australia!'[45]

The British Army in the Turkish city of Kut in Meso-potamia (modern Iraq), had been under siege from 7 December 1915 until 28 April 1916, before it sur-rendered to the Turks. Conditions were very harsh during the 147-day siege; it was bitterly cold, with low rations of food and limited medical supplies. Besides this, many of the besieged were suffering from malaria, dysentery and mal-nutrition even before the surrender. After the surrender of the British Army at Kut, the most embarrassing British humiliation after the military disaster at Gallipoli, some 11,890 Allied prisoners were taken on a long march to the town of Bor Nigde in central Turkey on 6 May. More than 67 per cent of the 2,592 British troops – that is about 1,750 men – who surrendered at Kut died at the hands of the Turks, either on the long march to the prison camps, or in the prisons such as at Bor Nigde. Three of the men who died following the surrender at Kut were from County Clare.[46]

Conditions in Turkish prisons seem to have been very harsh indeed. Sgt Fred Perry of Tulla had joined the army on 29 November 1914. He served at Gallipoli and was captured by the Turks and was a prisoner for a couple of years. According to his family, he weighed only 4 stone when he was released in 1918! In his diary he refers, among other things, to cricket matches with other prisoners. He shared the prison with other nationalities such as Indians, Russians, Romanians, British and French prisoners. He wrote several letters to his family from the prison camp at Bor Nidge.

A Letter from Somewhere in Turkey

In one letter, written on 7 February 1918, Perry describes the weather as being very cold, with snow every day. In his letter he requested the County Clare Prisoners of War Aid Committee to send him some food parcels, including tea, sugar and bacon, but unfortunately, the Clare Prisoners of War Aid Committee were only able to send relief to prisoners being held in Germany. In another letter to his mother, dated 8 September 1918, he wrote a sentimental letter about home and family matters, as the Turkish authorities would not have allowed him to be critical of his conditions of detention:

My dearest mother

I hope you and all at home are quite well and enjoying life. I have not had a letter from you for over a month. I very often think of you all at home these days, as I have plenty of time for reflection and my mind takes me back to times when I was very small ... I wish you all a very happy Xmas ... Although I am miles away from the children, yet they are ever with me in my thoughts, and are as it were, a part of my life and soul. You are now in the fall of the year and busy with the harvest. I hope you have a heavy one and that everything is thriving. The weather here is glorious and has been so since last March. The people here have finished threshing and are busy with the vineyard collecting grapes and making wine for the winter. We get very good potatoes here, much drier than in Ireland, as they do not get as much rain, with love to all, keep smiling and write. Au revoir,

Your affectionate son, Fred.[47]

Soldiers and Sailors Club

Within a short time of the war ending a branch of the Discharged and Disabled Soldiers' Federation was formed in Ennis and the first meeting, held on Wednesday 18 December 1918, highlighted their concerns and hopes for the future. The secretary, M.L.Hegarty, stated that the town of Ennis, with a population of 5,000 had given 1,100 of its men voluntarily since the outbreak of the war. They hoped that a Land for Soldiers Act would become law and urged the Irish MP to support it, 'as the labouring men of the county had played a major part in the war and a good many had paid the big sacrifice.' They demanded proper houses to live in, 'not death traps, which so many poor fellows have to face when they turn homewards broken up men'.

'What was it all for' they asked, and 'will labour have to wait again?' 'No', they stated. 'We have waited a long time and patience has its limit and that limit is reached, we don't want that weary wait and see again'. The secretary also pointed out that the Irish MPs showed very little interest in their welfare. 'Only one man ... Major Willie Redmond MP, was always anxious to do a good turn ... He was a soldier and was endowed with all that goes to make one ... He also paid the big sacrifice and now we miss his helping hand to steer us clear to our destination ... God rest his soul'.

'Any requests for assistance had now to be made to English Members'. (Note, the Sinn Féin MPs were pursuing a policy of abstention at this time, while only six Home Rule MPs were elected in 1918.) 'Now is the time we want to get over our difficulties, which are many. In the New Year we will want the help of all whole-hearted to gain our object which is Justice'.

Early in the New Year they formed a committee to establish a club in the town. The Soldiers and Sailors Club occupied the house in Church Street formerly used as a recruiting office for the British Army. Mrs G. de Willis set up a fundraising committee to pay the rent and carry out repairs. She organised a song recital and lecture on the songs of Robert Burns at 1 Bindon Street, Ennis, to be arranged by Revd Capt. J. Reid Christie, chaplain to the Scottish Horse. Singers included Mrs F.N. Studdert and Pte Gault of the Scottish Horse.

An appeal was also made for gifts for the club such as a billiard table, gramophone, books and magazines.[48]

The County Clare Belgian Relief Committee also wound up its affairs in May of the following year. Mr George McElroy, RM, honorary secretary of the Ennis committee, thanked all their supporters for contributing money totalling more than £1,000. He said that two of the refugees had died in Ireland, while all of the rest had returned to their 'ruined and pillaged homes in Belgium, with fervent expressions of undying gratitude to all who in Clare stood by them during the long dark years, 1915-1919'.[49]

In the meantime the county remained under martial law and hundreds of troops and extra RIC men tried to keep law and order in the county, while the members of Sinn Féin, the Irish Volunteers and the local members of the Irish Republican Brotherhood were growing in strength and becoming more defiant of the British Government. The election of 1918, with an overwhelming victory for Sinn Féin, gave the republicans a moral mandate to pursue their aims against the British, and the Irish Volunteers were determined to fight for Ireland's cause.

Just before Christmas an editorial in the *Clare Champion* expressed a sincere wish for peace:

> The Christmas of 1918 will be welcomed by all as one of general joy and thanksgiving at the lifting of the horrid nightmare which has enveloped our people for the past four-and-a-half years and we can only hope that it will be the forerunner of a long period of universal peace through the countries of the world. It has come at the time of the most awful war that has ever chastised mankind, which has brought empires and kingdoms rocking to their downfall, and wrought an upheaval, of which we can yet barely realise the extent.
>
> Our poor country has been by no means the least sufferer, though thank God, we have been spared the worst blows of the Red Demon of warfare. But many homes through the length and breadth of the land have given of their best and bravest to the great sacrifice, and willingly borne the attending tears and sorrow.
>
> The bright lining of the dark cloud which has so long hung over us is, however, now to be seen shining on our people, and we hope we are emerging from the shadow into days of prosperity and plenitude, though many hours of hardship and suffering have yet to be endured. But the worst is over, and the bells of the New Year, it will be the prayer of all, will ring out the thousand wars of old, and ring in the thousand years of peace. We wish all our readers a Happy Xmas and a prosperous New Year.[50]

Some Gallant Clare Men and Women

The following soldiers and nurses from Clare received awards for distinguished service in wartime: Sgt J. Slattery, from Kilrush, of the Canadian
Army was awarded the DCM. He had the distinction of serving with the
armies of three countries and fighting wars on three continents – Africa,
America and Europe. His citation read as follows, 'During an attack he led a
flanking party which rushed an enemy pill box. He personally shot eight of
the defendants, and succeeded in cutting off a party of the enemy who were
retreating. The success of the enterprise was largely due to him'. Sgt Slattery
served in the South African (Boer) War, where he won two medals. Then he
went to America where he joined the United States Army. While there he
was sent to Mexico and served during the troubles in that country. He next
went to Canada to volunteer for the Great War and was sent to France as part
of the Canadian Army.

Cpl Frank Gordon, of Clare Castle, serving with the US army was posthumously awarded the Croix de Guerre, the highest award of the French Army,
and the DSC from the US Military, for his heroic sacrifice in attempting to
rescue a wounded colleague in France.

Private Stephen Scully, RMF, from Ennistymon was awarded the Military
Medal for 'gallantry and fearless conduct on the battle field'.

> On August 28th during an attack this stretcher-bearer rendered most valua-
> ble assistance to the wounded of his own battalion and of the battalion of the
> King's Liverpool Regiment. He worked fearlessly and untiringly from 2 pm
> on the 28th until 6am on the 29th, and cleared a whole area of wounded. After
> the battalion had been relieved he refused to come out until he had rescued
> those who were lying in shell holes outside his own area. On September 2nd
> he displayed the same gallantry working in an intense barrage, bandaging the
> wounded, and later returning carried them to the aid post.

Military awards were granted to two brave Clare nurses for their services in military hospitals during the war. Miss Nellie Galvin, of Caherbanna, a member of
Queen Alexandria's Imperial Military Nursing Service, was one of 135 women
from the British Empire to whom the MM was awarded. Nurse Galvin trained
in the Meath Hospital, Dublin and in the County Dublin Infirmary. She joined
the Civil Hospital Reserve in October 1914 and served throughout the war
in casualty clearing stations and hospitals in France at places such as Etaples,
Bailliul, Abbeville, St Omer, Wimereaux, Malassie and Ebbinghem. Her citation
in the *London Gazette* of 31 July 1918 was as follows:

For bravery and devotion to duty during an enemy air raid, (at no. 10 Station Hospital, St Omer, on the night of 22-23 May), when four enemy bombs were dropped on the hospital, causing much damage to the ward in which Sister Galvin was on night duty. She remained in the ward attending to the sick, several of whom were wounded, and carried on her work as if nothing had happened. She displayed the greatest coolness and devotion to duty.

Miss Galvin was invited by King George V to Buckingham Palace on 18 December 1919. In addition, Miss Galvin received the 1914 Star as a member of the Civil Hospital Reserve, as well as British War and Victory medals.

(Miss Galvin was sister-in-law of Mr Sarsfield Maguire, editor of the *Clare Champion* and she took over the management of the paper from 1937 until her death in 1965.)

Miss Nellie Galvin SRN with the Military Medal. (Courtesy of the Galvin family, Ennis)

Another Clare nurse, Miss Cissie Moore, Kilrush, was awarded the DSM by the Greek Government for bravery and distinguished service at Salonika in Greece during the war. She was the only Irish nurse to have received such an honour.

Another Clare lady, Miss Mary (Molly) O'Connell Bianconi, from Ballylean House, Kildysart, was also honoured for her bravery during the war and was awarded the MM 'for conspicuous devotion to duty during a hostile air raid in 1918, when she showed great bravery and coolness'. Molly O'Connell was born on 22 December 1896. She was educated at Lack National School and later at Laurel Hill, Limerick and in Jersey. She went to 'finishing school' in Belgium and in Paris, but her education was interrupted by the outbreak of war. She joined the Voluntary Aid Department in 1915 and later the First Aid Nursing Yeomanry. She was transferred to France in 1917 and served in field hospitals at Amiens and St Omer, where she worked in the Women's Transport Service, ferrying wounded soldiers from the front line to hospitals and railway stations. She was

Mary (Molly) O'Connell Bianconi, SRN, MM. (Courtesy of the Irish War Museum)

presented with the MM by King George V in 1919. She served with the British forces again during the Second World War. Afterwards, she inherited Longfield House, Cashel, County Tipperary, where she opened a hotel. Mary O'Connell Bianconi died in 1968. In 2009 the new Department of Nursing and Healthcare at Waterford Institute of Technology was named the Mary O'Connell Bianconi Building in her honour for her services to nursing, by the Minister for Health and Children, Ms Mary Harney TD.

Sgt Clune, Kilrush, RGA, was presented with a DCM for 'gallantry and devotion to duty under continuous shellfire' by Gen. Sir Archibald Murray; Fr Clune, a chaplain with the Anzacs, a native of Ruan, was awarded the MC for his services at the front; Fr Moran, CF, a chaplain from Tulassa, Ennis, was awarded an MC for gallantry; Capt. P. Hickey, RE. Indian Expeditionary Force, Mesopotamia, from Kilkee, was awarded the DSO, while his brother, Capt. A.J. Hickey, Royal Army Medical Corps, received the MC for valour in France; Lt J.B. Maclachlann of Knockerra got the MC for bravery; Sgt W. Hickey of Clare Castle received the Meritorious Service Medal; 2nd Lt Henry Busker of Carrigoran, was awarded the MC for 'conspicuous bravery' serving with the Leinster Regt. in the field of battle in France, he was also awarded the Divisional Card of Honour; L-Cpl W.H. Cooks of Killaloe was awarded a bar to the MM;

Capt. W.F. Cullinan, Bellvue, Ennis, was awarded the Most Distinguished Order of St Michael and St George, in 1919; Lt F.J. Slattery, 7th Field Co. was mentioned in a despatch dated 7 April 1918, from Field Marshall Sir Douglas Haig, for 'gallant and distinguished service in the field'. This posthumous award was granted to the parents of Lt F.J. Slattery, Fergus View, Darragh in a letter from the Secretary of State for War, Winston Churchill, on 1 March 1919.[51]

Roll of Honour

By the end of this year at least 125 Clare people had died because of the war, including six women who drowned in the sinking of the SS *Leinster*. The majority of the soldiers were killed on the Western Front in Belgium and France, due to the German push in the spring, but others died in new fronts in Greece (Salonika) and in Palestine.[52]

> Calm fell. From Heaven distilled a clemency;
> There was peace on earth and silence in the sky;
> Some could, some could not, shake off misery;
> The Sinister Spirit Sneered: 'It had to be!'
> And again the Spirit of Pity whispered: 'Why?'[53]

7

IN MEMORIAM

Though the victims and survivors of the Great War were remembered by their families, that was largely a private grief. Most of those who died are buried far away from home in places such as Belgium, France, Turkey, or further afield and many have no known grave at all. So most of the people could not easily visit the graves of their family members, as it was too costly. There was no official commemoration of the fallen in the new Free State. The Protestant churches did make some efforts to commemorate the dead, with memorial plaques and stained-glass windows in many churches in memory of the fallen.

There are memorial tablets in the Church of Ireland churches of Ennis, Killaloe, Ennistymon, Kilnasoolagh, Spanish Point, and Tuamgraney. Indeed, in the Church of Ireland in Bindon Street, Ennis, there is a wooden cross which was originally placed over the grave of Lt John Frederick Cullinan Fogerty, who died on 8 August 1915 in Gallipoli. One brass plate in St Columba's commemorates six men from the parish of Dromcliffe, who died in the Great War. These memorials were erected by the families of the wealthier Protestants in County Clare, the landed gentry and professional classes.

There is no similar tradition in the Catholic churches, despite the fact that well over 95 per cent of the Clare dead of the First Word War were Catholics, even though many of the Catholic soldiers may have been persuaded by the Catholic hierarchy to enlist in defence of Catholic Belgium. So, there is no reminder in the Catholic churches of County Clare of those who died. However, in the old graveyard of Shanakyle in Kilrush, the Kilrush Ex-Servicemen's Association erected a wooden cross to commemorate their comrades who had fallen in the Great War. This was erected in the early 1920s.[1]

On the other hand, the republicans who died in the War of Independence in County Clare are buried in their native parishes, and monuments have

Memorial plaque for G.W. Maunsell at Ennis. (Courtesy of Eric Shaw and John Power)

been erected where they were killed. It was easier to cherish the memory of the twenty-four republicans from County Clare, who died during the War of Independence than that of the 600 or so men and women from County Clare who died during the First World War. Incidentally, the twenty-four Clare civilians who died during the War of Independence are also largely ignored by the public.[2]

Michael Brennan, in his memoir, contrasted the manner in which he and other republicans were treated immediately after the Easter Rising with the reception they received eight months later when they returned from English prisons:'At Limerick station we had been sent off by a crowd of British soldiers, "separation allowance ladies" ("viragoes"), who howled insults, pelted us with anything handy and several times had to be forced back physically by the military escort, when they tried to get us with fists or nails.'

'Eight months later, when I got off the train in the same station I was met by a crowd numbering several thousands, who cheered themselves hoarse and embarrassed us terribly by carrying me on their shoulders through the streets.

It was all very bewildering, but it made clear that the Rising had already changed the people.'

Michael Brennan's welcome on his return in January 1917 was similar to that given at Ennis in December 1918 to James Madigan of Ennis, when he was greeted at Ennis railway station after serving more than twelve months jail in Belfast for his republican activities. Hundreds of supporters turned out to greet him and he was given 'a most enthusiastic reception'. The Volunteers organised a parade into O'Connell Square, but the RIC interrupted the procession into the town centre with a baton charge.[3]

It was almost the reverse with those who volunteered to join the British forces in 1914 and 1915. After enlistment they may have received notice in the local papers and been cheered off by their families and friends

Memorial Cross for Lt John F. Culligan R.E. (Courtesy of Eric Shaw and John Power)

at local railway stations, but there were no cheering crowds to welcome home the 'gallant' men as heroes, who had served in the British Army or Royal Navy during the Great War. Instead, they came home quietly after demobilisation, to a country that no longer acknowledged their sacrifices and bravery.

Armistice Day

After the war the British Legion was active in many of the large towns and cities, assisting those ex-servicemen who had fallen on hard times. In 1919 Earl Haig became the patron of the Poppy Fund to raise funds to assist the wounded soldiers and sailors. In the large towns and cities, especially in Northern Ireland, there were Armistice Day services to commemorate the dead.

Some attempts were made to have Armistice Day ceremonies in County Clare after the War of Independence and the Civil War. It would have been very difficult to sell poppies in County Clare for the British Legion during the years of the 'troubles', 1919-1924. However, there was some commemoration in Ennis on the first anniversary of Armistice Day, which did not please some republicans in Clare as Michael Brennan, Commandant of the East Clare Brigade described in his memoir:

> On Armistice Day 1919 I was in Ennis. British soldiers, ex-soldiers and their women folk were demonstrating to celebrate the victorious end of the war and Union Jacks were flying in a few places. We didn't interfere until the English flag appeared on the County Infirmary. I went at once to the hospital and demanded an explanation as to why an enemy flag was flown on a hospital owned and maintained by the people of Clare. I learned that it had been done on matron's orders. I pulled down the flag and burned it in the street in the presence of a crowd which had gathered.
>
> I anticipated reactions and they came quickly. I went to the Old Ground Hotel and was talking in the garden with Canon O'Kennedy and other members of the Clare Sinn Féin Executive when a shrieking and apparently drunken mob of soldiers and civilians arrived … I fired three shots over their heads and they disappeared hurridly … I made a strategic retreat over various walls until I reached the convent where the nuns kept me until it was dark. Two of the local priests called then in a motor car and I went with them to St. Flannan's College. I learned from them that the 'hunt was up' and that the town was being combed for me by military and police … A day or two later I left St. Flannan's and motored to Cork dressed as a woman, complete with the flowing motoring veil of those days …[4]

There were many ex-servicemen living in the town of Ennis and indeed in many towns of Clare after the war. They were a significant presence in the community. Indeed, during the local elections of 1920, one candidate, James Frawley, stood as a candidate for the Comrades of the Great War party. He received eighty-four votes, the third highest, and was elected a member of the Ennis Town Council. In that election six Sinn Féin and five Labour councillors were also returned. Another ex-soldier, Martin McCarthy, was co-opted onto Kilkee Town Commissioners in 1919.[5]

The Ennis branch of the Comrades of the Great War held a committee meeting at the Comrades Club, Church Street (now called Abbey Street) on 30 October 1925, in which they expressed their gratitude to Mr G. de Willis and Mr Schofield and others who assisted Mr F. Connolly, who suffered severe financial difficulties after the death of his wife. Mr E. Reynolds (chairman) presided at the meeting. The resolution of thanks was proposed by Mr Michael M. Hegarty and seconded by Mr James Frawley.[6]

Shortly after this meeting, a notice of an Armistice Day Choral Evensong to be held at Ennis parish church, Bindon Street, was put in the *Saturday Record*. The preacher was to be Revd R. Boyd, MC, HCF. A collection would be taken up afterwards for the Soldiers' and Sailors' Association of County Clare.[7]

Over the following nine years Armistice Day ceremonies at Ennis were recorded in the *Saturday Record*. The newspaper reports give us some idea of the work and influence of the British Legion in distributing relief in the town of Ennis to wounded and disabled ex-servicemen. W.H. Ranalow was honorary secretary of the Ennis branch of the British Legion around this time.

In 1926, two parades took place, one on Remembrance Sunday, 7 November, and the second on Armistice Day, 11 November. The parades started from the British Legion Hall in Mill Road and the men marched with medals and other awards. The parade was led by Maj. G. Studdert and was inspected by Gen. Parker. The route of the parade was from Mill Road, via Harmony Row and Abbey Street into O'Connell Street for 10 o'clock Mass at the Pro-Cathedral. On Armistice Day the men marched to the Franciscan Friary for 11 o'clock Mass, after which there was a two-minute silence in O'Connell Square, followed by the Last Post and Reveille. Later that afternoon a choral evensong was held at Bindon Street church, where the preacher was Revd H. MacManamy, MC, Legion of Honour. Afterwards, a collection for Earl Haig's Poppy Fund was held. According to one report, 'about 120 ex-servicemen, proudly wearing medals and decorations, formed into ranks four deep and, led by the Ennis Brass and Reed Band, paraded to the church'. The ceremonies were described as 'solemn'.[8]

There was a similar parade on Remembrance Day in 1927, again under the command of Maj. G. Studdert, with services in the Franciscan friary and in the Protestant church at Bindon Street. The parade was inspected by Lord Inchiquin of Dromoland. Also, a dance was held in the Legion Hall (women's section), in aid of Earl

ARMISTICE DAY

Choral Evensong

IN ENNIS PARISH CHURCH

at 8.30.

PREACHER—REV. R. BOYD, M.C.,H.C.F.

COLLECTION FOR THE SOLDIERS AND SAILORS ASSOCIATION OF COUNTY CLARE.

Notice of Armistice Day Service, *Saturday Record*, 28 October 1925.

Haig's Poppy Fund. The *Saturday Record* of 12 November published a letter from Earl Haig appealing for the charity. The ceremonies in Ennis were 'quiet, but impressive'. The parade was led by the band of the United Labourers' Association. Lord Inchiquin, in addressing the assembly spoke 'of the hardship and distress prevailing among many ex-servicemen, owing to the dearth of employment'. He advised them 'to remain united in the comradeship which had been formed, fostered and cemented during the Great War'. During the day 'Flanders Poppies were worn by many in the streets of Ennis'.

Mrs Olive Gordon Stewart was in charge of the poppy sellers and organised several entertainments during the week on behalf of the Wounded and Disabled Soldiers. A 'most successful' dance was held at the British Legion Hall on Monday night, 14 November, which was attended by more than forty-five couples from Ennis and its environs. Music was supplied by the D'Vine Band from Dublin and dancing was non-stop from 9.30 p.m. until 4 a.m.! The dance and catering was organised by Mrs Pearson, Provincial Bank and Mrs Gordon-Stewart.[9] It would seem that those who went to the dance were middle-class people, as 5s was a significant sum of money during these years.

There was only a brief mention of British Legion activities in 1928. There was a dance in the British Legion Hall on 21 November. H.W. Ranalow, hon sec., also wrote a letter to the paper stating that £157 had been collected through the sale of poppies in 1926, but that more than £300 had been distributed in County Clare to ex-servicemen in need.[10]

Similarly, in 1929 little was written about the Remembrance Day ceremonies. The men marched from the Legion Hall to the friary, where Mass was celebrated. A two-minute silence was observed at O'Connell Square at 11 a.m. Later that afternoon a memorial service was held at Ennis Parish church, Bindon Street, where the preacher was Revd Canon Adderly, Hon. CF. The new honorary secretary of the British Legion Ennis Branch was H.V. White, who stated that poppies would be sold on 9 and 11 November. He also said that grants to disabled men in County Clare amounted to three times the amounts raised in Clare by the sale of poppies. There was also a poem by John McCrae, called 'In Flanders' Fields':

> In Flander's fields the poppies blow
> Between the crosses row on row,
> That mark our place; and in the sky,
> That larks still bravely singing, fly
> Scarce heard amidst the guns below.
>
> We are the dead. Short days ago
> We lived, felt dawn, saw sunset glow

Loved and were loved, and now we lie
In Flander's fields.

Take up your quarrel with the foe;
To you from failing hands we throw
The torch; be yours to hold it high.
If ye break faith with us who die,
We shall not sleep, though poppies grow
In Flander's fields.[11]

The only news reports in 1930 and 1931 were that the annual fundraising Poppy Dance would be held in the Legion Hall. Tickets would be 5*s*. Dancing was from 9 p.m. to 2 a.m. in 1930, but from 9 p.m. to 3.30 a.m. in 1931! Supper was included in 1931. In 1932 an average of £100 was distributed in County Clare, while it was reported that much more was collected in the county.[12]

In 1933 More than sixty ex-servicemen took part in the parade on Remembrance Day led by Capt. Jack Corry DCM from Labasheeda. There were ceremonies in the Ennis Friary and at the Church of Ireland church in Bindon Street. It was reported that 'poppies were worn by many people in the streets of Ennis and that the anniversary passed off as quietly as to be unnoticed'.[13]

The last newspaper report of the 1930s relating to an Armistice Day ceremony at Ennis dates from 17 November 1934 when, 'A parade of about 100 ex-servicemen under the command of Capt. Corry, DCM, Labasheeda, took place from the British Legion Club to the Friary. Following Mass there was a two-minute silence followed by the Last Post and Reveille. In the evening there was a commemoration service in the Ennis parish church, Bindon Street, where Canon Griffin gave a sermon'.[14]

Unfortunately, the *Saturday Record* closed down in September 1935 and there were no further reports of Remembrance Day ceremonies at Ennis or elsewhere in the county until 1948. That is not to say that they did not occur, but they were rarely reported during the forties and fifties in the only remaining Clare newspaper, the *Clare Champion*, which had pursued a more nationalist policy since 1917. The ceremonies may have continued, as there were at least 100 marchers in 1934, which was a significant number. There were no hostilities shown to the ex-servicemen by the IRA or other militant republican groups in the county. The Second World War began in September 1939 and Ireland declared neutrality. This is perhaps another reason why the surviving combatants of the First World War may have been sidelined. The Irish people had more important things on their minds.

After the Second World War ended in 1945 there was no mention of a Remembrance Day ceremony. Instead the *Clare Champion* was more focused on the erection of a memorial to four members of the East Clare Brigade of the IRA who were shot at the bridge of Killaloe on 17 November 1920.[15]

On the thirtieth anniversary of the Armistice, in November 1948, a Remembrance Day service was held in the Church of Ireland church at Bindon Street, Ennis. Afterwards there was a collection for Earl Haig's Poppy Fund. It must be remembered that the Poppy Fund was now catering for veterans of both world wars. There was no report of any publicly advertised Mass in any of the chapels in Ennis in memory of the deceased.[16]

There was no mention of a Remembrance Day ceremony in Ennis in 1958 on the fortieth anniversary of the armistice. Of course, this was during the years of the so-called IRA 'Border

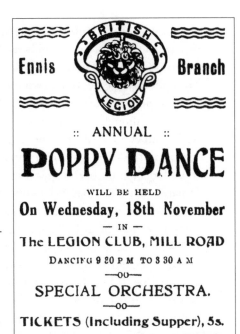

Ennis   BRITISH LEGION   Branch

:: ANNUAL ::

POPPY DANCE

WILL BE HELD

On Wednesday, 18th November

— IN —

The LEGION CLUB, MILL ROAD

DANCING 9 20 P M TO 3 30 A M

—oo—

SPECIAL ORCHESTRA.

—oo—

TICKETS (Including Supper), 5s.

Saturday Record, 6 November 1931.

Campaign' of 1956-62 and national republican sentiment was high at the time. As a matter of interest, the Great War memorial at Limerick, which had been erected by the Limerick Branch of the British Legion in 1929, was blown up in August 1957. A significant factor in this was that Sean South, an IRA Volunteer from Limerick, was killed while taking part in the IRA 'Border Campaign' on 1 January 1957.[17]

IRA memorials were erected at Miltown Malbay and at Lahinch to honour two local IRA Volunteers. There was also a memorial service in Tuamgraney with a Mass for the repose of the souls of the deceased members of the East Clare Brigade IRA and members of Cumann na mBan, with a procession to the Garden of Remembrance. The year 1958 was also the centenary of the foundation of the Fenian movement and there was a huge parade around Ennis from O'Connell Square to the Maid of Éireann monument at the Mill Bridge to honour the memory of the 'Manchester Martyrs'. Perhaps it was prudent not to have a Poppy Day collection in Ennis at this time.[18]

Ten years later, in 1968, to mark the fiftieth anniversary of the Armistice, there was a notice in the front page of the *Clare Champion* that the Annual Poppy Collection would be made on 8-9 November in Ennis. The report stated that £245 had been collected in the previous year and that war veterans in County Clare had benefitted from grants of £400 from British Legion funds. They had received help to purchase coal and groceries. It mentioned that

membership of the British Legion in Clare now amounted to about seventy
men. (Again, it must be remembered those who benefitted were survivors of
two world wars.) By now, those who had fought in the Great War were probably in their late sixties or older and the numbers were dwindling rapidly.[19]

The annual Remembrance Day collection continued in Clare for a few
more years, though it received only intermittent mentions in the local papers.
In November 1970, during the height of 'the troubles' in Northern Ireland,
a report in the *Clare Champion* stated that a three-day Poppy Day collection
would be taken up in the streets of Ennis between 5-7 November. The article stated that £201 had been collected in 1969 for the Irish men who had
fought in two world wars. The newspaper report stated that at least forty
needy cases had been helped, with the provision of clothes, groceries and
coal. Widows were also assisted and three of them had been given grants for
funeral expenses during the year. It was stated also that for every £1 collected
in Clare, the HQ of the British Legion returned £4 to the county. During
the early years of 'the troubles' membership of the Limerick Branch of the
British Legion declined steadily. The branch was closed and their premises in
Hartstonge Street Limerick was sold. The Clare members and friends were also
affected by 'the troubles'. There were no more reports in the local papers of
Poppy Day collections after 1970. Incidentally, the special issue commemo-
rating the seventy-fifth anniversary of the foundation of the *Clare Champion*
printed in 1978 hardly mentioned the Great War at all.[20]

Some Veterans of the Great War

Time was marching on and the number of Clare veterans of the Great War was
shrinking rapidly. Belatedly, some local people and historians began to take an
interest in the few known surviving Great War veterans living in Clare. But,
even if they wished to discuss the war, the memories of the old men were
fading.

Tommy Kinnane

One of the few ex-British Army veterans who were honoured in his community after the war was Tommy Kinnane of Clare Castle. This was because
after he left the army in 1918, he joined the IRA and took an active part in
the War of Independence. Born in 1882, he joined the Ordnance Survey in
his teens and was many years with the British Army. He then left the army for
a few years. During this time he was captain of the Robert Emmet's football

Gillespie Collection

Tommy Kinnane
Old I.R.A. Clare Castle
1882-1947

Tommy Kinnane, Old IRA.
(Courtesy of Eric Shaw, per the Gillespie Collection)

team that won the county football title for Clare Castle in 1908. When the Great War broke out he joined the Royal Engineers and spent two years in France. When home on leave in 1918, he was arrested by the RIC for possession of a Sinn Féin flag and was sentenced to six months in jail. While in jail he made contact with some members of the IRA and upon his release, he joined the IRA and became a member of the flying column of the mid-Clare brigade. His military training and experience was quite useful to the IRA in Clare and he served on many engagements during the War of Independence. He took the anti-treaty side in 1922 and was badly wounded in an engagement with Free State forces in 1922, losing an eye. After his death in 1947, his friends in Clare Castle and in the Old IRA erected a Celtic Cross at Clarehill Cemetery, Clare Castle, in his honour. An IRA firing party gave him a gun salute, firing three volleys over the grave and the Last Post and Reveille was sounded in his honour. Mr Bernard Power, Clare Castle gave the oration at the graveside on 22 July 1950.[21]

John 'Pal' Horan

There was an interesting article in the *Clare Champion* of 27 September 1958 about John Horan of Madden's Terrace, Clare Castle, a veteran of the Great War, who was then 84 years old. This was, I believe, the first interview with a Great War veteran in the *Clare Champion* since the war ended in 1918. In this article

John 'Pal' Horan in 1958.
(Courtesy of Eric Shaw)

headed PROFILE OF A GRAND OLD MAN, he was described as 'a fine elderly character, who had many years service with the British Army.'

He played at full forward position on the Clare Castle football team that won the Clare Senior Football championship in 1908 and he also played for the county against Limerick in the Munster Football Championship.

John 'Pal' Horan had joined the Clare Militia in 1894 for a soldier's pay of 9*d* a day, trained in Dover and Plymouth and served in the Coastal Defence Artillery at Queenstown in defence of Cork Harbour. He retired from the army as a reservist, but was 'called up' in August 1914, at the start of the Great War. He was assigned to the 9th Battalion of the Munster Fusiliers and was sent to France in 1915 after some training in Buttevant County Cork.

He took part in many engagements with the Germans, had numerous narrow escapes in the trenches and came through without any wounds. In 1917 he was transferred back to the Coastal Defence Artillery. But, shortly afterwards, he was assigned to the Labour Corps in France and he ended his war years on the ground staff of the Royal Flying Corps. He was then 44 years old.

In the interview John Horan, like so many other Great War veterans, did not mention much about his wartime experiences, except to say 'we had good times and bad times in the army'.[22]

Michael 'Robineen' Gallagher

Another veteran was Michael 'Robineen' Gallagher of Burton Street, Kilrush, who was interviewed by a *Clare Champion* reporter in August 1985. He was then 88 years old. In the interview he gave a brief account of his early life and war service.

I was born in 1897 at Fermoy, Co. Cork, where my father was a quarter master in the army. Within a few weeks of being born my father was killed by a horse and my mother moved to Kilrush. Times were tough then. We had a small house because we could not afford anything else. My mother had one shilling a week to pay for the house and look after us. This wasn't enough and she was forced to go out to work to earn more money.

When I was 17 Lord Swinbourne [*sic*], Lord Lieutenant of Ireland was in Kilrush recruiting for the army and along with a good number of locals I joined up. It was the last day of December 1914 at the old Post Office in the Square here in Kilrush. I joined the army not to serve anyone, but to get the money to feed ourselves.

After signing up we went to Aghada Camp in Cork … and from there we were sent to Durham for further training and from there to the Dardenelles. Three of us were picked up and sent to Egypt because we were too young. After being sent to a few different places we were brought back to England and discharged as we were under-age.

I came back home to Kilrush, but a couple of weeks later re-enlisted with the Royal Garrison Artillery and went to Spike Island in Cork in early 1916. From there we were sent to fight in all the major battles of the war.

For a bed we used to spread a ground sheet on the wet, use our fists for a pillow and we had the sky over us for a blanket. On many occasions we slept in vaults, which were swarming with rats. I remember arriving at a little church during the war which had no roof. As we went in the doorway there was a big drop. There was a vault underneath for coffins but there were no headstones. The Englishmen took out the remains of the coffins to make beds, but I, being a Catholic, just could not do this. I recall that I slept standing up against a wall in the wet and dirt on many occasions.

Michael 'Robineen' Gallagher. (Courtesy of the Gallagher family, per Peadar McNamara Collection)

On one occasion (during the Battle of the Somme in July 1916) I was sent by an officer to get a container of water and ended up buried under a pile of rubble after a shell landed. When I was dug out by my comrades I could not lift my legs and I was moved to hospital for a few weeks before being moved to Warrington in England for further treatment.

After the war I came home to Kilrush, where I stayed for a month, but I enlisted again in 1919 and was sent to Dacca in India, where I stayed until 1924 when I left the British army …

Michael 'Robineen' Gallagher died at the end of December 1988, aged 91. He was, reputedly, the last survivor of the hundreds of men from Kilrush and the district of West Clare who had served in the Great War.[23]

Joe Hawes

Joe Hawes was another Clare war hero, who had served with the British Army from 9 January 1916 to the end of the war, and continued his service with the British Army for a few years afterwards. He was sentenced to death for his republican actions in 1920, but was fortunately reprieved and returned to Ireland as a hero. Indeed he was one of the few British soldiers who was accorded hero status at that time, but that was due to his brave protest in opposition to British atrocities in Ireland during the War of Independence.

Joe Hawes was born in Kilkeedy, Tubber on 20 August 1883, the son of a tailor. He enlisted in the 4th Battalion Munster Fusiliers in Galway on 9 January 1916 and served with the regiment until it was disbanded after the war on 18 February 1919. His military career started in Tralee Barracks. He was then posted to the 6th Battalion Munsters Mediterranean Expeditionary Force on 28 August 1916. He served in

Joe hawes, *c.* 1950. (Courtesy of Oliver Hawes)

Salonika and Palestine and was wounded in action on 15 March 1918 at Garza on the Nablus Road, Palestine.

Between 16 May and 26 October he was posted to France with the British Expeditionary Force. He returned to barracks at Plymouth on 28 September 1918. Fortunately, he survived these battles. When the war ended the Munster Fusiliers were disbanded on 18 February 1919. However, Joe decided to stay with the British Army and joined the Connaught Rangers the next day, 19 February 1919. He was sent to the Punjab in India and arrived at Bombay on 24 November 1919. From there he was sent to Wellington Barracks at Jallundar in the Punjab, on the North West Frontier.

While home on leave in 1920 he heard about and witnessed the activities of the British Army and the atrocities committed in Clare and elsewhere by the British Army and by the 'Black and Tans' during the War of Independence. When he returned to duty in India Joe Hawes told his Irish comrades what was happening at home and he was the instigator of what became known as the 'Connaught Rangers Mutiny' on 29 June 1920, when he led a number of Irish soldiers in protest against 'British atrocities in Ireland'.

Joe and the other mutineers were court-martialled at Dhagsai Prison on 23 August 1920. For his actions as one of the ringleaders, Joe, along with sixteen other Irish soldiers, was sentenced to death on 4 September 1920; but fortunately for him only one Irishman, John Daly, was executed for the mutiny. Joe's death sentence was commuted to life imprisonment. He spent some time in solitary confinement in British prisons such as Maidstone, Portland and Shrewsbury and went on hunger strike to protest against his barbaric treatment.

Under the amnesty agreement after the Anglo-Irish Treaty, Joe Hawes was released on 4 January 1923. On the next day he returned to Ireland a hero and settled in Kilrush for the rest of his life. He joined the 12th Battalion of the Irish Army on 8 May 1923 at Union Barracks, Clonmel. He was discharged on medical grounds on 19 March 1924. He then set up a business as a barber in Kilrush. He married Mary Quinn at Tubber on 29 April 1923 and had five children, two sons and three daughters. He died on 29 November 1972 while on holiday in Birmingham and was buried in Shanakyle, Kilrush on 6 December, where his tombstone has the following inscription: '... Joseph Hawes, leader of the Connaught Rangers Mutiny, India 1920 ...'[24]

Patrick 'Pappy' Neville

The last known Ennis-born Great War veteran to pass away and perhaps the last Clare-born surviving veteran of that terrible conflict was Pappy Neville, who died in Carrigoran Nursing Home at Newmarket-on-Fergus on

5 January 1993 about seventy-five years after the Armistice. He was 103 years old! His centenary was marked by family and friends at a special Mass in Carrigoran. One of his visitors on that occasion was Lady Inchiquin of Dromoland Castle. The *Clare Champion* article was headed, 'War Hero Celebrates a Century'.

It is noteworthy that the word 'hero' has been used by journalists in the local Clare publications since the early 1990s to describe veterans such as Pte 'Pappy' Neville, who survived the war into extreme old age in 1993 and Pte Thomas Davis, who was executed by the British in 1915. That term was not used to describe First World War combatants between the 1920s and the 1990s in the local papers of County Clare. That word 'hero'

Patrick 'Pappy' Neville, *c.* 1990,
(Courtesy of the Neville family and Eddie
Lough, per the Peadar McNamara Collection)

in itself reflects a cultural change, an acceptance of the bravery of the men and women from the county who served in the Great War as 'one of our own'. It was an acknowledgement of their sacrifices, a rehabilitation of their character and a welcome integration into national and local historiography.

Patrick 'Pappy' Neville was born in Ennis on 5 August 1890. He trained as a tailor, but joined the Royal Irish Regiment in January 1912, enlisting at Clonmel. After training and service in India, Pte Neville, Reg. No. 10568, was transferred to France at the outbreak of the war after doing some training at a home barracks from 13 October to 18 December, 1914. On 19 December he was sent to France to fight in Flanders. During the early spring of 1915 he was seriously wounded at the Battle of Ypres, suffered frostbite, had one foot amputated and had another partially amputated. He was invalided out of the army and discharged on 14 May 1915 and he returned to Ennis in 1916. He had served fifty-nine days in the trenches at the front.

He later married and had a family and settled in one of the ex-servicemen's cottages at Clonroad, Ennis. These cottages for disabled ex-servicemen were built in many towns and villages in County Clare around 1923 under the aegis of the Soldiers' and Sailors' Association.[25]

(Note, according to this newspaper article of 20 July 1990, at least 538 Ennis men served in the Second World War of whom seventy-one were killed serving with the Munster Fusiliers and seventy-one others died while serving in other regiments. When the war ended there were 382 Ennis men still in the services. Of these, twenty-three were from the Turnpike Road, where Patrick Neville had lived.)

Thomas Davis Pardoned

Between October 2001 and April 2009 several articles were written in the *Clare Champion* by various writers about the fate of Ennis man Pte Thomas Davis, who was executed by the British Army at Gully Beach, Gallipoli on 2 July 1915 after being found guilty of leaving his post. The purpose of these articles was to highlight the issue and seek a posthumous pardon for Pte Davis and more than twenty other British soldiers executed during the war. He was finally exonerated and described as a World War 'hero' in these reports. These articles also served to raise awareness of the Clareman who served in the First World War.[26]

Public Acknowledgement

The Clare war dead were publicly acknowledged in other ways also around this time. Two war memorials were erected in 1999 in Clare, one at Kilrush and the other at Ennistymon. The erection of these memorials may have been partly due to the peace in Northern Ireland, after The Belfast Agreement of Good Friday 1998. The belated interest of journalists in the local papers and the work of Peadar McNamara and other interested people in places such as Kilrush and Ennistymon may also have been significant in this.

At Kilrush 'a very moving prayer service' in remembrance of the men and women from Kilrush and West Clare, who served in the Great War was held at Old Shanakyle graveyard on Sunday, 14 November 1999. A 'poignant moment' during the prayer service was when the names of the thirty-seven members of the Royal Munster Fuslilers Regiment from Kilrush who died in the war were read out. The keynote address was delivered by Mr Tom Prendeville, NT, a Fianna Fail member of Clare County Council. After he unveiled the plaque a wreath was laid and the ceremony concluded with a rendition of 'The Green Fields of France'. The ceremony was organised by Mr George Harratt of Kilrush. Since then, Remembrance Day ceremonies have taken place annually at Old Shanakyle.[27]

A memorial was also erected at Churchill cemetery, Ennistymon, in November 1999. However, this memorial plaque is not exclusively related to men and women from Ennistymon and North Clare, who fought and died in the Great War. It is an all-embracing one including all Irish men and Irish women who fought and died in all wars before and after the Great War. Furthermore, it commemorates all members of the permanent defence forces of Ireland who died in service at home and abroad, especially those who died on the United Nations peacekeeping missions.

This memorial plaque was erected in 'a spirit of peace and reconciliation' by the North Clare War Memorial Committee. After a special commemoration Mass was held at Ennistymon church the plaque was unveiled on Sunday, 21 November 1999 by Mr Paddy Harte, former Fine Gael TD from Donegal, who was Joint Co-executive Chairman of A Journey of Reconciliation Trust.[28]

The development of more friendly relationships between Britain and Ireland during the late twentieth century, with a joint ceremony at Messines Peace Park in Belgium attended by Queen Elizabeth II and President McAleese on Remembrance Day 1998, Queen Elizabeth's historic visit to Ireland in 2011, and the state visit by President Higgins to Britain in 2013, combined with power-sharing administrations in Northern Ireland, has removed much of the legacy of bitterness in Anglo-Irish relations.

The centenary of the outbreak of the Great War also acted as a spur to individuals and local communities to commemorate those who took part in that terrible conflict and has led to a deeper appreciation of the bona fides of the men and women who participated in that awful tragedy. Parishes throughout the county are now beginning to acknowledge the people from their communities who served and suffered during the First World War. This is reflected in parish newsletters, booklets, newspaper articles, memorial plaques and a greater interest in the story of the men and women from County Clare who served in the Great War.

Historiography of the Great War in Clare

'The only thing worse than being talked about is not being talked about.'

Oscar Wilde.

Apart from the Remembrance Day ceremonies in the various churches and Poppy Day collections, besides the occasional references to Great War veterans such as John 'Pal' Horan, 'Pappy' Neville and Michael 'Robineen' Gallagher, little was written about the contribution of Clare men and women to the Great War between the years 1918 and 1988.

The seminal historical work on the years 1913-1921 in Clare was written by David Fitzpatrick in his book, *Politics and Irish Life 1913-1921, Provincial Experience of War and Revolution*, which was published in 1977. However, the main focus of this great study is the rise of Sinn Féin in the county, while the Great War looms in the background.

Gen. Michael Brennan, a native of Meelick, was a leading republican in Clare and became commandant of the East Clare Brigade IRA during the War of Independence. His memoir, *The War in Clare 1911-1921, Personal Memoirs of the Irish War of Independence*, which was published in 1980, gives a very impressive first-hand account of these troubled times from a republican perspective, but it does not say much about the Great War.

Martin Staunton published an article in *The Irish Sword*, the Journal of the Military History Society of Ireland, Vol. XV1 (1984–85) on 'Kilrush Co. Clare and the Royal Munster Fusiliers'. This was a detailed study of the men from Kilrush who fought in the war, and, as such, the first academic study of the impact of the Great War on County Clare.

Other academic studies on the county during the war years include Daniel McCarthy's, *Ireland's Banner County, County Clare from the Fall of Parnell to the Great War, 1890-1918*, which was published in 2002. This book devotes several chapters to the war and indeed more than 110 pages to County Clare during the war years. This volume also has an appendix listing more than 500 Clare men and women who died in the war.

Paul O'Brien has also written a study of recruitment in Kilrush during the war entitled 'Provincial Recruiting in the First World War: The Glynns of Kilrush', in militaryheritage.ie. This was published in 2013, based on his study of the Glynn papers.

Tom Burnell's, *The Clare War Dead*, published in 2011 gives a comprehensive list of more than 600 people associated with County Clare who died in the Great War. There are also biographical sketches about those who died, citing among other things, age, rank, military service, regiment, place of death and site of grave or war memorial. It is an excellent reference book.

Burnell's book has been complemented by Ger Browne's publication, *The Great War 1914-1918, The Clare War Dead World War 1*, which classifies the war dead by parish. This booklet was published by the Clare Roots Society in 2014 to mark the anniversary of the war and to highlight the development of a Peace Park in Ennis.

The vast majority of local history books, even those recently published in the county have largely ignored the impact of the Great War in Clare, while most, if not all of them, have a chapter, or more on the War of Independence in the respective parishes. One notable exception is Sean Kierse's *The Killaloe Anthology*, published in 2001, which has a chapter listing the casualties of war from Killaloe and district and has a chapter on 'Soldiers and Sailors Trust Houses' in Killaloe.

Pádraig Óg Ó Ruairc, *Blood on the Banner, The Republication Struggle in Clare*, published in 2009, is a study of the rise of the Volunteers from 1913 to the end of the Civil War. It barely touches upon the Great War, but gives good insights, unfortunately without references, into political developments in Clare – the split in the Volunteers after 1914, plans for a 1916 Rising in Clare and the conscription crisis of 1918.

A recent major study, *Clare History and Society, Interdisciplinary Essays on the History of an Irish County*, edited by Matthew Lynch and Patrick Nugent, series editor, William Nolan, Geography Publications, Dublin, 2008, only mentions the Great War indirectly in one out of twenty-eight chapters – chapter 15 by Brendan O'Cathaoir, 'Another Clare: Ranchers and Moonlighters, 1700-1945', pp. 359-424. O'Cathaoir mentions the East Clare election and 'cattle drives' after 1916 (see pp. 385-395).

One man who did Trogan work to reclaim the memory of the Great War veterans and victims from County Clare was the late Peadar McNamara of Inch, an art teacher at Ennis Community College. Peadar's interest was sparked off when he joined a committee, called 'The Clare Historical Project', set up by Michael Connolly, an inspector with the Department of Education in 1987, to compile a manual of local history studies in the county. One of Peadar's areas of specific interest was 'the involvement of Clare people in the Great War'. Peadar engaged enthusiastically with this project and began to compile a mass of information on the topic. Over the years he even visited the sites of battles and war graves in France, Belgium and Turkey.

One year after the formation of the committee, Peadar organised an exhibition in Clare County Library on the theme of 'Clare and the Great War'. This was done in conjunction with the Clare County Library Service and the Western Front Association. The exhibition also toured the other libraries in Clare and later went to Dublin.[29] Peadar compiled the first list of the Clare war dead, which he published in the *Clare Champion* of 11 November 1988, on the seventieth anniversary of Armistice Day. Peadar kept up the interest and continued to highlight the war. He published another list of the Clare war dead in the *Clare Champion* of 2008, on the ninetieth anniversary of Remembrance Day.

Peadar, along with Revd Bob Hanna, Church of Ireland rector of Drumcliffe and Fr Tom Hogan, administrator of Ennis parish, was the instigator of the revival of an ecumenical Remembrance Day ceremony in Ennis in 2008. On that occasion some dissident republicans protested outside Ennis Cathedral. Since then, Remembrance Day ceremonies have taken place annually at Ennis Cathedral.

Other fruits of his work were shown in an article, 'The Great War (1914–1918) and some effects on Clare', published in the *Other Clare* of March 1989. This was in fact the first local historical study of the impact of the Great War in the county published in that journal. Peadar's article ended with a quote from Ben Johnson: 'Cursed be he who first invented war!'

Peadar's written works and the revival of the Remembrance Day ceremonies at Ennis have done much to generate interest in the Great War and the contribution of Clare people to that terrible conflict. Before his untimely death Peadar had a vision of erecting a suitable monument in Clare to commemorate the Clare war dead. Unfortunately, Peadar did not live to see this project brought to fruition, but members of his family are part of a committee set up in 2013 to erect a war memorial in a peace park in Ennis to commemorate the Clare men and women who died in the Great War.

While the general public and local newspapers have, until fairly recent times, largely ignored the men who fought and died in the Great War, there was also a remarkable silence, an historical amnesia, and a seeming lack of interest among local historians in the impact of the Great War in Clare. The major historical journals circulating in the county include *The Other Clare*, and *The North Munster Antiquarian Journal* (*NMAJ*). Other publications have included *Dal gCais*. There have been remarkably few historical articles on the Great War published in these journals.

The *NMAJ* which circulates mainly in the old Thomond area of Clare, Limerick and North Tipperary, has been published by the Thomond Historical and Archaeological Society in Limerick since the 1930s. In all that time, in the fifty-three editions up to 2013, only two articles relating to the Great War were published, one about the Belgian refugees in Limerick (Vol. 39, 1989) and the other relating to the economic impact of the Great War in Limerick (Vol. 50, 2010). There was nothing written on the Great War in County Clare.

Dal gCais, published in Miltown Malbay, had only one article on Eamon de Valera in 1917 in Issue No. 4. While the *Old Limerick Journal*, published in Limerick also had only one article on 'The Volunteers, the 1916 Rising and afterwards', in Vol. No. 39 (1993).

In Slieve Aughty, *East Clare Heritage*, which has been published in Tuamgraney since 1989, there has only been one article relating to the Great War, 'Willie Redmond, a Forgotten Hero', in Vol. 10, 2002.

The Other Clare has been published annually by The Shannon Archaeological and Historical Society since 1977. In the thirty-seven

publications up to 2013 there has been only one historical study relating
directly to the impact of the Great War in Clare out of a total of 686 articles
and that was Peadar McNamara's article in Vol. 13, published in 1989. Eight
other historical studies were published about this era (1913-1923), but all of
them were related to republican or Sinn Féin activities in the county at this
time, dealing with such topics as 'Sectarianism in Co. Clare during the War of
Independence',Vol. 34 ; 'The experiences of a Sinn Féin priest, 1919-21',Vol.
31; 'The Patrick Hennessy letters',Vol. 30; 'Sinn Féin hunger strikers',Vol. 36;
'British servicemen secretly buried in Clare during the War of Independence',
Vol. 36; 'The prison letters of Canon O'Kennedy',Vol. 37; 'The Waldron
family in Co. Clare',Vol.17; and 'Kathleen Talty and de Valera's escape from
Lincoln Jail',Vol. 12.

Surprisingly, even the thirty-eighth volume of *The Other Clare*, published in
September 2014, on the 100th anniversary of the Great War does not have an article relating to the Great War, but it does have an interesting article on the Battle
of Clontarf in 1014. As a matter of interest, Brian Boru did not survive the Battle
of Clontarf in 1014, but his direct descendant, the Hon. Donough O'Brien, later
16th Baron Inchiquin, was injured in 1917, while another descendant, the Hon.
Desmond O' Brien, was killed in 1915.

'History', it is said, 'is written by the victors'. The survivors and political heirs
of the 1916 Rising and the War of Independence have dominated Irish political life since then the 1918 election. Their struggle has taken priority over the
tragic story of those who fought in the Great War. The struggle in the War
of Independence in Clare, involving a few hundred Volunteers, has eclipsed
the memory of the combatants of the Great War in which perhaps more than
4,000 Clare men and hundreds of women were involved. The Easter Lily has
blossomed while the Flanders Poppy has withered.

The republicans who fought for Irish freedom were honoured as patriotic
heroes, while the First World War veterans, who fought bravely and courageously
in hellish conditions in places such as the Western Front and in Gallipoli were
ignored. Those who died in the cause of Irish freedom have been enshrined in
the martyrology of Irish patriots. The republican story is celebrated in visual art
in works such as Sean Keating's 'The Men of the West'), in song and in story.
Their deeds are proudly recorded in local history books published throughout
the county, while the courageous deeds of the brave men who fought in the
First World War were rarely mentioned, or, worse still, ignored. Hopefully, this
publication, along with others recently published, will cherish the memory of
and acknowledge the bravery and sacrifices of the many thousands of men and
hundreds of women from County Clare who served, fought, suffered and died in
the terrible Great War of 1914-1918.

CONCLUSION

County Clare was one of the most Catholic counties in Ireland, with over 98 per cent per cent of the population of more than 104,000 in the census of 1911 being Catholic. There was a small scattered Protestant community in the county comprising about 1,900 people. Though small in number the Protestants were significant in economic matters in the county, with substantial land holdings. They were also significant in middle-class professions such as law, finance and medicine. Though they had lost political power since the 1870s at parliamentary level and at local level since the Local Government Act of 1898, they were still prominent as deputy lieutenants of the county and as magistrates.

The passage of the Third Home Rule Bill in 1912 was widely welcomed by the vast majority of the people of Clare and the Thomas Davis song, 'A Nation Once Again', became almost a national anthem at this time in nationalist circles. However, while the nationalists of Clare were rejoicing at the prospect of Home Rule in 1914, the small unionist community in the county were apprehensive at the prospect of living in a state and county dominated by a large majority of Catholics and nationalists. Some spokesmen for the Protestant community, especially Revd Armstrong, rector of Kilrush and H.V. MacNamara, DL, of Ennistymon, a prominent landlord in north Clare, raised fears of sectarianism in County Clare. There was much controversy and publicity in the local news-papers such as the *Clare Journal* and the *Saturday Record*, both owned by the Protestant Knox family of Ennis, highlighting the fears and concerns, whether real or imagined, among the Protestant and unionist community when Home Rule was due to be implemented in 1914. To some extent, the land agitation campaign, a continuation of the Land War in County Clare, was inextricably linked with the Protestant fears, as many of the landlords were Protestant, while the majority of their tenants were Catholic.

However, events in Ireland were significantly transformed in 1914 due to the activities of the unionists in the north of Ireland. Their actions, both legal and illegal, involving such actions as the formation of the Ulster Volunteers, and gun-running at Larne, combined with the 'Curragh mutiny' among the Protestant and unionist army officers based at the British Army HQ in Kildare, cast a gloom over the prospects for a peaceful transition to Home Rule for Ireland. Also, political developments in England, granting concessions to the unionists, such as the right of temporary exclusion of six northern counties, further undermined the Home Rule Act. The threat of force by the unionists had paid off.

In response to these developments the National Volunteers were founded after a call by Eoin MacNeill in February 1914. Within a couple of months branches of the National Volunteers were established in almost every parish in county Clare. The Irish Home Rule Party, led by John Redmond, MP, was a significant factor behind the formation of the National Volunteers, along with the AOH, which had branches in many parts of the county. Some prominent local politicians, such as Councillor P.J. Linnane, JP, chairman of Ennis Urban Council, and Catholic clergy, with the encouragement of the Catholic Bishop of Killaloe, Dr M. Fogarty, were active in the formation of the Volunteers throughout the county, to ensure that the British Government would keep its promise and grant Home Rule to Ireland. The main nationalist newspaper in the county, the *Clare Champion*, also enthusiastically supported the formation of the National Volunteers throughout the county.

Despite the formation of the National Volunteers as a countervailing force to the threats from the Ulster Volunteer Force, there were further disappointments in March. British Prime Minister Asquith granted some concessions to the unionists, allowing them the right to temporarily opt out of a united Home Rule Ireland. Despite these concessions by the Liberal government and by John Redmond, MP, there were still hopes that the unionists were bluffing and that Home Rule would still be introduced as originally promised under the 1912 Act.

But the unionists were not bluffing and there was much talk about the prospect of civil war in Ireland over the introduction of Home Rule. The Church of Ireland Bishop of Killaloe and Kilfenora, Dr Berry, expressed a sincere wish in July that there would be peace in Ireland and appealed to the Protestants and unionists of County Clare to remain in the county and live in harmony with their Catholic neighbours after Home Rule became law.

In July Asquith made further concessions to the unionists at the Buckingham Palace Conference. John Redmond agreed to the suspension of Home Rule, while Asquith suspended the proposed partition of Ireland to exclude six counties. Thus, in the words of UCD historian Ronan Fanning, 'Redmond nourished the nationalist delusion that the partition of Ireland was avoidable'.[1]

With the outbreak of war in early August 1914, the Home Rule Bill was formally passed in September 1914, but its enactment was temporarily shelved until the end of the war. Ironically, the outbreak of the Great War prevented the development of a civil war in Ireland, which many feared over the proposed introduction of Home Rule in 1914.

In 1914 the Home Rule Party and the AOH were the main political forces in County Clare. These political organisations were backed by the Catholic Church and by the *Clare Champion*. With the outbreak of war there was strong support for John Redmond's policy committing the National Volunteers to fight with the British Army. However, as the war dragged on and as casualties mounted due to the horrific slaughter on the western and indeed other fronts, support for the war dwindled, as did support for the Home Rule Party.

From a small nucleus of opposition the Irish Volunteers, also known as the Sinn Féin Volunteers, became a significant force in local and national politics, especially after the 1916 Rising, when the leaders were executed and turned into martyrs. Though they numbered only between 300 and 400 men in the county, they were active and vocal in promoting their cause. Men such as the Brennan brothers of Meelick openly defied the British authorities by brazenly parading in uniform even under arms. Some Catholic priests, such as Fr McGrath, CC of Clare Castle, and Ballyea parish and Fr Culligan, CC of Carrigaholt, were also prominent in promoting Sinn Féin in the early years of the war.

The Irish Republican Brotherhood, taking advantage of England's difficulties, opportunistically planned a rebellion for 1916, to strike a blow for Irish freedom. The Easter Rising of April 1916 laid the foundations for the modern Irish state and brought about a sea change in Irish politics, with the rise of Sinn Féin and the terminal decline of the old Home Rule Party. Though County Clare, like most of Ireland, was relatively quiet during Easter Week, many republicans in Clare, such as Art O'Donnell, Michael Brennan and others, were expecting a rising and did indeed turn out at Easter, expecting orders to rise up, but the orders never came.

The death of Willie Redmond, MP in 1917, and subsequent election of Eamon de Valera showed the decline of Redmond's Home Rule Party. The rout of the Home Rule Party was completed in the general election of 1918 when the Sinn Féin candidates in Clare were not even opposed. Significantly, the two leading bishops in the county, Dr Fogarty of Killaloe and Dr O'Dwyer of Limerick, had publicly abandoned their support for Redmond's party and strongly endorsed Sinn Féin after 1917. Even the conservative Bishop of Galway, Kilmacduagh and Kilfenora, Dr O'Dea, supported Sinn Féin after the 1918 election. The *Clare Champion*, the leading nationalist paper circulating in the county also abandoned Redmond's party after the death of Willie Redmond, MP, and gave strong backing to the Sinn Féin Party.

With the outbreak of the war in August 1914 there was an initial sense of shock in the county. The loyalist and unionist community in the county responded to the king's call from a sense of duty and loyalty to the crown. This view was fully endorsed by the *Clare Journal* and the *Saturday Record*. The nationalist MPs for Clare, Willie Redmond and Arthur Lynch, fully supported John Redmond's policy urging the National Volunteers to join the British war effort. This policy also received the backing of the Bishop of Killaloe, Dr Fogarty, and the Bishop of Galway, Kilmacduagh and Kilfenora, Dr O'Dea, but was not supported by Dr O'Dwyer of Limerick. However, the vast majority of the National Volunteers in Clare were reluctant to join the army and they also abandoned the National Volunteers, in case they were conscripted into the British Army.

The prosecution of the war involved much propaganda, with a great deal of emphasis on the fate of 'poor Catholic Belgium'. This was an appeal to the instincts of the Irish Catholics. Almost all the local papers carried huge advertisements appealing to Irish men to volunteer and fight against German tyranny. They were urged to fight for the freedom of small nations, for the Catholics of Belgium, and for liberty, democracy and civilisation. Men were urged to 'do their duty' and fight for the 'honour of Ireland'.

There were also cinematic shows of the war scenes in France and Belgium that were shown at the cinema in Ennis. There were colourful campaigns in the county when the bands of the Munster Fusiliers and the Irish Guards toured the county during the summer of 1915, seeking recruits.

Attempts were also made to put pressure on young men to volunteer by insinuating that they were cowards. The words 'shirkers' and 'slackers' were frequently used in the media during 1915 and 1916 through letters and other comments to shame young men into joining the colours.

Perhaps the highlight of this phase of the recruitment campaign was the tour of West Clare by the Lord Lieutenent, Lord Wimborne in late August 1915. He was greeted enthusiastically and given a warm Irish welcome in the main towns such as Kilrush, Kilkee, Miltown Malbay and Ennistymon. The Lord Lieutenant hoped that a modern version of 'Clare's Dragoons would win glory and honour in the battlefields of France against the Germans'.

The Catholic Church in the county was initially broadly supportive of John Redmond's policy towards the war, as outlined at Woodenbridge, County Wicklow on 20 September 1914. However, there was no unanimity either at hierarchical level or indeed at parochial level on support for the war. Initially, it could be argued that of the three bishops with ecclesiastical jurisdiction in the county – two of them, Dr O'Dea and Dr Fogarty – were supportive of Redmond's policy, while, Dr O'Dwyer was not enthusiastic for the war, as he took Pope Benedict's pleas for peace seriously. It would also seem to be the case, judging by C.E. Glynn's list for West Clare, that the vast majority of the parish priests in the county were also supportive of recruitment for the war. Only a small minority of curates, apparently four in all in the county, spoke out against the war and against recruitment in the early years of the war.

However, over the course of the war years the support of the Catholic hierarchy was gradually undermined, firstly by political developments in Britain in 1915 and secondly by political events in Ireland during 1916. Bishop Fogarty privately lost faith in Redmond and the Home Rule party after Carson, the Unionist leader, was included in the British War Cabinet in 1915. Bishop O'Dwyer publicly turned against John Redmond's party over Redmond's rejection of the pope's pleas for peace in August 1915 and over the treatment of Irish emigrants in Liverpool in 1915. Both of these bishops regarded the men of 1916 as martyrs. Bishop O'Dwyer publicly endorsed Sinn Féin after the 1916 Rising, while Bishop Fogarty came out publicly in support of Sinn Féin after the 1917 by-election caused by the death of Willie Redmond, MP, in July 1917.

Bishop Fogarty, who had, in the early years, publicly described the war as 'a sign of God's anger at sinful humanity', welcomed it as a divine purgative of Providential good, 'its purifying waters', he wrote, 'would cleanse society of corruption, sensuality and socialism'. However, by 1917 he had become totally disillusioned by the war and he began to publicly oppose it. By then, it had become 'an accursed war', and 'a war of plutocrats'.

Bishop O'Dwyer, part of whose diocese was in South East Clare, was the moral and spiritual leader of the nationalist opposition to the war and he contributed significantly to the rise of Sinn Féin after 1916. Bishop Fogarty's letters to O'Dwyer confirm that Bishop O'Dwyer's opinions were widely circulated and hugely influential in the county. After Bishop O'Dwyer's death in 1917, Bishop Fogarty of Killaloe became the moral voice of the opposition and the ecclesiastical champion of Sinn Féin.

All three bishops in the county supported the anti-conscription campaign in 1918 and the policies of Sinn Féin during the November election of 1918. Besides the bishops, it can be seen, judging by the numbers of clergymen assenting to de Valera's election in 1917 and 1918, that a majority of the younger clergymen in the county, especially the curates, were broadly sympathetic to the Sinn Féin policies, while many of the older parish priests were still loyal to the Home Rule Party, now led by John Dillon after the death of John Redmond in 1918.

Religion played a significant role in the Great War and the outbreak of the war was used by the Catholic Church and indeed other churches as a spur to a religious revival. To Pope Benedict XV and Bishop Fogarty, the outbreak of the war was a sign of God's anger at man's apostasy from God and the spiritual malaise and secularisation infecting mankind at this time. Religion was used by some prominent churchmen and by politicians as a factor in motivating the Catholics of Ireland to enlist. In a fusion of propaganda and patriotism they cited the fate of Catholic Belgium and Poland, which were at the mercy of the 'barbarous Huns'. Some clergy also mentioned the Armenian Christian massacre at the hands of the Muslim Turks as a motivating factor. The Great War became a great Christian crusade, a just war. Even Fr Moran became outraged at the behaviour of the 'Prussian butchers', 'the Prussian beasts', who, he said, were a cancer in the German army to be eradicated.

In 1942, an American chaplain Revd T. Cummings wrote, 'there are no atheists in a foxhole'. The evidence from many Clare correspondents testifies to the vital role of prayer and sacraments in the lives of the soldiers. The letters from the Catholic chaplains, Fr Glynn and Fr Moran testify to the importance of religion to the soldiers facing death on a daily basis. Maj. Willie Redmond in his letters to Bishop Fogarty, to P.J. Linnane and in the book *Trench Letters*, published posthumously, mentions the deep faith of the Catholic soldiers at the front, with religious devotion to the Mass and the sacraments before they went 'over the top' and the importance of the rosary and the rosary beads to the men. Redmond stated that the revival of religion was one good consequence of the war. The letters of Pte John Power also highlight the importance of his religious duties before he went 'over the top'.

Besides the diligent practice of their faith in the trenches, their relatives at home in Clare must have been besieging Heaven with their prayers for the safety of their loved ones at war. There were benedictions, novenas and constant prayers for peace. The 'white gloves' given to the local judges between the years 1915 and 1917 testifies to a highly moral society where crime and drunkenness were virtually absent.

Society in County Clare under the influence of war and the Catholic Church seems to have become more puritanical. By 1917 Bishop Fogarty was still justifying the war as a dreadful instrument of divine wrath, purging social evils. He denounced feminism and the suffragettes, the 'demoralising' cinemas, as well as pubs and clubs in the towns, which, he said, were promoting scandal. He also denounced 'frivolity, fancy costumes and hedonism' and even welcomed restrictions on excursions by train.

The Catholic clergy played a major role in society and they had huge influence in politics. It was indeed ironic that Col Arthur Lynch, MP, in his book, *Ireland: Vital Hour*, published in 1915, wanted to reduce the power of the Catholic Church in Ireland, when in fact he had been proposed for the vacancy in West Clare in 1909 by Fr James Monahan; and the Catholic clergy of Clare probably had a strong influence in his nomination and election. With this book Col Lynch made an implacable enemy in the Catholic Church. The political power of the Catholic Church in Clare and elsewhere was seen in the role of the clergy in supporting John Redmond's party and policies up to 1916 and in the rise of Sinn Féin after the Easter Rising. It was also displayed during the anti-conscription crisis when the Catholic churches were used as venues for signing the petition, when all public meetings were banned during Martial Law.[2]

Women, of course, were also victimised by the war. Thousands of Clare women had husbands, brothers and sons serving in the British, American, Australian and Canadian forces. The women suffered psychologically, constantly worrying about and praying for their loved ones at war. They mourned the losses of their beloved sons, husbands and fathers and had to care for the wounded men after the war ended.

The absence of conscription in Ireland and the reluctance of young Claremen to enlist reduced the need for the women of Clare to do work in jobs and professions traditionally associated with men. One Clare woman who fought and won a battle for equality at work was Ms Georgina Frost who was rejected for the post of clerk of the Petty Sessions at Sixmilebridge in 1917, though she had been assisting her father in that position for several years and had been unanimously appointed by the local magistrates. She was re-appointed to the post in 1920, after an appeal to the Supreme Court.

The 'separation women', the wives of soldiers and sailors, received separation allowances, which perhaps gave them some economic freedom and financial control for the first time in their lives, while their husbands were away at the front. Though there were occasional references to 'drunken' women', there was no evidence of widespread abuse in County Clare of the separation allowances through alcohol abuse. Widows were granted pensions for the rest of their lives. However, the cost of living more than doubled during the war years and the poor women and their families were very badly off.

Clare nurses outside the County Home, Ennis.
(Courtesy of the Peadar McNamara Collection)

The 'separation women' were naturally supportive of their husbands and quite vocal in their opposition to Sinn Féin during the war years, as Michael Brennan recorded in his memoirs, referring to them as 'viragoes'.

Many Clare women played a vital role in the Great War. Women trained as nurses and served in the field on the western, or other fronts, or else in military hospitals in Britain and elsewhere. Indeed, two Clare nurses, Miss Nellie Galvin of Caherbanna and Miss M. O'Connnell-Bianconi, of Kildysart were awarded the MM for their services in field hospitals in France, while Nurse Cissie Moore of Kilrush was awarded a DSM for service in Salonika. Unfortunately, at least five Clare nurses, Misses Nora and Delia Davoren from Claureen, Ennis; Margaret and Brigid O'Grady from Newmarket-on-Fergus, and Miss Nellie Hogan of Ralahine, Newmarket-on-Fergus were among the nine Clare people, six of whom were women, who drowned in the sinking of the SS *Leinster* on 10 October 1918.

The upper-class women of Clare, mainly Protestant, had a huge role in fun-raising for war charities, such as the Red Cross, wounded and disabled soldiers and sailors, prisoners of war, Belgian refugees, etc. In the early years even the women's branch of the AOH, a Catholic nationalist body, organised a fundrais-ing concert to assist the men at war. The female relatives of the men serving abroad also supported them privately by sending food parcels, cigarettes, wool-len socks and especially letters. These supports from home were most welcome by the troops and sailors who were enduring horrific conditions far from home. However, it is notable that County Clare contributed the lowest amount of money to charity in Ireland during the war years. Lord Inchiquin summing up the charitable donations in 1919 was very grateful to the 'few who had contributed so much'.

Many women of Clare took a very active part in the recruitment cam-paigns of late 1915 and early 1916. Ms Florence Glynn, Kilrush, chaired the inaugural meeting of the West Clare Ladies Recruitment Committee, while Lady Inchiquin of Dromoland chaired the East Clare Ladies Recruitment Committee. The membership of these committees came largely from the Protestant community in Clare. The women may have been very persuasive in encouraging reluctant young men to join up.

Of course, some women of Clare took a very different view of the war. They came from a more republican background and they opposed John Redmond's policy of supporting the war. These women became more active after 1916, when they joined Cumann na mBan and they had a prominent role in the anti-conscription campaign of 1918.

Clearly, the war had had a profound impact upon politics in the county, with the destruction of the Home Rule Party and the rise of Sinn Féin to prominence. In 1914, though Home Rule was on the cards, there was a strong hint of parti-tion. The events of 1916-1918 confirmed in the minds of most Irish people that

Ireland could expect little or nothing from the British Government. Home Rule would only bring nominal freedom and Ireland would be partitioned.

Within a short time it was obvious to the military authorities that the war would not be over quickly and Kitchener appealed for a million men to join the new army. Advertising in the papers would not be sufficient to meet this demand and the military authorities decided to organise recruitment in a more professional manner. The Department of Recruitment in Ireland was set up and recruitment organisers were appointed in each county. Two recruitment organisers were appointed in County Clare, Mr M. O'Halloran of Tulla in East Clare and Mr C.E. Glynn of Kilrush in West Clare. These local recruitment committees, which involved the most significant people in each district, especially the Catholic parish priests, played a major role in encouraging voluntary recruitment. The local public bodies such as urban and county councils, as well as boards of guardians in the county also passed resolutions in support of voluntary recruitment. Because of the activities of these local recruitment committees and local organisers, recruitment peaked in 1915 and looked set to increase in 1916, but the 1916 Rising changed everything.

It is remarkable that there were few reports of recruitment meetings in the county after 1916. It is also significant that the Glynn papers had no references to recruitment activities after the Easter Rising up to the end of the war.

The Sinn Féin members and Irish Volunteers actively opposed recruitment in the county. Their activities became much more significant after the 1916 Rising and recruitment declined sharply.

With the war of attrition on the Western Front and indeed on many other fronts, there was a voracious demand for new soldiers, but the majority of eligible young men of military age in the county, mainly farmers' sons, were reluctant to enlist. Attempts were made to shame young men into enlisting by referring to them as 'slackers' and 'shirkers'; but, despite these accusations, many young men refused to enlist. Eventually, desperate for recruits, the British tried to introduce conscription in Ireland in 1918, but led by Dr Fogarty, Catholic Bishop of Killaloe, the people of Clare almost unanimously rejected conscription. The British, faced with such nationalist opposition were forced to abandon its proposal to introduce conscription. They had to rely upon voluntary recruitment and even granted the Boer War rebel, Arthur Lynch, MP, for West Clare, whom they had sentenced to death in 1903, a commission as a colonel in the army to organise an Irish Brigade in 1918.

War news was carefully censored in the national and local press, with propagandist press releases issued by the War Office, usually highlighting Allied successes and demonising the Germans. Some more details of the war campaigns were filtered through letters published in the local papers, by combatants, especially in the army. Some perceptive letters were written by clergymen, especially Catholic chaplains, to their friends in Clare. Examples of these included letters from Fr Moran to Councillor P.J. Linnane, Ennis and Fr Gwynn SJ to Dr Garry of Trinaderry. These were published in the local papers and brought the horrors of war to the people of Clare. Some other soldiers' accounts were written privately and not published in the papers.

While many soldiers wrote short accounts of their experiences in Gallipoli, the most comprehensive account of the campaign in Gallipoli was written by Capt. Poole Hickman from Kilmurry MacMahon, shortly before his death in 1915. Through all these sources people in Clare became familiar with the struggles in France and Belgium such as at Ypres and the Somme, as well as more distant places such as Gallipoli.

The two Clare MPs also made observations about the war. Col Arthur Lynch, MP, gave illustrated lectures in Clare about the trench warfare in France and discussed war tactics. However, he managed to alienate his most powerful Clare supporters in the Catholic Church and in the nationalist paper, the *Clare Champion,* by writing a highly controversial book, *Ireland: Vital Hour* in 1915. He was finally given a commission as a colonel in the British Army to form an Irish Brigade in 1918, but he had very limited success in forming it before the war ended.

On the other hand, Willie Redmond, MP, who had enlisted in January 1915, sent letters from the front line to significant people in Clare, such as his friend Councillor P.J. Linnane, JP, and to Bishop Fogarty. He also wrote articles for a British paper, the *Daily Chronicle*, which were posthumously published in a book called *Trench Pictures from France*. Willie Redmond had an idealistic vision that the unionists from the north, men of the 36th Ulster Division and nationalists from the south in the 16th Irish Division, would, by fighting together in France and elsewhere against the common enemy, forge a bond between themselves and help bring about Irish unity on the battlefields. Although the 16th Irish Division fought alongside the 36th Ulster Division at Messines in July 1917, and a fatally wounded Willie Redmond was cared for by men of the 36th Ulster Division, the unity in the battlefield did not translate into unity in Ireland. Willie Redmond's 'naive vision' died, as did Willie Redmond, on the Western Front.

The economy had mixed fortunes during the war. Initially, there was a panic and a run on the banks. Tourism was badly hampered by the war, especially in places like Kilkee, Lahinch and Killaloe as reserve officers were called up, and the bathing lodges were shut down for the rest of the season. However, tourism seems to have recovered by the summer of 1918 as the resort of Kilkee was crowded in early August of that year. Trade was also affected and dock workers in ports such as Clare Castle and Kilrush were badly affected by the downturn in commercial traffic as British coal was difficult to secure due to war priority needs in Britain.

On the other hand, war was good for business and the farming and fishing economy of Clare got a significant boost through the government purchases of horses for cavalry as well as for transport purposes and provisions for the army and navy. The price of agricultural products increased sharply from the first months of the war and the cost of food had more than doubled by the end of the war. E.E. Lysaght, writing in 1918, stated that 'Irish farming had become more profitable and more self-sustaining than it had been in the previous 70 years'. Likewise, the value of fish stocks also increased by more than 66 per cent in weight and by 400 per cent in value between 1914 and 1918.[3]

The food supply in Ireland and in Clare became more urgent as the war continued and shipping losses mounted due to German submarine attacks. The farmers benefitted from this increased demand for food, but the weather was not always favourable to good harvests. This was especially the case during the years 1917 and 1918, when, due to terrible weather conditions, there was a real and genuine fear of famine. The shortage of food in the UK motivated the government to introduce compulsory tillage, with farmers obliged to till up to 15 per cent of their land, while farmers with over 200 acres were legally obliged to till at least 20 per cent of their land. This may explain why some of the extensive landowners were prepared to let out some of their large farmlands on conacre for grazing, as it would reduce the need for ploughing up their lands. The Tillage Act also created problems in a county such as Clare, where only about 30 per cent of the land was actually suitable for tillage, and only about 8 per cent of the total acreage in County Clare was deemed to be of 'moderate to very good' tillage land.

The damper weather of Clare was not conducive to tillage either, compared with the sunnier and warmer east and south-east Ireland. The food shortages and genuine fears of famine during the years 1917 and 1918 sparked off a wave of illegal agrarian agitation with cattle drives and illegal ploughing in many parts of the county. The economy of Clare was also badly hampered by the introduction of Martial Law in 1916 and in 1918, with severe restrictions on movement into and out of the county, and the banning of all public meetings, even fairs and markets.

The price of food and many other products such as coal more than doubled during the war years and the poor people were very badly off as wages were not increased to compensate for the rise in prices. The economic impact on the poor was cushioned a little by the payment of separation allowances for the wives and children of serving soldiers and sailors while the men were at war.

While many, especially young men of the farming class, sought to escape the war through emigration in the early years of the conflict, that avenue was largely closed off by 1918. Emigration from Ireland fell from 20,314 in 1914, to 2,111 in 1915 to only 980 in 1918.

Other sectors of the economy also suffered due to shortages. For instance a shortage of newsprint forced the closure of one of the county's oldest newspapers, the *Clare Journal,* in 1917. Its sister newspaper, the *Saturday Record,* had to increase its price by 50 per cent, from 1*d* to 1½*d,* while at the same time reducing the volume of the paper from six to four pages by the end of the war. The nationalist rival newspaper, the *Clare Champion,* was closed down by the British authorities for about six months in 1918 for political reasons. Thus, for more than six months the *Saturday Record* had a monopoly of circulation in the county.

This temporary closure of the *Clare Champion* probably had little impact upon the spread of republican ideology and information in the county, but the general public were probably more affected. According to one police report 'the general standard of education was so low that the views of the people were drawn from the local paper, the priest and the national schoolmaster'.[4] Nationalists and republicans would probably not have purchased the unionist papers in Clare. Unionists, such as Lord Inchiquin, relied upon *The Irish Times* and the *Clare Journal* for news.

Other businesses also suffered the downturn in trade and profits, for example, coal importers in ports like Clare Castle, who could not get adequate supplies due to the war demands in Britain and to the shortage of shipping. The dockers in the ports also suffered the loss of employment due to the reduction of coal imports. The grocers and traders of Ennis and other towns in the county took advantage of the poor economic outlook to stop the practice of giving 'Christmas boxes' to their customers in 1915.

Sport and leisure was also affected by the war. Initially in 1914 events such as the County Agricultural Show at Ennis and the South of Ireland Golf Championship at Lahinch were cancelled. But these events were organised in the following years of the war. Business at tourist resorts like Kilkee and Lahinch seemed to have recovered after the initial setback of 1914. More British-type minority sports such as cricket, hockey and soccer were more affected by the war, especially cricket and hockey, as most of the players of those games were from the unionist community, who had probably enlisted in the army or navy for the duration of the war.

Other country sports in the county such as fowling, fishing and hunting, as well as horse racing continued, though many of the younger male members of the gentry, the main supporters of these sports, were absent on military service. Big race meetings at Limerick and Galway attracted large numbers of fans throughout the war years, while race meetings were banned in England.

However, the GAA seems to have been largely unaffected by the war, except during emergency periods of martial law in 1916 and in 1918, when all major sports meetings were banned. But, as seen above, the GAA publicly and successfully defied the ban on all unauthorised meetings on 'Gaelic Sunday' 4 August 1918. Fortunately, the Clare senior and junior hurling teams won All-Ireland titles in 1914, while the Clare footballers were beaten in the All-Ireland senior football final in 1917.

The war seems to have had a limited impact upon the GAA in Clare, probably affecting some urban clubs such as Ennis and Kilrush more than rural clubs. There were a number of reasons for this. First of all, the 'Ban' on members of the British forces from playing Gaelic games may have discouraged many young men from joining the British forces. It seems that there was only one high-profile member of the GAA who joined the army and that was Jack Fox of Newmarket-on-Fergus in 1915. His enlistment did not encourage large numbers of Gaels to join him in the army or navy. Secondly, it would appear to be the case that the Irish Volunteers were closely linked to the GAA in many instances. Thirdly, there was little recruitment among the farmers' sons, who would have made up the majority of GAA members in the rural clubs throughout the county.

Recruitment in County Clare seems to have largely been an urban phenomenon. Also, the vast number of recruits joined before the 1916 Rising, and there were very few after that date. According to reports, Kilrush was 'weeded out', sending more than 450 men, Ennistymon sent more than 200, while Ennis contributed around 800 men.

Therefore, the GAA clubs in towns such as Ennis and Kilrush may have had difficulty in fielding teams during the war. 'Ennis Dals' contested six county football finals between 1909 and 1915, winning three in a row between 1909-1911, and two in a row, 1913 and 1914. They were defeated in 1915, and did not contest another county football final until 1927. The decline of the team after 1915 may have been due to the loss of some players to the British forces during the war.

Kilrush Shamrocks were bound to have been affected by the loss of players also, when about 30 per cent of the young men of the parish had gone to war before the Easter Rising. The 'Shams' won the county football final in 1912, but they did not contest another final until 1924.

There was a similar pattern in hurling. Ennis Dalcassians won the county finals of 1914 and 1915, and they were beaten in the final of 1916, but they did not contest another senior hurling final until 1924. These were strong clubs before the war, but they did not achieve much after 1915. Recruitment into the British forces may have been a significant factor in this decline, but this cannot be stated definitively, as other clubs may have had better players at the time.[5]

Apart from agrarian crimes such as cattle drives, illegal ploughing and the occupation of the large ranches, there were very few other indictable crimes committed in the county during the war years, except political crimes committed by the activities of the Irish or Sinn Féin Volunteers under the Defence of the Realm Act (DORA). This was remarked upon by resident magistrates and by the press during the war years. Even during the crisis of Easter Week 1916, the county was remarkably quiet and 'white gloves' were presented to magistrates at petty sessions courts in various parts of the county in the years 1915, 1916 and 1917. The fact that a significant number of the normally unemployed or casually employed working classes had joined the army or navy and were temporarily out of the country for most of the war years and had secured regular pay as well as support for their families, was probably a significant factor in this regard.

Towards the end of the war County Clare, like the rest of Ireland and much of the world, was affected by the outbreak of the dreaded 'Spanish Flu' in 1918. Thankfully, the number of casualties was relatively small in the county, compared with other counties in Ireland. In fact County Clare had the lowest level of mortality in the country, with a mortality rate of only 0.4 per cent compared with a national average mortality rate of 2.5 per cent. The local newspapers noted about twenty Clare people who died because of the Spanish Flu.

The war had lasted slightly more than four years and three months, from 2 August 1914 until 11 November 1918, and it had an immense impact upon County Clare. Estimates of the mortality from among all nations engaged in the conflict suggest that about 15 per cent of those who enlisted died directly or indirectly because of the war. McCarthy published a list of 500 people of Clare origin who died due to the war.[6] On the other hand, Burnell suggests that over 600 people associated with County Clare died in this war.[7]

It seems that about half of the recruits joined the Royal Munster Fusiliers, the local regiment for Clare, Limerick and Kerry. Fitzpatrick states that of 411 Clare men recruited between 15 October 1914 and 15 August 1915, 204 were recruited in Ennis and Kilrush. Fitzpatrick also states that 949 Clare men were recruited into the army from 4 August 1914 up to 15 October 1916. However, County Clare seems to have been among the counties with the lowest percentages of recruitment in Ireland. Indeed between 4 August 1914 and 15 April, only 3.5 per cent of the available manpower of Clare officially joined the forces, the lowest percentage in Ireland. He also notes that by the end of 1915 only about 300 National Volunteers had enlisted. That was about 6 per cent of the county force of 3,200 Volunteers in sixty companies at the middle of August 1914. Up to the middle of August 1915, Clare had contributed only 324 reservists and 519 army recruits from a population of more than 100,000. His table 3.1 of Irish Recruitment, 1914-18, shows that 344 Clare recruits joined in 1915 and an estimated 208 Clare men joined up in 1916. There were no figures for 1917 and 1918. It seems that Fitzpatrick has underestimated the number of those who enlisted. Nevertheless, it seems that despite the encouragement of the Home Rule Party, the two local MPs, Willie Redmond and Arthur Lynch, and the Catholic Church, the people of Clare were not as enthusiastic about the war as their political and religious leaders.[8]

The list of casualties in the county, as suggested by Burnell and Browne, has a total of Clare war dead numbering about 600 men. Of these, approximately thirty-six were drowned and six were killed in air crashes. More than 275 Clare soldiers were laid to rest in the battlefields of France where they died. At least ninety-six Claremen are buried in Belgium, while ninety-eight more are buried in the UK. At least forty-eight Claremen are buried in Turkey, mainly in Gallipoli. Seventeen men have graves in Greece (Salonika) and at least fifteen are laid to rest in Iraq. A few soldiers are buried in Ireland, including a couple in County Clare. At least twenty Clare victims of the war, including sailors and civilians, men and women are buried at sea. The rest of the Clare war dead are buried in various other countries, including Egypt, Israel, Germany, India, Pakistan, Australia, Burma, Canada, Chile, Sudan, Tanzania and South Africa.[9]

According to Patrick Casey, County Clare had the second lowest percentage of casualties in Ireland of the total of 35,000 estimated Irish casualties, with 1.27 per cent of the eligible males, based on the 1911 census.[10]

The majority of those who enlisted were from the towns of Clare, especially from Ennis and Kilrush, from where about 800 and 400 men, respectively, joined the colours. The evidence is anecdotal for Ennis, as this figure was merely mentioned by several politicians and others in favour of recruitment. Indeed, one of the ex-soldiers noted in 1918 that Ennis alone had provided more than 1,200 men for the war, but that number cannot be verified and it does seem very high.

However, C.E. Glynn, recruitment organiser for West Clare, drew up a list of men from Kilrush, who served in the army and navy. His list, which was compiled just after the war, ended in November 1918 and is probably quite accurate, as he recorded the men who enlisted on a street-by-street basis. His list totalled 416 men. He also drew up a separate list of men who were former employees of Michael Glynn and Co., Flour Millers, Kilrush, who had enlisted. In all, he counted 106 former employees of his family company who had served in the forces.

Henry R. Glynn, brother of C.E. Glynn, mentioned in several of his letters how many of their employees, and others from Kilrush, had joined the forces. On 5 August 1914 he told John Redmond that about 100 men had left the town of Kilrush for the war. (It would seem that many of these men were reservists.) In March 1915 he informed the vice-admiral at Queenstown that eighty of the firm's former employees had enlisted and that more than 200 men had gone from Kilrush to the war. Later in the month, he wrote to Maj. Ievers, of Mount Ievers, Sixmilebridge, saying that more than eighty-five of their former employees had enlisted. At the end of March 1915, he informed the admiralty in London that more than 100 of their men, who had worked part-time or full-time for the company, had joined the services and that about 300 Kilrush men out of a population of 3,600 had enlisted up to then. Around this time he wrote to Prime Minister Lloyd George, informing him that more than 260 men were serving in the army and navy and that during the previous week fifty more had volunteered to join up.[11]

Taking the figures produced by H.R. Glynn and C.E. Glynn as being reliable sources, it would seem that about 75 per cent of the total recruitment from

Kilrush town took place before 1 April 1915. C.E. Glynn also wrote that he had enlisted more than 100 recruits from the time he was appointed recruiting organiser in November 1915 up to early February 1916, but these men were drawn from all over West Clare. The figures for Kilrush clearly indicate that recruitment dropped off sharply after March 1915, with about 300 enlisting in the first six months and only 116 men joining up over the next three-and-a-half years. One reason for the decline may be the high mortality rate during 1915, which may have deterred young men from enlisting. From Glynn's list of soldiers enlisted in the Royal Munster Fusiliers, thirty-five men died in service over the four years. However, half of those men died in the year 1915 alone, with six Kilrush men dying on 9 May. Staunton gives the Kilrush mortality in the Royal Munster Fusiliers by year as: two in 1914, eighteen in 1915, seven in 1916, four in 1917, and four in 1918. Staunton also states that Kilrush, as a port, provided an above average number of men to the Royal Navy and most of them came through the war unscathed. It seems that a number of men from other coastal locations in Clare, such as Quilty, also joined the navy during the war.[12]

Overall, from Glynn's list, about 15 per cent of the soldiers and sailors of Kilrush died in the war. This is consistent with the average mortality rate among all the belligerent nations during the war. If we take McCarthy's fatality list of Clare casualties in the Great War as accurate and apply the 15 per cent mortality rate to the 504 names on that list, then we can estimate that about 3,300 Clare-born people enlisted. This is not an unreasonable assumption, if we accept that about 1,200 came from the towns of Ennis and Kilrush alone. On the other hand, if we accept Burnell's list of over 600 casualties and apply the 15 per cent mortality rate, then it would seem that over 4,000 men of Clare origin enlisted in the war. This is much higher than Fitzpatrick's estimate. Overall, therefore, it would seem that 3-4 per cent of the county population taken at the census of 1911, had enlisted in the British forces.

The majority of those who enlisted seem to have come from the 'working classes'. About 80 per cent of those on C.E. Glynn's list of Kilrush veterans are described as 'general labourers'. Perhaps their motives for enlistment were mercenary, as many of them may have been unemployed, or in low wage employment, or indeed in abject poverty. The prospect of regular pay was attractive for men who were unemployed or under-employed. Privates would earn a shilling a day, 'all found'. Furthermore, their wives and families would also benefit. Wives of soldiers would receive 12s and 6d per week, with 5s for the first child, 3s 6d for the second and 2s for each extra child. Pensions for wholly disabled men were between 25s and 40s a week; 'separation money' was welcome in towns such as Kilrush. One Kilrush man, Michael 'Robineen' Gallagher, who enlisted early in the war said that he joined up because 'there was nothing in Kilrush only poverty in 1914, I joined for no other reason than to have a job … it was the only way, there was nothing here, England before the 1914 war was no better'.[13]

Mercenary motives alone cannot explain why men enlisted and the matter was much more complex. Some may have been inspired by a moral duty to fight for the Catholics of Belgium following the many appeals by churchmen and politicians on behalf of Catholic Belgium. Many followed 'Redmond's call', believing that by joining an Irish regiment they would help to secure Home Rule. Some may have joined up for a sense of adventure. Others may have been persuaded by their friends, for example those who joined the 'Pals Battalion' – the 7th Dublin Fusiliers. Many left secure employment positions to join up, with the promise that they would, if they survived be re-hired, or get preference for jobs.[14]

Some, especially those from the Protestant minority of Clare, enlisted from a sense of duty and loyalty to their king and country. The memorial brass plate for Capt. Robert H. Cullinan of Bindon Street, Ennis in the local Church of Ireland church states that he died 'for king and country'. Addressing the annual synod of the united dioceses of Killaloe and Kilfenora in September 1915, the Rt Revd Dr T. Sterling Berry observed that there were few families who had not given members to serve in the forces. He said that there were about 400 members of the Church from the united dioceses – that is from the dioceses of Killaloe and Kilfenora, who were serving in the army or the navy. This was a very high proportion of that cohort of the population. It suggests that almost all of the adult male population of military age must have joined the services, and only the very young and the elderly remained behind. Nevertheless, he said that there were many lingering at home from an 'apathetic indifference'.

Dr Berry had warned that 'conscientious scruples about warfare should not be a cloak for apathy, cowardice or greed'. 'They should make it clear', he said, 'that selfish apathy, unmanly cowardice and worldly-minded greed were sins against God, as well as blots and blemishes on human character.' Dr Berry paid tribute in 1916 to those who gave their lives in the Great War: 'We mourn the loss of so many brave sons of our empire, who in obedience to the call of duty counted not their lives dear to them in order to fulfil the task to which their patriotism and loyalty summoned them'.[15]

Many descendants of the landed gentry of Clare had come from families with a long military tradition. Some of the young men from this background may also have enlisted from a sense of adventure. T.R. Henn from Paradise House, Kildysart wrote: 'The war … left little mark on my life, except that my brother, my Gore-Hickman cousins – in fact, all the young men among the 'gentry' of the west – joined immediately, having no need or compulsion, for the unreasoning adventure of it. By 1916 many of them were dead, among them my first cousin. My brother was three weeks wounded and missing at Suvla Bay with the 7th Munsters'.[16]

Undoubtedly, many were reluctant to enlist, they belonged to several categories, those who seceded from Redmond's National Volunteers to form the Irish Volunteers; then there were 'the shirkers' and 'slackers', and, finally, those who were of farming stock. At the outset, there were, according to Inspector Gelston's testimony to the Royal Commission on the 1916 Rising, only about 300 or 400 Irish Volunteers in the county in September 1914, who refused to follow 'Redmond's call', with many others sympathising; but this number probably increased sharply after Easter 1916.

Mr Gelston also observed in June 1916 that 'recruitment was very good in County Clare, especially among the labouring classes and in the towns, but there was no recruiting at all from the farming classes'. Col C.E. Whitton, historian of the 16th Irish, Leinster Regiment, wrote that recruiting in Ireland had been confined largely to two classes, the gentry and the town labourers – 'the farmers' sons and the "shop boy" class were conspicuous by their scarcity'.[17]

As Jeffery, observed, 'rural prosperity undermined the economic impulse to enlist'.[18] Puirseil adds another group who were reluctant to enlist: 'in effect, it was the Protestants and working class men who joined the colours, while middle class Catholics largely abstained'.[19]

> Nor law nor duty bade me fight,
> Nor public men, nor cheering crowds,
> A lonely impulse of delight
> Drove to this tumult in the clouds.[20]

Those who fought in the First World War were brave men, who faced death on a daily basis with great courage in what Siegfried Sassoon called 'the desolation of the trenches'.[21] The contemporary accounts all testified to their bravery and gallantry under fire. Maj. Bryan Mahon, Commander of the 29th Brigade at Gallipoli, wrote of them in 1918: 'Never in history did Irishmen face death with greater courage and endurance than they did at Gallipoli and Serbia in the summer and winter of 1915 ... Ireland will not easily forget the deeds of the 10th Irish Division at Gallipoli.'[22] However, the sacrifices at Gallipoli seemed all in vain, as Harris observed: 'To Ireland, Gallipoli means V Beach, the River Clyde collier and the 10th Irish Division ... it was a disastrous failure, hopeless bravery, a useless slaughter of brave men ... It cost the British empire more than 200,000 dead and it achieved nothing'.[23] Commander Guy Nightingale wrote 'two splendid Irish regiments were wiped out, reduced from more than 2,000 to 778 men'.[24]

The bravery of the men who fought on the Western Front was also well documented, as Gen. Sir Douglas Haig, commander-in-chief of the British Army wrote, 'Irish regiments which took part in the capture of Guillemont behaved with the greatest dash and gallantry, and took no small share in the success gained that day.' Willie Redmond recorded, 'A captured German officer declared that his people believed that Ginchy could not be taken, but', he added, 'you attacked us with devils not men, no one could withstand them!'[25]

Bryan Cooper had observed in 1918, 'Ireland will not easily forget the deeds of the 10th Irish Division at Gallipoli.' However, the sacrifices by the Irish at Gallipoli and on the Western Front have been largely forgotten or ignored by successive Irish generations. As Denman observed, 'After the armistice the veterans returned to an Ireland little prepared to give them a heroes welcome ... the men of 1916 and the War of Independence were regarded as heroes, patriots and martyrs, while the men of the Somme and Gallipoli were ignored and forgotten ... the fate of 35,000 dead was largely ignored'.[26]

However, while the sacrifices of the men who fought in the war may have been largely ignored, some traces of that terrible conflict are found in the place names of a few scattered locations around the county, where names such as 'Shellshock' and the 'Dardanelles' are still used. 'Shellshock' is an unofficial name for the townland of Ballynote West in Kilrush, where presumably, ex-soldiers suffering from shellshock were housed after the war. The 'Dardanelles' is a name used to describe a back lane called The Creggaun in Clare Castle, where ex-soldiers lived. There is also a place called 'The Dardanelles' in Newmarket-on-Fergus where some First World War veterans were housed in cottages erected for disabled ex-servicemen. It was located near the Catholic church in the village.

Stephen Gwynn MP, speaking in London to the Irish Literary Society in London shortly after the death of Willie Redmond asked a few pertinent questions about the indifference of Irish society towards the soldiers in 1917: 'perhaps now in the face of Maj. Redmond's death, the Irish people will make up their minds what is their attitude towards the troops who are fighting in the name of Ireland. Is Ireland going to be proud of the Irish troops, or is she going to be ashamed of them? Are the Irish soldiers to be set down as West Britons? And were the real heroes those who stayed at home?'

Gwynn wrote after the war; 'And when the time comes to rejoice over the war's ending was there anything more tragic than the position of men who had gone out by the thousands for the sake of Ireland to confront the greatest military power ever known in history, who had fought the war and won the war, and who now looked at each other with doubtful eyes'.[27]

It was indeed to be the tragic fate of the Irishmen who fought and died in the Great War to be largely ignored and forgotten by Irish society. They were eclipsed by the men of 1916 and those who fought in the War of Independence. It is right and proper that the bravery of the men of 1916 and the War of Independence should be honoured and celebrated, but not at the expense of those thousands of brave Clare men who fought in the First World War.

Willie Redmond wrote an article for *Irish Life* published on 11 May 1917, about a month before he died, asserting that the combatants in the war would not be forgotten. 'When the war is over, the names of those who fight for all that life makes worthwhile will be remembered with gratitude by generations yet unborn … for the two Irish divisions, the 16th Irish and the 36th Ulster, undivided in their splendid devotion to the cause they believed just, there will ever be gratitude and honour in Ireland, no matter what will be said to the contrary'.[28]

In a letter to his solicitor Willie Redmond justified his attitude towards the war, 'If I should die abroad I shall die a true Irish Catholic, humbly hoping for mercy from God, through the intercession of His blessed mother, whose help I have ever implored throughout my life. I should like all my friends to know that in joining the Irish Brigade and in going to France, I sincerely believed, as all Irish soldiers do, that I was doing my best for the welfare of Ireland in every way'.[29]

Willie Redmond, like tens of thousand of Irishmen who fought in the First World War, genuinely believed that he was fighting for Ireland's cause. He believed that Home Rule was virtually achieved in 1914 and that Ireland had a duty to fight for the empire and the freedom of small nations such as Belgium in a great struggle for civilisation against the threat from Imperial Germany. While many people in Ireland and Clare may have shared those views, what Jeffery called 'naïve patriotism', in 1914, support for those views rapidly evaporated within a couple of years, especially after the 1916 Rising.[30]

After the Great War ended the survivors returned to an Ireland that was radically different to the country they left when they had enlisted. When they departed for the front line they may have received accolades in the newspapers and been cheered off at railway stations and at ports as heroes and patriots, fighting a gallant cause. However, this was not the case when they returned. The mood of the country had changed and men in British uniforms, perhaps the only clothes they had worn for years, were not welcomed home by cheering crowds as heroes, victorious in the war.

This was in marked contrast to the treatment of the men and women who took part in the 1916 Rising. Immediately after the Rising they were reviled and abused by hostile crowds as they were shipped out as prisoners to England. However, about eight months later, they were welcomed home as patriotic heroes by thousands of supporters.

The Irish Volunteers and Sinn Féin now dominated the political life of the country after the general election of 1918. The ex-soldiers and sailors were now being viewed with suspicion, men who had served with an alien force. They were stigmatised. The returning servicemen were traumatised, demoralised and disillusioned by their wartime experiences, which now seemed all in vain, and they were rejected, or ignored at home. The population in general did not wish to publicly acknowledge their heroic struggles and sacrifices. The British Army was perceived by the majority of the Irish people as being an enemy force, and the Great War veterans were tainted by association with it.

The ex-servicemen who returned to Ireland seemed unable to discuss their traumatic experiences. For about twenty years after the war ended some Great War veterans marched from the British Legion Hall in Ennis to church services on Remembrance Day, but these parades gradually faded away as the number of surviving veterans declined.

Many of the people of Ireland, during the years of the War of Independence and later were not interested in their story. The effect of all this was that there was a great silence about the war in Ireland. It was not publicly discussed and the men who survived it were reluctant to talk about their experiences. Ireland, for the Great War veterans, was not 'a country fit for heroes'. Perhaps the horrors of war had psychologically damaged them and many probably suffered what we now know as 'post traumatic stress disorder'. Few wrote their memoirs and many must have suffered in silence.

While one war was ending, some men of Clare, with very different motivations, were preparing to fight a totally different kind of war for Ireland's cause, this time on Irish soil. The War of Independence was about to commence. The new heroes in the Ireland of the post-war years were the Irish republicans, who had fought the British in the 1916 Rising and in the War of Independence.

As time went on the great silence intensified, especially after de Valera came to power in 1932, when anti-British sentiment increased. During the Economic War and later the Emergency Years, when Ireland was neutral in the Second Word War, the sacrifices of the Great War seemed to be irrelevant and most Irish people preferred to forget that awful conflict and the heroism of the men who fought in it. The sacrifices of the Protestant gentry and the Catholic working class men of urban Ireland were ignored in a republican bourgeois Ireland. Their struggle was air-brushed out of the public consciousness. This was their tragedy. Whatever the motivation, each man's decision to enlist in the British forces fighting in the Great War was personal and voluntary. Their contribution has been ignored for too long. The brave men who fought in the battles at Etreoux, Guillemont, Ginchy, Gallipoli and indeed many other battles on land, sea and in the air during the Great War deserve to be remembered.

> They shall grow not old, as we that are left grow old;
> Age shall not weary them, nor the years condemn.
> At the going down of the sun and in the morning,
> We will remember them.[31]

POSTSCRIPT

'BETTER TO WEAR OUT THAN TO RUST OUT'

There was much apprehension amongst the Protestant unionist community in Clare about their prospects of living in Clare after the proposed introduction of Home Rule in 1914. They feared that 'Home rule would be Rome rule'. They were reluctant to face the prospects of living in a Catholic dominated state and county. Some of them feared for their lives, livelihoods and their properties in sectarian conflict.

Naturally, when the War of Independence broke out in 1919 many Protestants in Clare feared that a sectarian war would break out and that there would be 'ethnic cleansing'. This, however, does not seem to have been the case. Both Henry V. MacNamara and George O'Callaghan Westropp, who had raised the fears of sectarianism during their tour of the north of Ireland in 1911, survived the war. Col George O'Callaghan Westropp became a member of the Irish Senate in 1922 and was elected president of the Irish Farmers' Union in 1926. Their large estates, like all other landed properties, were divided up by the Land Commission after 1923. However, they remained in County Clare for many years afterwards.[1]

Some large gentry houses were burnt down during the War of Independence, but the motives for these actions seem to have been political rather than sectarian, in reprisals for the burnings of nationalists' homes by the Black and Tans. Some of these houses were also being used by the British Army or by the RIC, so they were deemed to be military targets. Those burnt included Doolin House (H.V. MacNamara); Beechlawn House, Newmarket-on-Fergus; Woodpark House, Scarriff (Mr Hibbert); Violet Hill, Broadford; Richmond House; Hazelwood House, Quin, (Mr Studdert); Strasburgh House, (R.J. Stacpoole); Fortfergus House, Kildysart, (Mr Ball); Williamstown House, (Mr Brooks); Kilmore House, Knock, the home of Capt. Hickman who was killed in Gallipoli in 1915 and Kiltannon House, Tulla (home of Col Molony). Compensation was paid in all of these cases. The RIC report on the burning of five gentlemen's homes in 1920-21 described the motives as 'political'.[2]

What was inexcusable, of course, was the destruction of several Church of Ireland buildings around this time. These reprehensible actions were clearly evidence of naked sectarianism. The church at Clare Castle was burnt on 18 April 1920; the church at O'Briensbridge was set on fire on 29 June 1920 and the church at Miltown Malbay was burnt on 14 December 1922. These burnings were not authorised by Sinn Féin and indeed were denounced by the organisation at local and national levels. These burnings may have been in reprisal for the burning of Catholic chapels in the north of the country by Orange bigots around this time. Meanwhile, Dr Berry, Church of Ireland Bishop of Killaloe and Kilfenora, stated in 1920 that 'hostility towards Protestants was almost unknown in the twenty-six counties where Protestants were in a minority'.[3]

On the other hand, there must have been sufficient evidence of sectarianism in the country by 1923 to motivate Bishop Fogarty, who was lucky to escape an assassination attempt by the Black and Tans on 23 November 1920,[4] to appeal for a higher sense of patriotism among the Irish nationalists, noting that 'their Protestant fellow countrymen – he regretted to have to say it – were persecuted and dealt with in a cruel and coarse manner'.[5]

The Protestant community in Clare declined greatly over the following decades, due to a number of reasons, but not, apparently, due to sectarian bigotry. Some, such as the MacDonnells of Newhall and the Stacpooles of Eden Vale sold their houses and estates and moved away in the early 1920s. The reasons for this were largely economic, during the War of Independence and Civil War, which was accentuated during the Great Depression and the Economic War, followed by the Second World War. Difficult economic conditions followed in the 1950s that caused a massive haemorrhage of Irish people of all persuasions. Another factor was the long-term impact of the Ne Temere decree upon the Church of Ireland community after 1904.[6]

In 2014, 100 years after Bishop Berry's appeal to the Church of Ireland members in the diocese to stay after the introduction of Home Rule, the number of Church of Ireland members has declined somewhat. But, so has the population of County Clare to about 86,000. It must be remembered, however, that this decline in religious infrastructure and religious practice also applies to the Catholics of County Clare in the twenty-first century. There is a great variety of other denominations and religions in the county, including Jehovah Witnesses, and Muslims, Presbyterians, Methodists and other Christian churches.

There are at least ten Church of Ireland churches still in use in the county in 2014: Ennis, Clonlara, Killaloe, Kilfenora, Kilnasoolagh, Kilkee, Mountshannon,

Shannon, Spanish Point and Tuamgraney. Some of these are shared with other Christian churches, while others have seasonal or monthly services. Some former churches, such as Kilrush and Sixmilebridge, have been turned into libraries or heritage centres. There are two serving ministers in the county. There are no Church of Ireland schools in County Clare.[7]

APPENDIX
ONE

The war diary of the Hon. Donough E. F. O'Brien,
(later 16th Baron Inchiquin of Dromoland), 2nd Lieutenant,
Kings Rifle Regiment, from 25 October 1916 to 14 December 1916:

Sir Donough
O'Brien, 16th Baron
Inchiquin, c. 1965
and his war diary.
(Courtesy of the Hon.
Grania R. O'Brien)

Wednesday 25 October	Ordered to join Expeditionary Force in France. Left London 11.40 am. Sailed from Southampton 8 p.m. Beautiful crossing, arrived Le Havre 3 am. Farmer, Pugh, Jones and Baker came out with me, we sailed in the 'Archangel'.
Thursday 26 October	Rained all day, reported to Camp Adjutant by 11 a.m., Allotted quarters (no. 11 camp), which consisted of minute canvas and wood shack, holding two, which I shared with MacGeorge – bed, table, and work stand made of packing cases.
Friday 27 October	Posted to 1st Batt. Went up to Central Training Camp (CTS). Lectures on bombing, skirmishing and patrolling, poured with rain all afternoon, nights frightfully cold.
Saturday 28 October	Trench work, excellent lecture on fatigue duties, had tea in house, rained a good deal. MacGeorge went up the line; he'll come back for one night, just recovered from fairly slight shell wound in the back.
Sunday, 29 October	On fatigue party whole day, 6am-6pm, removing empty shell cases from Aod, there must be three million empty shell cases in the yard. Poured rain all day. Hill went up the line.
Monday 30 October	Went for a ten mile route march, column counting about 5,000 men, drenching rain the whole time (three and a half hours) everyone wet through to the skin.
Tuesday, 31 October	Beautiful day.
Wednesday 1 November	Went through course of every kind of gas and smoke, did night wiring in the evening, had tea in Le Havre. Lecture on trench sketching, and details which should be put in.
Thursday, 2 November	Rained all day, attended most excellent lecture on spirit of bayonet fighting, also gas and work to be done in trenches by company and platoon officers, went to watch boxing competitions.
Friday, 3 November	Bayonet fighting all morning, in the afternoon I went down to Havre to meet Aunt Marguerite, who was on her way to Paris, but couldn't find her anywhere.

Saturday, 4 November	Revolver shooting in the morning, went down to Havre for tea, wrote and censored letters in the evening, rained most of the day.
Sunday, 5 November	Went to most excellent church parade service in cinema hut, rained all day.
Monday, 6 November	Was Orderly Officer, spent day, except during duty, censoring letters, generally between 300 to 500 letters to censor, rained all night.
Tuesday 7 November	Another draft of 85 came from England, came in to my detachment, 1st Co., I have already got 270 men, this makes my lot bigger, I should think, than all the other 5 detachments put together.
Wednesday 8 November	Rained most of the day, details were for interior economy, in the afternoon paid out my detail (1st Batt.), dined with Blake and Rowley in K.R.R. mess about 9 pm, worst storm of thunder, lightning, rain and hail I have ever seen.
Thursday 9 November	Spent the day in Central Training School, heavy showers of hail during day, beautiful night, absolutely full moon.
Friday 10 November	Spent the whole day at Havre docks with a party of about 300 Royal Garrison Artillery, and four other officers, unloading hay and corn etc. from ships into the hangar Au Coton (a shed 700 yards by 150 yards).
Saturday 11 November	Central Training School in morning, went down to Havre in afternoon.
Sunday 12 November	Took RC [Roman Catholic] church parade and attended their service, (my first service in RC church). Went to opera (Faust) in evening in the Grand Theatre du Havre! This is my first opera.
Monday 13 November	On musketry all day, 30 yards range. In evening went to excellent concert given for the soldiers in Woodbine Hut (Miss Vera Askwell).
Tuesday 14 November	Interior economy; rifle inspection in the afternoon.
Wednesday 15 November	C.T.S. all morning, paid out my detail, 1st Batt., which consisted of 425 men in the afternoon, took two and a half hours.
Thursday 16 November	I was Orderly Officer, bitterly cold day, had to wash in water with ice on it in the morning.

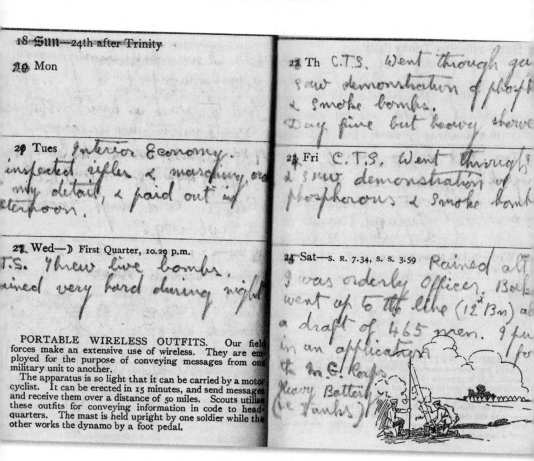

Extract from the war diary of Lt the Hon. Donough O'Brien. (Courtesy of Grania R. O'Brien)

Friday 17 November	Asst. Orderly Officer, draft of 190 men left my detail, bitterly cold day, snowed in the evening.
Saturday 18 November	C.T.S., had tea in Havre.
Sunday 19 November	Took Roman Catholic church parade and attended the service.
Monday 20 November	-
Tuesday 21 November	Interior economy, I inspected rifles and marching orders of my detail and paid out in the afternoon.
Wednesday 22 November	Threw live bombs, rained very hard during the night.
Thursday 23 November	C.T.S., went through gas and saw demonstration of phosphorous and smoke bombs, day fine, but heavy showers.
Friday 24 November	C.T.S. , went through phosphorous and smoke bombs.

Saturday 25 November	Rained all day, I was Orderly Officer, Baker went up to the line [front line] 12 Batt., also a draft of 465 men. I put in an application for Ing. Corps, [heavy battery, i.e tanks].
Sunday 26 November	Rained all day.
Monday 27 November	I took a platoon in special drill for a good part of the morning, very heavy showers.
Tuesday 28 November	Interior economy, I inspected men, rifles and kit, also paid out. Had tea in Havre and met Leyland Barnett, who has got the Military Cross.
Wednesday 29 November	-
Thursday 30 November	Felt very seedy all day with chill, stayed in.
Friday 1 December	Felt better today, went for along walk with Patterson on the far side of the valley. I enjoyed it more and felt better after it than I have for a long time.
Saturday 2 December	Musketry, 30 yards range all morning, billiards, Leake brought over draughts. Dinner in Havre at Hotel Moderne, Patterson went up to the line, 1st Batt.
Sunday 3 December	Church and RC [parade] went for a long walk in the afternoon.
Monday 4 December	C.T.S. all day, a draft of men from King Edward's House came to my detail.
Tuesday 5 December	Capt. Orr and Jack Davison arrived also Chamberlain from the 5th Batt. Interior economy, rained most of the day.
Wednesday 6 December	Orr went up to the line to the 2nd Batt.
Thursday 7 December	I was Orderly Officer; Capt. Page arrived from the Royal Berkshire Regt.
Friday 8 December	A large draft was suddenly called for and about 500 men were sent up to the line this evening. I spent practically the whole day censoring letters.
Saturday 9 December	Morgan, Grenville and Adair brought a draft over from England. Jack and I had tea and dinner with them in Havre. Macintosh went up to the line to the 4th Batt.
Sunday 10 December	Extraordinarily good sermon in church by one of the padres. Had tea and dinner in Havre with Jack.
Monday 11 December	Had day off due to a sore heel.

Tuesday 12 December   Interior economy, Bridgeman, Hobbs and Reid
                             went up to the line, I received my orders to
                             join my unit and conduct a draft of K.R.R.s
                             (King's Rifle Regiment).

Wednesday 13 December   We marched down to Havre and left at 11.30
                             pm; roads very bad and we were heavily laden;
                             we drew three days rations and iron rations,
                             detrained at Rouen 8 am.

Thursday 14 December   Took the men to a rest camp in Rouen. Had a
                             very good bath and excellent lunch at Officer's
                             Club; entrained at 2.30 pm, men travelled in
                             ordinary luggage vans, 30 per van.

APPENDIX TWO

Menu for Christmas Dinner held at the Officers' Mess, King's Rifles Regt., at the Somme on 17 January 1917:

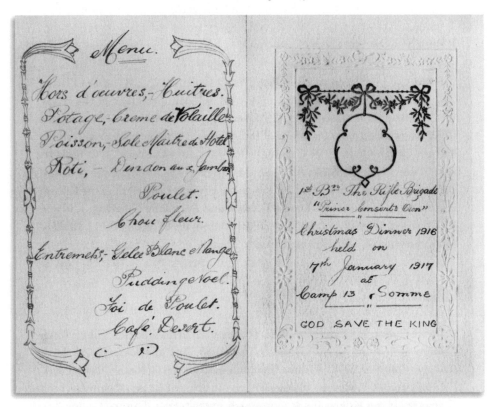

Menu for Christmas Dinner held at Officer's Mess, King's Rifles Regtiment held at the Somme on 17 January 1917. (Courtesy of the Hon. Grania R. O'Brien)

APPENDIX THREE

Members of West Clare Recruitment Committees March 1916. (Information taken from the Glynn Papers.)

Kilrush

V. Revd Canon McInerney, PP; Revd Fr O'Gorman, CC; Revd L. O'Brien, CC; V. Revd Canon Armstrong, rector; M. Killeen, president of the AOH; W. Counihan; H.R. Glynn, DL; J.S. Dowling, JP; W.J. Glynn, JP; B. Culligan, JP; W. McNamara, vice-president of the AOH; T. Ryan, vice-chairman of the Kilrush Urban Council; W. Carmody, JP, Poor Law Guardian; T.J. O'Doherty, JP; J. Ryan, National Bank; R. Welsh; M. Hennessy, manager of the National Bank; G.V.Watson, manager of the Provincial Bank; T. Kelly, clerk of the Kilrush Union; M. Crotty, Kilrush Urban Council and Poor Law Guardian; T. Nagle; M. O'Meara, Kilrush Urban Council; P.J. Dillon; P.J. O'Shea, NT; J.J. Bradley; M. Slattery; and T. Lillis, Kilrush Urban Council.

Kilkee

V. Revd Canon P. Glynn, PP; W.C. Doherty, chairman of the Kilkee Town Commissioners and Kilrush Board of Guardians; Dr P.C. Hickie, JP; P.S. Brady, RM; Dr C.O. Hickie; G. Collins, Town Commissioner; P. Keane, Town Clerk; J.T. Doherty; H. Rountree, manager of the Provincial Bank; M. Scanlan, vice-chairman of the Kilkee Town Commission; J. Murray, County Councillor; J. Kett, chairman of Clare County Council.

Ennistymon

Revd Fr Cassidy, PP; E. O'Dwyer; M. Griffy, clerk of the Ennistymon Union, and president of the AOH; P.J. Hurley; Dr Keane, JP; Dr O'Dwyer, JP; J. McInerney, JP; J. Nagle; M. Leyden, JP, chairman of Ennistymon Rural District Council; Joseph Leyden; J.J. Matthews, manager of the National Bank; J.M. O'Riordan, manager of the Munster and Leinster Bank; P. Kerin; P. Daly; John O'Dea; M. McCarthy; J. Roughan; and M. Linnane.

Miltown Malbay

V. Revd Canon Hannon, PP; T. O'Brien, T. Burke, Clare County Council; M.J. Kenny, KC; J.T. O'Brien; M. McDonagh; Mat Lynch; Dr Hillery; Dr McClancy; P. Clancy, JP; Gould Ellis, JP; W. Hynes; James McMahon; Revd A. Elliott, rector; J.F. Davis; A. Jones; M. Moroney; and Dr Healy.

Cooraclare

Revd Fr Hehir, PP; M. Mescall, JP, chairman of the Kilrush Rural District Council; J. Kenny; and M.B. Kelly (Cree).

Mullagh

Revd Fr Glynn, PP; Revd J. Considine, CC; Revd M. McCormack, CC; P.J. Talty, Rural District Councillor; and M. O'Dwyer, Rural District Councillor.

Kildysart

V Revd Fr F. O'Dea, PP; J. Bianconi, JP; J. Casey; Thomas Kenny; Timothy Kenny; P. McNamara; John Meehan; M. Griffin, JP, chairman of the Kildysart Rural District Council; P. McMahon, clerk of the Kildysart Union; and M. Shannon.

Kilshanny

Revd Fr McGurran, PP, and J. Murphy, technical instructor.

Kilmihil

J.F. Daly; Francis Ryan; and James Griffin, JP.

Carrigaholt

W.C.V. Burton, DL; Dr Studdert, JP; P.J. O'Kelly; T.D. Roughan; A.O'Dwyer; and James Lillis,(Querrin).

Doonbeg

V. Revd Fr Vaughan, PP, and M. McInerney.

Knock and Killimer

V. Revd P. Barrett, PP; F.W. Hickman, DL; P. Hassett, JP; Capt. Poole Gore; James Blake; and P. McInerney

APPENDIX
FOUR

This letter, by James Wood, was sent to Lord Inchiquin to appeal for an increase in wages. It is reproduced here courtesy of the Hon. Grania O'Brien.

'An example of a man's weekly expense, *c.* 1918.'

Weekly wages	£1 12s 0d
Flour 3st, at 3s per st	9s 0d
Tea , 1lb at 4s per lb	4s 0d
Sugar, half a stone 6d per lb	3s 6d
Butter 2lbs at 2s per lb	4s 0d
Oil, half a gallon at 1s 8d per gal	0s 10d
3lbs American bacon at 1s 4d per lb	4s 0d
Milk, 7qts at 6d per qt	4s 2d
Meat for Sunday roast (beef or mutton),	
2lbs at 1s 2d per lb	2s 4d
National health insurance	0s 4d
Total :	£1 13s 6d

Leaving firing, clothing and necessaries essential for household to be supplied from little home industries, for example fowl rearing and pig rearing. Asking your Lordships consideration from this very chariatible [*sic*] example, as one of the many in your employment, James Woods, Ayleacotty (Family 5 inclusive).

APPENDIX
FIVE

War Charity in Clare

CLARE AND WAR CHARITIES.

Dromoland Castle,
Newmarket-on-Fergus,
County Clare,
13th August. 18.

Dear Sir,—I enclose a list of the donations which I have received, for the Irish Counties War Hospital, Marlborough Hall, Dublin.

I also enclose a list of all the money which has been subscribed to various war charities during the past four years.

This list will not compare well with what other counties in Ireland have done, but considering how very few people subscribe in this county, it shews how great has been their individual generosity, and I am sure grateful thanks are due to the "few" who have done so much.—Yours faithfully,

INCHIQUIN.

DONATIONS TO IRISH COUNTIES WAR HOSPITAL

The Hon Mrs Blood	1	0	0
J F Gelston, Esq, Co Inspector	0	5	0
Col F Tottenham	5	0	0
Mrs Frost	0	10	0
Capt. E S O'Brien	2	0	0
R G Parker, Esq.	1	0	0
Brigadier Gen. R G Parker	1	0	0
W M F Counihan, Esq, M.D.	1	1	0
F N Studdert, Esq.	1	1	0
H V Macnamara, Esq.	2	0	0
W Wilson-Lynch, Esq.	1	0	0
Torlogh O'Brien, Esq.	2	2	0
Mrs H Studdert	1	0	0
Bonacord Jock	3	3	0
W J Glynn, Esq.	4	0	0
The Hon: Edward O'Brien	1	0	0
Miss F K Knox	1	0	0
W H MacDonnell, Esq.	5	0	0
T F H Crowe, Esq.	1	0	0
Clara Lady Fitzgerald	5	0	0
A B Stoney, Esq.	2	2	0
W W Burton, Esq.	3	0	0
Mr and Mrs R F Hibbert	5	0	0
Mrs D C Parkinson	1	0	0
F F Cullinan, Esq.	3	3	0
Miss Henrietta Butler	5	0	0
The Misses Scott	2	2	0
The Rev Canon Stanistreet	1	1	0
The Lady Inchiquin	25	0	0
The Lord Inchiquin	15	0	0
W F Corbett, Esq.	1	1	0
The Lord Bishop of Killaloe	1	1	0
Total	**103**	**12**	**0**

TOTAL MONEY SUBSCRIBED TO ALL WAR CHARITIES SINCE THE BEGINNING OF THE WAR.

Clare Needlework Guild	548	11	4
Sailors and Soldiers Associa'n	1086	12	6
Irish War Hospital Supply	735	0	0
Prisoners of War Fund	1459	13	3
Belgian Refugees, Ennis and Clare Castle	920	0	0
Belgian Refugees, Newmarket-on-Fergus	1475	1	0
Irish Counties War Hospital	221	10	0
Queen's Work for Women	200	0	0
Total	**6646**	**8**	**1**

War charities in Clare, news cutting from the *Saturday Record*, 18 August 1918.

NOTES

Introduction

1. Fitzpatrick, David, *Politics and Irish Life 1913-1921* (Dublin: Gill and Macmillan, 1977), p.90.
2. Dungan, Myles, *Irish Voices from the Great War* (Dublin: Irish Academic Press, 1995), Chapter 1.

1. Prelude to War

1. *Clare Journal* (*CJ*), 22, 25 January 1912. The statements repudiating the assertions of sectarianism were re-published in Lynch, Arthur, *Ireland: Vital Hour* (London: Stanley Paul and Co., 1915), pp. 49-50. The Unionist Club of Clare included the most prominent Protestants in the county. They were a select group drawn from the landed gentry, Church of Ireland ministers and county officials in the police and local government. Among those in attendance in 1912 were the following: Lord and Lady Inchiquin, Lord and Lady Dunboyne, The Hon. Edward O'Brien, Col and Mrs Tottenham, Col and Mrs O'Callaghan Westropp, Revd J.B. Greer, The Misses Butler, Mr Charles MacDonnell, Mr George Studdert, Dr Charles Blood, Mr and Hon. Mrs Blood, Mr Blackwell, Mr Hunter, Mr Patterson, Mr R.G. Parker, Mr G. MacNamara, Mr Marcus Keane, Mr W.J. MacNamara, Mr R.J. Stacpoole, The Misses Mahon, Mr and Mrs H.V. MacNamara, Revd Canon Birch, Miss V. MacNamara, Mr W.A. Fitzgerald, Revd M. Greer, Mr and Mrs J.A. Studdert, Revd R. Twiss-Maclaurin, Revd Canon King, Mr Barker, Mr Bryan Mahon, Revd Canon Stanistreet, Mr Dudley Perrse, Mr Charles Bailee, Mr and Mrs A.R. Martin, Mr W.F. Henn, Mr R. Archdall, Mr Burton, Mr James Wakely, Mr R. O'Brien Studdert and Revd Mr Abrahall.

2. *CJ*, 12 October, 1911; *Clare Champion (CC)* 31 January, 7 February, 14 February 1914.

3. *CC*, 23 May 1914.

4. *CC*, 25 July 1914. In 1912 Mr A. Capon, Secretary of the Oddfellows Star of the West Lodge, Ennis Branch, wrote a letter to the editor of the *Clare Journal* outlining the presence of the friendly society in Ennis since 1854 and the work it was doing for its members in distributing sickness, disability and funeral benefits to members. In essence it provided insurance for its members. Mr Capon stated that all money raised by the society from its members in Ennis was retained for the use of its members and spent in the Ennis area. *CJ*, 15 July 1912.

5. *CJ*, 8 and 12 January 1914. Among the members of the Clare Hunt at the outing in Buncraggy were the following: The Master, Mr Roche-Kelly and Mrs Roche-Kelly, Lady Beatrice O'Brien, Capt. and Mrs Brady Brown, Capt. and Mrs Molony, Mr and the Misses Henn, Mr Studdert, the High Sheriff and Mrs Studdert, Mr and Mrs Maunsell, Mr and Mrs R. Lane-Joynt, Mr and Mrs T. O'Gorman, Mr Fitzgerald-Blood, Col Butler, Miss Creagh, Mr W.H.A. MacDonnell, Mr J.W. Scott, Mr and Mrs C.O. Keane, the Misses Mahon, Mr and Mrs Studdert, Mr de Clare-Studdert, Mrs O'Callaghan Westropp, Mr J. A. Parker, Mr and Mrs T.H. Pilkington, Mr J.M. Regan, DI, Mr P.J. Howard, MRCVS, Mr and Mrs Loftus-Studdert, Mr P.F. O'Halloran, Capt. O'Brien, Mr G.H. Walton, Mr P. White, Mr Bernard Lynch, Mr B. Moloney, Mr J. Kelly, Mr Lynch, Mr T. Crowe Jnr, the Misses Crowe, Mr McMahon, Mr James Butler-Ivers, Capt. Standish O'Grady, Mr Montfort-Westropp, Mr Kelly (Porte), Mrs Healy, Mr McNamara, Mr L. Ryan, Mr G.H. MacDonnell, Mr Ernest Corbett, Mr Hogan, Mr Brennan, etc. For the Subscription List of the membership of the Clare Hunt for the 1912-1913 season see, McCarthy, Daniel, *Ireland's Banner County, Clare from the Fall of Parnell to the Great War 1890-1918* (Ennis: Saipan Press, 2002), p.74.

6. For a comprehensive account of sport and social life in Clare see Joe Power, 'Aspects of Sport and Social Life in Clare' in *The Other Clare*, published by the Shannon Archaeological and Historical Society, Vol. 33, 2008, pp. 42-44.

7. Bacon, Peter, *Land, Lust and Gun Smoke, a Social History of Game Shoots in Ireland* (Dublin: The History Press, 2012), pp. 181-205.

8. *CC*, 16 March, 28 April 1914, also *Saturday Record (SR)* and *CJ* around these dates.

9. *CC*, 14 February and 4 July 1914.

10. *CJ*, 2 February 1914; *CC*, 18 April 1914.

11. *SR*, 4 March, 11 April, 2, 23 May 1914; *CC*, 14 February, 18 April 1914.

12. There was extensive coverage of the Derrymore murder trial, in which two men were charged with the murder of John Kildea at Derrymore on 30 November 1913, in all the local papers, for example, *SR*, 14 February, 13 June, 4 July; *CJ*, 4 May; *CC*, 2 May, 1 August 1914.

13. Hansard, Commons Debate, 21 May 1914; *SR*, 23 May 1914.

14. Denman, Terence, *A Lonely Grave, the Life and Death of William Redmond* (Dublin: Irish Academic Press, Colour Books, Dublin, 1995), p. 78, as reported in *The Times* of 2 April 1913.

15. Power, Joseph, *A History of Clare Castle and its Environs* (Ennis: privately published, 2004), pp. 348-50.

16. *CC*, 25 July 1914; 4 January 1915. At the start of each year around this time a summary of annual weather, taken at various sites around the county, was published in the local papers. The weather reports, only giving details of the amounts of rainfall each month, occasionally accompanied with a yearly summary, were taken by gentlemen amateur meteorologists at places such as Carrigoran, Moy and Broadford. Carrigoran was chosen as the representative station for the weather report from the county, as it is in a central location, is of low altitude, being less than 100m (110 yards), and the weather reports were submitted and published for the duration of the war years, unlike some other areas.

17. *CJ*, 3, 10 January, 14 February, 1 August 1914; *SR*, 17 July 1915.

18. *CC*, 14 February 1914.

19. *CC*, 14 March 1914; *SR*, 14 March 1914. For a modern scholarly view of Home Rule and the Ulster crisis, see Fanning, Ronan, *Fatal Path, British Government and Irish Revolution, 1910-1922* (London: Faber and Faber, 2013).

20. Col Arthur Lynch's letter to John Redmond is cited in Finan, Joseph P., *John Redmond and Irish Unity, 1912-1918* (New York: Syracuse University Press, 2004), pp. 139-140.

21. *CC*, 28 March 1914. *SR*, 28 March 1914, referred to the Curragh 'sensation'; see also R. Fanning, op cit., pp.110-117.

22. *CC*, 21 March 1914.

23. *CC*, 23 March 1914; *SR*, 28 March 1914.

24. *CJ*, 27 April, 4 May, 7 May 1914; *CC*, 2 May 1914. R. Fanning, op cit, p.122.

25. *SR*, 28 March,16, 23, 26, 30 May, 6 June, 27 June, 4 July, 25 July, 19 September, 1914; *CC*, 21 March, 21 April, 30 May, 6 June 13 June, 27 June, and 4 July 1914. Fitzpatrick, David, *Politics and Irish Life, 1913-1921* (Dublin: Gill and Macmillan, 1977), p.107; Denman, Terence, *A Lonely Grave, The Life and Death of William Redmond* (Dublin: Irish Academic Press, Colour Books, 1995), p.81.

26. *CC*, 25 April 1914.

27. *CC*, 3 January 1914.

28. *CC*, 30 May 1914; *SR*, 26, 30 May, 6 June, 1914.

29. *CC*, 1 September, 1914; *SR*, 8 August 1914; R. Fanning, op. cit, pp. 128-9.

30. *CC*, 8 August 1914.

31. National Archives, Bishop Street, Dublin, CSORP/1914/6307. The letter was received on 18 April 1914; however, despite several searches, (17 April 1914 and 29 July 1914), this letter was not found in the archives. It may have been destroyed, or else removed to the archives in Kew, London, England.

32. *SR*, 8 August 1914. Denman, Terence, *Ireland's Unknown Soldiers, the 16th Irish Division in the Great War, 1914-18* (Dublin: Irish Academic Press, 1992), p.73, states 'Ironically the Great War prevented the outbreak of civil war in Ireland'.

2. 'For the Freedom of Small Nations'

1. Jeffrey, Keith, *Ireland and the Great War* (Cambridge: Cambridge University Press, 2000), p.84;

2. Denman, Terence, *A Lonely Grave, The Life and Death of William Redmond* (Dublin: Irish Academic Press, Colour Books, 1995), pp. 85-86. *CJ*, 19 April 1915.

3. *SR*, 8 August 1914; *CJ*, 8 August, 24 August, 5 November 1914; *CC*, 17 October 1914.

4. *CJ*, 6, 17 August, 1914.

5. *CJ*, 22 March 1915.

6. *CJ*, 10 August 1914

7. *CJ*, 29 August 1914.

8. De Wiel, Jerome Aan, *The Catholic Church in Ireland, 1914-1918, War and Politics* (Dublin: Irish Academic Press, 2003) pp.5-14; *William Henry, Galway and the Great War* (Cork: Mercier Press, 2006), p.57.

9. *CC*, 17 October 1914; *SR*, 5 December 1914.

10. *SR*, 15, 22 August; *CC*, 22, 29 August 1914; Fitzpatrick, David, op. cit., pp.63-64. McCarthy, Daniel, *Ireland's Banner County, Clare from the Fall of Parnell to the Great War 1890-1918* (Saipan Press, Darragh, 2002), p.95. McCarthy cites the Col Maurice Moore papers in the NLI, Moore Mss, 10547, no. 5. See *Australian Dictionary of Biography* for a summary of the career of Arthur Lynch, http://adb.anu.edu.biography/lynch-arthur-alfred-7270.

11. Jeffery, Keith, *Ireland and the Great War* (Cambridge: Cambridge University Press, 2000), pp.40-46.

12. Fitzpatrick, op. cit., p.64; Burnell, Tom, *The Clare War Dead* (Dublin: The History Press Ireland, 2011), see under various names; O' Brien, Grania R., *These My Friends and Forebears, the O'Briens of Dromoland* (Whitegate: Ballinakella Press, 1991), pp.206-209; *CC*, 22, 29 August 1914; Stacpoole, John, *Stacpoole: The Owners of a Name* (published privately, Auckland, New Zealand, 1991), p.106. Incidentally, Capt. Alexander Moore Vandeleur, Life Guards Regiment, of Cahercon and Kilrush was one of the prominent Protestant and unionist officers from Clare who was killed in October 1917. His body was never found. Graves, Robert, *Goodbye to All That, an Autobiography* (London: Penguin Classics, 2014), first published by Jonathan Cape, in 1929, pp.83-4. Graves admired the spirit of the Hon. Desmond O'Brien, a fellow schoolmate at Charterhouse Public School, 'He was the only schoolboy in my time, who cheerfully disregarded all the school rules … at last having absented himself from every lesson and chapel for three whole days, he was expelled. He was killed early in the war while bombing Bruges [from the air]'.

13. Clare Museum: 'Claremen in the First World War' Exhibition, which was held in November 2012. There was a list of thirteen soldiers, among them John Cunneen, Burnell, op. cit., p.61.

14. Staunton, Martin, 'Kilrush, Co. Clare and the Royal Munster Fusiliers', in *The Irish Sword*, Vol. XVI (1984-'85), *Journal of the Military History Society of Ireland*, edited by Harman Murtagh, PhD., Athlone. Tom Johnstone, *Orange, Khaki and Green, the Story of the Irish Regiments in the Great War, 1914-18* (Dublin:

Gill and Macmillan,1992), pp.29-33. See also, McCance, Capt. S., *History of the Royal Munster Fusiliers, Vol. 11.1861 to 1922* (Sussex, The Naval and Military Press Ltd) pp.113-120, for a detailed account of the heroic struggle of the Munsters against the X Reserve Corps of the German Army, at least six times more numerous than the Munster Battalion. See also, Jervis, Lt Col, Sir Herbert S.G. Miles, *The 2ndMunsters in France* (first printed in 1922, Aldershot, UK, edition, Cork: Schull Books, 1998), Chapter 1, pp.1-7.

15. *SR*, 19, 26 September, 1914; *CJ*, 17, 26 September, 2 October, 2, 7 November, 17 December and *CC*, 7 November, 1914. See also *CC* 14 February 1997. See an interview with Gerard Halloran, his grandnephew, in *An Cosantoir*, October 2002. Amazingly, all five surviving Halloran brothers answered the call to arms and joined the American and British armies in the Second World War against Hitler and all of them survived. Jeremiah and Martin took part in the D Day landings with the American forces, while John, William and Michael joined the British forces.

16. *CC*, 3 October, 14 November 1914; *SR*, 24 October, 31 October 1914.

17. *SR*, 14 November, 5 December 1914.

18. *SR*, 14 November 1914.

19. McCarthy, Daniel, op. cit., p.89; Fitzpatrick, op. cit., pp.89, 105; also, Maleady, Dermot, *John Redmond the National Leader* (Kildare: Merrion, an imprint of Irish Academic Press, 2014), p.359; *SR*, 31 October 1914. According to the report in the *Saturday Record*, the attendance on the reviewing stand included: Bishop Fogarty; Fr O'Connell, president of St Flannan's College; Fr Slattery, PP Quin; W. Grace, PP; Fr J. O'Mara, *CC*; J. Hogan, *CC*; Fr M. McGrath, *CC* Clare Castle; P.J. Linnane, JP; W.H. Ball, DL Fortfergus; Mr and Mrs G. de Willis; Mr S.N.P. Waring; Mr F.F. Cullinan; Mr J.B. Lynch; Mr and Mrs T.J. Hunt; J. Lynch; Dr Coughlan; Dr Garry; Dr Geary; Dr Counihan; Dr O'Mara; Mr B. Crowe; Mr E.A. Ellis, JP; and Misses Burns, McGeogh and O'Brien, etc. See also Staunton, Martin, 'Kilrush Co. Clare and the Royal Munster Fusiliers, the experience of an Irish town in the First World War', in *The Irish Sword*, Vol. XVI (1984-86), Journal of the Military History Society of Ireland, edited by Harman Murtagh, Athlone, pp.268-272. See also, Ó Ruairc, Pádraic Óg, *Blood on the Banner, the Republican Struggle in Clare* (Cork: Mercier Press, 2009), pp.34-36 on the split in the Clare Volunteers after Redmond's 'Woodenbridge speech'. Unfortunately, O'Ruairc does not include references in his book. See also Denman, Terence, *A Lonely Grave, the Life and Death of Willie Redmond* (Dublin: Irish Academic Press, Colour Books, 1995), p.84.

20. Bureau of Military History 1913-21, W.S. 1,322, testimony of Art O'Donnell of Tullycrine, formerly OC West Clare Brigade, dated 14 December 1955.

21. *CJ*, 2 October; *SR*, 19 October 1914. Jeffery, op. cit., p.12.

22. *SR*, 14 November 1914. The chorus verse of the famous song written by Jack Judge and Harry Williams.

23. Glynn papers, H.R. Glynn to Redmond, 5 August 1914; H.R. Glynn to Birrel, 29 August 1914; William Healy, Clerk of Crown and Peace to H.R. Glynn, 26 September, 1914; H.R. Glynn to Mr H.H. Asquith, Prime Minister, 23 November 1914; H.R. Glynn to Sir Michael O'Loghlen, HML,

30 November, 1914.

24. *SR*, 21 November, 12 December 1914.

25. Crane, Stephen, *The Red Badge of Courage*, first published 1895 (New York: Bantam Classic edition, 1985), p.3.

26. *CC*, 29 August 1914.

27. *SR*, 14 November 1914; *CJ*, 15 December 1914 and 7 January 1915.

28. Based on lists of war dead in three publications, McCarthy, Daniel, op. cit., appendix 165-174; Burnell, op. cit., passim, and Browne, Ger., op. cit., passim.

3. Propaganda, the Western Front and Gallipoli

1.   *CC*, 1 February, 22 May, 18 December 1915 and *SR*, 6 February 1915.

2.   *CC*, 20 February 1915.

3.   Bishop Michael Fogarty to John Redmond, 8 June 1915, NLI, Redmond Papers, Ms 15188; *CC*, 1,8 ,15 May, 15 November, 1915.

4.   *SR*, 20 November, 11, 25 December 1915.

5.   Mark Tierney, Paul Bowen and David Fitzpatrick, 'Recruiting posters' in Fitzpatrick, David, editor, *Ireland and the First World War* (Mullingar: Lilliput Press and Trinity History Workshop, 1988), pp.47-58, passim.

6.   *SR*, 23 January 1915.

7.   *SR*, 30 January, 4 September 1915; Martin Staunton, op. cit.p 270, casts doubt upon the figure of over 200 recruits at Kilrush, stating it seems too high. Nevertheless, it does highlight the recruits from the area being cheered off by large crowds. *CJ*, 6 December 1915.

8.   *SR*, 13 February; *CJ*, 13 May 1915.

9.   Limerick Diocesan Archives, LDA/B1/ET/7 (episcopal correspondence Fogarty to O'Dwyer), 9 December 1915; De Weil, op. cit., pp.65, 71-74; *CJ*, 3 June, 15 November; *SR*, 15, 20 and 30 November 1915; *CC*, 15 November 1915.

10. Bowman, Timothy, *Irish Regiments in the Great War, Discipline and Morale* (Manchester: Manchester University Press, 2003), p.27; see also, Jane Leonard, *The Catholic Chaplaincy in Ireland and the First World War*, David Fitzpatrick (ed.), (Mullingaer: Lilliput Press and Trinity History Workshop, 1988), pp. 1-16 passim; Graves, Robert, *Goodbye to All That, an Autobiography*, first published in 1929, by Jonathan Cape in 1929, (London; Classic Penguin Edition, 2014), with an introduction by Andrew Morton, pp.240-241. Graves, a captain in the Welsh Fusiliers during the First World War, 'who was brought up with a horror of Roman Catholics', had great praise for the Catholic chaplains, who risked their lives to comfort the wounded and dying soldiers. He said, 'No soldier could have any respect for an Anglian chaplain, who obeyed the orders' (that is, to stay safely behind the front lines).

11. *CJ*, 13 May 1915; *SR*, 16 January 1915; *SR*, 20 February, 6, 20 March, 1 May, 26 June, 7 and 15 August 1915.

12. *SR*, 28 August, 4, 11 September 1915; *CJ*, 13 August 1915; *CC*, 18 September 1915; Glynn papers, 'programme of their excellencys' visit to County Clare'; Sir Basil Blackwood, secretary to Lord Wimborne, to H.R. Glynn, DL, 30 August 1915.

13. *SR*, 31 July, 6 December 1915.

14. *CJ*, 19 July; *SR*, 19 July, 6 November 1915. Fitzpatrick, David, *Politics and Irish Life, 1913-1921*, p.65. I remember on one occasion in the early 1960s when Martin Faulkner was in Clare Castle on an occasional visit, my father, Bernard Power, treated him to a glass of Guinness telling me that he had been an old soldier in the Great War. I am grateful to Mr Con Woods of Newmarket-on-Fergus for telling me the anecdote on 4 August 2014 about how Martin Faulkner, a Traveller, saved Jack Fox, the All-Ireland winning hurling star from Newmarket-on-Fergus, during the war. See article by Con Woods, 'From Jones Road to the Somme' in *CC*, 31 October 2014, p.22. See also an article by Joe O'Muirceartaigh, 'Fox slashing, fearless and free' in *Clare People*, 23 December 2014, pp.50-52.

15. *CJ*, 29 July 1915.

16. *SR*, 17 July 1915. Blythe was Minister for Finance in the Free State Government between 1922 and 1932.

17. Brennan, Michael, *The War in Clare, 1911-1921, Personal Memoirs of the Irish War of Independence* (Dublin: Four Courts Press, 1980), p.11.

18. *CJ*, 21 June, 4 October 1915; *SR*, 31 July 1915.

19. Dungan,Myles, *They Shall Not Grow Old, Irish Soldiers and the Great War* (Dublin: Four Courts Press, 1997), p.26.

20. *CJ*, 5 July 1915.

21. *SR*, 20 November, 18 December ; *CJ*, 13 December 1915. Glynn Papers, Kilrush: C.E. Glynn to Sir Charles Barrington, Baronet, DL, 30 October 1915; Capt. Browning to Mr C.E. Glynn, 3 November 1915; Mr C.E. Glynn to Capt. Browning, 4 November 1915, Sir Charles Barrington, Bart., to C.E. Glynn, 17 November 1915; C.E. Glynn to Capt. Browning, Ennis, 4 November 1915, HQ, Irish Command, Dublin to C.E. Glynn, 8 December 1915; C.E. Glynn to Sir Charles Barrington, 9 December 1915; Col H.V. Cowan, HQ, Irish Command to C.E. Glynn, 8 December 1915.

22. Glynn Papers, H.R. Glynn to Sir Grey Wilson, 19 January 1915; H.R. Glynn to J. Redmond, 4 February 1915; H.R. Glynn to E.C. Blanchflower, Queenstown, 11 March 1915; H.R. Glynn to Director of Contracts, Admiralty, London, 30 March 1915; H.R. Glynn to David Lloyd George, 1 April 1915; H.R. Glynn to Maj. Ivers, 18 March 1915; Maj. Ivers to H.R. Glynn, 20 March 1915; H.R. Glynn to Secretary, Recruitment Department of Ireland, Dublin, 20 November 1915.

23. Grania R. O'Brien, op. cit, pp.208-09; *SR*, 9 January, 15 February, 28 May; *CJ*, 4, 11, 14 January, 22 February, 1 April; *CC*, 9 January, 3 April, 1 May, 1915. See letter by one Belgian refugee, Charles Nissen, who was housed in Clare Castle for some time, describing how he and family escaped from Belgium, in *CJ*, 11 January 1915.

24. *SR*, 28 May 1915; *Irish World*, 23 October 1915, cited in Daniel McCarthy, op.cit., pp.104 and note 43,p. 191.

25. *CJ*, 22 March; *SR*, 16 October 1915.

26. *CC*, 27 November; *CJ*, 13 December and *SR*, 18 December 1915.

27. *SR*, 24 July 1915.

28. M.J. Gardiner and T. Radford, *Soil Associations of Ireland and their Land Use Potential*, explanatory Bulletin to Soil Map of Ireland 1980, An Foras Talúntais, Dublin, 1980, pp.139-140; also, T.F. Finch, E. Culliton and S. Diamond, *Soils of County Clare*, soil survey Bulletin no. 23, An Foras Talúntais, Dublin, 1971, p.49.

29. *SR*, 2, 9, January, 20 February, 29 May, 17 July, 7 August, 20 November and 25 December; *CC* 9 March, 6 November, 4 December, *CJ*, 4 January, 1, 4, 18 February, 17 May and 4 October 1915 and 29 January 1916.

30. *SR*, 30 January, 6, 13 March, 24 July, 6 November, 25 December 1915, *CJ*, 23 December 1915. The full list of fifty prisoners was included in the *SR* of 25 December 1915: *Royal Munster Fusiliers* Sgt Maj. J. Browne, Sgt J. Scanlan, Sgt P. Ryan, L-Cpl John F. Ryan and L-Cpl J. McCarthy. Ptes P. Crowe, John Hynes, T. Costello, Pat Ensko, John Hynes, M. Moroney, T. Timmins, T. Kelly, Ed Moloney, John Hanly, A. Hegarty, James Considine, Martin Kenny, W. Malone, Mat Dynan, D. O'Connor, Joe Manning, W. McCowan, Mat Gorman, John Stafford, John Danaher, John Hogan, P. McSparrow, John Daly, Michael McCarthy, Thomas Cushin, Martin Kelly, D.I. Considine, Pat Burke, P. Collins, J. O'Shaughnessy, J. O'Brien, P. Cullinane and D. O'Connor. Pte P.O'Loughlin, Connaught Rangers; L-Cpl Patrick Connor, Gordon Highlanders; Ptes John Flynn and Mat Griffey, Leinster Regiment; Lance Cpl Mat Leyden and Ptes M. O'Brien and John Thynne, Royal Irish Regiment; Ptes John Mahoney and Pat Roche, Royal Dublin Fusiliers; Pte J. MacNamara, South Lancashire Regiment; Pte George Nolan, King's Own Royal Lancashire Regiment and Pte Pat Crimmins, Royal Army Medical Corps.

31. *SR*, 15, 22 May, 25 July 1915; Burnell, Tom, *The Clare War Dead, a History of the Casualties of the Great War* (Dublin: The History Press of Ireland, 2011), pp.89 and 90; See also www.rmslusitania.info/tag/irish. Dr Garry's heart-broken mother, Mary Garry, wrote several letters to the mother of another victim Mrs Pritchard: 'No one feels for you as we do, knowing what it is to lose a darling boy, RIP, our hearts go out to you in sympathy over your great loss ...'

    'God alone knows what suffering our darling boy was saved from, for life had plenty of trouble, sooner or later for all that my loved son had signed into going out to Serbia to attend to the typhus patients. This dreadful war will leave no son to father or mother; we have only to console ourselves with the thought that God knows what is best for all, welcome His holy will ...'

    'Isn't the war dreadful? I am always worrying, as I have a daughter at Birkdale Convent. I feel terrified fearing anything would happen to her. One can never know what those terrible Huns might do. They delight in taking the lives of poor innocent people...Yours, Mary Garry.'

    The letters are dated, 13 November 1915, 26 January and 23 February 1916, and are located in the Imperial War Museum, London. For a comprehensive analysis of the ill-fated voyage of the *Lusitania*, see Molony, Senan, *Lusitania: an Irish Tragedy* (Cork: Mercier Press, 2004), passim.

32. *SR*, 31 July 1915.

33. *SR*, 14 September 1915.

34. *SR*, 14 September 1915; See McCance, op. cit., pp.48-61 for an account of the Munsters in Gallipoli.

35. Burnell, Tom, *The Clare War Dead, a History of the Casualties of the Great War* (Dublin: The History Press Ireland, 2011), pp.104-109.

36. *SR*, 20 November 1915.

37. *SR*, 3 July 1915; Brian Dinan, 'A town I know so well', in Power, Joseph (ed.), *An Ennis Miscellany* (Ennis 750 Committee, 1990), p.198.

38. *CJ*, 13 September 1915.

39. Taylor, A.J.P, *The First World War, an Illustrated History* (Norwich: Penguin Books,1963), pp.77-100, passim; the names of the war dead buried in Gallipoli are found in Tom Burnell, *The Clare War Dead*, passim. Interestingly, one of the great anti-war ballads of the late twentieth century is Eric Bogle's 'And the band played Waltzing Matilda', to the tune of an old Australian ballad, which deals with the sacrifices of the Anzac forces (the Australian and New Zealand soldiers) in Gallipoli in 1915. The lyrics were penned by Eric Bogle in 1971. In one of the verses are the following words: 'I recall the day in the Hell called Suvla Bay, we were butchered like lambs at the slaughter.' These words could easily be attributed to all the British troops at Gallipoli and certainly to the Irishmen of the Munster and Dublin battalions, many of whom were from County Clare.

40. Tottenham family records, miscellaneous entries in Rain Gauge book at Mount Callan. I am grateful to Ms Jane Tottenham, who gave me this information on 25 and 29 April 2014.

41. Cooper, Bryan, *The Tenth Irish Division in Gallipoli* (Dublin: Irish Academic Press, 1993), pp.14, 37, 87 and 100.

42. *SR*, 2 December 1915.

43. *CJ*, 3 June 1915.

44. Lynch, Arthur, MP, Ireland: *Vital Hour* (London: Stanley Paul and Co., 1915), p.129.

45. *CJ*, 23, November, 2, 9,16, 23 December; *CC*, 27 November, 4, 11, 18 December, 1915.

46. *CJ*, 6 May, 3 July 1915; *SR*, 14 September, 6 August 1915. Harris, Henry, *The Irish Regiments in the First World War* (Cork: Mercier Press, 1968), Chapter 4, Gallipoli, described the Gallipoli campaign as 'useless slaughter of brave men … it cost the British empire, more than 200,000 killed and wounded and it achieved nothing'.

47. *CC*, 25 December 1915.

48. *CJ*, 30 December 1915.

49. *SR*, 22 May 1915.

50. Walker, Stephen, *Forgotten Soldiers, the Irishmen Shot at Dawn* (Dublin: Gill and Macmillan, 2007), see chapter on Pte Davis. Incidentally, his brother Francis was a war hero, receiving a citation for bravery. Following a prolonged campaign by relatives of the twenty-six Irishmen shot by the British Army during the First World War for alleged desertion, cowardice, or other reasons, the defence of which was supported by the Irish Government, Pte Tommy Davis was posthumously pardoned by the British Army. The Irish Minister for Defence stated: 'We believe a great injustice was done to these young

men and the Irish Government has given its full support to the "Shot at Dawn" campaign'. See article by Jessica Quinn in *CC* 18 August 2006; See also *CC*, 19 October 2001; 16 May, 2003; 26 January, 2007; 27 January 2006; 5 November 2007; 25 April, 2008; 24 October, 2008.

51. See lists of Clare war dead in, Browne, Burnell, and McCarthy, op. cit.

52. Owen, Wilfred, '*Dulce et Decorum Est*', in Kindall, Tim (ed.), *Poetry of the First World War, an Anthology* (Oxford: Oxford University Press, 2013), pp.154–55.

4. Recruitment and Rebellion

1. *CJ*, 13 April 1916; Glynn Papers.

2. Glynn Papers; See list published in *CJ*, 11 March 1916 and typed supplementary list, dated 16 March 1916 and *CC*, 25 March 1916. The following gentlemen were also members of the West Clare Recruitment Committee set up by Mr C.E. Glynn. Kilrush: L. O'Brien; P.J. Dillon; P.J. O'Shea, NT; J.J. Bradley; and M. Slattery. Kildysart: Thomas and Timothy Kenny; P. McNamara; John Meehan; F. O'Dea, Clerk of the Union; and M. Shannon. Knock and Killimer: Revd P. Barrett, PP; F.W. Hickman, DL; P. Hassett, JP; Capt. Poole Gore. Kilmihil: Francis Ryan and James Griffin, JP. Doonbeg: M. McInerney. Cree: Mr B. Kelly. Carrigaholt: Dr Studdert, JP; P.J. O'Kelly; T.D. Roughan; and A. O'Dwyer. Querrin: James Lillis. De Wiel, op. cit., p.25.

3. See McCarthy, Daniel, op. cit., p.113; de Wiel, op. cit., p.18.

4. *SR*, 4, 25 March 1916. The *CJ* of 13 April 1916, mentions the names of the ladies of West Clare in attendance: Miss Glynn, Mrs Hennessy, Mrs W. Glynn, Mrs Silles, Mrs T. Kelly, Mrs Killeen, Miss Supple, Mrs Watson, Mrs Dowling, Mrs Bradley, Mrs Kirby, Mrs Parker, Miss Nellie Walsh, Miss Rose Clancy, Miss Blake, Miss Culligan, Miss Carey, Mrs Nagle, Miss Napier, Miss O'Dea, Miss Slattery, Kilrush, Miss E. Ellis and Mrs Elliott, Miltown Malbay, the Misses Hassett, Burrane, and Mrs O'Dwyer, Clonadrum. Apologies were received from several ladies in Kilkee, Kildysart, etc. Mr F.W. Johnstone, Limerick and Mr C.E. Glynn, recruitment officer also attended.

5. *CJ*, 20 April 1916. The full list of East Clare ladies included Lady Inchiquin (president), Mrs G. de Willis (secretary), Lady Beatrice O'Brien, Hon. Mrs Blood, Miss Stackpoole, Miss Hester Mahon, Mrs Butler and Miss H. Butler, Mrs Loftus Studdert, Mrs Vere O'Brien, Mrs Bulger, Mrs and Miss Crowe (Dromore), Mrs MacDonnell, Mrs Allen, Misses Kerin, Mrs Fogarty, Mrs O'Callaghan Westropp and Miss O'Callaghan Westropp, Mrs H. Webster, Mrs and Miss O'Mara, Mrs T.M. Stewart, Mrs Healy and Miss Healy, Mrs Abrahall, Mrs J.A. Reardan, Mrs H. Mills, Mrs Marcus Keane, Mrs J.W. Scott, Mrs Tierney, Mrs J. Dawson, (Ballynacally), Mrs Charles Mahon, Mrs T.A. O'Gorman, Mrs Fitzjames Kelly, Miss Simpson, Mrs Hadden, Mrs Maunsell, Miss Byrne, Miss Cissie Lynch, Mrs M.V. O'Halloran, Miss O'Brien, Mrs McMahon, Miss Studdert (Bunratty), Miss E. Frost, Mrs C.W. Healy, Mrs J. Healy, Miss E. Mahon, Mrs Scanlan, Miss Scanlan, Miss M.C. McNamara, Mrs T.J. Hunt, and Mrs Penman. Letters of apology were received from Mrs Berry,

Mrs Ievers, Mrs Stackpoole, Mrs Hibbert, Mrs Marcus Patterson, Mrs F. Gore Hickman, Mrs F.N. Studdert, Mrs Sampson, and Mrs Mellett.

6. *SR*, 11 March 1916.

7. *SR*, 16 March; *CJ*, 20 March 1916. Those councillors who voted for the resolution in March included: Messrs J. Lynch; M. Leyden, JP; P.J.Linnane, JP; W. Purcell; P. Garry, JP; F. Burke; M.F. Nagle; M. Griffin, JP; W. O'Connor, JP; P.Culloo, JP; and S. Maguire. The councillors who voted against the resolution – Messrs P. McInerney, D. Healy, B. Crowley, L. Brohan, G. Frost and J. Collins. *SR*, 18 October 1916.

8. *CC*, 22 January 1916.

9. *SR*, 11 March; *CJ*, 20 January, 2, 27, March, 13 April 1916.

10. Glynn Papers, C.E. Glynn to Capt. Kelly, Dept. of Recruitment, Dublin, 22 February, 1916; C.E. Glynn to John Redmond, MP, 21 February 1916; Dinneen to Glynn, 25 February 1916; Glynn to Dinneen, 25 February 1916; Glynn to Capt. Kelly, 18 March 1916; Barrington to Glynn, 15 March 1916; Sir Charles Barrington to C.E. Glynn, 15 March 1916; Glynn to Barrington, 18 March 1916; Richard Stacpoole, Eden Vale, to C.E. Glynn about organising a motor service for the recruiting officer, 19 March 1916; Glynn to R. Stackpoole, Edenvale, 20 March 1916; *CC*, 30 March 1916; Glynn to F.N. Studdert, Sec. to Clare County Council, 22 March; Capt. Kelly to C.E. Glynn, 28 March, 1916. Lord Pirrie to H.R. Glynn, 27 March 1916. After a recruitment conference in Ennis on 9 March a deputation was appointed to wait on Clare County Council with the object of securing their assistance and co-operation in the recruiting scheme. Led by Lord inchiquin, the deputation included the following gentlemen: Sir Charles Barrington, Bart., DL; Capt. Kelly, Director General of Recruiting in Ireland; P.J. Linnane, JP; P. Kinealy, JP; M.S. Honan, JP; F.N. Studdert, DL; J. O'Regan, JP; G. Mcilroy, RM; M.V. O'Halloran, JP, controller of recruiting East Clare; H.R. Glynn, DL; B. Culligan, JP; Dr Scanlan, JP; M. Brady, JP; J. Daly, Solicitor; C. Healy, JP; M. McNamara, JP; and C.E. Glynn, controller of recruiting, West Clare. The dissension at the Kilrush Board of Guardians was noted in the local paper, *The Kilrush Herald*, of 31 March 1916, (news-cutting in the Glynn papers); newspaper cutting, *The Kilrush Herald, & Kilkee Gazette*, in the Glynn papers, Box no. 7.

11. The poem was published in the *CC* of 16 March 1916; the letter was in the *SR* of 29 January 1916. Presumably, the Patrick McMahon mentioned in the letter was referring to Lt Patrick McMahon, 8th Battalion, Royal Munster Fusiliers, of Knocknagun House, Newmarket-on-Fergus, who died of wounds in France on 29 December 1915.

12. *CJ*, 20 January 1916. According to the testimony of Chief Inspector Gelston of the RIC in Clare, speaking at the Inquiry into the 1916 Rising, 'recruitment was very good, especially among the labouring classes and in the towns, but there was no recruiting at all from the farming class', pp.180-181; *CC*, 3 June 1916. Also, Martin Staunton, 'The Royal Munster Fusiliers in the Great War', MA thesis, UCD, unpublished, p.12.

13. *CJ*, 20 January, 19 March; *SR*, 22, 29 January, 15 April 1916.

14. *CJ*, 1 May 1916. County Inspector Gelston's testimony was given at the

Royal Inquiry into the Easter Rising held at the Shelbourne Hotel, Dublin, in late May, early June, 1916. *CC*, 3, 10 June 1916; *SR*, 10, 20 June 1916, see minutes of the Inquiry, pp.180-181; for more detailed accounts from a republican perspective, of the organisation of the Volunteers in Clare between 1913 and 1916, see Brennan, Michael, op. cit., Chapter 1, passim; also, Ó Ruairc, Pádraig Óg, *Blood on the Banner, the Republican Struggle in Clare* (Cork: Mercier Press, 2009), pp. 30-40.

15. *CC*, 6 May, 3 June 1916; *SR*, 6, 13 May 1916.

16. *CC*, 20 May; *CJ*, 15 May 1916.

17. County Inspector Gelston's testimony, see note 14 above; Brennan, Michael, op. cit., pp.18-19; also, O'Ruairc, op. cit., Chapter 3, pp.41-58, passim, on the Irish Volunteers activities in Clare during the 1916 Rising. O'Ruairc states on p.54 that the parish priest of Carrigaholt had persuaded the local Irish Volunteers to hand up their weapons to him after the 1916 Rising and that he had given them to the RIC.

18. Letter from Lord Inchiquin to the Hon. Donough O'Brien, 2 May 1916. I am grateful to the Hon. Grania O'Brien, daughter of the 16th Baron Inchiquin, for showing me this correspondence. Judge Bodkin's observations are cited in the *SR*, 24 June 1916.

19. *CJ*, 27 April; *SR*, 6, 20 April, 6, 13, 20 May; *CC*, 5 May, 1916; Sheedy, Kieran, *The Clare Elections* (Bauroe Press, 2000), p.786.

20. LDA, /BI/ET/O/7 (episcopal correspondence), Fogarty to O'Dwyer, 31 July, 7, 10, 12 and 17 September 1916; Morrissey, Thomas, J., SJ, *Bishop Edward T. O'Dwyer, of Limerick, 1842-1917* (Dublin: Four Courts Press, 2003) with an afterword by Professor Emmet Larkin, p.380.

21. *CJ*, 1, 5 May; *SR*, 6, 13, 20 May, 3 June; *CC*, 6, 25 May 1916.

22. *CC*, 3 June (testimony of County Inspector Gelston), 10 June, 1 July, 19 August, 9, 30 September, 7, 28 October 1916.

23. Glynn Papers, Col Barrington to Glynn, 26 April 1916; Capt. Kelly to Glynn, 6 May 1916; Capt. Kelly to Glynn, 8 May 1916; Capt. R Kelly to C.E. Glynn, 3 June 1916. *SR*, 20 May 1916. H.R. Glynn to Lloyd George, 27 May, 1916; H.R. Glynn to Mr Birrel; Mr Lewis Gray, Director of Ministry of Munitions, Ireland, to H.R. Glynn, 28 October, 1916; M.E. White to H.R. Glynn, 23 October, 1916. For the flour contract with the British Army, see company accounts, Glynn Papers, Box no. 4.

24. Joe O'Muirceartathaigh, *Chronicle of Clare 1900-2000* (Ennis: Fag an Bealach, 2000), p.35; *CC*, 29 July 1916, 12 May 1917.

25. *SR*, 13 May 1916.

26. *CC*, 12 February, 1916; the eight prisoners mentioned in the newspaper included Pte T. O'Brien, Pte P. Collins, Pte P. Insko, Pte J. Hogan, Sgt J. Scanlon, Pte Martin Kennedy, L-Cpl A Hogarty and Sgt P. Ryan. *CJ* 20 November 1916. *SR*, 29 September 1917. Dungan, Myles, *They Shall Not Grow Old, Irish Soldiers in the Great War* (Dublin: Four Courts Press, 1997), pp.138-40, 155; Also Mitchell, Angus, *16 Lives, Roger Casement* (Dublin: O'Brien Press, 2013), pp.240-41, 243 and 206. Gilbert, Martin, *The First World War* (London: Weidenfeld and Nicholson, 1994), p.114.

27. Bowman, Timothy, *Irish Regiments in the Great War, Discipline and Morale* (Manchester: Manchester University Press, 2003), pp.128-9. Harris, Henry, *The Irish Regiments in the First World War* (Cork: Mercier Press, 1968), pp.53, 127.

28. Letter from Willie Redmond, MP, to P.J. Linnane; Linnane family papers, courtesy of Dr Michael Linnane, Shannon.

29. Maj. William Redmond, *Trench Pictures from France* (New York: George H. Doran Company, 1918) with a biographical introduction by E.M. Smith-Dampier, pp.106-109, 121. The letter to Dr Fogarty was published in *SR*, 12 February and the letter to Mr Linnane on 14 October 1916.

30. The death of Pte John Power was announced in the *SR*, 20 January 1917. The article stated, 'he had joined the "Pals" Battalion of the Dublin Fusiliers soon after its formation, and that he had taken part in many engagements. He had a promising career before him in the service.' I am indebted to Frank Power and John Power, Clare Castle for bringing these letters to my attention. Pte John Power was killed on 13 November 1916, about two weeks after writing the letter to his sister Mary. He died during the late stage of the Battle of the Somme, when the 10th Battalion of the Royal Dublin Fusiliers captured the village of Beaumont Hemel and rounded up 400 prisoners. The battle took place in terrible weather conditions, in a blinding snowstorm, which later turned to sleet and rain. His brother Timothy, who was in the Royal Army Medical Corps, never recovered from 'shellshock' as a result of his wartime experiences in the Western Front.

31. First World War diary of the Hon. Donough O'Brien (later 16th Baron Inchiquin of Dromoland), 2nd Lieutenant, Kings Rifles Regiment, entries from 25 October 1916 to 14 December 1916. The total entries in the war diary are given in Appendix One. Lt O'Brien was injured in the following summer, but was able to serve till the end of the war. After the war ended he served as an aide-de-camp to the Viceroy of India, Lord Chelmsford. See Grania R. O'Brien, op.cit., pp. 206-209.

32. De Wiel, op. cit., pp.111-114.

33. *SR*, 4 November 1916.

34. Johnstone, T. op. cit., p.254.

35. Harris, Henry, *Irish Regiments in the First World War* (Cork: Mercier Press, 1968), pp.140-141.

36. *SR*, 15 May; *CJ*, 17 July, 26 August 1916. *CJ*, 17 January, 1916.

37. *SR*, 23 November 1916.

38. See the various local papers in July, August and September 1916. See also, Joe Power, 'Sport and social life in nineteenth century Clare', in *The Other Clare*, Published by Shannon Archaeological and Historical Society, Vol. 33, 2008, pp.42-43.

39. *SR*, 24 January, 5 February, 15 April, 12 August, 9, 16, 30 September, 4 November 1916.

40. *SR*, 21 October 1916.

41. Based on published lists compiled by Burnell, Browne, and McCarthy, op. cit.

5. The Spirit of 1916

1. *SR*, 10, 17 February; 3, 24 March, 1917; *CJ* 15 March 1917.
2. *SR*, 24 February; *CC*, 27 February 1917;
3. *CJ*, 30 April 1917.
4. *SR*, 24 February 1917; *CJ*, 5 April 1917.
5. LDA/BI/ET/O/7 (Episcopal Correspondence), 17 and 25 February 1917; De Wiel, op. cit., p.170
6. Ó Ruairc, Pádraig Óg, *Blood on the Banner, The Republican Struggle in Clare* (Cork: Mercier Press, 2009), pp. 75-78, citing Thomas Macnamara; Brendan O'Cathaoir, 'Another Clare: Ranchers and Moonlighters, 1700-1945,' in Matthew Lynch and Patrick Nugent, editors, *Clare History and Society* (Dublin: Geography Publications, 2009), pp.392-398. O'Cathaoir cited the testimonies of O'Donoghue, Brennan, Barrett and O'Loughlin.
7. National Archives, Bishop Street, Dublin, CSORP, 7673 S, (13489 Secret) with respect to Fr Maher, Killaloe and Garranboy. Unfortunately no copy of this could be found on 17 April 2014; letter from Sgt Daughton (RIC No 55,619), Kilboy, enclosing reports by Constables Bray (RIC No 57577) and Folan (RIC No 65850) of sermons at Sunday Masses in Silvermines and Ballinclogh, dated 4 and 11 November 1917; Reports sent to Chief Secretary's Office, file number 13567S, dated 5 and 12 November 1917. Fr Charles Culligan was transferred to Kilmihil in 1918.
8. *CC*, 13 18 January 1917.
9. *CJ*, 1, 18 January, 2 April 1917.
10. *CJ*, 11 January 1917.
11. *CJ*, 15 January 1917.
12. *SR*, 17 March 1917. See also Richardson, Neil, *A Coward if I Return, a Hero if I Fail, stories of Irishmen in World War I* (Dublin: O'Brien Press, 2010), pp.157-58.
13. *SR*, 16 June 1917.
14. ibid.
15. *CC*, 9, 14 June; *SR*, 7 July 1917. Jeffrey, Keith, *Ireland and the Great War* (2000), pp.84-86; Dermot Maleady, *John Redmond The National Leader* (Kildare: Irish Academic Press, 2014), p.410.
16. Linnane family papers.
17. Jeffrey, op. cit, p.85; Sheedy, Kieran, *The Clare Elections*, (Dún Laoghaire: Bauroe Publications, 1993), see Chapter 12.
18. Redmond, William, *Trench Pictures from France* (New York: George H. Doran and Co., 1918), pp.20-23, 28-9.
19. Johnstone, Tom, *Orange, Green and Khaki, The Story of the Irish Regiments in the Great War, 1914-1918* (Dublin: Gill and Macmillan,1992), p.278.
20. Denman, Terence, *A lonely Grave* (Dublin: Colour Books, 1995), pp.135-136. Moloney, Timothy J., 'The Impact of WWI on Limerick', MA thesis, Mary Immaculate College, University of Limerick, 22 July 2003, p.63.
21. *SR*, 16 June 1917.
22. *CC*, 23 June 1917.

23. *CC*, 22 September 1917; McCarthy, Daniel, op. cit., p.113; *SR*,
    31 October 1914.

24. *CC*, 3 November 1917.

25. *SR*, 16 June 1917. The Election Committee chosen at this meeting
    included the following delegates: All the priests who were summoned to
    the Convention; Messers M. Quinn, chairman of Ennis Rural District
    Council; J. Murray; H. Hehir; J. Barrett; T. O'Brien; T. Kelly; Jas Brennan,
    DC; D. Healy; P. Roughan; P. McGrath; P.Casey; - McCormack; H.J. Hunt,
    DC; P. McInerney, County Councillor; O. Hegarty, DC; T. O' Loughlin,
    Carron; Austin Brennan; Joseph Keane, DC; F. Shinnors-Moran; Thomas
    Hogan; P. Duggan, Scarriff; J. Considine; A. Power; Dr Brennan; - Scanlan;
    Sean McNamara; J. O' Connor; Jas Lalor; Martin McInerney; Peter
    O'Loughlin, Carron; D.S. Steward; F. Breen; Arthur O'Donnell; J. Hoare,
    Caherea; E. Lysaght; T. Clune; - Bingham; P. Culligan, Spancilhill; J. O'Brien,
    Ogonneloe; and P.J. O'Loughlin, County Councillor, Ballyvaughan.

26. Brennan, Michael, op. cit., p.25. On the other hand, Eamon Gaynor in his
    book, *Memoirs of a Tipperary family, the Gaynors of Tyone* (Dublin: Geography
    Publications, 2000) p.73 states that his uncle Fr Patrick Gaynor, a curate in
    Kilmihil at the time, remembered Fr Tom Meagher, CC of Killaloe, shouting
    out de Valera's name at the convention. Gaynor also states that several other
    priests in the county actively supported de Valera, such as Frs Hewitt, Molony,
    Molloy, S. O'Donoghue, W. O'Kennedy and W. Gleeson. Gaynor states that
    the 'separation women' were fiercely opposed to Sinn Féin. He added that
    Fr A. Clancy was 'the best orator in the diocese'.

27. Denman, Terence, *A Lonely Grave*, p.134.

28. Gaynor, Eamon, op. cit., pp.73-74. Incidentally, Mr Patrick Power, Clare Castle,
    along with Canon Bourke, PP Clare Castle, were among those who proposed
    Mr Patrick Lynch for election. See the *SR* and *CC*, 15, 22 and 29 June and
    3 November 1917. Ó Ruairc, Pádraig Óg, *Blood on the Banner*, p.65.

29. Maleady, Dermot, *John Redmond, the National Leader* (Kildare, Merrion,
    an imprint of Irish Academic Press, 2014), p.439. The letter was also
    published in the *Freeman's Journal* of 29 September 1917. According to
    Maleady, Bishop Fogarty's letter was printed in a pamphlet, which was widely
    distributed at the funeral of Thomas Ashe.

30. 'The Great Bishop of Limerick', Panegyric delivered by Dr Michael Fogarty
    at month's mind in St John's, Limerick 18 September 1917, pamphlet
    published by MH Gill and Son Ltd, Dublin, 1917, p.18. De Wiel, op. cit.,
    pp.185,195; LDA/BI/ET/O/7 (Episcopal Correspondence), Fogarty to
    O'Dwyer, 5 May 1917.

31. *SR*, 16 June, 30 June, 7, 14 July, 11 August, 1, 8, 29 September 1917,
    5 January 1918; *CC*, 16, 23, June, 9, 14, 21, 28, July, 4 August, 6,
    13 October 1917.

32. *SR*, 16 June 1917; *CC*, 10, 24 November 1917. The list of hunger strikers,
    members of the Clare Brigade, IRA, included: P., A. and M. Brennan, Meelick;
    F. Gallagher, Meelick; J. Griffey, Meelick; H. Hunt, Corofin; J. Liddy, Cooraclare;
    William McNamara, Ennis; J. Madigan, Ennis; J. Murnane, Newmarket;

M. O'Brien, Ruan; A. O'Donnell, Tullycrine; P. O'Loughlin, Liscannor; F. Shinnors, Ennis; M. Murray, Newmarket; and John Minihan, Corofin. In all, thirty-eight Republicans went on hunger strike, including Thomas Ashe, who died after force-feeding. The hunger strike weapon was initiated by the first Clare republicans arrested, the three Brennan brothers from Meelick and P. O'Loughlin from Liscannor. See also, Ó Ruairc, Pádraig Óg, *Blood on the Banner, The Republican Struggle in Clare* (Cork: Mercier Press, 2009), pp.66–72.

33. *SR*, 15 September 1917.

34. *CC*, 28 April 1917. See notice of her original appointment in *SR*, 19 July 1915; also, de Bhaldraithe, Padraig, 'Sixmilebridge Clerks of Petty Sessions', in *The Other Clare*, Vol. XI, pp. 22–26. I am grateful to Eoin Grogan from Killimer, for drawing the case of Georgina Frost to my attention.

35. *CC*, 31 March; *SR*, 7 April 1917.

36. Junger, Ernst, *Storm of Steel*, first published in Germany as Stahlgewitten in 1920; final edition 1961, translated by Michael Hofmann (London: Penguin Classics, UK, 2004), pp.127–8. Incidentally, Junger mentions that his company captured some British soldiers, including a Lt Stokes of the Royal Munster Fusiliers. Perhaps some Claremen were involved in that engagement? Jurgen was also impressed by the 'bravery and manliness of the British soldiers'; op. cit., p.125.

37   *SR*, 30, December 1917; 12 January 1918.

38. *SR*, 31 March, 21 April, 16 June 4, 25 August, 8, 22 September, 3 November, 15 December 1917; *CC*, 26 February 1917.

39. *SR*, 16 June 1917.

40. *CC*, 24 November 1917, 19 September 1914 and 15 December 1916; *SR*, 1 December 1917. Power, Joseph, *The GAA in Clare Castle, 1887-1987* (Clare Castle: Clare Castle GAA, 1987), pp. 28-29; and Power, Joseph, *A History of Clare Castle and its Environs* (Ennis: privately published, 2004), pp.219–221; Ger Browne, op. cit., p.15.

41. Information leaflet from Mr John Rhattagan, curator of the Clare Museum, Ennis. Information supplied by the French War Office to the Barrett family. See also www.marytfamilytree/jackbarrett.

42. Sheedy, Kieran, op. cit., p.786.

43. *CC*, 27 December 1917.

44. Based on lists published by Browne, Burnell and McCarthy, op. cit.

6. From Conscription to Armistice

1. *CC*, 19 January, 16 February 1918.

2. *CC*, 9 February 1918.

3. *SR*, 9 February 1918.

4. *SR*, 23 February 1918.

5. *SR*, 9 February, 2 March, 1918.

6. *SR*, 2 March, 1918; See note 12, Chapter One above. For a comprehensive account of this tragic land dispute see Philomena Butler, 'Outrage at Drumdoolaghty, The Francie Hynes Affair,' in *The Other Clare*, Vol. 30, 2006, pp.15–22.

7. *SR*, 2 March 1918; O'Ruairc, op. cit., p.77, has a statement from one of the attackers, John Joe Neylon, who states that they were not masked, though the contemporary newspaper account states that they were masked.

8 Power, Joseph, *The GAA in Clare Castle 1887-1987*, pp.34-35; Joseph Power, *A History of Clare Castle and its Environs*, p.222; *CC*, 12 October, 1914, 9 February, 2, 16, 23 March; *SR*, 5, 26 January, 2 March, 4 May, 6 July, 17 August 1918. Records of interview between the author and the late Jim Reilly of Castlefergus, c. 30 July 1977.

9. Brennan, Michael, op. cit., p.33; *SR*, 9, 30 March, 15 June 1918.

10. *SR*, 2 March 1918; *CC*, 24 January, 2 February 1918.

11. *SR*, 9 March 1918; *CC*, 1 March 1918.

12. *SR*, 9 March 1918

13. *SR*, 2 March, 15 June 1918,

14. *SR*, 27 April 1917; Henry, William, *Galway and the Great War* (Cork: Mercier Press, 2006), pp.70-71; De Wiel, op. cit., p.213.

15. *SR*, 27 April 1918.

16. De Wiel, op. cit., p.217; *SR*, 22 June, 1918; see index under Bishop Michael Fogarty at Clare County Research Library for copy of Bishop Fogarty's letter to Sinn Féin.

17. De Wiel, op. cit., p.228.

18. *SR*, 15 June, 1918; *CC*, 22 January 1918, see also O'Muirceartaigh, Joe, *Chronicle of Clare* (Ennis: Fag an Bhealach, 2000), p.40.

19. *SR*, 28 September 1918.

20. *SR*, 11 May, 15 June 1918; Ronan Fanning, op. cit., pp xvii, 180-181 and 183-185; McMahon, Paul, *British Spies and Irish Rebels, British Intelligence and Ireland, 1916-1945* (Dublin: Boydell Press, 2008), p.24.

21. *SR*, 10 August 1918.

22. *SR*, 16 June 1918. Mrs Studdert stated in a letter to the editor of the *Saturday Record* that this was one of many similar letters of gratitude, which she had received from Clare prisoners of war.

23. *SR*, 2 February 1918.

24. *SR*, 29 June, 27 July, 17 August, 7, 28 September, 12, 19 October 1918.

25. *SR*, 29 June, 12 October 1918; 'Cycle and Motor Accessories from 1916 to 1918', No.7 Ledger, M.F. Tierney, Abbey Street, Ennis. I am grateful to Mr Anthony Scanlan, Clare Castle, for bringing this source of information to my attention. *SR*, 14 September 1918.

26. *SR*, 27 July 1918.

27 *SR*, 3, 17 August 1918; Col Arthur Lynch's appeal to Col Theodore Roosevelt was published, via Associated Press, in *The New York Times* of 8 July 1918. See also Denman, Terence, *Ireland's Unknown Soldiers*, pp.173-174; also, Henry, William, *Galway and the Great War*, p.67.

28. *SR*, 23, 30 November 1918. Much of the second part of the letter is not included here as it went into too much technical detail on the effects of different types of gas attacks. Though the letter is undated it was written shortly after the sinking of the *Leinster*, but the earliest publication date was 23 November. I suspect, because of the anti-German tone of the letter, that it

was written before the Armistice of 11 November.

29.   *SR*, 9 November 1918.

30.   *SR*, 7 September 1918.

31.   Johnstone, Tom, *Orange, Green and Khaki, the Story of the Irish Regiments in the Great War, 1914-1918*, (Dublin: Gill and Macmillan, 1992), p.64. For a German perspective on the Battle of Guillemont see Junger, Ernst, *Storm of Steel* (London: Penguin Classics, 2004), pp. 90-110.

32.   *SR*, 5 October, 1918.

33.   Cronin, Jim, Munster GAA Story, Vol. 1, printed by *Clare Champion*, Ennis, 1985; *SR*, 10 August 1918, p.108.

34.   *SR*, 19, 26 October 1918.

35.   rmsleinster.com; *SR*, 12 October 1918.

36.   The title of the famous German novel by Remarque, *Erich Maria, All Quiet on the Western Front*, originally published in 1929, from an edition translated from German by Brian Murdoch (London: Vintage Books, 2005).

37.   Denman, Terence, *Ireland's Unknown Soldiers* (Dublin: Irish Academic Press, 1992), p.174. The advertisement appeared in the *Irish Independent* of 3 December 1918. Among the clergy who proposed and endorsed de Valera were the following: Revd A. Clancy, PP Ballynacally; V. Revd Canon O' Dea, St Flannan's; Revd T. Molloy; Revd G. Clune; Revd W. Marrinan, PP; Revd J. Molony, CC; Revd M. Breen, PP; Revd W. Molony, CC; Revd P. Gaynor; Revd M. Considine, CC, Tulla; Revd W. O'Kennedy; Revd E. Vaughan, CC Kilkishen; Revd J. Greed, CC Killaloe; Revd P. Quinn, PP O'Callaghan's Mills; Revd D. Flynn, CC Broadford; M. Murray, CC Newmarket-on-Fergus; Revd J. Clancy, CC; Revd Thomas Neylon, CC Crusheen; Revd J. Smyth, CC Corofin; Revd Marcus McGrath, CC Clare Castle; Revd M. Scanlan, CC; Revd James McInerney, CC; Revd Pat O'Reilly, CC, Feakle; Revd D. Flannery, CC Mountshannon; Revd James Daffy, PP; Revd Dan O'Dea, CC; Revd M. Crowe, CC Doora; Revd John O'Donoghue, CC Tulla; Revd P.J. Hewitt, CC, Kilkishen. In Kilrush only a small attendance turned up for the nomination of Mr Brian O'Higgins. Among those present were the following clergy: Revd James Clancy, PP, Revd A.J. Molony, CC, and Revd M.J. O'Houlihan, CC.

38.   *SR*, 7 December 1918. Note, at a meeting of the Sinn Féin Executive in Kilrush, the chairman, Revd James Clancy, PP, stated that he was in favour of the selection of Peadar Clancy, the republican from Cranny, as a Sinn Féin candidate in West Clare, but stated that he was unable to contact him before the nomination day, *SR*, 30 November, 1918; O'Ruairc, op. cit., pp.85-86.

39.   *SR*, 18 January 1918, 28 September, 5 October 1918.

40.   Ferriter, Diarmuid, *The Transformation of Ireland, 1900-2000* (London: Profile Books, 2004), pp.184-185. Foley, Catriona, *The Last Irish Plague, the Great Flu Epidemic 1918-19* (Dublin: Irish Academic Press, 2011), p.16. See also 'The Spanish Flu Epidemic of 1918-19', *History Ireland*, Issue No 2, March-April, 2000. Dorney, John, Ireland and the Great Flu Epidemic of 1918, in www.theirish story.com-irelandandgreatflu-epidemicof1918/19

41.   *SR*, 2, 9, 16, 23, 30 November, 7, 16, 21, 28 December 1918; 18 January 1919.

42. *SR*, 2 March, 17 August, 14 September, 2, 23 November, 1918. See list of contributors in *SR*, 12 January, 30 March, 7 September, 23 November 1918. One generous subscriber was Mr John Power, Superintendent of Customs at Macao in South China, who sent a cheque of £10 in 1918 and £14 in 1917 for distribution among the returned prisoners of war from West Clare. His wife of Ivy Cottage, Kilrush, distributed the money at Christmas, (*SR*, 21 December 1918). For a summary of Red Cross contributions see Margaret Downes, 'The civilian voluntary aid effort', in Fitzpatrick, David (ed.), *Ireland and the First World War* (Dublin: The Lilliput Press and Trinity History Workshop, 1988), p.32, Table 6.

43. *SR*, 9 November 1918.

44. *SR*, 4 October 1919; David Fitzpatrick, *Politics and Irish Life, 1913-21* (Dublin: Gill and Macmillan, 1988), p.65.

45. www.ae2.org.au/wheat-john-harrison-able-seaman-ran-7681.

46. www.nationalarchives.gov.uk/pathways/firdtworldwar/battles/esopotamia. htm; also, miscellaneous images and www.winkleleighheroes.co.uk/level3/ kutdeathmarch.htm.

47. Fred Perry's letters and prison diary, courtesy of Emily Tuohy Fitzpatrick, The Crescent, Lucan, Co. Dublin, granddaughter of Fred Perry. My thanks also to Eric Shaw, Clare Castle for bringing this source to my attention.

48. *SR*, 21 December 1918, 15 February 1919. The recruiting office was located at 32 Church Street, now Abbey Street, Ennis. See Brian Spring, *A Broad History of a Narrow Street* (Ennis: Clare Roots Society, 2013), p.40.

49. *SR*, 19 April, 31 May, 1919. Mr McElroy specifically thanked Lord and Lady Inchiquin; V. Revd John Scanlan, PP; Mrs Silles, Kilrush; Lady Fitzgerald, Carrigoran and Mrs Vere O'Brien for their generosity and assistance.

50. *SR*, 21 December 1918.

51. *SR*, 19 January, 27 April, 25 May, 26 May, 22 June, 20 July, 3 August, 7 September and 5 October 1918; and 8 November 1919; www.clarechampion. ie/briefhistory. I am grateful to Mr John Galvin, general manager of the *Clare Champion* for the information on Nurse Nellie Galvin. For information on Mary O'Connell Bianconi, see Hehir, James, *Lack School and People* (City? Blurb Books, 2012), chapter on John O'Connell Bianconi; also www.waterfordtoday. ie/4121-commemoration; and www.wit.ie/dept of nursing and healthcare.

52. Based on lists compiled and published by Browne, Burnell, and McCarthy, op. cit. passim.

53. Hardy, Thomas, 'And There Was a Great Calm (On the signing of the Armistice, 11 November 1918)', poem cited in Kendall, Tim, *Poetry of the First World War* (Oxford: Oxford University Press, 2013), pp.12-13.

7. In Memoriam

1. McGuane, James, *Kilrush in Olden Times* (Kilrush: privately published, 1984), p.92.

2. Ó Ruairc, Pádraig Óg, *Blood on the Banner, Roll of Honour*, pp.25-26, 28.

3. Brennan, Michael, *The War in Clare, 1911-1921, Personal Memoirs of the*

Irish War of Independence (Dublin: Four Courts Press, 1980), pp.20-21; *SR*, 21 December 1918. See also *SR*, 4 January 1919 which noted the receptions given to Michael Brennan and Art O'Donnell on their release from prison.

4. Brennan, Michael, op. cit., p.39.
5. Sheedy, Kieran, *The Clare Elections* (Dún Laoghaire: Bauroe Press, 1993), p.758 and 808.
6. *SR*, 1 November 1925.
7. *SR*, 7 November 1925.
8. *SR*, 6, 13 November 1926.
9. *SR*, 5, 19 November 1927.
10. *SR*, 10 November 1928.
11. *SR*, 9 November 1929.
12. *SR*, 8 November 1930, 9 November 1931 and 5 November 1932.
13. *SR*, 18 November 1933.
14. *SR*, 17 November 1934.
15. *CC*, 10 November 1945.
16. *CC*, 6 November 1948.
17. Royal British Legion Limerick, history, in rbl-limerick.webs.com/branchhistory.htm; Also, Sean South of Limerick in Wikipedia.org/wiki/Sean-South.
18. *CC*, 9 November 1958
19. *CC*, 9 November 1968.
20. *CC*, 7 November 1970.
21. Power, Joseph, *The GAA in Clare Castle* (Clare Castle: Clare Castle GAA, 1987), pp.95-96; Also, Shaw, Eric, *Clare Castle and Ballyea, the Parish Remembers* (Ennis, 2011).
22. *CC*, article on Tommy Kinnane, 27 September 1958.
23. *CC*, 2 August 1985 and 30 December 1988.
24. Brew, Frank, *The Parish of Kilkeedy, a Local History* (Tubber: 1998), pp.214-216; See also Hawes, Joe, 'Mutiny Under the Sun,' passim; Kilfeather, T.P., *The Connaught Rangers* (Tralee: Anvil Books, 1969), Chapters 12-14 passim; Also O'Muircearthaigh, op. cit., p.47; *CC*, 4 July 1970, 19 January 1973 and 11 January 2013. Grave at Shanakyle, Kilrush. He is also named on the Connaught Rangers memorial erected by the National Graves Association at Glasnevin, Dublin, in 1983. It seems that there was another Clareman involved in the mutiny in India. A man named Michael Kearney, 'a native of County Clare' was sentenced to fifteen years' penal servitude for his part in the mutiny. He too was released under the amnesty and lived in London up to the 1970s. www.war-talk.com conaughtrangersrsmutiny; *History Ireland*, Spring 2001, Vol 9.
25. *CC*, 20 July and 3 August 1990; Also Records of Burials at Drumcliffe, Ennis. See Kierse, Sean, *The Killaloe Anthology* (Killaloe: Boru Books, 2001), Chapter 17, pp.176-181, for an excellent article on the 'Soldiers and Sailors Trust Houses' in Killaloe. He states that thirty-five houses were built for the ex-servicemen in this district. Similar houses were built in Ennis, Kilrush, Ennistymon, Clare Castle, Sixmilebridge, Tulla and Newmarket-on-Fergus and perhaps other places in Clare.

26. See reference note 4 in Chapter Four (Western Front and Gallipoli) on the execution of Tommy Davis.

27. *CC*, 19 November 1999, Kilrush Notes under a heading 'War Dead Remembered', p.14.

28. *CC*, 12 November and 26 November 1999.   See also, a booklet, written by Ger 'Guss' O'Halloran, '*The Men from North Clare and the Great War 1914-1918*', 2012, which has a photograph of the memorial. There is a copy of this booklet in the Local Resource Centre, Clare County Library, Ennis.

29. *CC*, 4 November 1988.

Conclusion

1. Fanning, Ronan, op cit., p.134.

2. See Jenkins, Philip, *The Great and Holy War: How World War I Became a Religious Crusade* (City?) Harper One, 2014). According to Jenkins, religion is central to an understanding of the war and the war triggered a global religious revolution.

3. Jeffery, op. cit., p31, citing E.E. Lysaght in Russell, G; Riordan, E.J.; Lysaght, E.E., and Malone, A., 'Four Years of Irish Economics, 1914-1918', in *Studies*, 7 June 1918, pp.310-327.

4. Fitzpatrick, D., *Politics and Irish life*, pp.90-91.

5. Crowe, Des, *For the Record, Clare GAA 1887-2002* (published privately, 2002), pp. 81 and 133; See also O'Reilly, Seamus, *Clare GAA, the Club Scene, 1887-2010* (Ennis, privately published, 2010). See the years 1912-1924 in both hurling and football.

6. McCarthy, Daniel, op. cit., Appendix 1, pp 165-174.

7. Burnell, Tom, *The Clare War Dead*, passim.

8. Fitzpatrick, David, *Politics and Irish Life, 1913-21* (Dublin: Gill and Macmillan, 1977), pp.110, 315.

9. Based on the lists of Clare war dead compiled and published by Browne, Burnell and McCarthy, op. cit.

10. Casey, P., 'Irish Casualties in the First World War', in *Irish Sword*, Vol. XX, 1996-7, *Journal of the Military History Society of Ireland*, edited by Harman Murtagh, pp.193-205.

11. Glynn Papers, list compiled by Mr Glynn, on Armistice Day, 11 November 1918. H.R. Glynn to Redmond, 8 August 1914; H.R. Glynn to Birrell, 29 August 1914; H.R. Glynn to Vice Admiral at Queenstown, 11 March, 1915; H.R. Glynn to Maj. Ievers, 18 March 1915; Maj. H.H. Ievers to H.R. Glynn, 20 March 1915; H.R. Glynn to Admiralty London, 30 March 1915, and H.R. Glynn to Lloyd George, 1 April 1915.

12. Martin Staunton, 'Kilrush County Clare and the Royal Munster Fusiliers,' in *The Irish Sword*, Vol. XVI, 1984-6, pp 268-271.

13. Paul O'Brien, Provincial Recruitment in the First World War: The Glynn's of Kilrush Co. Clare, in www. military heritage.ie/. Paul O'Brien, military-trust-article, July 2013, citing an interview that Michael Gallagher had with Sean Dunleavy in the *CC*, 2 August 1985.

14. *SR*, 20 March 1915; *CJ*, 4 November 1915. My late father, Bernard Power,
     from Clare Castle told me that his brother John was a dental student at the
     Royal College of Surgeons in Dublin and that the reason he joined the
     army was that his friends encouraged him to join them in the 'Pals' battalion,
     and perhaps infected by their enthusiasm, he joined the 10th Battalion Royal
     Dublin Fusiliers. Another brother, Timothy, probably enlisted for the same
     reason, or perhaps was inspired by his brother John to join up for a sense of
     adventure in the 'war fever' atmosphere of 1914 and 1915.

     Many years ago, sometime in the early 1970s, I interviewed the late Garda
     Sgt Jim Long, who was stationed at Clare Castle. He had served in the
     Great War and I asked him why he had enlisted. He said that he was then a
     young man living in Cork and he believed that preference would be given
     to those who had served in the war if there were employment opportunities
     afterwards. He told me that he did not particularly wish to fight, so he joined
     the Royal Army Medical Corps and served on the Western Front in France
     and Belgium. He did not wish to talk about his activities while he was there;
     perhaps the memories were too painful. He was profiled in an article in
     the *Irish Independent* of 10 March 1938, being described as 'a Clare Garda
     officer of many talents, poet, archaeologist, coin collector and camera-man'.
     In the article the description of his Great War career is brief: 'A native of
     Ballincolllig, Co. Cork, Sgt Long served as a stretcher-bearer with the 37th
     and 5th Divisions in France and Belgium during the Great War, and was
     gassed at Douai in 1917.' The article also noted that 'one of his most painful
     memories is the Drumcollogher Cinema fire, where many lives were lost'.
     He was stationed there at the time. (The cinema tragedy happened on
     5 September 1926 and forty-eight people were killed.) I am thankful to Eric
     Shaw for giving me a copy of this newspaper article.

     I remember a few other 'old soldiers', veterans of the Great War, who
     lived at Clare Castle until the 1960s and 1970s, such as Mick Moore, who
     lived at Barrack Street; Willie Kelly, who lived on the Ennis Road at Clare
     Abbey, and Stephen 'The Dad' Moloney who lived in Killow. There were
     also a few war widows living in the village, Mrs 'Mary Taylor' McMahon,
     whose husband Michael was killed in 1917, and Mrs Molly Callaghan, whose
     husband was killed while serving in the US Army in France. None of these
     people mentioned the war and its impact upon them.

15. *CJ*, 6 September 1915; Myles Dungan, op. cit., pp 15, 18, 23.

16. T.R. Henn, *'Five Arches, with Philocotes' and Other Poems* (Gerrard's Cross:
     Colin Smythe, 1980), pp.64–65.

     The following officers, with Clare connections were mentioned in the
     newspapers above, especially the *Saturday Record* and the *Clare Journal*,
     cited for bravery: H.M.C. Vandeleur, Ralahine; Lt G. Gore, Derrymore; Lt
     R. Studdert, Hazelwood; Lt H. Spaight, Killaloe; Capt. Lysaght, Raheen;
     Capt. Alex Vandeleur, Kilrush and Cahercon; Capt. Cullinan Bindon Street,
     Ennis; Gen. Sir O'Moore Creagh, Cahirbane; Maj. J.P. Butler, Knappogue;
     Lt B.E. Stacpoole Mahon, Corbally; Lt J.F.R. Massy Westropp, Doonass;
     Capt. R.H. Stacpoole, Edenvale; Lt Lane-Joynt, Carnelly; Capt. W.F. Henn,

Paradise; Capt. Bindon Blood, Templemaley; Lt Dan O'Brien, Clare Abbey; Capt. Poole Hickman, Kilmore, House, Knock; Lt J. Roche Kelly, Mullagh; Capt. Tottenham, Mount Callan; Lt Donough O'Brien, Dromoland; Maj. F.C. Sampson, Scariff; Commander Gore, RN, Derrymore; Lt Hugh Murrough Vere O'Brien, Ballyalla; Maj. George MacNamara, Ennistymon; Lt G.W. Maunsell, Island McGrath; Maj. R.H. Studdert, Hazelwood; Capt. Hume Crowe, Dromore; Lt Claude Molyneux Molony, Ennis; and Flight Lt, the Hon. Desmond O'Brien, Dromoland. Other Clare military men mentioned included, Gen. Sir Thomas Kelly Kenny, Doolough Lodge; Maj. Moloney, Kiltannon, Tulla; Maj. Ievers, Mount Ievers, Sixmilebridge; and Col O'Callaghan Westropp, Lismehane, Tulla. It is significant that almost all of these officers belonged to the old Protestant Ascendancy of Clare, who would have fought from a sense of duty for king and country.

17. Cited in Myles Dungan, op.cit, p.34.
18. Jeffery, op. cit., p.31.
19. Niamh Puirseil, 'War, Work and Labour', in Horne, John (ed.), *Our War, Ireland and the Great War* (Dublin: RIA, 2008), p.193.
20. W.B. Yeats, 'An Irish Airman Foresees his Death' (written in honour of Maj. Robert Gregory, who died in an air accident in 1918), poem cited in *W.B. Yeats, The Poems*, Everyman's Library (London: JM Dent & Sons, 1990) introduced by David Albright.
21. Sassoon, Siegfried, MC, *Memoirs of an Infantry Officer* (London: Faber and Faber, first published 1929), re-issued in 1965 and 1992, p.6.
22. Keith Jeffrey, 'Gallipoli and Ireland' in Macleod, Jenny, *Gallipoli, Making History* (London: Frank Cass, 2004), pp.98–110.
23. Terence, Denman, *Ireland's Unknown Soldiers, The 16th Irish Division in the Great War* (Dublin, Irish Academic Press, 1992), p.173.
24. *Cooper, Bryan, The Tenth Irish Division at Gallipoli*, (London: Herbert Jenkins, 1918), reissued (Dublin: Irish Academic Press, 1993), p.14.
25. Redmond, W., *Trench Pictures from France*, pp. 73, 82.
26. Denman, Terence, *Ireland's Unknown Soldiers*, p.173.
27. *The Irish Times*, 11 June 1917; Terence Denman, *A Lonely Grave*, p.181; See also pp.104 and 113.
28. Denman, *A Lonely Grave*, p.104.
29. *ibid.*
30. Jeffery, Keith, op. cit., p.14.
31. Laurence Binyon, 'For the Fallen', cited in Kendall, T., op cit., pp.43-44.

Postscript

1. Devas, Nicolette, *Two Flambuoyant Fathers* (London: Collins, 1966), passim; and O'Donovan, R., 'To Hell or to Clare, Donogh O'Callaghan, Chief of his name, a Transplanter' in *The Other Clare*, Vol. 9, 1985, p.74.
2. Ó Ruairc, Pádraig Óg, 'The distinction is a fine one, but a real one, sectarianism in County Clare during the War of Independence', in *The Other Clare*, Vol. 34, 2010, p.35-41, passim.

3. Power, Joseph, *A History of Clare Castle and its Environs* (2004), pp.259-60; also, Power, Joseph, *The GAA in Clare Castle, 1887-1987* (1987), p.45; *CC*, 23 April, 24 May 1920; Ó Ruairc, Pádraig Óg, 'Sectarianism in Co. Clare during the War of Independence', in *The Other Clare*, Vol. 34, 2010, pp.36-37.

4. *Irish Independent,* 4 October 1930; *SR*, 1 November, 1930. In a letter to the press written from on board the liner *Laconia*, en-route from Southampton to New York, Gen. F.P. Crozier confirmed that there was a plot to murder the Bishop of Killaloe in November 1920.

5. *The Irish Times*, 8 May 1923, also, Letter to the Editor from Prof. Brian Walker, School of Politics, Queens University of Belfast, *The Irish Times*, 19 January 2011.

6. For a general appreciation of the role of the churches, both Catholic and Protestant denominations in Ireland, see J.H. Whyte, *Church and State in Modern Ireland, 1923-1979* (Dublin: Gill and Macmillan, 1984), passim.

7. I am grateful to Dr Hugh Weir, Whitegate, a member of the Church of Ireland, for giving me this information.

BIBLIOGRAPHY

Australian Dictionary of Biography.

Bacon, Peter, *Land, Lust and Gun Smoke, the Social Life of Game Shoots in Ireland* (Dublin: History Press Ireland, 2012).

Barry, Sebastian, *A Long Long Way* (London: Faber and Faber, 2005).

Bowman, Timothy, *Irish Regiments in the First World War, Discipline and Morality* (Manchester: Manchester University Press, 2003).

Brennan, Michael, *The War in Clare, Personal Memoirs of the Irish War of Independence* (Dublin: Four Courts Press, 1980).

Browne, Ger, *The Great War 1914-1918, The Clare War Dead, WWI* (Ennis: Clare Roots Society, 2014).

Bunbury, Turtle, *The Glorious Madness: The Irish and World War One* (Gill and MacMillan, Dublin, 2014)

Burnell, Tom, *The Clare War Dead* (Dublin: History Press Ireland, 2011).

Cooper, Bryan, *The Tenth Irish Division at Gallipoli* (Dublin: Irish Academic Press, 1993).

Cousins, Colin, *Armagh and the Great War* (Dublin: The History Press Ireland, 2011).

Crane, Stephen, *The Red Badge of Courage*, originally published 1895 (New York: Bantam Classics Edition, 1985).

Cronin, Jim, *Munster GAA Story* (Ennis: *Clare Champion,* 1985).

Cronin, Mark, *Blackpool to the Front, a Cork Suburb and Ireland's Great War 1914-1918* (Cork: Collins Press, 1914).

Crowe, Des, *For the Record, Clare GAA 1887-2002* (published privately, 2002).

Denman, Terence, *A Lonely Grave, The life and Death of William Redmond* (Dublin: Colour Books, 1995).

Denman, Terence, *Ireland's Unknown Soldiers, the 16thIrish Division in the Great War, 1914-1918* (Dublin: Irish Academic Press, 1992).

Dennehy, John, *In a Time of War, Tipperary 1914-1918* (Kildare: Merrion, an imprint of Irish Academic Press, 2013).

De Wiel, Jerome Aan, *The Catholic Church in Ireland, 1914-1918, War and Politics* (Dublin: Irish Academic Press, 2003).

Dungan, Myles, *They Shall Not Grow Old, Irish Soldiers in the Great War* (Dublin: Four Courts Press, 1997).

Durney, James, *In a Time of War, Kildare 1914-1918* (Kildare: Merrion, an imprint of Irish Academic Press, 2014).

Fanning, Ronan, *Fatal Path, British Government and Irish Politics, 1910-1922* (London: Faber and Faber, 2012).

Ferriter, Diarmuid, *The Transformation of Ireland, 1900-2000* (London: Profile Books, 2004).

Finan, Joseph P., *John Redmond and Irish Unity, 1912-1918* (New York: Syracuse University Press, 2004).

Finch, T.F., Culliton, E. and Diamons, S., *Soils of Co. Clare* (Dublin: An Foras Talúntais, National Soil Survey of Ireland, 1971).

Fitzpatrick, David, *Politics and Irish Life* (Dublin: Gill and Macmillan, 1977).

Fitzpatrick, David (ed.), *Ireland and the First World War* (Dublin: Lilliput Press, 1988).

Gardiner, M. and Radford, T, *Soil Associations of Ireland and Their Land Use Potential* (Dublin: An Foras Talúntais, 1980).

Gilbert, Martin, *The First World War* (London: Weidenfeld and Nicholson, 1994).

Graves, Robert, *Goodbye To All That, An Autobiography*, with an introduction by Andrew Morton, Penguin Books, first published by Jonathan Cape in 1929 (London: Penguin Classics, 2014).

Harris, Henry, *Irish Regiments in the First World War* (Cork: Mercier Press, 1968).

Hart, Peter, *The Somme* (London, Cassell, 2005).

Hemingway, Ernest, *A Farewell to Arms*, first published by Jonathan Cape, 1929 (London: Vintage Books, 2005).

Henn, T.R., '*Five Arches, with Philocetes' and Other Poems* (London: Colin Smythe, Gerard's Cross, 1980).

Henry, William, *Galway and the Great War* (Cork: Mercier Press, 2006).

Horne, John, (ed.), *Our War, Ireland and the Great War* (Dublin: Royal Irish Academy, 2008).

Jeffrey, Keith, *Ireland and the Great War* (Dublin: 2000).

Jervis, Lt Col H.S., *The 2ndMunsters in France,* originally published by Gale and Polden in 1922 (Cork: Schull Books, 1998).

Johnston, Jennifer, *How Many Miles to Babylon?*, first published by Hamish Hamilton, London, 1974 (London: Penguin Books, 1988).

Johnstone, Tom, *Orange, Green and Khaki, The Story of the Irish Regiments in the Great War* (Dublin: Gill and Macmillan, 1992).

Junger, Ernst, *Storm of Steel*, first published in Germany in 1920, final edition 1961, translated by Michael Hofmann (London: Penguin Classics, 2004).

Kendall, Tim, (ed.), *Poetry of the First World War, An Athology* (Oxford: Oxford University Press, 2013).

Kierse, Sean, *The Killaloe Anthology* (Killaloe: Boru Books, 2001).

Lynch, Arthur, *Ireland: Vital Hour* (London: Stanley Paul and Co., 1915).

Lynch, Matthew and Nugent, Patrick, (eds), *Clare History and Society* (Dublin: Geography Publications, 2009).

MacCarthy, Daniel, *Ireland's Banner County, from the Fall of Parnell to the Great War, 1890-1918* (Darragh: Saipan Press, 2002).

McGuane, James, *Kilrush in Olden Times* (Kilrush: 1984).

MacLeod, Jenny, *Gallipoli, Making History* (London: Frank Cass, 2004).

MacMahon, Paul, *British Spies and Irish Rebels, British Intelligence and Ireland, 1916-1945* (Dublin: Boydell Press, 2008).

McCance, Capt. S., *History of the Royal Munster Fusiliers, Vol. 11, 1861-1922* (Aldershot: The Naval and Military Press Ltd, 1922)

Maleady, Dermot, *John Redmond, The National Leader* (Kildare: Irish Academic Press, 2014).

Martin, Thomas F., *The Kingdom in the Empire, a Portrait of Kerry during World War One* (Dublin: Nonsuch, Publishers, 2006).

Mitchell, Angus, *16 Lives, Roger Casement* (Dublin: O'Brien Press, 2013).

Moloney, Senan, *Lusitania, An Irish Tragedy* (Cork: Mercier Press, 2004).

Morrissey, Thomas J., SJ, *Bishop Edward T. O'Dwyer of Limerick, 1842-1917*, with an afterword by Professor Emmet Larkin (Dublin: Four Courts Press, 2003).

Myers, Kevin, *Ireland's Great War* (Dublin: The Lilliput Press, 2014).

O' Brien, Grania R, *These my Friends and Forebears, the O'Briens of Dromoland* (Whitegate: Ballinakella Press, 1991).

O'Comhrai, Cormac, *Ireland and the First World War: A Photographic History* (Cork: Mercier Press, 2014)

O'Comhrai, Cormac, *Revolution in Connaught* (Cork: Mercier Press, 2013).

O'Malley, Ernie, *On another Man's Wound*, first published in London, 1936 (Tralee: Anvil Books, 1979).

O'Muirceartaigh, Joe, *Chronicle of Clare, 1900-2000*, (Ennis: Fag an Bhealach, 2000).

O'Reilly, Seamus, *Clare GAA, The Club Scene, 1887-2010* (Ennis: published privately, 2010).

Orr, Philip, *The Road to the Somme* (Belfast: Blackstaff Press, 1987).

Ó Ruairc, Pádraig Óg, *Blood on the Banner, The Republican Struggle in Clare* (Cork: Mercier Press, 2009).

Power, Joseph (ed.), *An Ennis Miscellany* (Ennis: Ennis 750 Committee, 1990).

Power, Joseph, *The GAA in Clare Castle, 1887-1987* (Clare Castle: Clare Castle GAA, 1987).

Power, Joseph, *A History of Clare Castle and its Environs* (Ennis: privately published, 2004).

Redmond, Maj. William, *Trench Pictures from France, with a biographical sketch by E.M. Smith-Dampier* (New York: George H. Doran and Co., 1918).

Remarque, Erich Maria, *All Quiet on the Western Front*, translated from German by Brian Murdoch, first published Berlin, 1929 and re-published (London: Vintage Future Classics, 2005).

Richardson, Neil, *A Coward if I Return a Hero if I Fail – Stories of Irish Men in World War I* (Dublin: O'Brien Press, 2010).

Sassoon, Siegfried, *Memoirs of an Infantry Officer*, first published in 1929 (London: Faber and Faber, re-issued in 1965 and 1992).

Shaw, Eric, *Clare Castle and Ballyea, the Parish Remembers* (Ennis: Clare Roots 2011).

Sheedy, Kieran, *The Clare Elections* (Dún Laoghaire: Bauroe Press, 1993).

Stacpoole, John, *Stacpoole: The Owners of a Name* (Auckland: Published privately, 1991).

Spring, Brian, *A Broad History of a Narrow Street* (Ennis: Clare Roots Society, 2013).

Switzer, Catherine, *Unionists and Great War Commemoration in the North of Ireland, 1914-1939, People, Places and Politics* (Dublin: Irish Academic Press, 2007).

Taylor, A.J.P., *The First World War, an Illustrated History* (Norwich: Penguin Books, 1963).
Taylor, James, W., *The First Irish Rifles in the Great War,* (Dublin: Four Courts Press, 2004).
Walker, Stephen, *Forgotten Soldiers, The Irish Men Shot at Dawn* (Dublin: Gill and
    Macmillan, 2007).

Newspapers

Clare Champion   *Irish Independent*
Clare Journal   *Saturday Record*
Freeman's Journal   *The Irish Times*

Miscellaneous Papers

Glynn family papers, Kilrush
O'Brien/Weir papers, Whitegate
Linnane family records, Ennis and Shannon
John Redmond papers, National Library of Ireland
Peadar MacNamara papers, Inch
Power family records, Clare Castle
Shaw family records, Clare Castle
M.F. Tierney, family records, Ennis
Tottenham family records, Mountcallan

Unpublished Theses

Staunton, Martin, 'The Royal Munster Fusiliers in the Great War', unpublished MA
    thesis, UCD

Articles

Butler, Philomena, 'Outrage at Drumdoolaghty, the Francie Hynes Affair',
    in *The Other Clare*, Vol. 30, 2006, pp. 15-22.
Casey, P., 'Irish Casualties in the First World War', in *The Irish Sword*, Vol. XX, 1996-7,
    journal of the Military History Society of Ireland, edited by Harman Murtagh,
    pp.193-205.
History Ireland, special issue: Ireland and WWI, passim, Dublin, July – August 2014.
O'Brien, Paul, 'Provincial Recruiting in the First World War: the Glynns of Kilrush',
    in military heritage.ie – Paul O' Brien, military-trust-article, July 2013.
O'Donovan, R., 'To Hell or to Clare, Donogh O'Callaghan, Chief of his Name,
    a transplanter', in *The Other Clare*, Vol. 9, 1985, pp.69-75.
Power, Joe, 'Aspects of Sports and Social Life in Clare', in *The Other Clare*, Published
    by Shannon Archeological and Historical Society., Vol. 33, 2008, pp.42-44.
Staunton, Martin, 'Kilrush Co. Clare and the Royal Munster Fusiliers,' in, *The Irish
    Sword*, Vol. XVI (1984-85), journal of the Military History Society of Ireland,
    edited by Harman Murtagh.
'The Spanish Flu Epidimic', in *History Ireland*, No. 2 March – April, 2000.

INDEX